W9-CNN-474

217

Q4

DIPLOMATIC HISTORY
1713–1933

By the Same Author.

History.

THE HISTORY OF GOVERNMENT.

THE JACOBITE MOVEMENT.

THE HISTORY OF SPAIN (WITH LOUIS BERTRAND).

SPAIN.

THE FOUR GEORGES: A REVALUATION.

THE STUARTS.

WHEN BRITAIN SAVED EUROPE.

Biography.

THE LIFE OF GEORGE CANNING.

MUSSOLINI.

WILLIAM PITT.

WALTER LONG AND HIS TIMES.

BOLINGBROKE.

LOUIS XIV.

LIFE AND LETTERS OF SIR AUSTEN CHAMBERLAIN, 2 VOLS.

JOSEPH CHAMBERLAIN.

Letters.

THE LETTERS OF KING CHARLES I.

Political.

MONARCHY.

THE BRITISH PROBLEM.

LORDS OF THE INLAND SEA.

THE CHAMBERLAIN TRADITION.

TWENTY YEARS' ARMISTICE—AND AFTER.

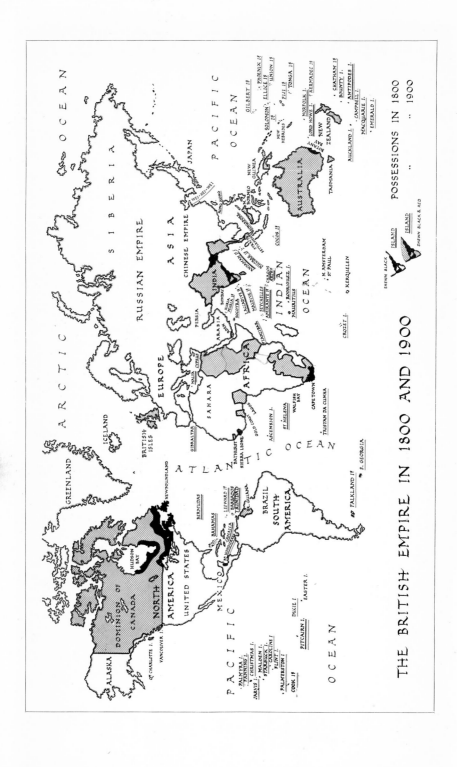

THE BRITISH EMPIRE IN 1800 AND 1900

POSSESSIONS IN 1800   " " 1900

DIPLOMATIC HISTORY

1713—1933

By

SIR CHARLES PETRIE, Bt.,

M.A. (OXON), F.R.HIST.S.

Corresponding Member of the Royal Spanish Academy of History.

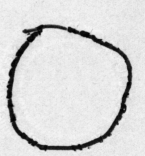

LONDON

HOLLIS and CARTER LTD.

1948

First published 1946
Second impression 1947
Third impression 1948

PRINTED IN GREAT BRITAIN FOR
HOLLIS AND CARTER LTD.

PREFACE

THIS book does not claim to be a complete history of international relations during the period which it covers; such a work would require many volumes, and would probably be beyond the capacity of any one man to write. In the following pages I have aimed rather at tracing the main threads which for more than two centuries have run through diplomatic history, and on occasion I have tried to point the moral as well as to tell the tale.

For reasons of space, accounts of campaigns, as well as of the domestic affairs of the various Powers, have been cut down to the minimum necessary to understand international relationships. The year 1933 has been chosen as the closing date, partly because the arrival of Hitler to power marks the end of one era and the beginning of another, but chiefly because of the lack, after that, of official documents upon which to base a narrative. Too much relating to the period 1933-1939 is still hidden for any final judgment to be passed upon the events of those years.

My thanks are due to Sir John Murray, K.C.V.O., for permission to reproduce in Appendix III an article which originally appeared in the *Quarterly Review*.

CHARLES PETRIE.

London, July, 1944.

CONTENTS

LIST OF MAPS

CHAPTER I

EUROPE AT THE TREATY OF UTRECHT

IN Britain, France, and Spain the sixteenth and seventeenth centuries were marked by the rise of strong national states and by the ensuing struggles between them. In Germany, on the other hand, the centrifugal forces gained the day, largely owing to the existence of the Holy Roman Empire, and their triumph was consecrated by the Treaty of Westphalia in 1648. Italy, too, failed to attain unity at this time, partly because of the continual interference of France and Spain in her affairs, and partly because of the international character of the Papacy, whose possessions comprised the central provinces of the peninsula.

During the whole of the sixteenth century, and the first decades of its successor, the leading Power had been Spain. Her armies were the best in the world, and as Flanders, the Franche Comté, and the duchy of Milan (at this period more usually termed the Milanese) belonged to her crown, she held her French neighbour as in a vice. In the reign of Philip IV (1621–1665), however, she rapidly declined, more particularly after her defeat by Condé at Rocroi in 1643, and France began to take her place. Nevertheless, the supersession of Spain was a lengthy undertaking, and the struggle was rarely confined to the two countries principally concerned. Habsburgs reigned in Vienna as well as in Madrid, and France, in her wars with Spain, had always to reckon upon the hostility of the Austrian branch of the Spanish dynasty.

Louis XIV came to the throne in 1643, when he was not yet five, and he did not assume full power until the death of Cardinal Mazarin in 1661; from then until he himself died in 1715 the control of French policy was entirely in his hands. It was of him that the late Lord Acton wrote, "He was by far the ablest man who was born in modern times on the steps of a throne", and there would appear to be no reason to question this verdict.

In 1659 war between France and Spain had come to an end with the Treaty of the Pyrenees, and although this settlement meant the cession to France by Spain of a number of towns on the former's northern border, it did not enable her to break the ring of Spanish possessions by which she had been surrounded for more than a century. Spanish troops could still march through

B

friendly territory from the Milanese to the Netherlands: it is true that the sea-route across the Bay of Biscay and through the Channel had been barred to Spain by the defeat of the Armada and the development of Dutch naval power, but these waters were only safe for France so long as she remained friendly with Britain and the United Provinces.

The Treaty of the Pyrenees was, in effect, little more than an expression of the lassitude of the two countries which had been at war for many years. Spain came to terms because Philip IV, though not old, was an invalid, while France was glad of the opportunity to profit by an advantageous military situation that might change, and also because, in the event of the King of Spain dying without male heirs, she wished to make in peace the necessary preparations to grasp the Spanish heritage. Thus the Treaty of the Pyrenees was far from marking finality, and France possessed no guarantee of security except the financial impoverishment and military weakness of the government at Madrid.

Throughout his reign Louis endeavoured to improve the situation of his country by three methods, namely the weakening of Habsburg power inside the Empire, alliances with states to the east of Germany, and the direct force of French arms.

Of all French statesmen, not excluding Napoleon I himself, Louis XIV displayed the greatest skill in his policy towards Germany. He fully realized that the old Germanic constitution was in decay, but he saw that the interests of France demanded that he should seek to profit by the fact, rather than create a fresh order on the other side of the Rhine. He sought to influence rather than to command, and to play upon the jealousies of the different states with a view to keeping the country disunited. Napoleon I, on the other hand, was bent on purely personal aggrandizement, consistent with neither the interests, nor the welfare, nor the ambitions of his French subjects. The Emperor's reforms removed many of the obstacles to German unity, while his oppressions and aggressions in the long run brought the Germans together in opposition to him. Napoleon, in short, prepared the way for that unification of Germany which was to prove the undoing of France. Louis XIV made no such mistake, and to the end of his reign he could count upon the support of some of the German states in his struggle with the Habsburgs, while German unity was as remote as when he ascended the throne.

He was less successful, especially in his later years, with the traditional allies of France, that is to say, Sweden, Poland, and Turkey. These Powers had interests, often conflicting, of their own, which they were not prepared to subordinate to those of France. For example, it was the Polish King, John Sobieski, who saved Vienna from the Turks in 1683 when it would have suited Louis very well for the Emperor to have lost his capital. Similarly, at a critical moment in the War of the Spanish Succession, in 1707, the King of Sweden, Charles XII, marched away to fight the Russians instead of coming to the aid of the hard-pressed French. On the whole, however, the efforts of Louis in eastern Europe, not least his encouragement of the Hungarian malcontents, did distract the Emperor to no inconsiderable extent.

Diplomacy without force behind it can achieve little, and Louis XIV and his minister, Louvois, may be said to have created the French army. Previously, the forces of the French Crown had looked to their leaders rather than to the King, for they were a kind of armed militia which regarded soldiering as an interlude, not as a profession. Louvois reorganized the army into brigades, regiments, battalions, and squadrons, and subjected it to regular discipline. The officers, too, were made to realize that they were under orders. The drill was improved out of all recognition, a proper commissariat was established, and a medical service was inaugurated. France was also fortunate in the possession of some first-class generals, of whom Turenne, Condé, Villars, and Berwick were the most notable.

In the pursuit of this policy the attitude of Britain was of great importance to Louis. In foreign affairs Cromwell had been anachronistic, and by espousing the cause of France against Spain he had shown himself unmindful of the change which was taking place in the balance of power in Europe. Charles II had many internal difficulties, and it was the aim of Louis to keep his cousin neutral by exploiting them. In the main he was successful, though he suffered a severe, if temporary, reverse in 1668 at the hands of the Triple Alliance of Britain, Sweden, and the Dutch. The French monarch never trusted Charles II, whom he once accused of "drawing back with one hand what he tended with the other". Charles knew quite well that the English forces could not save the Spanish Netherlands from the French, but he was determined at all costs to prevent the naval power of France from becoming unduly strong in the Narrow Seas. So it came about that neither monarch ever placed any real reliance upon the other in spite of *paid Charles II, not Whigs, Puritans*

the pacts, agreements, and secret treaties which they made between them. The consequence was that the strange spectacle was
seen of the greatest autocrat in western Europe encouraging the
Puritans and Whigs in England to undermine the throne of
Charles II, while the Stuart never missed an opportunity of show-
ing the Bourbon what a nuisance he could be unless he was
properly treated.

The year 1678, in which was concluded the Treaty of Nime-
guen, marked the apogee of the reign of Louis XIV. By this date
he had obtained all that France had fought for since the Treaty of
Vervins eighty years before. The Pyrenees and the Alps were
secure frontiers to the south and south-east. A powerful navy defended the seaboard alike in the Mediterranean, the Atlantic, and
the English Channel. The Spanish Netherlands had been in part
absorbed, and the safety of Paris was assured by the possession of
strongly fortified border towns; while with the recent acquisition
of the Franche Comté the Spanish line of communication between
the Milanese and the Low Countries had been cut. All that Louis
had to do was to wait until the death of Charles II of Spain
enabled him to force the division of the latter's inheritance on his
own terms. What he did was to set to work to carry the frontier
of France to the Rhine, and in the process he passed the point
where defence of French interests became defiance of the rest of
Europe.

The revocation of the Edict of Nantes in 1685, whereby the
exercise of the reformed religion was forbidden throughout France,
was a serious blunder, for not only did the country sustain great
economic loss owing to the quality of the Huguenots who went
into exile, but the military and political damage was considerable.
Huguenot soldiers taught the English and Dutch troops much of
the discipline and drill which had made the armies of Louis irresistible, and among those who left the French service in consequence of the revocation were Ruvigny and Schomberg. Nor was
this all, for the measure roused strong feeling in the Protestant
countries against France, and in England this had not a little to
do with the Revolution of 1688. Suspicion of the French King's
designs had been growing for years among the princes and statesmen of these Powers, but when the Huguenot refugees began to
pour in, the ordinary citizen, too, became disquieted, and a public
opinion was gradually formed which was bitterly hostile to
France.

During these years the leadership of the opposition to Louis became incarnated in William of Orange. An admirable judge of character, few men in the course of history have seen more closely into the motives of others, and he played with those by whom he was surrounded as if they were pieces upon a chessboard. Calculating as Bismarck, unscrupulous as Walpole, and pitiless as Napoleon, he became the symbol of antagonism to France, which threatened the land of his birth. Every other consideration was subordinate to this struggle, and the throne of England, to which he attained in 1689, only attracted William as a means to the great end of checking Louis.

As the seventeenth century drew to its close it became clear that Charles II of Spain had not much longer to live, and that it behoved those who considered themselves his heirs to bestir themselves. The claimants were three in number, namely the Dauphin, the Electress of Bavaria, and the Emperor. The Dauphin was the nearest heir by blood, for he was the son of the eldest daughter of Philip IV, but his mother had renounced all claim to the Spanish crown when she married Louis XIV, though it was a moot point whether this renunciation stood, in view of the fact that the dowry had never been paid. The Electress of Bavaria, the daughter of the Spanish King's younger sister and of the Emperor Leopold I (1658–1705), was next in succession, but her mother had likewise renounced her rights when she married the Emperor. Lastly, there was Leopold himself, for his mother, the aunt of Charles II, had made, unlike her nieces, no renunciation. If, therefore, the renunciation held good, the Emperor's claim was the best; but if not, then the Dauphin was the rightful heir.

In spite of this it was clear from the beginning that in the regulation of the succession legal interpretations would have to give place to practical considerations, for in spite of the encroachments of France during the previous forty years the Spanish monarchy was still by far the greatest of all Christian realms. If the Emperor succeeded to this inheritance the empire of Charles V would be revived, whereas if the prize went to France the rest of Europe would not unnaturally feel its very independence threatened. Accordingly, the two protagonists, Louis and William, negotiated a compromise which was effected without any great difficulty. This settlement is known as the First Partition Treaty, and it was concluded in October, 1698. The Electoral Prince of Bavaria, the weakest of the three claimants, was to have Spain, the Indies, and the Low Countries; Naples, Sicily, the Tuscan ports, and Guipuzcoa were to fall to the Dauphin; and the Milanese was to go to Leopold's son by his second wife, the Archduke Charles.

Scarcely had this solution been reached than the Electoral Prince died, and months of hard bargaining took place before the Second Partition Treaty was concluded in May, 1700, between France, Great Britain, and the Dutch. By this the Archduke Charles was given Spain, the Low Countries, and the Indies, while the Dauphin was to have Naples and Sicily, the Milanese and Guipuzcoa. It was not a very satisfactory arrangement from the point of view of France, but, even so, the Emperor protested against it. As for the Spaniards, their indignation at this division of their empire knew no bounds: the Queen of Spain broke all the furniture in her room, and the Spanish Ambassador in London used such strong language that he was requested to leave the country.

The dying King of Spain then further complicated the situation by making a will in which he left the whole of his dominions to Philip, Duke of Anjou, the younger son of the Dauphin; if Philip refused to accept the inheritance it was to pass wholly to the Archduke Charles. There was to be no partition. Having sown this crop of dragon's teeth, Charles the Bewitched, the last of the Spanish Habsburgs, died on November 1st, 1700.

Louis was now called upon to take the most important decision of his reign, and it was not an easy choice that had to be made. Only a few months had elapsed since the conclusion of the Second Partition Treaty, and for the French King to go back on his word would make him an object of contempt in every Court in Europe. Moreover, France was in urgent need of a prolonged period of peace, and to accept the will meant war, for it was impossible to believe that the other Powers would make no effort to prevent such an increase of French influence both in Europe and in the Americas. It is true that the Second Partition Treaty would have placed an Austrian Habsburg on the Spanish throne, but it also meant an enormous increase of French territory when the Dauphin should succeed his father. The Archduke Charles was, too, but the second son of the Emperor, and there was always the possibility that with the passage of time relations between Madrid and Vienna would become less friendly; in any event it would not be easy for the two branches of the House of Habsburg to come to one another's assistance with the French dominant in the Italian peninsula. Lastly, if the will was accepted Louis must abandon all hope of advancing the frontiers of France in the direction of the Low Countries.

There were equally weighty arguments on the other side. The attitude of the Emperor left no doubt that he would fight sooner than agree to the terms of the Second Partition Treaty, and if Louis had to go to war it was surely better to do so for the whole than for a part. In the latter case, too, he would have Spain against him, while it was more than likely that the English and Dutch would prove unable or unwilling to come to his assistance. Then, again, with a Frenchman on the Spanish throne the influence, if not the frontiers, of France would be immeasurably increased, and in future wars Spain, far from being an enemy, as for so long, would prove an invaluable ally. Louis called a council consisting of the Dauphin, the Chancellor, the Minister of Finance, and the Foreign Secretary, and after hearing their views he decided to accept the will.

At first it appeared as if the Emperor alone would withstand Louis by force of arms, for both England and the United Provinces recognized Philip as King of Spain. The French monarch, however, proved, not for the first time, to be his own worst enemy: on the death of the exiled James II in September, 1701, he recognized his son as King of England, and he proceeded to prohibit the importation of all British-manufactured articles into France. The former act showed a singular lack of understanding of the English character, for however much the ordinary Englishman might dislike the morose Dutchman who reigned over him, he was not prepared to accept a monarch at the dictation of the King of France, while the interference with their trade alarmed the whole commercial community. Leopold thus found allies in London and at The Hague, and the War of the Spanish Succession began.

It was not long before it became evident that Louis had undertaken a task beyond even his strength. The attempt to end the war at one blow by the capture of Vienna was foiled by Marlborough at Blenheim in 1704, and the following years witnessed the disasters of Ramillies, Oudenarde, and Malplaquet. In Germany and Italy the French and their allies steadily lost ground, and the Elector of Bavaria was driven from his dominions. In Spain alone were French arms ultimately successful, and that because the bulk of the Spanish people made Philip's cause their own against the Catalans and the Portuguese who were supporting the Archduke Charles. Louis was reduced to seeking peace upon the most humiliating terms, but his opponents thereupon hardened their hearts, and refused to hear of any compromise. The British Parliament, at the end of 1707, passed a resolution to the effect that "no peace can be safe or honourable for Her Majesty and her allies if Spain and the Spanish West Indies be suffered to continue in the power of the House of Bourbon", and as an indispensable preliminary to peace Louis was bidden to dethrone his own grandson. Observing, "If I must continue the war, I will fight against my enemies rather than against my own family", the French King determined to continue the struggle.

Meanwhile, events were gradually improving his prospects. Leopold I had died in 1705, and six years later his elder son and successor, Joseph I, followed him to the grave. The Archduke Charles had thus become the Emperor Charles VI, with the result that the Allies found themselves fighting not merely to force an unwanted monarch on the Spaniards, who were every day displaying an increasingly marked preference for Philip, but also to make the new Emperor the master of Europe by resurrecting the empire of his namesake Charles V. As these developments came to be realized in England, the paymaster of the Grand Alliance, opposition rapidly began to grow to a war in which English lives and English money were being sacrificed for what were felt to be no longer English ends. This feeling was later stimulated, after the accession of the Tories to power, by the appearance of Swift's pamphlet, *The Conduct of the Allies*.

The diplomatic history of the next two years is inextricably connected with the working of the party system in England, for its chief interest lies in the struggle between Harley and St. John on the one hand, and the Whigs, backed by the Emperor, on the other. The contest was of the bitterest, and the Tories made the widest use of the charge that Marlborough was prolonging the war for his own ends. Full advantage was also taken of Queen Anne's increasing resentment at the imperious airs of the Duchess of Marlborough. Finally, the Tories carried the day at Court, at Westminster, and in the country, and negotiations for peace were energetically conducted.

The actual Peace Conference opened at Utrecht in January, 1712, but as St. John soon wrote to the British representatives there, "Her Majesty is fully determined to let all negotiations sleep in Holland", little was done in the Dutch town, while the real business was transacted directly between London and Paris.

The position of the British government was a delicate one in spite of the victory over the Opposition at home. In the previous year the bases of a settlement had been agreed between England and France, much to the discontent of the former's allies, and the French were taking advantage of this situation to impose terms upon the Emperor and the Dutch in the knowledge that their own agreement with England had rendered her suspect at Vienna and The Hague. Torcy, a nephew of Colbert, was the French Foreign Secretary, and he enjoyed the great asset that he had free hands, except for the Franco-British understanding, while St. John was hampered by the Barrier Treaty with the Dutch. This was one of those undertakings which are so lightly given during the course of a war, and which prove so inconvenient at the succeeding Peace Conference. It had been negotiated in 1709, and went far to establish the supremacy of the United Provinces in North-West Europe. It admitted the right of the Dutch to close the Scheldt, which they had obtained sixty years before, and it pledged England to obtain for them Spanish Guelderland: the Dutch were also allowed to garrison more towns on the French frontier than had previously been the case. Bad as this arrangement was from the British standpoint, it nevertheless existed, and it tied St. John's hands.

A further difficulty arose at this point, and it came very near to wrecking the negotiations altogether, in view of the fact that the Franco-British understanding of the previous year had provided for the retention by Philip of Spain and the Indies. At that time there had been four lives between Philip V and the throne of France in the event of the demise of Louis XIV, but the situation was suddenly changed by the death of the Dauphin, of his son the Duke of Burgundy, and of his grandson the Duke of Brittany. This left only a sickly child, later Louis XV, between Philip and the crown when the old King should die. St. John and the government saw themselves placed in the same difficult position as the Whigs had been at the death of Joseph I, for it was no more to the interest of Great Britain to see Philip King of France and Spain than to assist Charles to become both Holy Roman Emperor and Catholic King.

The first of these complications was solved by recourse to the unilateral denunciation of the Barrier Treaty. Swift prepared the way with a pamphlet entitled *Some Remarks on the Barrier Treaty*, and the House of Commons then debated the matter. A vote was passed that the treaty contained "several articles destructive to the trade and interest of Great Britain", and the ministers who advised its ratification were declared "enemies to the Queen and kingdom". On March 1st the Commons addressed to Anne a long "representation on the state of the nation", and St. John contributed an article to the *Amsterdam Gazette* in its support. The States-General answered the allegations in a formal memorial, which the Lower House voted to be a "false, scandalous, and malicious libel". By the summer of 1712 the majority in the Commons (and probably in the nation) was so incensed against the Dutch that any attempt to carry out the terms of the Barrier Treaty was clearly impossible. St. John had skilfully surmounted his first difficulty.

The complication caused by the deaths of the French princes proved less easy of solution. St. John's first suggestion was that Philip should renounce the succession to the French throne, but Torcy advised him that this was impossible, since the Paris lawyers held that no renunciation by the rightful heir could be valid. However desirous the British statesman might be of reaching a settlement, he was not prepared to sacrifice a vital national interest out of respect for the French constitution, and he therefore made an alternative proposal. If Philip will not abandon his prospect of becoming King of France, let him hand Spain and the Indies over to the Duke of Savoy; in return he can have the Savoyard territories with the addition of Montferrat, Mantua, and Sicily; if and when Philip succeeds to the French crown, these north Italian provinces are to be incorporated in the French dominions, while Sicily is to go to Austria. This suggestion met with the entire approval of Louis XIV, who did not believe that his great-grandson would live, and who rejoiced in what appeared to him to be the practical certainty of a large extension of French territory to the south-east. Philip, however, preferred Madrid to Turin, even with the possible reversion of Paris, and the scheme came to nothing.

Meanwhile no effort was being spared by the Emperor to prevent the conclusion of peace, and early in 1712 he sent his great general, Prince Eugene, to see what could be effected by his prestige, but the government rose to the occasion, and saw that he became nothing more than a social lion. Indeed, there appears to have been a Tory conspiracy to keep him drunk as the surest method of rendering him harmless. On the Continent hostilities had ceased so far as Great Britain was concerned. Marlborough had already been displaced as commander-in-chief by the Duke of Ormonde, and in May the latter received orders to "avoid engaging in any siege, or hazarding a battle": St. John, who had now become Viscount Bolingbroke, also communicated these instructions to the French.

Ormonde accordingly announced to the Allied troops that the British government was arranging an armistice for two months, to which he invited them to accede. He then marched towards Dunkirk, which, by arrangement with the French, he was under orders to occupy, but the Dutch governors of Bouchain, Tournai, and Douai refused to open their gates. Ghent he easily secured, as it had an English garrison, and he occupied Bruges without resistance. The Dutch and Austrians soon proved unable by themselves to resist the French, and the campaigning season of 1712 closed with Marshal Villars not only as victor in the field, but as master of several fortresses, including Douai and Bouchain.

With an armistice concluded, and the renunciation of the French crown completed, it became desirable to settle the outstanding points as soon as possible, and with this end in view Bolingbroke himself went to Paris at the beginning of August. His journey from Calais to the French capital was in the nature of a royal progress, so desirous were the French of peace after the long and exhausting war. When he arrived in Paris he took up his residence at the house of the Marquise de Croissy, Torcy's aunt, and the two statesmen soon became personal friends.

The business of Bolingbroke's mission was easily concluded. It was agreed that the Duke of Savoy was to have Sicily, and that his right to succeed to the Spanish throne after Philip and his heirs should be acknowledged in the acts by which the inheritance of the Bourbons was settled. Other points at issue were seemingly arranged with equal ease. On the Saturday after his arrival Bolingbroke was taken by Torcy to Fontainebleau, where he spent the night, and next day was received by the King. Louis expressed his desire for peace, and his respect for Anne; but he spoke so fast, and his articulation was so indistinct, that the Englishman, although an excellent French scholar, had some difficulty in understanding him. Everywhere Bolingbroke met with the most flattering reception, and when he went to the theatre to see

Corneille's *Cid* the whole house rose to receive him, and the performance was suspended until he had taken his seat.

When Bolingbroke returned to London he found, like many another British statesman both before and since, that what had seemed so easy and pleasant in Paris took on a very different complexion once he had left France. His colleagues in the Cabinet by no means relished the ovation which he had received on the other side of the Channel, and they were only too ready to create difficulties. The French were not slow in making capital out of this situation, and the reverses which their armies were inflicting upon the Dutch gave them an added advantage. Then an unfortunate quarrel took place between the lackeys of the French and Dutch representatives at Utrecht; this was elevated to the dignity of a national conflict, and the work of the conference was for a time suspended. At this point the British government decided to send the Duke of Hamilton to Paris to expedite matters, but before he could set out this nobleman was killed in a duel. A further delay thereupon ensued until his successor was appointed.

Fortune was certainly smiling upon Louis once again as the position of the British government became increasingly more difficult. It was impossible to meet Parliament until peace had been made, and indefinite prorogation was out of the question. By February, 1713, it had been prorogued eleven times, and a decision was essential. In that month, therefore, Bolingbroke sent Torcy what amounted to an ultimatum. He laid down in precise terms the British demands relative to the questions still outstanding, namely, the fishing rights off Nova Scotia, the monopoly of the navigation of the Amazon by the Portuguese, and the addition of Tournai to the Dutch Barrier: failing compliance war would be resumed in the spring. The threat had the desired result, and on Good Friday, April 3rd, 1713, about two o'clock in the afternoon, a post-chaise rattled down Whitehall: as it stopped at the Cockpit. there alighted, all covered with dust, Bolingbroke's half-brother, George St. John, with the Treaty of Utrecht in his hand. The statesman welcomed him on the doorstep with open arms, and his relief can be gauged by his words, "It is the Lord's work, and it is marvellous in our eyes". The lapse of a few months, and several defeats by Villars, were necessary before the Emperor gave way, and signed the Treaties of Rastadt and Baden.

By the Treaties of Utrecht, Rastadt, and Baden, generally

grouped together under the name of the Peace of Utrecht, the following arrangements were effected:—

1. Philip V was recognized as King of Spain and the Indies, on the condition that the crowns of France and Spain were never to be united on the same head.

2. Naples, the Milanese, Sardinia, and the Netherlands were given to the Emperor, subject to the right of the Dutch to the military government of Furnes, Ypres, Ghent, Tournai, Mons, Charleroi, and Namur as their barrier against France. The Scheldt was to remain closed.

3. France was permitted to retain Alsace including Strasbourg, but she had to surrender the fortresses of Kehl, Breisach, and Freiburg, which she had seized on the right bank of the Rhine.

important

4. The Electors of Cologne and Bavaria were restored, the succession of the House of Hanover in England acknowledged, and James banished from France.

5. England received Gibraltar, Minorca, Newfoundland (subject to certain rights of fishing on the banks), Hudson's Bay, Acadia, and St. Kitts, and acquired by an Asiento, or agreement, with Spain the right to trade under strict limitations with certain towns in Spanish waters set apart for the purpose.

6. The Kingdom of Prussia was recognized, and received Upper Guelderland.

7. Sicily and part of the Milanese were given to the Duke of Savoy, and it was agreed that the fortifications of Dunkirk should be demolished.

Had Bolingbroke been able to have his way, the treaty would have been followed by a commercial agreement with France and a large step in the direction of freedom of trade between the two countries. In this respect he was too far in advance of his age. The manufacturers rose in revolt, the Whigs did everything in their power to foment the opposition, and a number of Tories voted against the government. Bolingbroke was no longer in the Commons to sway members with his eloquence, and his colleagues were only too ready to give him a fall. The vital clauses in the proposed treaty were rejected by nine votes, and a commercial understanding with France had to wait until the time of the younger Pitt.

Such was the settlement which was principally the work of two relatively young men, for Bolingbroke was only thirty-four, while Torcy was forty-seven. The methods employed to effect this pacification certainly left a good deal to be desired where the British government was concerned, but some, at least, of the blame must surely be shared with the Whig administration whose bellicosity had placed the country in so impossible a position. For the rest, the great merit of the treaty was that it recognized existing facts. France was the first Power in Europe, Philip was the monarch desired by Spain, Great Britain was building a colonial empire, and Prussia and Savoy were rising states: all these incontrovertible realities were admitted at Utrecht. As for Louis XIV, he had completed the work of Richelieu and Mazarin, and had given his country security. It is true that the more unjustifiable ambitions of the middle years of his reign had not been realized, but he had effected a very great deal. Spain was a friendly, almost a client, state; Italy and Germany were as disunited as ever; and to the north it was invasion of, not from, the Low Countries that had become the order of the day. If proof be wanted of the security which Louis XIV won for France, it lies in the fact that while the monarchy stood no invader established himself on French soil.

CHAPTER II

AFTER THE PEACE, 1713–1740

Louis XIV ended his long reign little more than two years after the conclusion of the Treaty of Utrecht, and with his death there ensued a somewhat confused period in the history of international relations: the allies of decades became enemies almost over-night, while sworn foes found themselves acting together against their erstwhile friends. This state of affairs continued until disputed successions in Poland and Austria brought about a re-distribution of forces more or less along the traditional lines, that is to say Britain and the Habsburgs against the House of Bourbon, with the lesser Powers inclining to one party or the other, not without occasional changes of side. At the same time the Utrecht Treaties (if this name may be given to the whole group) remained the established basis of the relations between the European Powers.

Had Louis XIV lived, or had his immediate successors possessed his experience, it is possible that the Diplomatic Revolution of 1756, by which France became the ally of Austria, might have been anticipated by more than a generation. In the eyes of the old King there were two sets of Powers in Europe in 1713—the satisfied and the greedy: in the first category were France and Austria, and in the second Great Britain and Prussia. On January 3rd, 1715, he gave the Comte du Luc, whom he had just appointed ambassador to Vienna, very definite instructions in this sense. In view of the growing power of Hanover, which was now joined with Great Britain in a personal union under the Guelphs, and of the Hohenzollerns, who had been advanced at Utrecht from the Electoral to the Royal dignity, Louis told his representative to try "to establish between the House of France and that of Austria a union as advantageous to their interests as it will be essential to the general peace of Europe". There was much to be said for such a line. France and Austria had no longer any reason to fear one another. The former had been compelled to realize that she could not make head against a continent in arms, and her King's dreams of universal dominion had perforce been abandoned. As for the Habsburgs, they no longer reigned in Madrid and they were only in the Low Countries on sufferance, so France was at last free from the danger which existed while their dominions encircled her. The potential aggressors were Great Britain and Prussia, and as against them Versailles and Vienna had a common interest in the preservation of the *status quo*. So Louis regarded the situation, and the rest of the century was to prove him correct, but many years elapsed, once his dominating personality was removed, before those responsible for the conduct of French policy adopted his opinions, and by then it was too late. As the late Lord Salisbury wrote, "The commonest error in politics is sticking to the carcases of dead policies".

The deaths of Anne and of Louis XIV, in 1714 and 1715 respectively, seriously affected the mutual relations of their two countries, and for a short space there was something in the nature of an Anglo-French Entente. Neither the new dynasty in Britain nor the regency in France was particularly secure, and it is thus hardly surprising that the governments in question should come closer together. The Jacobites, therefore, were viewed askance by the Regent Duke of Orleans, while the British government could be relied upon to thwart any intrigue on the part of Philip V either to succeed, or to obtain control over, the young French King. On each side of the Channel there was a statesman who realized the advantage of peace between the old rivals, and while Sir Robert Walpole and Cardinal Fleury remained at the helm pacific counsels were predominant.

The earlier part of the eighteenth century witnessed the decline of three Powers which had been very prominent during its predecessor, namely Holland, Sweden, and Turkey. The United Provinces emerged from the War of the Spanish Succession victorious but exhausted. The effort to maintain their position as a Great Power was too much for the Dutch, whose resources were inferior to those of their neighbours, and they rapidly sank to the second rank of European States. William III had made The Hague one of the great political centres, but after 1713 it became a mere backwater.

Sweden was also exhausted by war, in which she had finally been unsuccessful, and she was no longer the Great Power of the North. Charles XII was killed in 1718, and three years later there was concluded the Treaty of Nystad, by which Russia became possessed of Livonia, Estonia, Ingria, and part of Finland. Earlier arrangements had necessitated the sacrifice by Sweden of Bremen and Verden to Hanover, and of a portion of Pomerania to Prussia.

The Treaty of Nystad may be said to mark the appearance of Russia as a Great Power, and in the Baltic area she henceforth took the place of Sweden. The accession of the House of Hanover in England also had the effect of increasing British interest in the problems of Northern Europe, though this interest had an economic, as well as a dynastic, foundation, for it was from the Baltic countries that Britain derived no small part of the timber and naval stores which she required for her growing fleet.

The decline of the Ottoman Empire was, perhaps, less apparent than that of the United Provinces and Sweden, but it was no less real. The revival under the Kiuprili viziers, which had brought the Osmanli to Vienna in 1683, had proved to be their last big offensive effort, and since then the Treaties of Carlowitz (1699) and Passarowitz (1718) had marked the decay of the Sultan's power. All the same, the Turks still constituted a respectable force, especially when on the defensive, and both Austrian and Russian armies sustained many reverses at their hands during the course of the eighteenth century. Turkey was by no means yet reduced to the position of "The Sick Man of Europe".

It will thus be seen that the decade following the Utrecht Treaties was marked by a general pacification in the north and west of Europe, and by the emergence of new factors as well as by a diminution in the importance of some of the old ones.

The first threat to the new order came from Spain, and to this several causes contributed. Philip V was embittered by the progress of events in France, and was prepared to listen to desperate counsels. In any event he was completely dominated by his second wife, Elizabeth Farnese, who wished to see her sons on Italian thrones, since the heirs to the Spanish crown were Philip's children by an earlier marriage. The feelings of the King and Queen were also shared by many of their subjects, who had abated none of their original dislike of the partition of the Spanish empire, and who wished for the return of the Italian provinces with which Spain had many an old tie.

Nevertheless those aspirations would have been of little practical importance had it not been for the work accomplished by Cardinal Alberoni in the regeneration of Spain. He had succeeded in creating a fleet, and in April, 1717, suddenly put the weapons which he had forged to their trial-stroke. A Spanish expedition sailed from Barcelona to Cagliari, and by the end of September all Sardinia, which had been assigned to the Emperor

C

at the peace, was in Philip's hands. Charles VI, who had no fleet of his own, was powerless, and when he turned to Britain for assistance he was informed that he must first of all settle his differences with the Dutch, whose right to garrison the frontier towns of the Spanish Netherlands he had hitherto refused to acknowledge.

These differences between London and Vienna encouraged Alberoni, and it was not long before he began to meditate nothing less than the wholesale revision of the Utrecht settlement. He aimed at overthrowing both the French regency and the House of Hanover by a combination of Sweden, Russia, and Prussia, while he endeavoured to rouse the Hungarians against the Emperor. These projects had the not unnatural result of bringing together those whom they threatened, and on August 2nd, 1718, the Quadruple Alliance to curb Spanish ambitions was concluded in London between Great Britain, France, Austria, and the United Provinces. By this time the greater part of Sicily, as well as Sardinia, was in Spanish hands, and it was not until Philip's fleet had been destroyed by the British off Cape Passaro that the tide began to turn. In spite, however, of this action diplomatic relations between London and Madrid were not broken off, and the British fleet was nominally an auxiliary of the Emperor.

Alberoni and his master still refused to submit. An expedition was got ready to restore James III to his throne, and in the following year a few Spanish troops did actually land in Scotland, while the so-called Cellamare conspiracy against the Regent was engineered in France. The Anglo-French reply was a declaration of war, and in due course a French army invaded Spain, while a British force captured Vigo. These disasters brought about the fall of Alberoni, but they did not end the war, as Philip fought on in the hope of securing better terms. His enemies, however, were adamant, and in February, 1720, he gave way. Sardinia passed to the Duke of Savoy, who henceforth took his regal title from the island, while Sicily was given to the Emperor. As for Philip, he was compelled to renew his renunciation of the French throne, and to recognize the Emperor's claim to the Italian provinces which he now occupied.

In this way the first attempt to upset the Utrecht settlement was frustrated, but it was only frustrated because in the last resort the Powers were prepared to go to war in defence of the peace treaties. At the same time they were wise enough to allow modifications, as in the case of Sardinia and Sicily, where these seemed advisable.

Elizabeth Farnese was not daunted by the failure of Alberoni to promote her projects in Italy, and when she found that the Congress of Cambrai (1724–1725) was unlikely, owing to the Emperor's opposition, to do anything for her children, she persuaded her husband and the Spanish government to make a direct approach to Charles. The emissary chosen for this purpose was Ripperdá, a Dutchman who had changed his nationality once and his religion twice, and who was one day to become a Moslem in the service of the Sultan of Morocco. The moment was not ill-timed, for the Emperor was on the worst of terms with Britain, partly owing to her opposition to the Ostend East India Company and partly owing to the German policy of George I as Elector of Hanover, which favoured the Hohenzollerns too much for the Habsburg taste.

The Emperor's terms were, all the same, high, and the negotiation might have come to nothing had not the new French Regent, the Duke of Bourbon, at that very moment (March, 1725) sent back the Infanta who was to be the bride of Louis XV. This insult threw Philip into the arms of the Emperor, and at the end of the following month the Treaty of Vienna was signed. By this, and a further, arrangement Charles promised that two of his three daughters should marry Don Carlos and Don Felipe, the sons of Philip V and Elizabeth Farnese, and that, if he himself should die before Maria Theresa became marriageable, she should wed Don Carlos. In the event of war Austria was to have the Franche Comté, Alsace, and Strasbourg, as well as Metz, Toul, and Verdun, while the Spanish share was to be Roussillon, Cerdagne, Navarre, Gibraltar, and Minorca. Spain also guaranteed to Austria the privileges of the most favoured nation in the Peninsula, and an opening for the Ostend Company in the Indies.

The Western Powers had once more drawn together in the face of the Spanish threat, and on September 3rd, 1725, there came into existence the Alliance of Hanover between France, Britain, and Prussia. It professed to be merely defensive, but it provided for the maintenance of the balance of power, threatened by the prospective marriage of Don Carlos and Maria Theresa. The fact was that the Powers concerned were seriously disturbed both on political and economic grounds: they could no longer patronize the Emperor at the expense of Spain, nor assume the protection of

Spain against the Emperor, while the commercial classes in England by no means relished the prospect of sharing their privileges with the subjects of Charles, and of the Spanish fleet protecting the operations of the Ostend Company.

In spite of the Treaty of Vienna the alliance of Spain and Austria was not a very happy partnership from the beginning. The Spaniards laid siege to Gibraltar, but the Emperor did nothing to assist them, and Ripperdá fell into disgrace. Meanwhile events in France were tending to bring the two Bourbon Powers together. The marriage of Louis XV considerably diminished any prospects of succession to the French throne which Philip might still entertain, and the dismissal of the Duke of Bourbon removed one who had become anathema to the King and Queen of Spain. Above all, Fleury was working for a general peace. In these circumstances it is not surprising that in May, 1727, an agreement was reached by which the Emperor promised to suspend the Ostend Company for seven years, and the Spaniards abandoned the siege of Gibraltar.

The Congress of Soissons met the following year to consider the general state of Europe, and as a result of its lengthy deliberations as well as of the death of the last Farnese Duke of Parma one of the Spanish Queen's ambitions was realized, for in March, 1732, Don Carlos formally took possession of that duchy with the consent of the Powers, including the Emperor. So long as Britain and France held together, all attempts to upset the Utrecht settlement by force had failed, and its modification had been effected, not by unilateral action, but by general agreement.

At this point the centre of interest shifted north to Poland, where the death of Augustus II, who was also Elector of Saxony, in 1733 raised one of those succession problems of which the eighteenth century was so prolific. The native candidate for the vacant throne was Stanislaus Leszczynski, who was duly elected by the Sejm. He and his supporters looked to France for help, and that on several grounds. In the first place his daughter, Marie, had married Louis XV, and in the second it was the traditional policy of France to maintain the independence of Poland, as of Sweden and Turkey, as a check upon the House of Habsburg. The French government was not slow to champion a cause so peculiarly its own. Four million livres were sent to Warsaw to be distributed among those Poles whose support of Stanislaus might otherwise prove somewhat lukewarm, while in a circular letter, addressed to all its representatives abroad, it declared that, as the Emperor, by massing troops on the Silesian frontier, had sufficiently revealed his intention of destroying the liberties of Poland by interfering with the free election of her King, his Most Christian Majesty could not regard with indifference the political extinction of a Power to whom he was bound by all the ties of honour and friendship, but would do his utmost to protect her against her enemies.

These were brave words, but they took no account of the new factor which had arisen in eastern Europe, namely Russia. Pressure could always be applied to the western possessions of the Emperor to compel him to moderate his ambitions elsewhere, but the remote position of the Tsar and his dominions rendered him unsusceptible to such methods. Russia and Austria had no desire to see a revival of French influence in Warsaw, and they therefore brought forward as their candidate the son of the dead King, also named Augustus. A Russian army entered Poland to give effect to this policy, and before long Stanislaus was besieged in Danzig, while the rest of Poland was in the hands of his rival and the Russians. A French expedition arrived too late to change the course of events, and in January, 1736, Stanislaus finally renounced his rights. France was unwilling to waste any more men or money on her ally, more particularly as she was finding ample compensation for her reverses on the Vistula in the triumphs of herself and her allies in Lombardy and on the Rhine. "Must we", asked Fleury, "ruin the King to aid his father-in-law?" There could be no doubt about the answer, but the traditional French influence in Poland had received its death-blow.

The repercussions of the War of the Polish Succession in Italy were not long in making themselves felt, for if France could do little to hamper the operations of Russia, she could attack Russia's ally, the Emperor. War was declared in October, 1733, and an offensive and defensive alliance made with the King of Sardinia. By this time the ties of friendship between Madrid and Vienna had been broken, and in the outbreak of war in Italy the Queen of Spain saw the opportunity of further advancement for her children. Accordingly, on November 7th, the two Bourbon Powers signed the Treaty of the Escorial. Louis and Philip pledged themselves and their posterity to eternal friendship: they guaranteed each other's possessions both in Europe and overseas: and Don Carlos was confirmed in his duchy as well as being promised the

reversion of Tuscany on the extinction of the Medici; in addition
he was to have Naples and Sicily. France further pledged her aid
to Spain if the latter were attacked by England. Finally, "all
earlier treaties made between France and Spain, and between
their majesties and other Powers, shall no longer have effect between France and Spain". Such was the first of the three Family
Compacts between Paris and Madrid which played so great a part
in the diplomatic history of the eighteenth century.

The progress of the war favoured the allied monarchs rather
than the Emperor, and Don Carlos was soon in possession of
Naples and Sicily. Victory would have been even more complete
had it not been for the extreme difficulty of working with Charles
Emmanuel of Sardinia, who would neither fight a decisive battle
nor lend his artillery for a siege. In consequence, he was suspected
both in Versailles and Madrid of being ready, for a sufficient
bribe, to change sides, and aid the Emperor to evict the Bourbons
from Italy. Nor were relations between the French and Spanish
troops in the field any too happy. Of the allied armies the
Spaniards unquestionably displayed the best military qualities,
and they were the most effectively supported by their Government. The French fought well, but their discipline was not what
it had been in the days of Louis XIV, and the war itself was unpopular in France, where it was believed to be the result of a low
marriage, for so the match between Louis XV and Maria
Leszczynska was regarded.

Cardinal Fleury had never, as has been shown, been an enthusiastic supporter of the war, and he neglected no opportunity
of bringing it to an end, but it was not until the summer of 1739
that, in consequence of yet another Treaty of Vienna, all the
Powers concerned were again at peace. Substantial modifications
were made in the Utrecht settlement (with the approval of Great
Britain and the United Provinces) as this affected Italy. Don
Carlos obtained Naples and Sicily, but he had to surrender Parma
to the Emperor in exchange, while the King of Sardinia received
the benefit of some frontier rectifications. Not less important were
the clauses relating to Lorraine and Tuscany. The French government, assuming that Francis of Lorraine would marry Maria
Theresa, and ultimately be elected Emperor, declared that an
Emperor holding Lorraine and Bar would be a standing menace
to the security of France. It was agreed, therefore, that Stanislaus
should renounce his claim to Poland, and should be indemnified

with Lorraine and Bar, which were to revert to France on his
death. The Duke of Lorraine, in his turn, was to succeed to the
Grand Duchy of Tuscany. The preliminaries of this treaty were
signed as early as October, 1735, but, as we have seen, nearly four
years elapsed before it was finally ratified.

So ended the War of the Polish Succession, and after many
alterations the alignment of the principal Powers was roughly
what it had been in the later years of Louis XIV. France and
Spain were allied against the Emperor, and the House of Savoy
was throwing its weight first into one scale and then into the
other. All that was required to restore the old balance was for
Britain to range herself on the side of the Habsburgs, and it was
not long before this development, too, took place.

The clause in the Treaty of Utrecht relating to the Asiento had
for some time been a fruitful source of trouble between London
and Madrid, for the days were passing when quarrels could be
confined to colonial waters. As the eighteenth century grew older
the world became a great deal smaller, and the action and reaction
of events inside and outside Europe began to be increasingly felt.
In any case the privilege of the Asiento lent itself to a variety of
interpretations. There can be no doubt but that the South Sea
Company grossly abused its right to send annually one large trad-
ing ship to the Spanish colonies, and a widespread illicit trade
sprang up, partly under cover, and partly independently, of the
Company, while smugglers went to and fro with great frequency
between Jamaica and the mainland. Spain replied by sending out
gunboats, called *guarda-costas*, whose captains sometimes behaved
with excessive severity. A notable example of this occurred in
1731, when one Jenkins was forcibly deprived of his ear, the display of which to sympathetic legislators in the lobby of the House
of Commons later had much to do with rousing Parliamentary
opinion against Spain.

In actual fact neither side had anything approaching clean
hands. If there were Spanish privateers off the coast of Jamaica,
there were English off Havana and Honduras. If Jenkins lost his
ear and some other captains their goods, Spanish shipowners had
suffered in their turn. If Englishmen had been seen working in
irons in the harbour of Havana, Spaniards had been publicly sold
as slaves in the British colonies. Popular fancy in both countries
was not slow to exaggerate what was taking place, so that, in
England it was believed that hundreds of sailors were rotting in

Spanish dungeons, and in Spain that an English captain had compelled a Spanish nobleman to cut off and devour his own nose. Nevertheless, public opinion was definitely more bellicose in Britain than in Spain, and religious hatred was freely invoked; indeed, had it not been for public-house Protestantism the differences between the two countries might well have been adjusted.

Throughout 1738 and 1739 negotiations continued, and although Walpole was sincerely desirous of preserving peace, his administration was every day growing weaker. The Opposition stormed at him for alleged subservience to a foreign Power, while the popular agitation increased rather than diminished. Nor did the British Prime Minister get the help from Fleury which he might have expected. If, the Cardinal seems to have argued, Spanish attention can be diverted westwards, Elizabeth Farnese may cease to worry me with regard to Italian matters. Accordingly he blew hot and cold, and in due course the pot boiled over, and in October, 1739, Britain declared war on Spain. This was one of the earlier examples of hostilities being forced by public opinion upon a British government contrary to its better judgment.

While Elizabeth Farnese was troubling the waters of the Mediterranean for her own better fishing for Italian thrones, and English captains and Spanish *guarda-costas* were boarding one another off the coasts of the Americas, the problem of the Austrian Succession was looming ever larger in the eyes of European statesmen. Like their Spanish cousins at the end of the previous century, the Austrian Habsburgs were without male heirs. Leopold I had endeavoured to meet this difficulty by providing that in such circumstances females should succeed, with the special proviso that the daughters of the Archduke Joseph were to take precedence of those of his brother Charles. This arrangement was altered, after the death of Joseph in 1711, by the enactment, in 1713, of a secret family law, known hereafter as the Pragmatic Sanction, according to which Charles VI gave his own daughter priority over his brother's, and at the same time insisted strongly on the indivisibility of the Habsburg dominions, a principle which was now adopted for the first time. It may be added that in making this change the Emperor was well within his rights.

The daughters of Joseph I accepted the Pragmatic Sanction, as in due course did Hungary and the hereditary dominions of the House of Habsburg. This was an important step gained, but to

secure the recognition of the European Powers was far more necessary, and for many years the foreign policy of Charles VI was
directed to this object. By the close of 1739 he had realized his
purpose, though more than once he had been compelled to pay
heavily, and among the sacrifices was the Ostend Company in
1731. Nevertheless, with the exception of Bavaria and the Pala-
tinate the Powers of Europe were pledged to support the accession
of Maria Theresa to the undivided Habsburg possessions, though
what that pledge was worth in the case of some of them was soon
to be seen.

Unfortunately for his daughter, the Emperor had omitted the
precaution of reinforcing his diplomacy by arms and money.
Years before, Prince Eugene had warned him that the best guarantees of the Pragmatic Sanction were a strong army and a full
treasury, but in 1740 he had neither. The treasury was all but
empty; the revenues had shrunk to half the income of 1733; while
expenditure and indebtedness had increased, and the taxes, at
once oppressive and unproductive, were causing widespread discontent. The army, demoralized by defeat, with its principal
leaders discredited, and its ranks depleted to half their proper
strength, urgently needed reorganization and reforms which the
financial situation rendered impossible. Above all, the control of
the central government over the provinces was weak and ineffec-
tive, while the Austrian Netherlands were too far away from the
main body of the monarchy to be adequately succoured if they
were seriously attacked. All these facts must be taken into account
in any estimate of the foreign policy of Charles VI.

At home he had been neither a strong nor a successful ruler;
he had done little or nothing to check abuses or to effect reforms;
his relations with his neighbours had been dictated rather by ambition than by interest; and his personal character was as far
from being estimable as his capacity was from being adequate;
yet the peculiar circumstances of the moment rendered his death
as inopportune as possible. Charles VI died on October 20th,
1740, and on December 16th the Prussians invaded Silesia. The
War of the Austrian Succession had begun.

CHAPTER III

THE RISE OF PRUSSIA, AND THE WAR OF THE AUSTRIAN SUCCESSION, 1701–1748

To understand the motives of Frederick II of Prussia in falling upon Austria in this way it is necessary first of all to examine the conditions then existing in the Hohenzollern dominions, which had so recently been erected into the Kingdom of Prussia.

The state had been formed out of wholly dissimilar components, and this fact never failed to exercise very considerable influence upon the government in Berlin. The most important of the Hohenzollern territories was the Mark of Brandenburg. This province had come into the possession of the ruling family in 1415, when it was conferred by the Emperor Sigismund on one of his most faithful adherents, the Burgrave Frederick of Nüremberg, of the House of Hohenzollern.

Of almost as great importance was Prussia, from which the new kingdom had taken its name, for the Emperor would not permit the Elector of Brandenburg to assume the regal title from territory within the Empire of which he himself was suzerain. The history of Prussia had been a stormy one ever since the Polish Duke Conrad of Masovia had invited the Teutonic Knights into his land in 1226 to combat the heathen Prussians. The Order successfully performed this task, but in due course it lost its original spiritual character, and as it refused to admit any of the local nobility into its ranks, its rule came to be resented by the inhabitants as an alien domination. In 1410 the Knights were defeated by the Poles at the battle of Tannenberg, as a result of which they were obliged to cede part of their territory: fifty years later a further cession was forced upon the Order, which also had to acknowledge the suzerainty of the King of Poland for the rest of Prussia.

In the early years of the sixteenth century the doctrines of the Reformation began to reach the Baltic lands, and at that time the Grand Master was Albert of Brandenburg, a grandson of the Elector Albert Achilles. In due course he became a Protestant, and, with the consent of the King of Poland, he proclaimed himself hereditary Duke of Prussia. His grand-daughter, Anna, eventually succeeded to the duchy, and as she married the Elector John Sigismund of Brandenburg, her Prussian possessions passed to the Hohenzollerns of Berlin.

There were other territories scattered about Germany which belonged to the dynasty. Anna was also co-heiress of the Dukes of Jülich, Cleves, and Berg, and although the Hohenzollerns did not succeed in laying hands on all this territory they did secure Cleves, Mark, and Ravensberg. The Treaty of Westphalia marked further gains, for the Great Elector was awarded Lower Pomerania, as well as the secularized bishoprics of Minden, Magdeburg, and Halberstadt. In 1701 his son, Frederick I, assumed the title of King of Prussia, and, as has been shown, at Utrecht the possessions of the Hohenzollerns were further increased by the addition of Upper Guelderland.

The fact that the Kingdom of Prussia was not a compact state exercised an influence upon the foreign policy of its rulers which it would be impossible to exaggerate. The aim of Berlin was to link up these various territories, which otherwise were by no means easy to administer. Frederick William I (1713-1740) took an important step in this direction when he obtained Stettin and its districts by the Treaty of Nystadt, but whole Polish provinces still separated Brandenburg and East Prussia, while the latter itself was almost bisected by Ermeland. The desire for territorial acquisition which was thus developed in the Hohenzollerns was to have the most important consequences in the next two centuries, first for Germany, then for Europe, and finally for the whole world.

Not only were the Hohenzollern dominions scattered, but they were, as the wars of the eighteenth century proved, largely indefensible. They had no natural frontiers, so that there was an added inducement to further expansion.

Frederick William I forged the weapons which his son wielded so skilfully. France at this time was reckoned to have a standing army of 160,000, Russia one of 130,000, and Austria one of 90,000. When the King succeeded his father the Prussian land forces numbered about 30,000, and were maintained by means of subsidies from other Powers, which, of course, were only available in time of war. By the time of his death he had raised the army to 80,000, and there was in addition a well-filled treasury, although the population of the country was not more than two millions. This feat was only rendered possible by organizing the state on a military basis, with an officer caste as its most distinguishing feature: in effect, Prussia during the reign of Frederick William I may well be described as a polity of officers.

He was not an attractive figure, but he did manage to prevent other European nations from fighting out their quarrels in North Germany. "It is no mere boast", he said, "that I have won honour for the House of Brandenburg. All my life I have never sought alliances, nor made advances to a foreign Power. My maxim is to injure no one, but not to let myself be slighted." This boast was not wholly justified, but Ranke was right when he said that Prussia might have advanced on other lines than those laid down by Frederick William I, for, more than any other state in modern history, she is what her rulers have made her. Yet when he died contemporaries did not realize what he had done. Everybody abroad ridiculed him as one who was always preparing for war and never fought, while the Austrians declared that his soldiers, trained by profuse thrashings, would desert by the thousand when the test came. It was not the last time that the world underestimated the strength which Prussia had been quietly developing.

Such was the Power which precipitated the War of the Austrian Succession. Her new King had, on the death of Charles VI, sent the most friendly letters to Maria Theresa, in which he not only confirmed his father's recognition of the Pragmatic Sanction, but also made an offer of military help in case of need. The Hohenzollerns had an old and unsubstantial claim to the Silesian duchies of Brieg, Liegnitz, Jägerndorf, and Wohlau which Frederick was determined to press if he found a suitable opportunity, and in the meantime he lulled Vienna into a false sense of security by his honeyed words. For a brief space it appeared as if he might be disappointed, since Europe gave some evidence of intending to abide by its promise to the late Emperor, but the Habsburg dominions formed too unprotected a mass of plunder for the Powers to resist the temptation to help themselves. Bavaria, in particular, soon began to display a hostile attitude, and Frederick realized that he would not be left to act alone. In December, 1740, he invaded Silesia with an army more than twice as strong as its Austrian garrison, and before long the greater part of the province, including Breslau, was in Prussian hands.

At the same time that he was seizing Habsburg territory Frederick sent Baron Götter to Vienna to offer Maria Theresa his vote at the forthcoming Imperial election, and also armed assistance against her enemies, if she would satisfy his Silesian claims.

Maria Theresa indignantly refused, and set about collecting an army with which to recover the lost province, while she appealed to the guarantors of the Pragmatic Sanction for assistance against this unprovoked aggression. Only Great Britain, however, showed any disposition to fulfil her obligations, and she was already at war with Spain: elsewhere, Frederick found imitators, not opponents. Saxony withdrew her recognition; Spain, Sardinia, and Bavaria began to push their claims; and although Fleury was desirous of peace he was nearing the end of his life, while there were many voices raised in France in favour of the traditional policy of crushing the Habsburgs whenever and wherever the opportunity should occur; now, it was urged, was the chance to destroy their power for ever.

Before long, nearly all the Powers were engaged in the struggle —or rather struggles, for there were three of them, namely that of England against Spain, of Frederick to retain Silesia, and of the Elector of Bavaria to obtain the heritage of Charles VI. Nevertheless, some little time elapsed ere all the Powers appeared as principals: France, for example, did not officially declare war on Great Britain and Austria until 1744—the year, significantly enough, after the death of Fleury—although three years before that Louis XV had sent one of his Marshals across Europe at the head of some thirty thousand Frenchmen masquerading as auxiliaries of Bavaria. The War of the Austrian Succession was, indeed, often marked by the ironical, not least in the coincidence that on the very day when the Elector of Bavaria was being crowned as the Emperor Charles VII, his ancestral capital, Munich, was capitulating to the Austrians to avoid being sacked.

There were three main theatres of war, namely Central Europe, Flanders and west Germany, and Italy, and it is necessary to trace the progress of events on these fronts in order to realize the influence of the actual fighting upon the policy of those who were engaged in it.

Frederick cared little what became of Maria Theresa's other enemies so long as he was allowed to retain Silesia, and his campaigns showed pretty plainly that he was playing solely for his own hand. He was aided by the efforts of British diplomacy to persuade Maria Theresa to buy him off with the cession of Silesia.

George II was fearful for Hanover, while ministers in London wished to revive the Grand Alliance of the earlier years of the century, when France, Spain, and Bavaria faced a Europe in arms; in short, they were thinking of the war against England's old enemy, France, and they considered a German duchy was a small price to pay for the accession of Prussia to their cause: Maria Theresa, who had to do the paying, not unnaturally took a different view.

All the same, the pressure upon Austria from all sides save the east was such that she must have succumbed had she not taken some step to reduce the number of her enemies: British sea-power could exercise but little immediate influence upon the campaigns in Central Europe, while the army under George II was held in check by the French threat to invade Hanover. There was no other choice than to buy off Frederick, and in June, 1742, the Preliminaries of Breslau ceded to Prussia both Upper and Lower Silesia, including Glatz, but not Teschen and Troppau, while six weeks later a definitive peace was concluded at Berlin. Saxony, which had also formed part of the anti-Austrian coalition, withdrew from it at this time. Frederick had the less compunction in deserting his allies since their co-operation with him in the field had been none too happy, while, like Bismarck but unlike more recent German rulers, he always knew when and where to stop.

The termination of hostilities by no means implied a cessation of diplomatic activity on the part of the Prussian monarch, for he felt far from secure in his conquest; he feared that if Maria Theresa's arms were too successful in other theatres, they might be turned against him once more, and such apprehensions were enhanced when, as a direct consequence of the Peace of Berlin, the Austrians drove out of Bohemia a French army which had invaded that kingdom. Accordingly, Frederick directed his energies throughout the year 1743 to encouraging the Emperor not to come to terms with Vienna, to embittering relations between Austria and Russia, and to endeavouring to persuade the Turks to enter the war. In May, 1744, his efforts took shape in the Union of Frankfort, by which Prussia, Hesse-Cassel, and the Elector Palatine bound themselves together to secure the restoration of Charles VII to his hereditary dominions, the maintenance of the Emperor in his rights, and the re-establishment of peace in Germany.

With this end in view Frederick re-entered the struggle in August, 1744, by invading Bohemia, and this fresh contest between Prussia and Austria lasted until the end of the following year. During its course an event took place which profoundly affected the political situation in Germany, namely the death of the Emperor in January, 1745. The new Elector of Bavaria was a mere youth, and there was no chance of his reviving his father's claims, which in any case had in the end proved of little benefit either to Charles VII or to his Bavarian subjects. A few months later a British defeat by the French at Fontenoy and the outbreak of the Forty-Five offered Frederick further opportunities of improving his position. George II saw himself menaced with the loss of his British throne to Prince Charles Edward, and of his Electorate to the Maréchal de Saxe, and he was in consequence only too willing to reduce the number of his enemies. Frederick, on his part, was in great straits for money, while he was very anxious in case success should crown the efforts of Maria Theresa to bring Russia into the field against him. The result was the Convention of Hanover in August, 1745: by this agreement the King of Prussia bound himself not to vote against the election of Maria Theresa's husband, Francis, as Emperor, and he guaranteed Hanover to George II.

The Convention of Hanover was extremely unwelcome in Vienna, not least because Austria was given no more than six weeks in which to accede to it or face the consequences. Before long, too, further pressure was applied by the British government in the shape of a threat that unless Maria Theresa came to terms with Frederick the subsidies which she was receiving would cease. In the circumstances it was only natural that she should protest against British bad faith, and many of her advisers recalled the diplomacy of Bolingbroke a generation earlier. Nevertheless the military situation eventually compelled Austria to give way, and on Christmas Day, 1745, the Treaty of Dresden definitely ceded Silesia and Glatz to Frederick, who in return acknowledged Francis I as Emperor and guaranteed the Pragmatic Sanction in so far as it related to Germany. Having for five years joined and deserted the various belligerent Powers with equal readiness as it suited his convenience, Frederick thus finally withdrew from the War of the Austrian Succession, the sole substantial gainer from the conflict.

If the interest in the struggle in central Europe had mainly centred round Austria and Prussia, in the west the war had not been long in assuming the old form of a Franco-British conflict. In this the French were greatly aided, not only by the generalship of the Maréchal de Saxe, but also by the outbreak of the Forty-

Five. As in the case of the Habsburgs, so in that of England, it had long been a cardinal maxim of French diplomacy to strike the enemy in the rear. While Scotland was still independent she had, as the ally of France, served this purpose admirably, and even after the union of the crowns she had been made to contribute to French ends. Both Richelieu and Louis XIV had sought to profit by the domestic difficulties of the Stuarts, and when that dynasty was dethroned France was not slow to take advantage of Jacobite feeling: it was solely due to the peculiar position of the Duke of Orleans that a different policy was pursued in respect of the Fifteen.

At no time was it the intention of the French government merely to replace the Guelphs by the Stuarts, for the dealings of Louis XIV with Charles II were not such as to encourage the belief that if the fallen dynasty were restored to the throne it would prove any more susceptible to French pressure. Rather was it the aim of France to revive the state of affairs which had existed before the union of the crowns. Louis XIV had hoped to create an independent Irish kingdom for James II which would have been a perpetual menace to William of Orange in London, and on more than one occasion his great-grandson pursued a policy which had as its end a Stuart restoration in Edinburgh alone: to their credit let it be said that the exiled dynasty steadfastly refused to lend itself to any such project. For the rest, when the general international situation did not admit of an attempt on a big scale, the fire of the Jacobite enthusiasm was always kept alight against the time when it might be advisable to fan it into a blaze.

That Jacobitism was still a very real force in the middle of the eighteenth century there can be no doubt, and the Whig Pulteney declared in 1743 that two-thirds of the nation was opposed to the reigning dynasty. On the other hand, the Jacobites drew much of their support from the national dislike of being ruled by a foreign monarch, and so French diplomacy was constrained to walk warily. The British had shown in no uncertain manner in 1701 that they would not accept a sovereign at the hands of the King of France, so there was always the difficulty that if the French government gave the Stuarts too much support, many of the latter's political supporters would, for patriotic reasons, refuse to move at the critical moment. These complications had come to be thoroughly appreciated at Versailles, where the policy was to aid the Jacobites just enough to distract the government in London, but not so much as to arouse the traditional British xenophobia or to restore James III to all the three kingdoms which his father had lost.

These tactics succeeded admirably during the War of the Austrian Succession. The original intention had been a direct invasion of England, and in February, 1744, Saxe was instructed to land at the mouth of the Thames and to occupy London: a month later, however, the expedition had to be postponed owing to the weather, and further storms, which destroyed a number of transports collected at Brest, caused its abandonment. In the following year Prince Charles Edward, with the most slender resources, came within an ace of success, and the advantages which France gained from his victory at Prestonpans, and subsequent advance to Derby, were enormous. Ten battalions of infantry were at once withdrawn from Flanders, and it was not long before the British forces there were reduced to a mere shadow: German troops as well were sent to suppress the rising, since it was by no means certain what amount of reliance could be placed upon the native British. In consequence, Saxe had a series of easy conquests in the Low Countries, and it was not long before he reached the frontier of the United Provinces. France certainly received a handsome dividend on what she expended for the Stuarts in the Forty-Five.

The third main theatre of war was Italy, where the death of Charles VI seemed to afford Elizabeth Farnese the chance of establishing yet another member of her family upon a throne. The struggle there assumed the time-honoured form of a contest between the Habsburg and Bourbon dynasties, with the House of Savoy taking its wares to the best market: in the present instance this proved to be the Austrian, for the danger to her Italian possessions compelled Maria Theresa to come to terms with the "Prussia of Italy". The British fleet also played its part in the Mediterranean campaign, for it appeared off Naples and threatened to bombard that city if Charles III (Don Carlos of former days) gave any assistance to his Bourbon relatives against Maria Theresa. On the other side France and Spain drew even closer together, and in October, 1743, was concluded the Treaty of Fontainebleau, more usually known as the second Family Compact. This pledged France to help her southern neighbour to recover Gibraltar and Minorca; to recognize the rights of Don Felipe (younger brother of the Neapolitan monarch) to the

D

Milanese, Parma, and Piacenza; and to declare formal war on Britain and Austria, which, as we have seen, she had not at that time yet done.

Thereafter the course of the war in Italy was marked by a good deal of fighting, but without any decisive victory for either side, though on balance Maria Theresa found herself in the better position. Thanks to her own energy and courage, and to the assistance of Sardinia by land and of England by sea, the Italian campaigns had left her not merely with her own territory undiminished, but in possession of that of the Duke of Modena as well. That at the peace she had to give up this acquisition, and also to sacrifice Parma and Piacenza, was due to what had happened elsewhere. Italy had to pay the debts of Flanders.

As the years passed there came over the principal combatants a desire for peace, though it must be admitted that friction between allies had on both sides much to do with the growth of such sentiments. Frederick II had already withdrawn from the conflict in circumstances noted above, while French intrigues with Savoy behind the backs of the Spaniards had, almost on the morrow of the Treaty of Fontainebleau, resulted in a coolness between Paris and Madrid. Then, in July, 1746, Philip V of Spain died, and his successor, Ferdinand VI, not only displayed little interest in the Italian ambitions of his half-brothers, but was by nature of a pacific disposition. Great Britain and the United Provinces were equally inclined towards peace. Indeed, Maria Theresa, who had at last secured a promise of Russian assistance, alone wished to continue the war, but she was powerless in the face of British opposition. Pelham's government informed the King of Sardinia that its financial aid would come to an end, and unwilling as that monarch was to see another Bourbon established upon an Italian throne, he could not fight without British subsidies. Maria Theresa had no means of bringing pressure to bear on London, but she could do nothing in Italy without the Sardinian army and the British fleet, so she had to give way.

Louis XV, whose arms had latterly been crowned with such success in the old cock-pit of the Netherlands, played a prominent part in the ensuing settlement: he declared that he wished to make peace, not like a merchant, but like a King. All the same there was a good deal of manœuvring for position before the final pacification was effected. Kaunitz, whose long ascendancy in Austrian counsels was just beginning, endeavoured to open direct negotiations with France, but the latter was found to be already in communication with Britain, with whom she preferred, if possible, to come to terms. The Congress of Aix-la-Chapelle had actually met in March, 1748, but, as in the case of so many similar gatherings, most of the real business was transacted privately and directly between the Powers chiefly concerned. Finally, on October 18th, a definite treaty was concluded between Britain, France, and the United Provinces; Spain adhered to it two days later; and before the end of the following month Austria and Sardinia had given their reluctant assent.

The basis upon which the Treaty of Aix-la-Chapelle was concluded was a general restitution of conquests, though there were some exceptions. Silesia and Glatz, for example, were guaranteed to Frederick, while the ambitions of Elizabeth Farnese were at last satisfied by the cession of Parma and Piacenza to Don Felipe. Charles Emmanuel of Sardinia, on the other hand, had to content himself with the recovery of Savoy and Nice, which had been occupied during the war by the forces of the Bourbon Powers. For the rest, the Pragmatic Sanction was guaranteed, except in respect of Silesia, Glatz, Parma, and Piacenza; Francis I was recognized as Emperor; the Duke of Modena regained his dominions; and in spite of the protests of Maria Theresa the Barrier fortresses were again committed to the proved inefficiency of their Dutch garrisons.

As between France and Britain the former agreed to conditions which were commensurate neither with her sacrifices nor with her successes. In addition to the restoration of all conquests in the Netherlands and in Italy, the French evacuated Madras, recognized George II and the Hanoverian Succession, and promised to demolish the fortifications of Dunkirk. Great Britain, on her part, reluctantly gave up Cape Breton, but received a pledge that Spain would carry out the commercial concessions promised at Utrecht. There was no determination of boundaries between the British and French possessions in America, and the only stipulation was that matters should be restored to their original footing.

In effect, the Treaty of Aix-la-Chapelle, like the war of which it marked the termination, was in the main indecisive, though some of its provisions were to stand the test of time. The territorial settlement of Italy, although upset during the Revolutionary and Napoleonic Wars, was substantially unaltered until the Risorgimento, while Silesia remained largely in Prussian hands until the second decade of the twentieth century. The struggle for maritime and colonial supremacy was left unsettled, since Britain and France had in reality suspended hostilities, not because they had abandoned their ambitions, but because they had exhausted their immediate resources. Otherwise the Treaty merely marked a stage in the rise of Prussia and Sardinia, in the decline of the United Provinces, in the relaxation of the old alliance between Britain and Austria, and in the intervention of Russia in the affairs of Central Europe.

Such was the close of that War of the Austrian Succession of which Macaulay wrote—with some exaggeration, it must be admitted: "On the head of Frederick is all the blood which was shed in a war which raged during many years and in every quarter of the globe, the blood of the column of Fontenoy, the blood of the mountaineers who were slaughtered at Culloden. The evils produced by his wickedness were felt in lands where the name of Prussia was unknown; and, in order that he might rob a neighbour whom he had promised to defend, black men fought on the coast of Coromandel, and red men scalped each other by the Great Lakes of North America."

himselbut - if he hadnt done it someone else was bound to.

CHAPTER IV

THE EXPANSION OF EUROPE, 1748-1783

WITH the turn of the eighteenth century overseas problems began to affect even more closely the course of events in Europe, and, as we have seen, it was becoming increasingly difficult for Powers to indulge in hostilities in the New World while remaining nominally at peace in the Old; indeed, the day was not far distant when Chatham could speak of Canada having been won on the battle-fields of Germany. The struggle between Britain and Spain over the right of search and the interpretation to be put upon the commercial clauses in the Treaty of Utrecht was, it is true, soon merged in the War of the Austrian Succession, but its very occurrence was prophetic of what lay ahead. The interest of the next international contest, namely the Seven Years' War, was at least as great outside the Old World as within it, and its results in the Americas and in India were to be far more lasting than in Europe.

Nor was it surprising that such should be the case. Just as the ambitions of Prussia and Sardinia were a disturbing factor in Continental politics, so were those of Britain overseas. Ever since the Restoration in 1660 she had been building a colonial empire, but this latter was still only in its early stages, and the Treaty of Aix-la-Chapelle had not taken the matter any farther. Thus, in the middle of the century it was as yet undecided whether North America was to be Latin or Anglo-Saxon, and in India he would have been a bold prophet who would have cared to forecast whether France or Britain would be the heir of the decadent Moghuls.

In spite of British acquisitions at Utrecht the American possessions of King George were shut in on three sides by the colonies of France and Spain. To the north lay Canada; to the west was a line of French forts, reaching from the Great Lakes to New Orleans; and to the south were Louisiana and the Spanish colony of Florida. Only to the east, on the Atlantic, were the British territories unthreatened, and that solely if the command of the sea was retained. Farther away were the

West Indies, that bone of contention between France, Spain, and Britain, and it would have been difficult to exaggerate their economic importance in that age. The success of Louis XIV in setting his grandson upon the throne of Spain had constituted a considerable menace to British interests in the Americas, for henceforth the French and Spanish colonial authorities tended to act closely together, whereas they had formerly been opposed. The Family Compacts were eyed askance by statesmen in London, not because of their effect upon the fate of Italian duchies, but on account of possible repercussion in the Caribbean Sea and the valley of the Mississippi.

In India the earlier years of the century had been for English and French alike a period mainly of commercial prosperity and silent growth, and both nations were occupied in warding off the worst consequences of the rapid decline of the Moghul Empire. During the War of the Spanish Succession various agreements for a local neutrality were made between many of the British, French, and Dutch settlements, and apart from some uneasiness as to the fate of incoming and outgoing ships, neither side seems to have feared aggression on the part of the other. In the War of the Austrian Succession it was otherwise, and the roar of the French guns off Madras in 1746 announced the beginning of a new era in the East, although in Bengal a strict neutrality continued to be observed between the British and French. The principle that peace or war between European nations necessarily involves peace or war between their distant possessions had received recognition.

While all this combustible material was lying about in India and in the Americas, every day that passed afforded further evidence that, in spite of the hopes of Louis XV, the Treaty of Aix-la-Chapelle was a mere truce. It had satisfied nobody, which is tantamount to saying that it had dissatisfied everybody. The French felt that they had been made the catspaw of the King of Prussia, while Maria Theresa still nourished a grudge against her British allies for compelling her to make peace when her prospects appeared so encouraging. For a few years the Powers concerned were content to lick their wounds, but in every case with the determination to renew the conflict when opportunity occurred.

One thing at any rate was clear, and it was that Frederick had by no means abandoned his designs upon his neighbours' possessions in the effort to link up his own scattered dominions in one geographical and political whole. In 1752, believing himself to be on the point of death, he had drawn up a political testament for his successor. In this document he stressed the desirability of acquiring by conquest the electorate of Saxony, Polish West Prussia, and Swedish Pomerania, but of these he attached the greatest importance to Saxony, both on account of its wealth and of its strategic position as a bulwark of defence for Brandenburg against attack from the south. The Prussian King proposed that the Elector of Saxony should be compensated with Bohemia, which would have the added advantage of further weakening the Habsburgs. The French knew of these designs, and, with a vivid recollection of what had happened in the War of the Austrian Succession, they saw no reason why they should again pull Prussian chestnuts out of the fire. In this attitude they were encouraged by Kaunitz, who, after representing Maria Theresa at Versailles for three years, had in 1753 returned to Vienna to become Chancellor. The stage was set for the Diplomatic Revolution and the Seven Years' War.

Long, however, before the first shots were fired in the European theatre hostilities had begun unofficially between Britain and France in America, largely as a result of the failure of the Treaty of Aix-la-Chapelle to define the boundaries of their respective colonies. The opening incident occurred near Fort Duquesne in June, 1754, and, after some fruitless negotiations, twelve months later a British squadron under Boscowen was sent into the Straits of Belle Isle to intercept French ships carrying soldiers and stores, and two transports, as well as a number of merchant-men, were seized. The government of Louis XV did not reply with an immediate declaration of war, but it was clear that this could not be long delayed, and the necessity of protecting Hanover compelled Great Britain to look for assistance on the mainland of Europe. Recourse was had at first to the old ally, Austria, and Maria Theresa was found to be quite willing to help in the defence of the electorate, but only on condition that the British subsidies should be on a sufficiently large scale to enable her to take up arms against Prussia: now, this was exactly what George II and his ministers did not want, for it would have exposed Hanover to attack by the Prussians as well as by the French, and so the Anglo-Austrian discussions came to nothing.

The next approach was to Frederick, who proved much more

[margin annotations: Diplomatic Revolution / Anglo-Prussian alliance / Franco-Austrian alliance]

amenable, and in January, 1756, he signed the Treaty of West-minster, by which he guaranteed the neutrality of Hanover: thus the French, who had been for many years united with him in a defensive alliance, found themselves prevented by their Prussian ally from attacking the German possessions of George II. In these circumstances it is not surprising that Frederick's action should have roused ill-feeling in France, and Kaunitz took full advantage of French resentment. Accordingly, on May 1st, 1756, was concluded the Treaty of Versailles between Austria and France: it comprised a convention of neutrality, a defensive alliance, and a secret agreement of five articles. Under the first of these heads Maria Theresa bound herself to observe absolute neutrality in the war between Britain and France, while Louis XV promised to respect the Austrian Netherlands and the other Habsburg possessions. By the defensive alliance the two Powers guaranteed to each other the security and reciprocal defence of their European dominions, and mutually promised an auxiliary force of 24,000 men in the case of either being attacked. Finally, by the secret convention, Austria signified her readiness to intervene in case a Power allied to England should invade the territory of His Most Christian Majesty, and Louis XV gave a similar promise to the Empress.

Such was the famous Diplomatic Revolution which put an end to a system of alliances which had lasted for two generations. A close examination of the conditions in which it took place would seem to show that, with the exception of Kaunitz, who from the beginning had a clear view of what he wanted, circumstances had as much to do with the new arrangement as had the deliberate resolve of the statesmen concerned, though general dissatisfaction dating at least from the Treaty of Aix-la-Chapelle played its part.

Thus came about that Franco-Austrian understanding which Louis XIV had envisaged in the last years of his life, but in very different circumstances from those in which Le Roi Soleil would have concluded it. Austria clearly was the gainer by the Treaty of Versailles. She changed the most formidable Power in Europe from an enemy into a friend; she freed herself from anxiety in respect of the Netherlands; and she recovered her freedom of action against Frederick. France, on the other hand, had allowed herself to be rushed into some dangerous concessions whereby she made it impossible for herself to obtain in the Low Countries any indemnification for potential overseas losses; nor was this all, for she converted Prussia, which had no particular quarrel with her, from a neutral into an enemy. French diplomacy was at its weakest in the middle of the eighteenth century: Saint-Sévérin, who represented France at Aix-la-Chapelle, and Cardinal de Bernis, who negotiated the Treaty of Versailles, both did their country an ill turn, though Louis XV must, of course, bear his share of the blame.

On the other side, Prussia stood to benefit very considerably. Frederick did not believe that the French would be of any great assistance to the Empress, owing to their war against Britain, while there was little chance of Spain giving them any active support so long as Ferdinand VI was on the throne. It was true that ever since 1748 there had been in existence a defensive alliance between Austria and Russia directed against him, but he reckoned, mistakenly as the event was to show, that Maria Theresa could depend even less on her Russian than on her French allies; the health of the Empress Elizabeth was none too good; the heir, Peter, was a fervent admirer of the Prussian monarch; and the leading Russian statesmen were in British pay. Furthermore, Frederick stood a much better chance of realizing his Saxon ambitions in concert with England than with France, for the Dauphine was a daughter of the Elector of Saxony. As for Great Britain, the Diplomatic Revolution was calculated to prove of greater advantage to the dynastic interests of her German ruler than to herself, though as events turned out the reverse proved to be the case.

The summer of 1756 was thus characterized by a situation of the most extreme tension, and little doubt existed in Vienna that Frederick would seize the first opportunity to attack the Empress. The movement of some Russian troops to the Russian frontier, subsequently countermanded at the request of Maria Theresa as unduly provocative, gave Frederick an excuse to mobilize. By the end of June he was writing to his representative in Vienna that war was inevitable, and to his sister that " we have one foot in the stirrup, and I think the other will soon follow ". It did follow very soon. Frederick addressed to the Empress an ultimatum as to her armaments and intentions, and, without waiting for her reply, invaded Saxony at the end of August. To an envoy from the Saxon Elector he announced, "If fortune favours me, the Elector will not only be amply compensated for everything, but I shall take as much thought for his interests as for my own". Frederick Augustus realized that this meant embroiling him with the Empress in an attempt to secure him the kingdom of Bohemia as compensation for the cession of his electorate to Prussia, so he retired to Poland: the Saxon army was compelled to lay down its arms, and by the middle of October the electorate was in Prussian hands.

The invasion of Saxony united the continental nations against Frederick, and not only Austria, Russia, and France, but the Empire itself and Sweden, resolved to take up arms against the disturber of the peace. A second Treaty of Versailles was signed in May, 1757, between France and Austria, and its terms are evidence that the two Powers intended to put an end to the Prussian menace once and for all. France bound herself to furnish, over and above the 24,000 auxiliaries prescribed by the previous treaty, the Austrian armies with 10,000 German soldiers, put 105,000 men of her own into the field, and pay an annual subsidy of twelve million florins. In return she was to obtain the towns of Mons, Ypres, Furnes, Ostend, and Nieuport: the rest of the Netherlands was assigned to Don Felipe whose duchies of Parma and Piacenza were to revert to the Empress. The two Powers further promised not to lay down their arms until the King of Prussia had been forced to cede Silesia and Glatz to Austria, and Magdeburg and Halberstadt to Sweden. In February, 1757, the Tsarina also promised not to make peace until Silesia and Glatz had been restored and Prussia had been finally enfeebled.

The stage was now set for the Seven Years' War, and during the earlier part of the ensuing conflict Frederick, who had the advantage of operating on interior lines, made headway against his enemies with surprising success. The French were defeated at Rossbach, while the Austrians, after being vanquished at Prague and victorious at Kolin, had been utterly routed at Leuthen. In April, 1758, a second Treaty of Westminster stipulated that neither Britain nor Prussia should make a separate peace, and Frederick was promised a subsidy of £670,000. The real danger to Prussia, however, came from the east, whence the Russians, although checked from time to time, pressed slowly forward, until in October, 1760, they occupied Berlin itself. The next twelve months saw Frederick, surrounded by foes, on the very brink of destruction, and he was only saved by the death, in

January, 1762, of the Tsarina Elizabeth. Her successor, Peter III, at once completely reversed Russian policy, and by June of the same year he was Frederick's ally. This new alliance was not destined to be of long duration, for Peter was soon murdered: Catherine II, however, remained neutral, and this fact was of enormous advantage to Prussia. Indeed, that Power was saved from destruction by the vacillation of Russia, who may be said to have intervened decisively in the affairs of Central Europe. What had been a threat in the War of the Austrian Succession developed into a very definite reality in the Seven Years' War.

While Frederick was thus experiencing to the full the vicissitudes of fortune, his British ally, after a bad start with the loss of Minorca, was going on from strength to strength under the inspiring leadership of William Pitt the Elder. The year 1757 had witnessed the victories of Clive in India, and the consequent resolving of any doubt as to which European Power was in future to be supreme in that country; its successor was marked by the capture of Louisburg; and in 1759 the capture of Quebec by Wolfe, entailed the loss of Canada by the French. Frederick was certainly earning the subsidies with which he was supplied by London, for in the circumstances France could provide neither the men nor the money to retain her overseas possessions.

At this point, yet another Power, namely Spain, began to show signs of entering the conflict. Ferdinand VI died in 1759 and was succeeded by Charles III, previously King of the Two Sicilies, who was frankly in sympathy with France. The Duke of Choiseul, who had by now succeeded the Cardinal de Bernis as chief minister of Louis XV, was determined to take full advantage of this unexpected piece of good luck, for the fortunes of France were at a very low ebb, after the loss of Quebec and the defeat at Minden, and he was not very well informed, as events were soon to show, about the condition of Spanish resources. The result was the conclusion of the third Family Compact, to which Naples and Parma also adhered, in August, 1761. After stipulating for the mutual aid to be afforded, the two Powers promised not to treat for peace "save by mutual and common agreement and consent". By a secret convention Spain undertook to declare war on May 1st, 1762, if peace had not been concluded by that date, and Portugal was to be compelled, if necessary by force, to embrace the cause of the Bourbon Powers. Further, any "Power which shall become the enemy of the one or the other of the two Crowns" was declared the enemy of both.

Not the least interesting aspect of the third Family Compact was the commercial. In the first place, Spaniards and Neapolitans were no longer to be classed as aliens in France, while the French were to enjoy the same advantages in Spain and the Two Sicilies. Further arrangements included liberty of import and export for subjects of each Crown in the dominions of the others; equal treatment in the matter of trade, taxes, and navigation; and a united attitude on the part of the representatives of the Bourbon Powers in their relations with foreign states. The growing importance of economic considerations is thus strongly emphasised in this otherwise largely dynastic agreement, and it may be observed that the prospect of freer trade between the Bourbon states did little to recommend the third Family Compact in British commercial circles.

While these negotiations were in progress Choiseul was also treating for peace with England, where the accession of George III in 1760 had considerably modified the existing political situation. What the French statesman appears to have had in view was to use the Family Compact either to induce the British government to modify its terms, or, if the war continued, to supplement the diminishing resources of France by the strength of neutral Spain. He over-estimated Spanish might, and he did not know Pitt. Whether the Englishman was at once aware of the details of the Family Compact is immaterial; he knew enough to realize what was at stake, and he became convinced, not only that war with Spain was inevitable, but also that it should be declared by Britain at once.

Pitt had little difficulty in persuading his colleagues to break off the negotiations with France, but the majority of them declined to go so far as an immediate declaration of war against Spain. Cabinet meetings in the middle of September, 1761, were in consequence stormy in the extreme. The Great Commoner laid before his colleagues an intercepted letter from the Spanish representative in Paris, which revealed everything. He showed, in an impressive speech, that the danger could only increase if Spain were left to declare war at the moment stipulated in the Family Compact. There was at present but one House of Bourbon. The Spanish fleet must be regarded as the French fleet. "Spain is France," he declared, "and France is Spain." It was all to no purpose. The peace party in the Cabinet raised the objection that action could not be taken on the ground of an intercepted letter without a previous declaration of war, and that the attack on the Spanish fleet off Cape Passaro in 1718, without such a declaration, still remained a cause of bitterness. Finally, it was decided merely to make a protest to Madrid, and to ask for an explanation; perhaps also to make some advances towards a settlement of Anglo-Spanish differences in the Americas. On October 5th, 1761, Pitt resigned. The outside world thus had another example of the fact that there are definite limitations to the power of even the greatest British minister, a fact which, if remembered more often, would save that outside world many disappointments.

However pacific may have been the intentions of the new King and his advisers, events soon hurried them into the course of action which Pitt had advocated, and on January 2nd, 1762, war was declared on Spain. Then was seen the falsity of Choiseul's calculations, for France merely involved her ally in her own down-fall. The campaign of 1762 entailed upon the French the loss of such possessions as they still held in the West Indies, while the British conquered Havana and the Philippines from Spain.

These successes, however, had in no way diminished the desire of George III and his new Prime Minister, Bute, for peace at the earliest possible moment. In these circumstances Frederick, surrounded by his foes, was clearly a liability, and Bute stopped the subsidies which the Prussian King had been receiving from England: instead he was offered good advice to the effect that he should make a sacrifice for the cause of peace. Frederick never forgot the treatment which he received from the British Government in 1762, and eleven years later he declined the suggestion of an English alliance because of "the indecent, I might almost say infamous, way in which England treated me at the last peace". It must be admitted that at this time the British Government had a bad reputation in the matter of the treatment of its allies. At Utrecht it had made peace with the enemy, and left them to get what terms they could, while at Aix-la-Chapelle the Austrians had been the victim of much the same manœuvre as that of which Frederick was now complaining. There was, indeed, much to be said against Britain's cynical dis-regard of her ally in 1762, but not by one with the record of the King of Prussia.

With Bute in power occasion was soon found for resuming negotiations with Choiseul, though at first these were, for the sake of secrecy, carried on through the medium of the Sardinian representative in the British and French capitals. The preliminaries were signed at Fontainebleau in November, 1762, but the treaty was not finally concluded until the virtual completion of the separate negotiation between Austria and Prussia. It may be noted that during the final stage of the discussions the British plenipotentiary, the Duke of Bedford, had been seriously handicapped by the fact that the Chevalier d'Eon had become acquainted with his instructions, and had passed on the information to Choiseul. So unhappy, however, were the relations between British statesmen at that time that Bedford never doubted for one moment but that he had been betrayed by Bute.

The Peace of Paris, finally concluded in February, 1763, greatly strengthened the position of Great Britain in the Americas. She received Canada and Cape Breton, but ceded to France the islands of St. Pierre and Miquelon as an unfortified station for French fishermen, who were guaranteed their rights under the Treaty of Utrecht. Britain also obtained St. Vincent, Dominica, and Tobago, while Guadaloupe and Martinique fell to France. Spain regained Havana and the Philippines, but she had to surrender Florida and Minorca, and to renounce her claim to participate in the Newfoundland fishing; on the other hand, the British government agreed, in exchange for a guarantee of a limited participation in the logwood trade, to dismantle forts which had been erected in the Bay of Honduras. It was agreed that the Mississippi from source to mouth should form the frontier in North America, except for Louisiana, which France ceded to Spain as compensation for the loss of Florida. In India the *status quo* of 1749 was restored, but the French also undertook not to keep an army in Bengal. Finally, the fortifications of Dunkirk were to be reduced to the condition stipulated by the Treaty of Aix-la-Chapelle.

A few days after the conclusion of peace between Great Britain and the Bourbon Powers the Treaty of Hubertusburg put an end to the Seven Years' War in Germany. To the very last Frederick had clung to the hope that he might acquire Saxony, and in his negotiations with Peter III he had expressed his willingness to hand East Prussia over to the Tsar in exchange for the electorate. Circumstances, however, were against him, and he had to be content with the return of Glatz by the Austrians, who had held it for two and a half years. The basis upon which peace was made was the *status quo ante bellum*. Between France and Prussia no peace was made, for the simple reason that although they had been fighting one another for nearly seven years neither had officially declared war on the other.

The Treaties of Paris and Hubertusburg settled several problems which had been envisaged at Utrecht and left unsolved at Aix-la-Chapelle. Great Britain, for example, definitely established her position as the leading maritime and colonial Power: it is true that had Pitt remained in office she would probably have obtained even more, but she was unquestionably the chief gainer by the Seven Years' War. In marked contrast was the decline of France both in Europe and overseas: her armies had been beaten in three continents, and the conditions which she was compelled to accept were the measure of her decadence. As for Frederick, his personal reputation as a general had been raised enormously, and all Europe, whether friend or foe, esteemed him as one of the greatest monarchs who had ever sat upon a throne; but this could not disguise the fact that he had failed to achieve the political object of the war, for the Prussian kingdom remained divided. One fact stood out above all others, and it was that the fate of Prussia depended upon the attitude of Russia. A century later this truth was clearly realized by another great Prussian statesman, Bismarck, but only to be forgotten by his successors, William II and Adolf Hitler.

The twenty years which followed this settlement were marked by the temporary eclipse of the very Power which in 1763 appeared to be in the strongest position, namely Great Britain. If the Treaty of Paris was one of the most gratifying international agreements which her representatives have ever signed, the Treaty of Versailles in 1783 was one of the most shameful. What, then, was the cause of this sudden reversal of fortune? It was due to two main factors—the isolation of Britain after 1763, and the repercussions of the Treaty of Paris in the New World.

The Diplomatic Revolution had put an end to the old Austro-British alliance, which had existed for two generations, and Frederick's anger at the treatment which he received in 1762 prevented the later understanding between London and Berlin from taking its place. With France and Spain there could be no real friendship, while Russia was too far away to constitute at that time an important factor in British policy. So long, however, as Britain was not in difficulties in other parts of the world her overwhelming naval supremacy rendered the attitude of the Continental Powers a matter of comparative indifference to her, and George III, unlike his two immediate predecessors, took no interest in the fate of Hanover. It was when trouble came else-where that the lack of friends on the mainland of Europe was so severely felt, and isolation proved to be far from splendid in the War of American Independence, as, indeed, was again to be the case when not dissimilar conditions obtained at the end of the following century when Britain was at war with the Boer Republics.

These facts were not appreciated by George III and Lord North, who were blinded to the risk of foreign intervention in the struggle against the American colonists by the fixed idea that the House of Bourbon would never ally itself with insurgents. They were speedily and rudely undeceived. There was not a Power which had not some grudge against Britain, and now that she was without a friend on the Continent the opportunity to humiliate her was too good to be missed. France and Spain took up arms in due course, and even the Dutch made a treaty with the American Congress. In the autumn of 1779 the Franco-Spanish fleet was able to sweep the Channel, while the British ships dared not put to sea. In the north the Armed Neutrality drew up its own list of contraband, and refused to accept the British interpretation of the right of search.

What had caused this situation to arise was, curiously enough, the Paris settlement of 1763. Canada may have been won on the battle-fields of Germany, but the American colonies were lost in the French capital. No longer threatened on three sides by the Bourbon Powers, they soon began to feel strong enough to stand alone, and it is no mere coincidence that only thirteen years after the conclusion of the Treaty of Paris the Declaration of Inde-pendence was signed. Rarely has there been so rapid a reversal of fortune as that which Great Britain experienced between 1763 and 1783.

This state of affairs found expression in the latter year in the Treaty of Versailles, which brought the War of American Inde-pendence to an end. France obtained St. Lucia and Tobago in the West Indies, together with Senegal and Goree in Africa, and regained her establishments in India, while the provisions of the Treaty of Utrecht were abrogated in what concerned the demolition of the fortifications of Dunkirk. Spain received Minorca and Florida, but she was forced to abandon all hope of Gibraltar, which she had besieged in vain during the course of the struggle. The clauses which recognized the independence of the United States were also expressive of the extremity to which Britain had been reduced. The boundaries of the country were enlarged unduly; the fisheries' concessions were too liberal; and, above all, the conditions as to the United Empire Loyalists were, so far as the Americans were concerned, insincere and inoperative.

With the greater part of her overseas empire lost, her finances in chaos, and disunity at home, Britain in 1783 appeared on the eve of descent to the rank of a second-rate Power. He would, indeed, have been a bold prophet who would have foretold that before another generation was past her fleets would once more control the seas, and that her soldiers would be in garrison on the soil of France.

CHAPTER V

THE PARTITIONS OF POLAND, 1763–1795

IN few countries have domestic politics exercised so profound an influence upon foreign policy as in the case of Russia. This is not to say that over a term of years her relations with her neighbours have not been conducted according to principles dictated, as in the case of all nations, by her geographical position, but rather that those principles have been applied in such a way as to reflect, more often than elsewhere, the idiosyncrasies of those who at various times have been her rulers. The government of Russia has been well defined as a despotism tempered by assassination, and never was that statement more true than in the eighteenth and nineteenth centuries, when the consequences of this state of affairs came to be felt far beyond the boundaries of the Russian state.

It was only natural that such should be the case in view of the ruling of Peter the Great that every Tsar should appoint his successor. Accordingly, although the Tsars were all members of the House of Romanoff, selection within the dynasty was wide, while there were long and glorious periods when the country was governed by Empresses. We have already seen, in the last stages of the Seven Years' War, how dramatically events in the palace at St. Petersburg could affect the destinies of other nations, and there were to be further examples of this in the future. Given the uncertain position of the Romanoff succession, and the frequent crimes by which it was marked, the reluctance of Metternich and other contemporary statesmen to accept Alexander I, himself suspect of at any rate connivance at regicide, as the apostle of legitimacy becomes easier to understand.

Such was the background against which Russian foreign policy was set, but of one thing there could be no doubt, and that was that the influence of Russia over her neighbours was increasing with every year that passed. Her intervention in the War of the Polish Succession had proved decisive, and the action of Peter III had alone saved Frederick the Great from destruction at the hands of his enemies. The Prussian King was never under any illusions on this score, and he made no secret of his belief that Russia was a "deadly neighbour and a peril to the whole of Europe". All the same, adversity proverbially makes strange bedfellows, and the truth of this adage was emphasized on the morrow of the Treaty of Paris. In spite of all his efforts Frederick had failed to obtain Saxony, and the Prussian dominions were as scattered as ever, while the Empress had been equally unsuccessful in her attempts to regain Silesia: in short, if Berlin and Vienna desired further expansion or compensation they must look beyond the frontiers of the Reich, and from this moment the partition of Poland became a distinct possibility. Not, indeed, that the idea originated at this time, for partition had been mentioned nearly a century before by Charles X of Sweden to the Great Elector.

The Russian government was certainly not prepared to hand Poland over either to the ambitions of Frederick or to those of the Empress, and for some time it wavered between the policy of an independent Polish state dominated by Russia and that of annexation in whole or in part. The same indecision on the part of St. Petersburg was to be observed in respect of Turkey in the following century during the reign of Nicholas I.

The path of the three Powers—Austria, Prussia, and Russia—was rendered easier by the eclipse of French influence in eastern Europe: this had been most marked at the time of the War of the Polish Succession, and the reverses which France had suffered in the Seven Years' War had still further lowered her prestige. It was the policy of Choiseul to retrieve the situation by means of the Austrian alliance. Whether he would have succeeded if left to himself is at least a moot point, but he was not left to himself. Louis XV was as distrustful of Vienna as he was of St. Petersburg and Berlin, and he consequently resisted any extension of Austrian influence in Poland or Turkey. It can hardly be denied that in the long run the King proved to be right, for the Austria of the later eighteenth century was far from being the "satisfied" Power which she had been on the morrow of the Treaty of Utrecht. Under the growing influence of the King of the Romans, after 1765 the Emperor Joseph II, her foreign policy became distinctly adventurous, and had Choiseul had his way France might have been involved in schemes which accorded ill with her true interests. In the meantime, however, the opposition between the official diplomacy of the country and the secret agents of the King caused such confusion as to reduce the influence of France to its nadir, at any rate in central and eastern Europe.

In Sweden, on the other hand, Louis XV was more successful.

For several decades there had been in that country a struggle between the Hats, who supported the traditional alliance with France, and the Caps, who looked rather to Russia: on the death of Adolphus Frederick in 1771 the Caps appeared likely to be triumphant, and it was clear that a great deal depended upon the amount of support which the new King, Gustavus III, would receive from the French Government. Louis XV was now in the last years of his life, in other words just at the time when both at home and abroad he was displaying an ability and an energy which, had he shown them earlier, might have had the most profound effect upon the history of his country. He readily promised to pay Gustavus unconditionally the outstanding French subsidies at the rate of one and a half million livres annually, and he sent as his representative to Stockholm one of the ablest French diplomats in the person of the Comte de Vergennes. With this backing Gustavus succeeded in the monarchical *coup d'état* of 1772: the influence of France in the north was thus re-established in the very year which witnessed its extinction in the east. The credit must go to Louis XV, for Choiseul had been dismissed more than eighteen months earlier.

In Poland, however, a very different state of affairs prevailed. The death of Augustus III in 1763 provided an excellent opportunity for foreign interference of which Russia and Prussia were not slow to take advantage. Frederick and Catherine had, in the first instance, a common interest in the continuance of the existing anarchy in Poland, since a strong and well-regulated state would prove an effective barrier to their ambitions. Their candidate was Stanislaus Poniatowski, who, as the Russian Empress very pertinently remarked, "had least right of all and must therefore feel more indebted to Russia than anyone else". In support of his election Russian troops were moved into Poland, and an agreement was made with Frederick by which he promised to exert military pressure on the Prusso-Polish frontier. In these circumstances it is hardly surprising that by the end of 1764 Stanislaus should have been elected King of Poland. Russian diplomacy had secured a notable triumph.

At this point Catherine became involved in a war with Turkey which complicated the situation, while Austria, in 1768, occupied the Polish district of the Zips, on the ground of a very dubious mortgage dating from the early years of the fifteenth century. It was at this point that the differences of opinion at the Russian

Court with regard to the policy which should be pursued in respect of Poland, to which allusion has already been made, were most marked. The one view, put forward by Count Nikita Panin, the Foreign Minister, was in favour of the country being brought into increasing dependence on Russia by continuous interference in its internal affairs, but without any curtailment of territory. The other standpoint, namely the annexation of Poland, was that of the War Minister, Count Zachary Chernuisheff, who quoted as a precedent the Austrian action in the Zips.

Actually Catherine had no such freedom of choice, for the Polish and Turkish questions were becoming intermingled, to her disadvantage. She was, in effect, on the horns of a dilemma, and she only extricated herself from the difficulties of her position by recourse to such masterful diplomacy that it won the reluctant admiration of no less a judge than the Austrian Chancellor, Kaunitz. The maintenance of Polish integrity might, it is true, bring Poland under Russian influence, but it had already been violated by Austria; moreover, Joseph and his mother were alarmed at Russian ambitions in the Balkans, and unless Prussia stood firmly by Russia there was a distinct possibility that Austria might come to the aid of the Sultan. In that event Catherine would have a first-class war on her hands, and while she was fighting it Frederick would be able to settle the affairs of Poland as he pleased.

The King of Prussia saw the situation no less clearly if from a different angle. Accordingly he had meetings with Joseph II both in 1769 and 1770, and as a result he came to the conclusion that only a partition of Poland could prevent a general conflict which, as the Seven Years' War had proved, would not serve any particular Prussian interest. Catherine was not long in discovering what was in Frederick's mind, and with the Turkish war on her hands, as well as with Austria assuming a threatening attitude, she was determined at all costs to retain Prussia on her side. In July, 1770, therefore, she took advantage of the presence of Frederick's brother, Henry, in Stockholm to invite him to visit her at St. Petersburg. It was at one of the parties held in honour of Prince Henry that the question of the partition of Poland was first broached on the part of Russia. "*Mais pourquoi pas s'emparer de l'évêché de Warmie?*[1] *Car il faut, après tout, que chacun ait quelque chose*", Count Chernuisheff observed to the Prussian prince, and the

---

[1] Ermeland.

Tsarina added, *"Mais pourquoi pas tout le monde se prendait-il aussi?"*

The suggestion quickly bore fruit. Frederick was determined to prevent war between Russia and Austria, into which he could hardly fail to be drawn, and he first of all averted this danger by obtaining, at the close of 1771, a declaration from Catherine to the effect that she would surrender the Danubian principalities. On February 17th, 1772, the Russo-Prussian Treaty of Partition was signed at St. Petersburg, and at the beginning of August the adhesion of Austria took place. The First Partition of Poland was an accomplished fact.

Poland was thus deprived of about one-third of its territory and of its population. Prussia acquired Ermeland and West Prussia with the exception of Danzig and Thorn, and thus realized Hohenzollern ambitions in the east by linking up Brandenburg with the outlying Prussian possessions. To Russia fell the strip of Livonia which had remained in Polish hands, as well as White Russia along the Dwina and the Dnieper. Catherine, it is not uninteresting to note, always maintained, even after the Third Partition, that she had not taken any genuinely Polish territory, and she represented the acquisition of White Russia, with its Orthodox population, as an act of national liberation. As for Austria, she obtained part of Little Poland, except Cracow, and the greater part of East Galicia. It is difficult to resist the conclusion that Austria had in reality the least to gain by the partition. She lost the former security of her north-eastern frontier, and she became encumbered with non-German territory which it was not to her interest to possess, but with which her enemies were only too pleased to see her embarrassed. She had taken the first step on the road to Sadowa—and Serajevo.

This was the first occasion on which a common interest in the affairs of Poland had brought together the Courts of Berlin, St. Petersburg, and Vienna, and it was not to be the last, but the First Partition had not long been concluded before the shadow of yet another disputed succession, this time in Bavaria, fell across Central Europe. For many years the Habsburgs had cast as covetous eyes in the direction of Bavaria as had Frederick in that of Saxony, and the marriage of Joseph with the sister of the childless Elector of Bavaria had been concluded mainly in order that the electorate might pass to the Imperial dynasty, but the Empress died without issue, and in 1777 her brother followed her to the grave.

The Elector Palatine succeeded to the inheritance, but he had little interest in Bavaria, and in January, 1778, he came to an agreement with Vienna by which he sacrificed the interest of the heir presumptive, the Duke of Zweibrücken-Birkenfeld, to Joseph II, who thus seemed to have secured, without striking a blow, a German land which not only carried the Habsburg monarchy into the very heart of the Reich, but also brought its dominions in Germany nearer to its Italian possessions. When the agreement was signed Joseph and Kaunitz thought that they had gained their point. They reckoned upon the French alliance, on the absorption of Russia in the affairs of Turkey, and on English pre-occupation with the American revolt; as for Prussia, they did not believe that Frederick had any other interest save to retain what he had already acquired.

Never were men more rapidly or more completely undeceived. Frederick, having persuaded the Tsarina that the least change in the Germanic Constitution would be prejudicial to the interests of Russia, espoused the cause of the disinherited heir. He put forward certain proposals of his own: when these were not accepted he invaded Bohemia at the head of 100,000 men, and advanced as far as the Elbe. Joseph at once appealed to France for support, but only to meet with the reply that the Treaty of Versailles, which had been invoked, did not cover the extension, but only the protection, of the Austrian dominions, and that the *casus fœderis* did not arise. Apart from these technicalities the French Government had no desire to see the aggrandizement of Austria at the expense of its old Bavarian ally.

That most extraordinary of European conflicts, the War of the Bavarian Succession, now ensued, and although some of the greatest generals of the age were concerned, there was neither a siege nor a battle of any moment. Frederick had merely taken up arms to oppose the acquisition of Bavaria by Austria, and he had no interest in fighting for its own sake—his reputation had been made long before. As for Joseph, when the moment came he was not prepared to put his fortunes to the test with the menace of Russia on the flank.

Peace was made by the Treaty of Teschen, and the settlement was as important as the war to which it put an end had been unexciting. Austria obtained that part of the territory of Berghausen which lies between the Danube, the Inn, and the Salza, and by this acquisition direct communication was established between the archduchy of Austria and the Tyrol. In return, Joseph and his mother renounced all claim to the Bavarian inheritance, and further bound themselves to assist in the eventual union of the margravates of Baireuth and Ansbach with the Prussian monarchy. In other words, the French alliance by which Kaunitz had set such store had failed Austria when she most needed its help, while the support of Russia had greatly strengthened the position of Frederick. The Habsburgs had sustained a severe reverse, and the consequences promised to be extremely serious.

Joseph was far from abandoning his Bavarian ambitions as a result of the Treaty of Teschen, and for some years he endeavoured to effect an exchange of the electorate against the Austrian Netherlands; these last, however, did not long remain a marketable commodity from the Habsburg standpoint, for in 1787 they rose in revolt against the reforms which the Emperor was endeavouring to force upon them. On the other hand, a common interest in the fate of Turkey was bringing the Courts of St. Petersburg and Vienna closer together, and in 1787 the two Powers jointly went to war with the Porte, as the Turkish government was then called. By this time Frederick the Great was dead—he died in 1786—but not before he had brought into being the *Fürsten Bund*, consisting of the Archbishop of Mainz, the Electors of Saxony and Hanover, and many other German princes, who thereby ranged themselves under the leadership of Prussia. Indeed, had Frederick left a successor of his own calibre the events of the sixties of the following century might well have been anticipated by two generations: as it was, Prussian policy was for the most part weak and vacillating for many years after his death until, in 1862, the reins passed into the capable hands of Bismarck.

While these events were taking place in Germany the unfortunate Poles were experiencing to the full the consequences of what had happened in 1772. Their country, or what was left of it, had become to all intents and purposes a dependency of Russia, whose troops were quartered in Poland and whose ambassador was as powerful at Warsaw as is the British Resident at the court of some petty Indian prince. Such being the case, there not unnaturally grew up a most violent antipathy to Russia and all her works, combined with a conviction that internal reforms of the most sweeping nature were inevitable if Poland was ever to regain her independence. Yet this was exactly what Russia, if not Prussia and Austria, could always be relied upon to oppose, and when, on

May 3rd, 1791, the Diet adapted a new constitution greatly strengthening the power of the monarchy it was clear that the gauntlet had been thrown down to the Tsarina.

At the moment Catherine was not in a position to take immediate action, as she was at war with the Turks, and the attitude of Austria and Prussia was causing her some anxiety. The Turkish War was soon liquidated by the Treaty of Jassy in January, 1792, but the other complication was not so easily removed. The new Emperor, Leopold II, a far shrewder and more balanced man than his predecessor, had a meeting with Frederick William II of Prussia at Pillnitz in August, 1791, and although their discussions were mainly concerned with France, the two monarchs ratified an agreement made in the previous month by which the integrity and free constitution of Poland were guaranteed, and an embargo was placed on the accession to the Polish throne of a prince from any of the three neighbouring states. It will thus be seen that under the direction of Leopold the initiative was again passing into the hands of Austria, who was not only departing from the Russophil policy which had marked the later years of Joseph II, but was taking Prussia with her.

The Tsarina was indeed checked, and she realized that her main hope of obtaining a free hand in Poland lay in implicating Austria and Prussia in the French Revolution. "I cudgel my brains", she said, "to urge the Courts of Vienna and Berlin to busy themselves with the affairs of France. I wish them to do this that I may have my own elbows free. I have many unfinished enterprises, and I wish these two Courts to be fully occupied so that they may not disturb me." It was not the last time that the fate of Poland was to be decided by the progress of events in western Europe.

The early months of 1792, however, were marked by changes extremely propitious to the furtherance of Russian ambitions. In January, as we have seen, the Turkish war came to an end, and in the same month the principalities of Ansbach and Baireuth reverted, on the abdication of their ruler, to Frederick William II, and this extension of Prussian power in South Germany was far from being relished in Vienna. In March the Emperor died, and under his young and inexperienced successor, Francis II, Austrian policy tended to revert to that reckless acquisitiveness which had characterized the reign of Joseph II. Above all, on April 20th the French Assembly declared war on Austria, and the conjuncture for which Catherine had been waiting was at hand.

The first step was to find an excuse for intervention, but that did not present any great difficulty. The chief opponents of Stanislaus, who had spent the winter in Russia awaiting their instructions from the Tsarina, returned to their own country, and at once formed the Confederation of Targowice. In their manifesto they denounced what they termed the establishment of despotism in Poland, demanded the restoration of liberty and the old constitution, and appealed to Russia for assistance. A few days later the Russian Minister presented to the Diet the Tsarina's formal declaration of her intention to support the Confederation, and on May 19th, 1792, one Russian army entered Poland and another crossed the frontier into Lithuania. The Poles themselves were as much taken by surprise at this move as if they had no reason to anticipate any such action on the part of Catherine. They appealed to Prussia to fulfil the provisions of a defensive treaty which they had made with her, when Frederick William II was desirous of raising his price to Russia, but only to be rebuffed on the ground that the Poland which Prussia had promised to defend was that of 1790, and that in view of the changes which had taken place since then the *casus fœderis* did not arise. Left to themselves, there was nothing the Poles could do but die bravely, and within six weeks all effective resistance was at an end.

Catherine owed her easy triumph to the pre-occupation of Austria and Prussia with revolutionary France, but she knew quite well that she would not be allowed to keep the whole of her prey to herself, whatever might be her own views in the matter. Even before the outbreak of the French war she had suggested to Berlin another partition of Poland, and the proposal took a prominent place in the somewhat acrimonious negotiations between Prussia and Austria which marked the summer and autumn of 1792. Claims and counter-claims to this or that territory were bandied to and fro between Vienna and Berlin, and Francis II revived the old project of exchanging the Netherlands for Bavaria. Events, however, moved faster than diplomacy. The Austro-Prussian forces were driven out of Champagne; the French invaded the Austrian Netherlands; and it became obvious that if the Germanic Powers were to acquire fresh territory it must be in the east, not the west.

Catherine once more displayed her diplomatic ability. A lesser statesman would have endeavoured to keep the whole of Poland, but she realized that it would be safer to be content with a smaller gain rather than to run the risk of bringing Berlin and Vienna closer together, and possibly of driving them to abandon the French war. So long as Francis and Frederick William were fighting France, and Russia was neutral, the Tsarina was mistress of eastern Europe: for this reason it was worth while to make some sacrifices to satisfy the appetite of Prussia.

Having once made up her mind on the point, the Tsarina acted quickly, and the terms of the Second Partition were soon drawn up. The Prussian share included Danzig, Thorn, and Posen, and was estimated to contain a population of a million and a half, while the provinces assigned to Russia were four times as extensive and included at least twice as many inhabitants. Austria got nothing, though the two Powers agreed to use their good offices to procure for her the exchange of the Netherlands for Bavaria with "such other advantages as may suit the general welfare". All the same, Catherine and Frederick William thought it as well not to say anything to Francis about what they had done until this fresh partition was an accomplished fact. The Prussians lost no time in claiming their share of the booty, though Frederick William thought it advisable to justify his action to the world by announcing his intention of saving Europe from Jacobin contagion by suppressing French revolutionary doctrines in Poland. By the end of March all resistance was at an end, and the actual terms of the arrangement were formally communicated to the Austrian government.

Francis II and his advisers were more annoyed than surprised. They knew perfectly well what was afoot, but they had never anticipated that Russia and Prussia would help themselves to Polish territory on quite so generous a scale as had proved to be the case: indeed, the Russian and Austrian frontiers now marched, and it had always been the aim of Vienna to prevent this. Austria had not only been over-reached, but also humiliated, and from these facts two important consequences ensued; one was a jealousy of Prussia which went far to paralyse the conduct of operations against France, and the other was a determination to acquire compensation, which, in its turn, led to the final extinction of Polish independence.

Under Russian pressure the Diet at Grodno accepted the Second Partition, but it was not long before the Polish people took up arms with Kosciusko as their leader. The struggle was hopeless from the beginning, but the Poles for a time did better than could have been anticipated, and the end did not come until the capture of Warsaw by the Russians on November 8th, 1794. The real beneficiary of the Polish rising was France, who was thereby enabled to drive the Allies from the left bank of the Rhine.

"The time has come", observed Catherine, "not only to extinguish to the last spark the fire that has been lighted in our neighbourhood, but to prevent any possible rekindling of the ashes." Austria held the same view, while the Prussian attitude was slightly different. Both Vienna and Berlin claimed the palatinates of Cracow and Sandomir, but they were actually in the possession of Prussia, and Frederick William declared that sooner than hand them over to Francis he would prefer not to have any partition at all.

The Tsarina might be approaching the end of her life, but her diplomatic skill was as great as ever, and so was her ability to see where her true interests lay. Prussia was a very useful ally against Poland, but quite valueless where Turkey was concerned, while precisely the reverse could be said of Austria. Now that Poland was about to be obliterated, the Prussian alliance ceased to be of any great importance, but the friendship of Vienna would be a definite asset when it came to the partition of Turkey, which was the next Russian objective. Above all, it was Catherine's determination to hold the balance fairly even between the two Germanic states. In 1793 she had given Prussia a substantial award, while Austria had received nothing: to the Tsarina this seemed a good reason for taking the opposite course two years later.

A good deal of haggling and some concessions proved necessary before Frederick William gave his consent to what was required of him, and a settlement was finally reached in October, 1795. The Russian frontier was to start from Galicia along the Bug to Brzesc in Lithuania, thence in a straight line to Grodno, and from that town along the Niemen to the border of East Prussia. Austria had hoped to receive Cracow and Sandomir, as well as to extend the province of Galicia by the inclusion of the whole district between the Pilica, the Vistula, and the Bug, but she had to cede part of this latter area in order to secure to Prussia the safe possession of Warsaw; Frederick William obtained the rest of Poland. A month later Stanislaus Poniatowski formally abdicated, not to be ungenerously treated by his conquerors, while in 1797 Paul (who by this time had succeeded Catherine), Frederick William, and Francis concluded a secret agreement recognizing "the necessity of abolishing everything which may recall the memory of the existence of the kingdom of Poland", and pledged themselves never to include such a designation among their various territorial titles.

CHAPTER VI

THE BACKGROUND OF BRITISH FOREIGN POLICY, 1713–1793

GREAT BRITAIN was exceptionally fortunate in the eighteenth century in that although she was twice the scene of civil strife there was never a War of the British Succession in which the others Powers participated. That this was the case was due rather to the existence of the English Channel than to any political factor. Accordingly, the British were able to fight out their dynastic differences undisturbed by foreigners, and so they avoided the misfortunes which in turn befell Spain, Poland, Austria, and Bavaria in that century of disputed successions. All the same, the change of dynasty in London had a more important effect upon the foreign policy of Great Britain than is sometimes realized.

The substitution of Guelph for Stuart implied an entirely different set of European connections. The fallen dynasty had been closely associated with western and southern Europe. Charles I had married a French princess, and one of his daughters had become the wife of the brother of Louis XIV. The wife of Charles II was a member of the House of Braganza, and when James II married a second time, his choice fell upon a princess of the Este family. The religious predilections of the later Stuarts were a further tie between Britain and those countries which owed spiritual allegiance to Rome. Furthermore, it was the period of the *grand siècle*, when every Englishman who made any claim to fashion or culture looked to Versailles for inspiration, and in this attitude he was certainly encouraged by his monarchs.

Whether this state of affairs would have continued had James II never lost the throne, or had his son ever regained it, is a moot point, but a change began soon after the Revolution of 1688. The accession of William III and Mary II meant the establishment of the closest ties with the Dutch, while Anne was married to a Danish prince: if George of Denmark is not a striking figure in English history, he was at any rate a further example of the tendency to look across the North Sea rather than the Channel. With the arrival of the Guelphs interest passed from Holland to Hanover, and the influence of that electorate upon British foreign policy has been shown more than once in preceding chapters. In effect, Germany tended to become the pre-occupation of the Court and statesmen in London until the elder Pitt once more showed both King and country where their true interests lay.

The official connection between Britain and Germany was further strengthened by the continued employment of German troops in the British Isles and in British wars overseas. The middle years of the eighteenth century marked the nadir of the British Army: the memories of Marlborough's campaigns were growing dim, and the victories of Wellington were still far in the future. An occasional genius like Wolfe made his appearance from time to time, but taken as a whole British generalship was neither competent nor inspiring, while British soldiers were not infrequently of very mediocre quality. The Whig oligarchy was fearful of the Jacobite sympathies of the mass of the people, and in moments of crisis it preferred the use of German mercenaries to the arming of its fellow-countrymen. Pitt did something to reverse this policy, but Hessians were hired in large numbers so late as the War of American Independence.

Strange to say, this neglect of all military preparation was far from unpopular, even in those circles which were by no means Whiggish in their outlook. Fear of anything approaching militarism was widespread, and the rule of Cromwell and his major-generals was far from being forgotten. In these circumstances it is hardly surprising that the militia fell into decay, and although Pitt did his best to revive it, the force could hardly, without excessive flattery, be described as effective. It was John Bull's navy and his purse that enabled him to hold his own in the world.

Between the King and the ruling oligarchy there was, during the reigns of the first two Georges, a compromise where foreign policy was concerned. The Whigs were in the main under no illusions as to the folly, from the British standpoint, of too much attention to German affairs, but unless they took some notice of the King's wishes there was always the risk that he might abdicate the British throne, and leave them to face James III and the triumphant Jacobites. The King, on the other hand, knew perfectly well that he ruled by the favour of the dominant party. The result was a compromise, rather on the basis of a little Hanover, but not too much of it, and the results of this can be traced in many a negotiation.

At the same time, German influence in the country, as apart

from the Court, was non-existent, and it was introduced not by the Guelphs in the eighteenth century, but by the Prince Consort in the nineteenth. Hanover was almost as unpopular among the Whigs as among the Jacobites, and xenophobia was one of the prevalent sentiments of the day. A politician might seek to curry favour with the monarch by an apparent eagerness to forward the interests of Hanover, but such a line was no recommendation to that monarch's British subjects. Pitt first acquired his hold upon the man-in-the-street owing to his opposition to any preference for Hanoverian, over national, needs. The reverse of the medal was the ease with which the British masses could be roused by agitators to jingoistic fury, as illustrated by the general attitude towards Spain in 1739. Fortunately these ignorant and turbulent masses had no votes, and generally speaking those who governed the country showed commendable firmness in their resistance to un-informed popular pressure.

In foreign, as in domestic, affairs the monarchy throughout the eighteenth century remained the pivot upon which everything turned, and the Sovereign had to be consulted, not only with regard to broad questions of policy, but also upon any detail of importance. The serious illness of the monarch could bring the whole machinery of the State to a standstill, and when George III went out of his mind in the winter of 1788-1789 the Foreign Secretary had to tell the British representative at Berlin, "I have not any commands to convey to you at present, the unhappy situation of His Majesty's health making it impossible for me to lay them (i.e., the despatches from Prussia) before him. The present situation of this country renders it impossible for me to send you any particular or precise instructions." The Marquess of Carmarthen went on to allude to "the present unfortunate interruption in the executive part of the Government".

The accession of George III soon resulted in an increase in the direct influence of the monarchy. It was the deliberate policy of that King to break the power of the Whig oligarchy, already undermined by the triumph of the elder Pitt, and in this he was highly successful. He was greatly assisted, it is true, by the divisions which manifested themselves in the ranks of that oligarchy, and also by the rapid decline of Jacobitism, which, in its turn, deprived the French of one of their opportunities of interference in British internal affairs. If the Tories had sacrificed most of their old principles, they still retained their devotion to the throne, and,

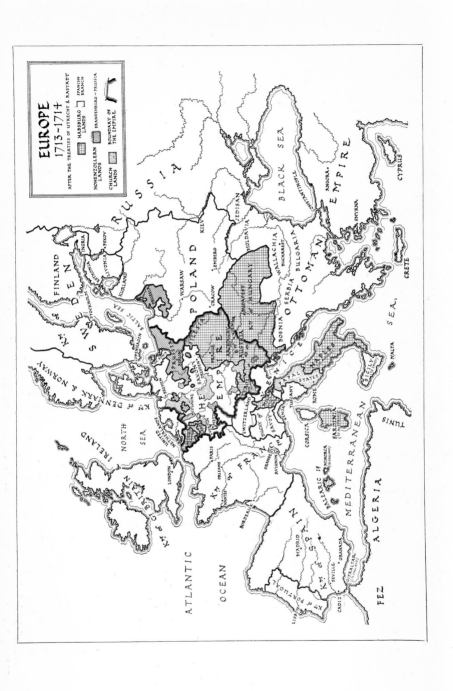

EUROPE
1713–1714

AFTER THE TREATIES OF UTRECHT & RASTADT

HABSBURG   SPANISH
LANDS   BRANCH

HOHENZOLLERN   BRANDENBURG – PRUSSIA
LANDS

CHURCH   BOUNDARY OF
LANDS   THE EMPIRE

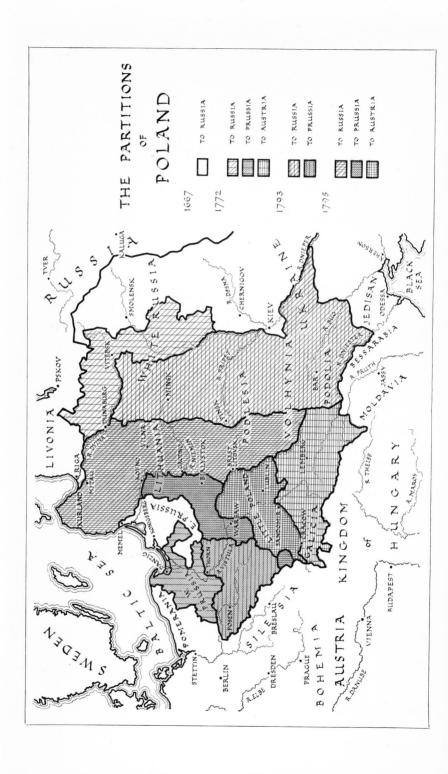

despairing of the restoration of the Stuarts, they were now prepared to transfer their loyalty to the House of Hanover. As Burke
said, "they changed their idol but they preserved their idolatry".
George III did everything he could to make this easy, and there
was soon a strong body of opinion throughout the country which
was prepared to support him in any attempt to increase the power
of the Crown.

For upwards of twenty years after the resignation of Pitt in
1761 the controlling influence in the shaping of British foreign
policy was George himself. He was, as has been shown, quite
indifferent to all that concerned Hanover, and in his desire for
peace he left Britain without a friend upon the mainland of
Europe: indeed, his lack of interest in Continental affairs was
remarkable in one who was both the great-grandson of George I
and the great-grandfather of Edward VII, and the ignorance
which arose from it had not a little to do with the disasters that
overtook his subjects during the War of American Independence.
When, in December, 1783, the younger Pitt became Prime
Minister the prestige of Great Britain among the nations of the
world was extremely low.

In any consideration of the foreign policy of the new Premier
it must be remembered that he was no dictator: indeed, his position was much weaker than that of many of his successors in his
high office. The rigid party machinery of a later age did not exist,
and ministers had to rely upon cajolery rather than threats to
secure their majority. Pitt was no exception. In March, 1785, his
government asked the House of Commons for £700,000 for the
fortification of Portsmouth and Plymouth, and met with a cold
reception. The leaders of the Opposition urged that such a step
was but the beginning of a despotism which would deprive the
country of its freedom. There was an all-night sitting, and when
the division was taken at 7 A.M. the numbers were found to be
equal, but the Speaker gave his casting vote against the administration. Where the navy was concerned Parliament displayed its
traditional generosity. Pitt, in spite of many claims upon his time,
devoted a great deal of attention to naval matters, and the fact
that he kept the country's first line of defence invincible enabled
him to play a decisive part in international affairs during the crisis
of 1786–1788. By the time of the Spanish war-scare in 1790, there
were no less than ninety line-of-battle ships ready for commission,
which was in marked contrast with the position little more than

F

ten years before, under Lord North, when the Franco-Spanish fleet had been mistress of the Channel.

At first the new government was content to pursue a policy of inactivity in matters of foreign policy, for there were more pressing questions at home which demanded attention; but the Prime Minister was no believer in isolation, for he knew its dangers only too well. Although he was both Head of the Government and Chancellor of the Exchequer, he took an active part in the work of the Foreign Office so long as the pleasant but unenterprising Carmarthen was Secretary of State; when war broke out with France he had naturally less time at his disposal for supervising departmental activities, and after 1791, the year in which Carmarthen was succeeded by Grenville, Pitt ceased to concern himself with details. Until that date the foreign policy of the administration was largely the emanation of a single brain.

One of Pitt's first successes was in the economic field, and here he was happier than Bolingbroke at the beginning of the century. The Treaty of Versailles had provided that commissioners should be appointed to make commercial arrangements between Great Britain and France, but nothing had actually been done. In 1785, however, the French government proceeded to restrict very drastically British imports, and Pitt was faced with the alternative of retaliation or negotiation: he chose the latter. William Eden, later Lord Auckland, was sent on a mission to Paris, and his efforts were crowned with success when a treaty was signed in September, 1786. By this agreement there was a reduction of duty on many of the principal articles of commerce of both countries, while others not specified were put on a most-favoured-nation footing. The subjects of either kingdom were to be free to enter the other without licence or passport, and were to enjoy complete religious liberty. The records of the negotiations prove that at every stage Pitt controlled them, and it is to him and to Eden, not to the Foreign Secretary, that the credit must go. He even tried to get inserted a clause for the limitation of armaments, but the French would not consent.

How long Pitt would have pursued the line of letting sleeping dogs lie if left to himself it is impossible to say, but circumstances soon forced his hand. These circumstances were a threat to the independence of the Low Countries, which no British government could ever regard unmoved. The attempts of Joseph II to exchange the Austrian Netherlands for Bavaria were at the root of the crisis, and occasioned growing concern in London. In spite of the French failure to support Austria during the War of the Bavarian Succession, the two Powers were still in alliance, while the Electors of Bavaria had for generations been the clients of France. This in itself was sufficient to cause Pitt to view the situation with the gravest suspicion, though after the Treaty of Teschen the relations of Louis XVI and Joseph II were not always so cordial as British statesmen appear to have imagined. The danger was still further intensified by the fact that in the United Provinces the party opposed to the House of Orange, always friendly to the British connection, was carrying everything before it, and was openly supported by all the resources of French diplomacy. The Stadholder, William V, was weak and irresolute, and it appeared to Pitt to be merely a question of time before the whole of the Low Countries fell under the control of France.

Fortunately for Great Britain, the interests of Prussia were also affected, for the Princess of Orange was the sister of Frederick William II, so that both dynastic and national considerations combined to cause Berlin to oppose the designs of France and Austria in the Low Countries. In June, 1787, matters came to a head when the Princess of Orange was prevented by the rebels from going to The Hague, and Prussia demanded satisfaction for the insult. The opponents of the Stadholder, who had by now suspended him from the exercise of his functions, refused to give way, and relied upon the support of France. Thereupon a Prussian army marched into the United Provinces, where it met with little opposition, and a British fleet appeared off the Dutch coast. For a moment peace hung in the balance, but before such a display of force France gave way, and abandoned the rebels to their fate. In 1788 there was formed the Triple Alliance of Great Britain, Prussia, and the United Provinces for mutual defence and the maintenance of peace. Within five years of the Treaty of Versailles, and without firing a shot, Pitt had safeguarded a vital British interest and had administered a sharp rebuff to France. That he had been able to do this was due to the fact that he had restored the predominance of Britain at sea and that he had secured an ally on the mainland of Europe.

The Triple Alliance was soon to exercise its influence elsewhere than in the Low Countries. As we have seen, this was the period when Russia and Austria were engaged in a joint war against the Turks, and when St. Petersburg was closer to Vienna than to Berlin. The Swedes, desirous of weakening the Tsarina, had invaded Russian Finland, but were in their turn being attacked by Denmark, the ally of Russia. The situation contained grave possibilities, for the overthrow of Sweden would make the Baltic a Russian lake, with disastrous consequences to British and Dutch trade in that sea: this was not, perhaps, of great concern to Frederick William, but he was glad of an opportunity to prove to Catherine that he could be a nuisance when he so desired. Pressure was, therefore, at once brought to bear on the Danes, and Sweden was saved, but the Tsarina was deeply offended, and she rejected all the offers of the Triple Alliance to mediate between herself and the Sultan.

Catherine was not the woman to sit down under a reverse of this nature, and circumstances soon enabled her to have her tit-for-tat with the British Prime Minister. Unlike his father and nearly all his contemporaries, Pitt regarded Russia with suspicion. The general attitude in Great Britain was to look on her as a useful counterweight to France, and to the latter's traditional allies, Sweden, Poland, and Turkey. Pitt did not take this view, and he was seriously alarmed at the progress of a Power whose appetite for Polish and Turkish provinces appeared insatiable: he believed the Tsarina to be determined upon the conquest of Constantinople, and he was apprehensive of the dangers which this would involve to the British trade in the Mediterranean. During the course of their operations against the Turks the Russians had captured the town of Ochakov, near the mouth of the Bug, and the Triple Alliance adopted the line that the place must be restored to the Sultan. Apart from his natural suspicion of Russian intentions, Pitt advanced this demand for two reasons: he had been led to believe that Ochakov was the key to Constantinople, and he desired to appease the Russophobe feelings of Prussia, to whom he had recently been compelled to point out that Great Britain would not permit the Triple Alliance to be used as an instrument for the aggrandizement of that country in Central Europe at the expense of Austria and Poland.

Catherine refused to give way, and she was encouraged in this attitude by Fox, who departed so far from customary diplomatic procedure as to send to St. Petersburg a representative of the Opposition in the person of Sir Robert Adair. It was just the situation to suit the Tsarina. An ultimatum to her was prepared, and war appeared imminent, when, in April, 1791, Pitt was forced to give way. More than one of his colleagues opposed his policy, which was also unpopular in the City and in the country as a whole. At this time, too, it began to be realized that Ochakov did not possess the strategic importance with which it had been invested. The ultimatum was accordingly never delivered, and the Russians retained their conquest. To the government the shock was considerable, and there was talk of its resignation. Pitt had gone too far ahead of public opinion. He managed, however, to weather the storm, though it cost him his Foreign Secretary. The Duke of Leeds, as Lord Carmarthen had become, resigned, and Lord Grenville was appointed in his place. In a few months the whole affair was forgotten as the progress of the French Revolution absorbed the attention of the population of Great Britain, while Frederick William, once more reconciled to Catherine, proceeded, by way of her guarantee of Poland, to another partition of that country.

Before, however, the course of events across the Channel had become the primary consideration in international politics there was a real danger of war between Britain and Spain. In 1790 a message from the King was laid before Parliament to the effect that British ships had been seized by the Spaniards while, so it was alleged, peacefully fishing at Nootka Sound. An address was presented; a million was voted; and both countries expected war. In July, on the contrary, a convention was signed by which Spain agreed to release the British vessels, to restore the land and property seized, and to pay compensation. On the other hand, there was to be no further disturbance with the fisheries on either side; no illicit trade with Spanish settlements; and no British fishing within ten leagues of Spanish territory on the Pacific coast.

What had happened was that the Spanish government had called upon France to fulfil its obligations under the Family Compact, but the National Assembly, after grandiloquently declaring that the French nation had renounced wars of conquest, proceeded to offer assistance on terms which included the restitution of Louisiana. In this dilemma the Spanish ministry preferred to treat with Britain, and the alliance between France and Spain was clearly at an end.

CHAPTER VII

THE FRENCH REVOLUTION, 1789–1802

THE French Revolution reintroduced the ideological factor into international politics. Between the Reformation and the Treaty of Westphalia religious differences had played no inconsiderable part in diplomatic calculations, and the leading Catholic and Protestant monarchs could always count upon the support of some at any rate of their co-religionists in the countries with which they might from time to time be at war. After 1640 religion played a decreasingly important *rôle* in the relations of states, and Oliver Cromwell was the last statesman of the first rank who refused to acknowledge the change which was taking place in this respect. The spectacle of a Prince of the Church, such as Richelieu, giving his support to the German Protestants had not a little to do with this development, and, in his earlier years, Louis XIV was not slow, particularly where Britain was concerned, to follow the churchman's example. This is not to say that religion could not still be used to whip up popular enthusiasm, as we have seen at the time of the War of Jenkins' Ear, and later still Frederick the Great—of all people—became a Protestant hero to the average Englishman. Nevertheless, it remains true to say that religion was not a major consideration in the diplomacy of the western and central European Powers during the eighteenth century. Cosmopolitanism, rather than any form of internationalism, was still the order of the day.

With the consolidation of the French Revolution a new era began, and the end of this is not yet. The revolutionary forces in every country looked to Paris for inspiration and support, and for many years the success of the French armies was in no small measure due to the sympathy of large sections of the people in the countries which they invaded, a sympathy which transcended any loyalty felt towards their legitimate rulers. With the advent of the Empire these Francophil sentiments began to disappear, and it was not until 1848 that France again—and then only for a brief space —became the hope of Continental Liberalism. Meanwhile moderate reformers all over Europe were beginning to look to London, and this tendency was accentuated by the foreign policy of such British statesmen as Canning, John Russell, Palmerston, and Gladstone. Later still, after 1917, Russia played the part once enacted by revolutionary France, while, by way of reaction, the parties of the Right, discarding their old allegiance to throne and altar, nearly everywhere gave open or tacit support to the movements associated with the names of Mussolini and Hitler.

These developments date from the outbreak of the French Revolution, and they bear a striking resemblance to certain aspects of sixteenth-century Europe, when the dividing-line was religious, not political. Not that this new state of affairs was by any means unprecedented, for it recalled that in Greece in the fifth century before Christ, when the democracies were sponsored by Athens and the oligarchies by Sparta: if London and Paris be substituted for Athens, and St. Petersburg and Vienna for Sparta, the parallel is striking.

For many years it was taken for granted that Continental Europe at least must be either wholly democratic or wholly absolutist, as once that it must be entirely Catholic or entirely Protestant: gradually, as in the seventeenth century, more moderate counsels prevailed, and, the impossibility of uniformity being realized, the lion lay down with the lamb. Such was the situation on the eve of the Four Years' War, but the Russian Revolution, together with the rise of Fascism and Nazism, produced a new clash of ideologies which was once more to drench the world in blood.

Coincident with this development was another that was in marked contrast, namely the growth of nationalism, which at first was the ally of democracy, but later became its foe. It would be absurd to say that nationalist feelings did not exist before 1789, and the history of Ireland, Scotland, and Poland, to quote but three examples, proves the direct opposite; but the record of diplomacy in the eighteenth century is proof that the sentiment was neither widespread nor, save in a few cases, very deep. Duchies and provinces could still be bandied about without any marked opposition on the part of their inhabitants, and men thought it neither shameful nor exceptional to take service with a foreign Power.

France was without question the most homogeneous state in Europe, and thus she was in a peculiarly favourable position to exploit on nationalist grounds the difficulties of her neighbours who were not so happily placed. In Ireland there was as much discontent as ever, and now that Jacobitism was dead it was by no means difficult to direct the feeling into hatred of the Saxon oppressor: in this way revolutionary France was enabled to pursue, in a somewhat different form, the old policy of Louis XIV, namely to strike at England from two sides at once. In the Low Countries there was also much inflammable material, and French ambitions in that quarter were greatly assisted by an appeal both to the political and to the national sympathies of those who re-belled against the rule of Vienna. In Italy it was the same, and dislike of Austria was a very valuable asset in the hands of Paris. In short, if the policy of revolutionary France was fundamentally that of the Valois and of the Bourbons, it possessed certain ideo-logical and nationalist assets which had been denied to them.

What must, of course, never be forgotten is that the drama of the French Revolution unfolded itself comparatively slowly. The storming of the Bastille took place on July 14th, 1789, but it was not until June, 1791, that the French Royal Family attempted to escape, and another year elapsed before Louis XVI was suspended from the exercise of his functions. On more than one occasion during these years it appeared highly probable that the Revolu-tion would be crushed (as it certainly would have been had Louis shown the firmness displayed by George III during the Gordon Riots), or that France would settle down under a constitutional monarchy. In addition, the governments and peoples of Europe had other matters to distract their attention from Paris. For the Englishman there had been a crisis in the Near East, another in the Pacific, and a General Election, while Austria, Prussia, and Russia were at least as interested in the affairs of Turkey and Poland as in those of France. By the time that Europe awoke to what was afoot in Paris it was too late.

The attitude of the Powers towards the Revolution naturally varied, and to understand their diplomacy it is necessary to examine their point of view when the storm first broke.

When Louis XVI began to get into difficulties there was, for a variety of reasons, considerable satisfaction in Great Britain. In the first place, the part played by France in the War of American Independence was far from being either forgiven or forgotten, and there was a natural tendency to rejoice over her troubles. Then the Bourbons had always been the enemies of England, so that their misfortunes were hardly calculated to bring tears to the eyes of the ordinary Englishman. Lastly, it appeared at first as if all that was happening in France was the substitution of a limited for an absolute monarchy, and this naturally made a strong appeal to that section of the British people which believed it had done the same thing a century before. Fox, whose heart always ran away with his head, in particular thought that the French Revolution was the counterpart of the English, and declared of the fall of the Bastille, "How much the greatest event it is that ever happened in the world! and how much the best!"

Certainly the British government could not be charged with precipitating the conflict, and its policy was definitely pacific. The General Election of 1790 had given Pitt an increased majority, and ministers were not unnaturally feeling exceptionally complacent in consequence. As late as the beginning of 1792 the Army Estimates provided for the reduction of each regiment by seventy men, which left the total force in the British Isles at 13,701. When Pitt introduced his Budget that same year he radiated optimism in a speech during the course of which he declared that "unquestionably there never was a time in the history of this country when, from the situation of Europe, we might more reasonably expect fifteen years of peace that at the present moment". All the same, in spite of its efforts to reduce expenditure, the government had never economized on the Navy.

Although himself distrustful of democracy, Pitt did not see the struggle against the French Revolution in the light of a monarchical crusade: rather did he look at the progress of events from the point of view of a British statesman, and to the very last he hoped that it would not be necessary for him to interfere. Moreover, British public opinion would not have supported any drastic action in those early days. It had a healthy distrust, which the Prime Minister shared, of the motives of Austria and Prussia, and for some months it continued fondly to hope that France was merely curtailing the power of the throne. The change of feeling did not really begin to make itself felt until November, 1790, when Burke published his *Reflections on the French Revolution*, and even then it is permissible to suppose that at first Burke made a greater impression outside political circles than at Westminster. Indeed, his judgment was as a rule so ill-balanced that his insight into the progress of the revolutionary movement in France is the more remarkable, and it was this insight that brought him in his declining years that fame which has ever since been associated with his name. Pitt certainly was not carried away by the arguments of the *Reflections on the French Revolution*, for as late as September,

1791, Burke wrote to his son, after dining with the Prime Minister and the Foreign Secretary, "They are certainly right as to their general inclinations, perfectly so, I have not a shadow of doubt; but at the same time thay are cold and dead as to any attempt whatsoever to give them effect".

From the moment that Pitt delivered his singularly optimistic Budget speech in February, 1792, events began to move at an accelerated pace. France was represented in London by the *ci-devant* Marquis de Chauvelin, a vain young man, who did nothing to improve his already difficult position by maintaining close relations with those who were working for an upheaval of the French type in England. As adviser to the French Embassy there was Talleyrand, an old acquaintance of Pitt, but his desire to improve his country's relations with England was thwarted by the jealousy of his official superior, as well as by the rapid changes of policy in Paris. The Prime Minister continued to hope that peace might be preserved, and carefully avoided any action calculated to antagonize France. In this attitude he was supported by Grenville, but the King, and more than one member of the Cabinet, was decidedly Gallophobe.

In Paris the situation was going from bad to worse, and anarchy was the order of the day. Pitt still adhered to his policy of neutrality, and when Lord Gower, the British ambassador, asked permission to make representations to the French Assembly on behalf of the King and Queen it was refused. On August 10th the Tuileries were stormed, and Royalty in France was suspended. This led to the recall of Gower, but only because the monarch to whom he was accredited was no longer reigning. Before he left he expressed the desire of Great Britain to remain neutral, but he warned the French government that any violence to the Royal Family "could not fail to produce one universal sentiment of indignation throughout every country of Europe". Pitt may possibly be accused of culpable inactivity during those critical months, but he can hardly be charged with forcing the pace.

Events now began to move very fast. In September there occurred the massacres of Royalist prisoners and the battle of Valmy, French armies over-ran Belgium, and in January, 1793, British public opinion was horrified by the execution of Louis XVI, a great deal more horrified, incidentally, than French opinion had been over a similar event in London a hundred and forty-four years before. When the news reached the English capital in the late afternoon of January 23rd there was a feeling of universal disgust; the theatres were closed, and all who could afford it wore mourning, while in Paris, to quote *The Times*, "the playhouses are open and the city is illuminated every night; as if the French wished to make their wickedness more visible". Certainly the new rulers of France made no effort to conciliate British opinion, and they spared no pains to stir up trouble in the three kingdoms.

Yet when war finally came it was not for ideological reasons. Belgium had been overrun by the French without interference, for since the Diplomatic Revolution the integrity of the Habsburg dominions had not been a British concern. The case of the Netherlands was different, for the Dutch alliance was one of the bases of national policy, and only a few years had elapsed since Britain had intervened to protect that country from France; furthermore, if the Cape of Good Hope passed into hostile keeping the route to India would be gravely threatened. Pitt was therefore determined to keep Holland out of the war as long as possible, and when Austria and Prussia tried to draw her into their combination against France he exerted himself to prevent it. "This country and Holland", wrote Grenville in November, 1792, "ought to remain quiet as long as it is possible to do so." At the same time a guarantee of British armed support was given to the Dutch in the event of attack by France. The necessity to implement this soon came, for the French government declared the Scheldt open, thus violating the Treaty of Utrecht, and subsequent negotiations proved futile. Chauvelin was accordingly given his passports, and on February 1st, 1793, France replied by a declaration of war upon Great Britain and the Netherlands. The Low Countries, for which England has so often had to fight, were thus the immediate cause of hostilities, and Pitt was only stating the truth when he said, "The war is not only unavoidable, but, under the circumstances of the case, absolutely necessary to the existence of Great Britain and Europe".

Austria was affected by the course of events in France both earlier and more closely, for not only was Leopold II the brother of the French Queen, but his frontiers marched with those of France. The initial cause of dispute between the Habsburgs and the Revolution was, however, connected with the Empire. The Constituent Assembly had abolished feudalism throughout all the dominions of Louis XVI, and the question at once arose whether

France had the right to deprive the landowners of Alsace of the feudal privileges which she had more or less guaranteed by the Treaty of Westphalia, and had confirmed by subsequent agreements. In February, 1790, those affected sent a protest to the French government, only to be told that the unity of France and Alsace rested on the unanimous decision of the Alsatians, and that ancient treaties and the stipulations of their former rulers could no longer bind a free people. An offer of monetary compensation was, it is true, made to the sufferers, but it was refused by the majority, which took its case to the Imperial Diet.

This was not the only cause of friction between Vienna and the Revolution. The King and Queen in secret, and the Comte d'Artois (the future Charles X) and the Prince de Condé openly, had asked for the assistance of the other European Powers to enable them to suppress the Revolution by force. In December, 1790, Leopold sent a protest against the treatment of the Alsatian landowners, and he offered the French Royal Family an asylum at the time of the flight to Varennes. In August, 1791, he had that conference with Frederick William at Pillnitz, to which allusion has already been made, and where the French question was fully discussed. It was agreed that, since the preservation of the French monarchy was an object of universal interest, an invitation should be sent to the other European Powers calling on them to aid in restoring the King of France to his rightful position, but at the same time safeguarding the liberties of the French people. To attain this object the two Kings promised to mobilize their forces, provided that the other Powers would aid them.

This was very largely bluff on the part of Leopold, who did not want war if it could possibly be avoided. He was much more interested in the safety of his sister and the maintenance of the French alliance than in the constitutional position of Louis XVI. It was his object to intimidate the French people, for he knew that Pitt would not intervene, and that Spain, Prussia, and the Dutch all had very different aims. In pursuit of this policy he discouraged the militant emigrés, but circumstances were against him. Gustavus III of Sweden was at Spa giving every assistance to those of whom Leopold disapproved, while the Tsarina was doing all in her power to embroil Vienna and Berlin with France. Such being the case, it is not surprising that in February, 1792, an offensive and defensive alliance was concluded between Austria and Prussia: on the first day of the following month the restraining influence of Leopold II was removed by his death.

War was, indeed, very near, and on April 20th, 1792, it was declared by France against Austria. On August 3rd there appeared a manifesto by the Duke of Brunswick, who had been appointed to command the Austro-Prussian forces, which did a great deal to rally moderate French opinion to the side of the Revolution. This document began by disclaiming any desire for conquest or intention to meddle in the internal affairs of France, but it called on the sane majority of the French people to declare themselves against the "odious schemes of their oppressors": it went on to threaten with all "the rigour of the laws of war" those who dared to defend themselves against the invading armies, while if further violence was offered to Louis XVI the citizens of Paris were threatened with an "exemplary and never-to-be-forgotten vengeance", by "giving up the town to military execution and total subversion, and the guilty rebels to the death they had deserved".

Neither side was ready for war, but from the beginning the French took the struggle seriously, while the Germanic Powers looked on it in the light of a punitive expedition, their real attention being directed towards Poland. The result was the Austro-Prussian reverse at Valmy, and the invasion of the Rhineland and the Austrian Netherlands by French armies which found many local sympathizers. In effect, the jealousy of the Austrian and Prussian governments, and their disputes over the spoils of Poland, gave France a breathing-space, and allowed the Revolution to establish itself.

In these circumstances it was hardly to be expected that the other neighbours of France, namely Piedmont and Spain, would be able to remain at peace, nor was such the case. In the autumn of 1792 the French seized Nice, and this event, combined with the close relationship which existed between the Houses of Bourbon and Savoy, caused Sardinia to declare war on France, and the aid of Austria against the common enemy was secured. Spain commenced hostilities on the execution of Louis XVI, so that by the spring of 1793 the war had become general. This is not, however, to say that the enemies of France acted together—far from it: they were more numerous, it is true, but they failed to bring their strength to bear at the right time in the right place, while France had the advantage of a single control and of interior lines. As the months went by the bonds connecting the allies grew steadily weaker, and it was only the English subsidy that kept Prussia at war at all. By the end of 1794 the French were masters of the

United Provinces as well as of the Austrian Netherlands, and in both they were far more popular than the regimes they had overthrown. The only compensation, from the Allied point of view, was Lord Howe's victory at sea on June 1st, 1794, which freed England from any immediate danger of invasion.

Such being the case, it is not surprising that the year 1795 should have witnessed a striking reduction in the number of France's enemies. The first to make peace was Prussia. Since October, 1794, Pitt had withdrawn the subsidy, on the ground that Britain was no longer getting value for her money, and Frederick William was by no means sorry for the excuse to retire from the war and to concentrate on the affairs of Poland. On April 5th, 1795, Barthélemy on behalf of France and Hardenberg on behalf of Prussia signed the Treaty of Bâle, whereby Prussia gave France a free hand on the left bank of the Rhine, while France in return undertook to respect a line of demarcation which virtually placed northern Germany under Prussian control: a secret article arranged for compensation for Prussia should French territory be extended to the Rhine. The next of the Allied Powers to give in was the United Provinces, which in May accepted terms rendering the Dutch to all intents and purposes dependent on France, and compelling them to bear their share in the war against Britain. Two months later Spain followed the example of Prussia and Holland at the price of the surrender of the Spanish half of San Domingo. By the end of the year Saxony, the two Hesses, Portugal, Naples, Parma, and the Pope had all made peace with France.

The First Coalition was clearly in the last stages of dissolution, and the situation was in no way changed by the conclusion, in September, 1795, of the Triple Alliance between Great Britain, Austria, and Russia. It was obvious that Russia would not, and Great Britain could not, do much, and everything thus depended upon Austria. The Directory in Paris was not slow to appreciate this fact, and at the beginning of March, 1796, it appointed Napoleon Bonaparte to command the French army in Italy.

As the international situation steadily deteriorated, even Pitt, much against the wishes of the King and several of his colleagues, decided to make an effort to bring the war to an end by negotiation. The reverses of the past two years had cured the optimism which had earlier encouraged him to say, "It will be a short war, and certainly ended in one to two campaigns", nor was there any sign of that complete collapse of the social and financial structure of France in which he had once fervently believed. On the contrary, he now felt that, with the Directory, some form of stable government had been established which might be willing to make peace on reasonable terms. The cost of the struggle was frightening him; he was informed that the anti-war party on the other side of the Channel was strong enough to carry the day; and he feared that at any moment Austria might be compelled to make peace, thus leaving Britain to carry on the conflict alone. The British Prime Minister little knew the men with whom he was dealing. To an overture in the early spring of 1796, suggesting peace on the basis of the restoration of the Low Countries, the Directory haughtily replied that no proposition for the surrender of any of the countries declared by France to be "reunited" to herself would be entertained.

Nevertheless Pitt persevered in his efforts; he may still have believed in the possibility of an accommodation, but he was certainly also influenced by a desire to prove to his opponents at home that peace with France was out of the question on any other terms than complete surrender. In September, 1796, therefore, the British government requested the Danish ambassador in Paris to ask for a passport for an English plenipotentiary, but the Directory rejected the mediation of Denmark, and would only receive an envoy on the direct request of London. Great Britain, in effect, was to sue for peace; but even to this Pitt agreed, and Lord Malmesbury was sent over to Paris to negotiate for a settlement on the basis of the evacuation of the Low Countries by the French in return for the restitution of all conquests made by British arms. Unfortunately for Pitt, his old enemy and present ally, Catherine, died at this moment, November 16th; she had been distinctly Gallophobe of late, but her successor, Paul, adopted a policy of neutrality. This news emboldened the French to reject Pitt's terms, and Malmesbury was unceremoniously bundled out of the French capital at twenty-four hours' notice.

Meanwhile in Italy the Austrian armies were going down to disaster before the hammer-strokes of young General Bonaparte. The closing weeks of 1796 witnessed their defeat at Arcola, and in January, 1797, came another French victory, this time at Rivoli. In April so far reduced was Francis II that he was compelled to sign preliminaries of peace at Leoben, by which he gave up all claims to the Austrian Netherlands and "recognized the limits of France as decreed by the laws of the French Republic". The next few months were spent, paradoxically enough, by the general of that republic in destroying the republics of Venice and Genoa. In neither case did these old states expire in a manner worthy of their past.

Peace between Austria and France was signed at the village of Campo Formio, near Udine, on October 17th, 1797. Austria received Venice and the whole of Venetia as far as the Adige and the lower Po, together with Dalmatia and the islands belonging to the Republic of St. Mark, but the Ionian Isles went to France—an interesting indication of the eastern ambitions which Napoleon already entertained. Francis re-affirmed his cession of the Austrian Netherlands, and he recognized the independence of the Cisalpine Republic, which had been formed out of the Milanese, Modena, and the adjacent territories. Secret articles stipulated that the Emperor would use his influence to procure the extension of the eastern boundary of France to the Rhine, while in return the French Government promised to help him to acquire the arch-bishopric of Salzburg and a frontier strip of Bavaria. For all practical purposes the dream of the Valois had been realized, and Italy was a French protectorate.

The surrender of Austria left Britain to face France alone, and in the most difficult circumstances. She had at that time no possessions of her own in the Mediterranean with the exception of Gibraltar, though from 1794 to 1796 she had exercised a precarious hold upon Corsica. When the Italian mainland fell into French hands the British position became untenable, and in 1797 the Mediterranean had to be abandoned altogether. Nor was this all, for financial panic necessitated the suspension of payments in cash, while there were naval mutinies at Spithead and the Nore.

These various calamities induced Pitt to approach France once more with proposals for peace, and negotiations were resumed in June, 1797: on this occasion they took place at Lille, with Malmesbury as the chief British delegate. The Prime Minister's position was one of considerable difficulty, for the failure of the previous year's attempt to end the war had prejudiced the King against any further similar discussions, and several members of the Cabinet, including the Foreign Secretary, shared the Sovereign's opinion. Such being the case, the Under-Secretary, George Canning, was called upon to act as an intermediary between Pitt and Malmesbury, for Grenville was by no means always informed of what was taking place. In effect, Malmesbury wrote three types of reports:

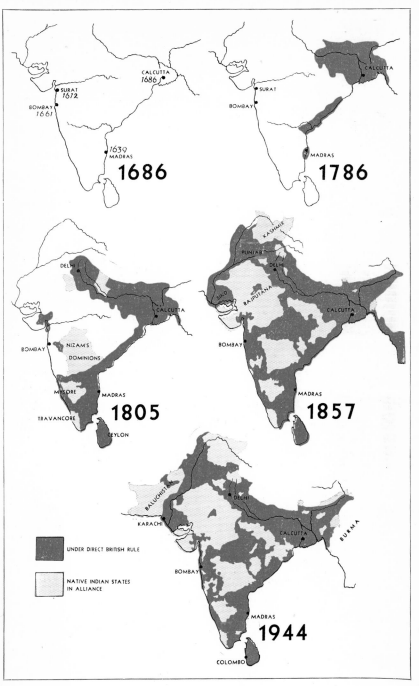

1686

1786

1805

1857

1944

UNDER DIRECT BRITISH RULE

NATIVE INDIAN STATES IN ALLIANCE

GROWTH OF BRITISH RULE IN INDIA

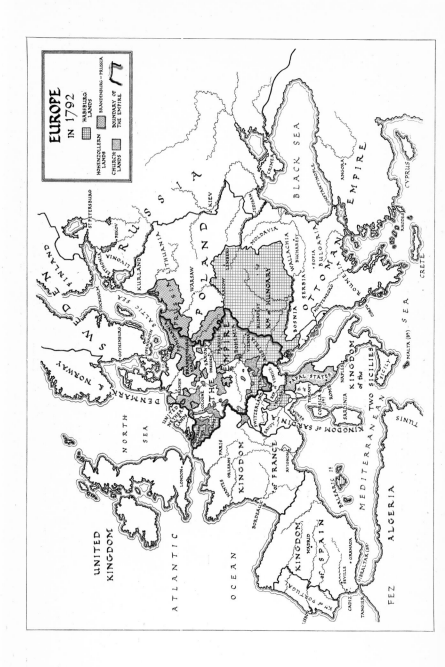

EUROPE
IN 1792

HABSBURG
LANDS

HOHENZOLLERN
LANDS

BRANDENBURG-PRUSSIA

CHURCH
LANDS

BOUNDARY OF
THE EMPIRE

those that were for Pitt, those that were for Pitt and Grenville, and those that could safely be communicated to the whole Cabinet. For all these despatches the young Under-Secretary of twenty-seven served as the clearing-house. He himself warmly supported the Prime Minister in this resumption of negotiations, and he believed that the policy to be pursued towards France was a question of expediency rather than of principle.

Malmesbury's instructions were a mirror of the French successes of the previous six months, for he was empowered to recognize the sovereignty of France over Belgium, Luxembourg, Savoy, and Nice, and to promise that Great Britain would restore all her conquests save Trinidad and the Cape of Good Hope, while Ceylon was to be exchanged if possible. These terms were, from the French point of view, a marked advance upon those suggested in the previous year, but they formed the only possible basis for an understanding between the two countries in view of Napoleon's victories in Italy. Moreover, in France itself there appeared a distinct possibility of a Bourbon restoration, and it was believed that the adoption of a conciliatory attitude would encourage the moderates in Paris. These hopes were soon disappointed. In September came Napoleon's *coup d'état* of the 18th Fructidor, and the aspirations of the French Royalists were frustrated for another seventeen years. The influence of events in Paris was soon felt at Lille, and Malmesbury was informed that the French government would only treat on the basis of a restitution by Great Britain of all conquests made by her from France and her allies. This was too much for Pitt, and Malmesbury was recalled to London.

The year 1797 marked a definite turning-point in the struggle between France and her neighbours. The contest was no longer one to permit the French to choose their own form of government, or to safeguard their frontiers. The France of the Revolution, like that of Louis XIV, had passed from defence to defiance, and had come to believe that security was a synonym for the domination of Europe. Moreover, Napoleon's eastern ambitions, of which he had already given evidence and was shortly to give more, gave a colonial and commercial bias to French policy, which brought it into sharper conflict than ever with that of Great Britain, and this accounts for the much greater energy displayed by the British government in the prosecution of the war.

The next twelve months witnessed Napoleon's campaigns in

G

the Near East and, in August, 1798, the Battle of the Nile; the absence of Napoleon and the British victory inspired the Tsar to suggest another attempt against France, and in this way the Second Coalition came into existence. At first all went well, and both the Russians and the Austrians pushed back the French armies, but before long there were the inevitable differences among the Allies which paralysed their military operations. If the Russian fleet, instead of operating in the Adriatic, had helped to close the Egyptian ports, as Nelson urged, Napoleon could hardly have returned to Europe, but the Russians, like the Austrians, thought more of seizing territory than of serving the common cause. Thus, for lack of that frank understanding and co-operation which Pitt was trying to effect, the efforts of the Allies both by land and sea hopelessly miscarried, and in spite of their naval supremacy they failed to shut up in Egypt the one man whose presence in Europe was most to be dreaded.

The task that awaited Napoleon when he returned to France in October, 1799, was thus by no means as difficult as might well have been the case. The Coalition had lost the aid of the Tsar, who accused his allies of breach of faith, and refused to have anything more to do with them, while Prussia would not depart from a neutrality which left her free to turn against France should fortune at any time smile upon the Coalition. The victories of Moreau in Germany and of Napoleon, now First Consul, in Italy brought Austria once more to her knees, and on February 9th, 1801, there was signed the Treaty of Lunéville. By this France acquired, in addition to the German districts on the left bank of the Rhine, Belgium and Luxembourg. In Germany she gained the right to take part in deciding the indemnities to be granted to dispossessed princes, and she imposed the principle of secularization. In Italy her advantages were no less substantial: she occupied Piedmont; the Cisalpine Republic and Liguria were under her protection; Tuscany, which had been converted into the kingdom of Etruria, was governed by the young Duke of Parma, who was completely under the influence of Napoleon; Rome was at the mercy of the First Consul; and the King of Naples was compelled to maintain a French garrison.

The need of a breathing-space to organize all these acquisitions, rather than any real desire for peace, inclined the new master of France to come to terms with his remaining enemies. In Russia there had been a palace revolution; Paul had been murdered, and had been succeeded by his son, Alexander I. This change of Tsar was followed by one of foreign policy, as so often happened at St. Petersburg. Paul, after his breach with the Second Coalition, had assumed a definitely Anglophobe attitude, and had hampered British strategy by a revival of the Armed Neutrality of twenty years earlier. His successor held very different views, and in June, 1801, Alexander concluded with Great Britain the Treaty of St. Petersburg, by which all the outstanding questions between the two Powers were settled. Two months earlier Nelson had won the battle of Copenhagen. These events made Napoleon realize that if he wanted peace with Britain or Russia he must have it with both, and peace had become a necessity. To organize the French Republic, as well as the governments of Italy, Holland, Germany, and Switzerland, not forgetting the supremacy of the First Consul, was a task which could not be deferred.

Negotiations were therefore opened simultaneously with the Powers still at war. France undertook to settle in conjunction with Russia the indemnification of the German princes, and also any outstanding problems relating to Italy; this really meant Piedmont, which Napoleon had no mind to restore to the King of Sardinia. In the end the Tsar had to be content with a clause whereby France and Russia promised "to concern themselves in friendly concert with the interests of His Majesty the King of Sardinia, and to treat them with all the consideration compatible with the actual state of things". This was in October, 1802: in the previous May the price of Prussian neutrality was paid with some bishoprics, and William V, the Stadholder, received compensation in the same way for the surrender of his rights in the United Provinces.

Above all, there was the settlement with England. When Napoleon became First Consul he wrote to George III expressing his desire for peace, but Pitt had had enough of negotiations with France, and he referred to the new ruler of that country as "this last adventurer in the lottery of revolutions". The British government therefore returned a haughty reply to the effect that the best guarantee France could give of her desire for peace was the immediate recall of her legitimate monarch. This recommendation came ill from the regime which compelled the grandson of James II to live in exile, as Talleyrand was not slow in pointing out. The fact was that Pitt believed neither in the stability nor in the sincerity of Napoleon. He proved to be as wrong on the first point as he was right on the second.

Pitt, however, was not to be in office much longer, and his

successor, Addington, was ready to come to terms. The war had reached a stalemate. The French were supreme upon the mainland of Europe, and Britain had failed to shake the enemy's position either by means of alliances or by expeditions of her own. On the other hand, Nelson's victory at Copenhagen and the French failure in Egypt testified to the ever-growing British supremacy at sea. On the economic side a cessation of hostilities was becoming imperative. The export trade of Great Britain might have increased, but there was considerable distress at home. The average price of wheat in 1800 was 112s. 8d. a quarter, whereas the highest annual average in the fifty years before the war had been 64s. 6d. On March 5th, 1801, the price of the quartern loaf was 1s. 10½d. True to his Whig traditions, Pitt had refused to consider any fixing of wages. Yet Britain was in a stronger position than her rival, and during the negotiations at Amiens the First Consul admitted to Lord Cornwallis that France had "entirely lost its commerce and in a large degree exhausted its pecuniary resources".

What had happened was that the British Empire was becoming a self-sufficing economic unit, knit together by the operations of the Navy, and able to exist and prosper in spite of the French control of the Low Countries, Germany, and Italy. British gains, too, were mostly in tropical lands which supplied vital needs, while the French successes, though superficially far more impressive, were in neighbouring countries which could ill support exclusion from the tropics. Moreover, the acquisitions of France necessitated large armies of occupation, and the expenses of these could not always be met by local requisitions. Consequently, in 1801 the Finance Minister admitted a deficit of 100,000,000 francs. By rigid economies he reduced this to 11,500,000 francs in the following year, but when war broke out again in 1803 he foresaw financial ruin ahead, and he declared that it was "retarded solely by prodigies of valour and genius".

Great Britain was thus in a relatively strong position after eight years of war, but Addington was not the man to make the best use of his opportunities. He did not realize that in all bargains the man who is most warmly bent on obtaining the object of discussion is inevitably the weaker, and he made no secret of his desire for peace. The result was a treaty involving sacrifices far greater than had been contemplated even in the blackest months of 1797. Great Britain agreed to restore to the French all her naval conquests, namely Martinique, St. Lucia, Tobago, and other sugar islands, as well as all their ports and factories in India, and Goree in West Africa. To the Dutch she returned the Cape of Good Hope, Demarara, Essequibo, and Surinam, besides Curaçoa and several other small islands, retaining only the Dutch ports in Ceylon. Of her conquests from Spain she retained only Trinidad. She further consented to evacuate Egypt, Malta, and Elba, the first reverting to Turkey, and Malta to the Knights of St. John in certain circumstances. The Ionian Isles became the Republic of the Seven Islands.

By comparison, the sacrifices made by France were slight. She recovered every one of her former colonies, and shifted on her Spanish and Dutch allies the burden of loss, namely Trinidad and Ceylon. She agreed, it is true, to evacuate South Italy, but she retained all her other Continental conquests, and she continued to exercise control over the Batavian, Helvetian, Ligurian, and Cisalpine Republics. Such was the Treaty of Amiens of March, 1802, and a more extraordinary document has rarely been signed by British statesmen. If the war had resulted in stalemate, then, as in 1748, the concessions should have been equal on both sides, whereas in actual fact Britain allowed herself to be jockeyed out of the advantages she had so laboriously acquired.

In these circumstances it was small wonder that both the treaty and its authors were severely censured. Pitt, indeed, was silent, but Canning dilated on "the gross faults and omissions, the weakness and baseness and shuffling and stupidity of the agreement". Grenville and Windham criticized an arrangement which placed Malta in the hands of an Order whose total income could not possibly maintain sufficient troops to defend it, even with the assistance of a garrison of two thousand Neapolitans, whose own country was, moreover, always at the mercy of the French; Grenville described the surrender of Malta and the Cape as "purchasing a short interval of repose by the sacrifice of those points on which our security in a new contest may principally depend". Perhaps the best case that could be made out for the treaty was presented by Sheridan when he said it was "a peace which all men are glad of, but no man can be proud of". Nevertheless, Addington and his colleagues, by stressing the commercial benefits to be derived from the peace, obtained large majorities in both Houses of Parliament. They had yet to learn that the mind of the master of France was set, not on commerce, but on power, and that the very idea of compromise was wholly foreign to his character.

CHAPTER VIII

NAPOLEONIC EUROPE, 1802–1814

FEW periods in modern history so well illustrate the inter-play of strategy and diplomacy as the era which began with the conclusion of the Treaty of Amiens in 1802 and closed with the abdication of Napoleon in 1814. Communications might be slow, but there were master-minds at work, and the rapidity with which their decisions were put into effect, as well as the vastness of their designs, cannot fail to fascinate and astonish even a generation which has itself witnessed a similar titanic conflict, the central figure of which, however, was hardly cast in the same mould as the Corsican. Posterity has much to learn from the strokes and counter-strokes of the statesmen and soldiers who controlled the destinies of the world when France was making her great—and last—effort to dominate Europe. It was not only war and politics, but also gripping drama in the grand manner.

We have seen the extent to which in the earlier days of the Revolution the French armies were assisted by the divided counsels of their opponents and by the sympathy of many of the inhabitants of the countries which they invaded: during the twelve years in which Napoleon towered over Europe like a colossus the position was reversed. The very nationalism which the Revolution had itself inculcated turned against France until she found herself no longer fighting princes but peoples, while her opponents, taught by bitter and bloody experience, learnt to close their ranks until victory was won. Such was the background against which the career of Napoleon was set.

It is no exaggeration to say that throughout these momentous years the French Emperor's most tenacious foes were the British. Other nations might retire from the fray for a longer or a shorter space, but Britain hung on to his coat-tails like her traditional bull-dog. No inconsiderable time elapsed before some of her statesmen realized with what manner of man they were dealing, but Napoleon never understood the British at all. "His great mistake", wrote Albert Sorel, "was to imagine that he could frighten the English with words, restrain them by threats, and reduce them to bankruptcy by closing the Continent to them."

He knew that Britain lived by her commerce, but he never realized
that without command of the sea, which always eluded him, no
blockade could be effective. His famous Continental System,
designed to prevent trade with the British Isles, certainly resulted
in terrible losses to Great Britain, but the sufferings of the smaller
European nations were far greater. Napoleon doubtless expected
that trade with France would make up for the lack of that across
the sea, but the event signally falsified his hopes, and was one of
the reasons why such countries as Russia and Sweden turned
against him when they thought it was safe to do so.

Indeed, to no inconsiderable extent he defeated himself in
the end. It has been said that in his last years as Emperor his
health was failing, but his fall cannot really be attributed solely
to that. It was rather his judgment that had deteriorated.
Megalomania led him to enlarge his responsibilities, and at the
same time impaired his faculty for meeting them aright. Both
in war and in diplomacy he continued the strategy which had so
often brought him success in the past, forgetful that circumstances
had changed, and that his opponents were at last on their guard
against him, until at Waterloo he despised Wellington, and said
the battle would be the affair of a *déjeuner*.

Much of this lay ahead when the Treaty of Amiens was
signed, though it was not long before it became obvious that
nothing more than a truce had been concluded. The British
government, however, took a more optimistic view, and proceeded to reduce the number of sail-of-the-line in commission
from 104 to 32, while some thousands of British people set out to
indulge in the luxury of a holiday abroad. Napoleon appears
to have acted on the assumption that nothing would induce
Great Britain to take up arms against him again; at least, no
other construction can be placed upon his words and actions.
By the autumn of 1802 he was already declaring that the British
government wished to force upon him a renewal of hostilities
which it was his great desire to avoid. His deeds were no less
provocative than his words. He annexed the Duchy of Parma,
and the continental possessions of the King of Sardinia. He
sent troops into Switzerland to occupy the chief passes of the
Alps, and he ordered the Cisalpine and Batavian Republics to
put crushing duties on British goods. This was bad enough,
but worse was to follow. He requested Addington to expel
those members of the French Royal Family who had taken up

Treaty of Campo Formio - 1797
Treaty of Luneville - 1801
Treaty of Amiens - 1802

their residence in Great Britain, and asked for the suppression of certain newspapers which had criticized his methods of government. These demands were refused.

Events were clearly working up to a climax, and this came over the question of Malta. The Knights of St. John were not yet ready to return to the island, but Napoleon insisted that the British troops should nevertheless be withdrawn at once. In view of the fate of Parma and Sardinia, this would have been tantamount to handing Malta over to the French, and the British government refused to agree. Napoleon then resorted to threats, and on March 13th, 1803, he publicly upbraided the British ambassador during a reception at the Tuileries. The object of the outburst, which was soon repeated all over Paris, was to work French opinion up in favour of war, and to place the responsibility upon Britain, for there was a strong peace party of which Talleyrand, Fouché, and Joseph Bonaparte were the leading members.

Yet Napoleon could have achieved his end had he only acted upon the principle *suaviter in modo, fortiter in re*, so averse were the British government and people from another war. By conceding a few points and concentrating on his navy, the First Consul would have had the world at his feet. The trouble was that he always looked at a problem from the point of view of a soldier, not from that of a statesman. For the prosecution of his designs in the East he must secure control of the Mediterranean, and for this the possession of Malta was essential: therefore he was prepared to fight for Malta. In these circumstances it is in no way surprising that war between Britain and France should have begun again in the middle of May, 1803.

The opening moves well illustrated the nature of the struggle between Land Power and Sea Power. The British seized the French island possessions in the Americas, while Napoleon occupied Hanover and South Italy. These actions were prophetic of the future, for the First Consul was committed to the attempt to acquire an absolute control of the Continent, to which the British replied by mastering the resources of the Tropics. In no previous war had economic considerations exerted so great an influence upon strategy and diplomacy.

The First Consul neglected none of the old weapons of French policy: he sent for Louise of Stolberg, the widow of Bonnie Prince Charlie, and asked her if she had a son, while Emmett attempted a rising in Dublin, but it proved impossible to re-kindle the flames of Irish rebellion after what had happened five years before. The main blow, however, was to be delivered direct, and the ports of Boulogne, Calais, Dunkirk, Ostend, and Antwerp hummed with the preparations for ferrying the veterans of France across to Britain. So obvious a threat brought Pitt back to office, and as Napoleon in the interval had become Emperor, "the two protagonists now stood face to face—Napoleon, Emperor of the French, President of the Italian Republic, Mediator of the Swiss Republic, Controller of Holland, absolute ruler of a great military Empire; Pitt, the Prime Minister of an obstinate and at times half-crazy King dependent on a weak Cabinet, a disordered Exchequer, a Navy weakened by ill-timed economies, and land forces whose martial ardour ill made up for lack of organization, equipment, and training". So wrote the late Professor Holland Rose.

Napoleon might be crowned Emperor of the French, but he was as far from London as ever. "Let us be masters of the strait for six hours, and we shall be masters of the world." The weather and British naval supremacy thwarted him, and French public opinion was becoming restive. Accordingly, Napoleon began to work out a manœuvre which should at the same time lure the British ships away from European waters and strike a damaging blow at British finance; this was an attack on the West Indies. This task appeared to be made the easier when, in December, 1804, Spain joined France, and the whole Spanish empire became available as a base for operations against the British overseas possessions.

"The Indies are ours when we want to take them", declared the French Emperor, and in this frame of mind he ordered the preparation of three expeditions; the first, carrying 3500 troops, was to reinforce the garrison of Guadeloupe, and to capture Dominica and St. Lucia; the second, of 4000 men, was to retake Surinam and the other Dutch West Indian possessions, besides bringing help to San Domingo; while the third, some 1500 strong, was to seize Goree and other African posts, as well as an island with which in later years Napoleon was to become better acquainted, namely St. Helena, where "the English are in blind security." The island was then to be used for commerce-raiding. "Thus the English, attacked simultaneously in Asia, Africa, and America, and being long accustomed not to feel the war, will have the proofs of their weakness brought home to them by these successive blows at the focal points of their commerce."

Nelson foresaw the danger, and at the beginning of September, 1804, he was prophesying a blow at the West Indies, "and in that case England would be so clamorous for peace that we should humble ourselves". At the same time Pitt and his colleagues acted with a boldness which had not characterized them in earlier crises, and with the full approval of Nelson they decided to strike where the Napoleonic system was most vulnerable, namely in the Mediterranean. Accordingly in the spring of 1805 they prepared a force under Sir James Craig to proceed to Malta, and its commander was warned that the protection of Sicily from the French was to be his principal object. It was a singularly courageous decision to take in view of the imminent danger of invasion.

Meanwhile the French Emperor was putting the final touches to his project. The destruction of his enemy's commerce now assumed almost as prominent a place as the invasion of Britain. He decided to concentrate in the West Indies the fleets of Brest, Ferrol, Toulon, and Cadiz, which were to convey some 4700 troops for action against the British colonies: they were then to return with a united force of more than forty sail to the English Channel for the great stroke on which hung the destinies of the world. Pitt, however, had not been inactive, and before these plans could mature Napoleon had been called away from the Channel to battle in Bohemia. Contrary to popular belief, therefore, Trafalgar was fought, not to save Britain from invasion but to assure her position in the Mediterranean.

With Pitt, as with Napoleon, arms and diplomacy now went hand in hand. Twelve months before Trafalgar was fought on October 21st, 1805, he was hard at work forming yet another coalition against France, but he had learnt by bitter experience that in persuading potential allies deeds spoke louder than words, so he determined to strike a blow which would impress the world with Britain's determination and might. Spain had been warned that if she continued to violate her neutrality by giving underhand assistance to Napoleon the consequences would be unpleasant, and when she showed no signs of listening to the advice, three Spanish treasure-ships were seized on the high seas without a previous declaration of war. It was, of course, the very blow which Chatham had wished to deliver over forty years before, but which his colleagues in the Cabinet had vetoed, and which thus brought about his resignation.

Britain might thwart Napoleon at sea, but she could not hope to overthrow him without the assistance of Continental allies. While Addington was still in office Gustavus IV of Sweden had suggested another coalition, this time between Britain, Russia, Austria, and Sweden, to withstand French aggression, and in due course the Tsar and the Emperor signified their adherence. The object of this alliance was defined to be the expulsion of French troops from north Germany, the assured independence of Holland and Switzerland, and the restoration of the King of Sardinia to his continental possessions. Russia and such other Powers as might join were to provide 500,000 men, while Great Britain, instead of furnishing troops, was to supply £1,250,000 a year for every 100,000 men engaged in the campaign. After the war there was to be a conference to define more clearly the law of nations, and to establish a European federation, where the states were to be independent, enjoying constitutions "founded on the sacred rights of humanity." In other words, there was to be a system of collective security, based on the aggrandisement of Austria and Sardinia in northern Italy to check the ambition of France. Pitt was dead long before there was an opportunity to put these plans into execution, but they foreshadow what was effected by Castlereagh in the Treaty of Chaumont nine years later.

Napoleon, in face of this threat, did not allow the initiative to pass out of his hands. The Austrians refused to believe that he could reach the Danube in force before the second week of November, but already, on August 29th—nearly two months before Trafalgar was fought—the "Army of England" had become the "Grand Army", and on September 2nd it began its march towards the Rhine in almost full strength. Its commander was probably by no means sorry for the excuse to abandon the projected invasion, and to silence his critics by success in fields to which he was more accustomed. On October 25th the Austrian vanguard capitulated at Ulm. Everything now, so far as the coalition was concerned, depended on Prussia.

The long line of French communications stretched across Germany, and in front of Napoleon lay the bulk of the Austrian, and the whole of the Russian, army, still unbeaten. Had Prussia taken advantage of the opportunity, the overthrow of the French Emperor would almost certainly have been anticipated by seven years, to the incalculable benefit of Europe, which would thus have been spared the loss of blood and treasure that took place between 1805 and 1814. Talleyrand's diplomacy, however, kept Berlin neutral by dangling Hanover under the nose of Frederick William III, and on the snow-covered hillside of Austerlitz on December 2nd, 1805, the Third Coalition collapsed before the disciplined fury of the French charge. Napoleon's domination of the Continent was more firmly established than ever.

In the following year the French Emperor established his "new order", as a later generation would have termed it, in Germany. His object was to dissolve the Empire, and to form a Confederation of the Rhine from which Austria and Prussia were to be excluded. The principal states in this new organization would be obliged to look to France for support, while the smaller Princes, who had hitherto leaned on Austria, were, with a few exceptions, to be swept away. The treaty constituting the Confederation was drawn up by Talleyrand, and was ratified at Saint Cloud in June.

The affairs of the Confederation were to be managed by a Diet at Frankfort, consisting of a College of Kings and one of Princes. The former was composed of the Kings of Bavaria and Wurtemberg, together with the Grand Dukes of Baden, Hesse-Darmstadt, and Berg. The minor members of the Confederation, of whom there were nine, formed the College of Princes. The secularizations of 1803 were completed by wholesale mediatization, and a further step was thus taken in the direction of that German unity which was one day to spell the ruin of France. Napoleon was declared Protector, and an alliance was made between the Confederation and the French Empire, binding each to help the other in any Continental war. On August 1st, 1806, the representatives of the several states announced their withdrawal from the Empire, and Napoleon declared that he no longer recognized its existence. Vienna had no choice but to accept the inevitable, so Francis II resigned the Imperial dignity, and became Francis I, Emperor of Austria. In this prosaic manner the Holy Roman Empire came to an end, after an existence of more than a thousand years.

The battle of Austerlitz had necessitated the withdrawal of the British troops which had been sent to northern Europe on the assumption that Prussia would join the coalition against Napoleon, and in January, 1806, Pitt had died. His ministry was succeeded by the administration of "All the Talents", and at the Foreign Office was Charles James Fox. The Whig statesman had lost a good deal of his earlier enthusiasm for the principles of 1789 since they resulted in a military dictatorship, but he still hoped that some accommodation with Napoleon might prove possible. He was speedily undeceived. The French Emperor was quite ready to talk peace, or even to make it, so long as it was on his own terms: particularly did he want Sicily, for the possession of that island was essential to the success of his Mediterranean ambitions. Fox soon discovered with what manner of man he was dealing, and he wrote to his nephew, "It is not Sicily, but the shuffling, insincere way in which they act, that shows me they are playing a false game". Napoleon's diplomacy, in effect, always assumed the same form, that is to say, separate treaties with different countries, combined with the hurried continuance of aggression while negotiations were taking place, so as to compel the other party either to accept the aggression or to fight in unfavourable circumstances.

By the autumn of 1806 the turn of Prussia had come. Her neutrality had served its purpose in the preceding years, and she could now be crushed with impunity. The execution of the publisher, Palm, may well have been deliberately carried out to provoke hostilities, which thereupon ensued. At Jena and Auerstadt the system of the great Frederick collapsed like a house of cards, and before long the French were in Berlin. All was not, however, over, for there were still the Russians to be taken into account. At Eylau, in February, 1807, they administered a severe check to the master of Europe, and it was not until the following June that they were defeated in the bloody fight of Friedland. Meanwhile, Danzig had surrendered in the previous month, and with its fall the resistance of Prussia ceased.

While these events were transforming the face of Europe, the British government was every day giving fresh proof of its lack of understanding of the connection between strategy and diplomacy. It seems at first to have believed that the best way to negotiate with Napoleon was to parade its unquestionably sincere pacific intentions. Accordingly it refused to support a vote of thanks to those who had come forward when invasion threatened, and it abolished their pay and allowances; it repealed the Additional Force Bill; and it suspended the ballot for the Militia. Finally, it replied to Jena by holding a General Election, in the hope of thereby weakening the Tories in the House of Commons.

Abroad it adopted the policy of frittering away British strength in a number of isolated operations: the war was never seen, as Napoleon saw it, as one connected whole. Two expeditions were sent to the Near East in the hope of coercing the Sultan into a rupture with France, and both failed dismally. Admiral Duckworth succeeded in getting his fleet through the Dardanelles, but failed to persuade the Turks, and only managed to re-pass the Narrows after considerable loss. A force that was sent to Egypt surprised Alexandria, but was repulsed before Rosetta, and the only result of these attempts to gain cheap laurels in the Near East was to throw the Porte into the arms of Napoleon. In the West an incompetent general was ordered to take Buenos Aires, which he not only failed to do, but also lost Monte Video, which had been conquered earlier in the year, and British prestige was hardly repaired by the court-martial that dismissed him from the service. The solitary success that the administration could claim to its credit was a victory at Maida, in Calabria, which demonstrated the superiority of the British line over the French column. After this battle, however, Craig prudently withdrew his troops from the mainland to Messina, and thus began that occupation of Sicily which was destined to last for eight years and to prove a firm barrier to the eastern ambitions of the French Emperor.

In the early weeks of 1807 the ministry of "All the Talents" fell (Fox having died in the previous year), and was succeeded by a very different administration, under the Duke of Portland, in which George Canning was Foreign Secretary and Castlereagh was at the War Office. It was, however, by then too late to retrieve the situation on the Continent, though a force was sent to Rügen.

The Russians had fought the French at Friedland in the middle of June, as we have seen, and by the end of the month the Tsar was Napoleon's ally. Russian diplomacy has always been remarkable for its realism, but this *volte face* recalled the course of events in the latter part of the Seven Years' War, when Peter III succeeded Elizabeth. There was, however, something to be said in favour of the Tsar and his advisers: the Russian armies had been beaten in the field, Prussia was at her last gasp, Gustavus IV of Sweden was proving himself impossible both as an ally and as a monarch, and, most important of all, the British government had done nothing of real value to assist in the struggle against the common enemy. These were certainly reasons for peace, but hardly, one would have imagined, for a peace which had as its basis an alliance with France directed against Russia's former friends. In this connection the personal factor cannot be left out of account: when, in years to come, Canning faced the Holy Alliance, it is not surprising that he should have remembered this earlier experience of Russian policy, and should have been inclined to see in the idealistic Alexander the co-conspirator of Napoleon on the famous raft in the middle of the Niemen.

The two Emperors had their first meeting on June 25th, and on the 7th of the following month the Treaty of Tilsit was signed. The public articles provided for the reduction of Prussia to the rank of a second-class Power, but the secret ones concerned Great Britain. By these the two monarchs agreed that if the British government did not mitigate the severity of the Orders in Council, which had forbidden trade with France and her allies, and restore all maritime conquests since 1803, they would summon Portugal, Denmark, and Sweden to close their ports against British shipping, while any of these three Powers which refused to comply with the order was to be treated as an enemy.

The threat to Britain could hardly have been more serious, and Napoleon seemed to have turned the tables on the islanders. When he marched away from the Channel in the late summer of 1805 he realized that the invasion of England would not become a practicable proposition until his rear was safe from attack by his Continental enemies; that condition was now fulfilled. It was true that France and Spain had lost a large part of their naval strength at Trafalgar, but if Napoleon could obtain possession of the fleets of Portugal, Denmark, and Sweden, he would more than repair his losses. The Emperor himself estimated that he could muster 180 sail-of-the-line; "with the aid of such a fleet, and my immense flotilla, it was by no means impossible to lead a European army to London".

Canning and his colleagues were under no illusions as to the danger which hung over them. The Franco-Russian agreement had hardly been concluded before the Foreign Secretary knew all about it, including the secret provisions regarding Great Britain. The source of his information is one of the mysteries of diplomacy, and for many years credence was given to the story that when Napoleon and Alexander met there was an agent of the Foreign Office behind a curtain listening to their conversation. Unfortunately for those who would like to believe this romantic legend, the accounts of the expenditure of Secret Service money for this year give it no support, and the probability is that Canning received the news from somebody in the Tsar's household, where Anglophil sympathies were strong and the most important secrets were rarely kept. In any event it is clear that what reached London was a report of the preliminary conversation between the two Emperors on June 25th, and not a copy of the secret clauses of the actual treaty, for Canning believed that every moment was of the most vital importance if the Franco-Russian plans were to be forestalled, whereas had he been acquainted with the terms of the treaty itself he would have realized that he had until December to take the necessary precautions.

In the light of the knowledge available, the danger thus seemed to the British government to be imminent, and of the three quarters from which it threatened, the Danish was the most menacing, for Sweden was still at war with France, while before Napoleon could lay hands on the Portuguese fleet he would have to come to terms with Spain. Under the influence of Canning the Cabinet acted in a manner reminiscent of Chatham. Before the end of July a naval squadron under Admiral Gambier, and a military force commanded by Sir Arthur Wellesley, had left for Copenhagen, and with them went a Mr. Jackson, whom Canning sent to negotiate an offensive and defensive alliance with the Danish Crown Prince, afterwards Frederick VI, who was at that time regent for his father, the mad King Christian VII.

Jackson was far from being the luckiest or the most skilful of diplomats, but he had little latitude in his instructions. He had to insist, as a preliminary to the conclusion of the alliance, upon the surrender of the Danish fleet, which the British government pledged itself to return intact at the end of the war. In any case the negotiation would have been a difficult one, for Great Britain had been unpopular in Denmark ever since the attack on Copenhagen six years before, but Jackson did not improve matters by very obviously offering the alliance at the cannon's mouth. The Crown Prince refused to negotiate, and Jackson called on Gambier and Wellesley to enforce the British terms. Wellesley defeated the Danes at Roskilde, and Copenhagen was bombarded by land and sea. Thereupon the Crown Prince made an unconditional surrender, and the Danish fleet was incorporated in Admiral Gambier's squadron.

At once there was an outcry in many quarters, from the Tuileries to the House of Commons. Napoleon, whose hands were still wet with the blood of Palm and the Duc d'Enghien, was horrified at so flagrant a violation of the rights of small nations, of which he declared himself to be the protector; and he set the tone for all who drew their inspiration from him when he declared that "blood and fire had made the English masters of Copenhagen". By the strict letter of the international law of the time the British government was justified, but in its defence to Parliament it was handicapped by its inability, for obvious reasons, to cite the information in its possession concerning the Tilsit negotiations.

Meanwhile, there were the Swedish and Portuguese fleets to be considered, and the British government displayed the same promptitude where they were concerned. In respect of Sweden it soon became obvious that Gustavus IV was impossible. Sir John Moore was, indeed, sent with a force to co-operate with the Swedes, but he was then withdrawn, and in any event the Swedish fleet was too small by itself to affect the balance of naval power in Europe. With Portugal the case was very different, for not only was she Britain's oldest ally, but events were moving so fast that the slightest delay was fraught with the greatest danger to British interests.

Portugal was governed by a Prince Regent, afterwards John VI, on behalf of the mad Queen Maria I, and Canning lost no time in coming to terms with him. John agreed to surrender the Portuguese fleet, and to retire to Brazil, but he was dilatory in carrying out his promises. In the meantime Napoleon had been far from idle. In October, 1807, he concluded the Treaty of Fontainebleau with Spain, by which he secured permission to march French troops across Spanish territory in return for a promise to partition Portugal, and he then sent Junot to occupy Lisbon. It was not until the French were in the very suburbs of the Portuguese capital that the Prince Regent handed his ships over to the British, and set sail for Rio de Janeiro. Canning had won the race with Napoleon by a very short head indeed; but he had won; and the Portuguese fleet, like the Danish, was under the White Ensign, not the Tricolour.

A French invasion of the British Isles was once more out of the question, and the ambitious schemes concocted by Napoleon and Alexander at Tilsit had come crashing down like a house of

H

cards. The Danish and Portuguese fleets were in British, not French, ports and the Corsican's triumphant entry into London was as far off as ever. On the other hand, Britain had neither an ally nor a soldier on the mainland of Europe. Napoleon was master of the Continent, but he could never feel secure so long as the British were undefeated. In short, if the war was not to end in a stalemate, both Powers must adopt new tactics, and this they proceeded to do. Britain intensified her blockade of the countries under the control of France, and Napoleon retaliated by endeavouring to strike at the most vulnerable part of his adversary, namely her commerce. As Admiral Mahan put it, "The battle between the sea and the land was to be fought out on commerce. . . . The Imperial soldiers were turned into coast-guardsmen to shut out Great Britain from her markets; the British ships became revenue cutters to prohibit the trade of France. The neutral carrier, pocketing his pride, offered his services to either for pay, and the other then regarded him as taking part in hostilities."

CHAPTER IX

NAPOLEONIC EUROPE, 1802–1814 (*continued*)

IN this new phase of the war against Great Britain the French Emperor clearly enjoyed many advantages. He controlled nearly the whole coast of Europe from Hamburg to Leghorn; the sovereigns of Russia, Austria, and Prussia were at his bidding, and the Spaniards, Dutch, West Germans, and Italians were his vassals. In these circumstances Napoleon may well have felt justified when, at Berlin in November, 1806, he had decreed that the British Isles were henceforth in a state of blockade and isolation, had forbidden on the part of all his dependent countries any commerce with them, and had declared every subject of George III found in a country occupied by French troops to be a prisoner of war. The British government retaliated by a series of Orders in Council which were issued at intervals during the year 1807. By the first of these orders vessels were forbidden to trade between any ports in the possession of France, or of her allies if under her control. By the second, issued after the extension of Napoleon's Continental System to the Mediterranean, general reprisals were granted against the goods, ships, and inhabitants of Tuscany, Naples, Dalmatia, and the Ionian Islands. By the third, all ports from which the British flag was excluded were declared in blockade, all trade in their produce unlawful, and their ships a prize, while all vessels carrying certificates of origin, a measure upon which Napoleon had insisted to prevent evasion of his system, were declared liable to capture. By the fourth, the sale of ships by a belligerent to a neutral was declared illegal, because the French had managed to preserve much of their commerce by fictitious sales, which enabled them to trade under neutral flags.

Napoleon heard of the last of these Orders in Council when he was in Italy in November, 1807, and in reply he issued the Milan Decrees. In these he declared every neutral ship which submitted to the Orders to be denationalized and good prize of war; and the same judgment was passed upon every vessel sailing to or from any port in the United Kingdom or its colonies or possessions. In short, each combatant had now instituted a total blockade of the other, and it remained to be seen which was in the better position to effect its purpose.

The countries under the domination of France were not long in feeling the consequences of this extension of the war into the economic sphere. They were cut off from all those tropical productions which the progress of civilization had rendered necessary for the modern world, especially sugar and coffee, together with most of the silk, cotton, and dyes needed for textile manufacture. It is true that some sub-tropical products could be grown in Italy or in the south of France, but their transport in any quantity by land to north Germany, Prussia, or Russia was impracticable. The result was a feverish endeavour to find substitutes for the commodities which could no longer be obtained. The lack of coffee was greatly felt, and frantic efforts were made to manufacture alternatives out of chicory, dried carrots, acorns, and sunflower seeds. The Danes, who always did their best to carry out Napoleon's orders, had seventeen factories at work upon these substitutes, while in place of tobacco men were reduced to getting what satisfaction they could out of a mixture of the leaves of gooseberries, chestnuts, and cabbages. The deprivation of sugar was even more serious, for of late years consumption had greatly increased. The imports into Great Britain had nearly doubled during the previous decade, and about half of this was normally re-exported to the Continent. To meet the shortage Napoleon encouraged the sugar-beet industry and a process of extracting sugar from grapes, but neither did much to satisfy the demand: cane-sugar was what was wanted, though by 1812 it cost nine times as much in Paris as in London.

Not unnaturally the ports of Germany and the Netherlands were considerable sufferers from the Continental System. In 1807–1808 a citizen of Hamburg wrote of that city, "There is no longer any trade as it existed formerly . . . more than 300 vessels are laid up". When John Quincy Adams went as American ambassador to Russia in 1809 he found the people very hostile to France, and one of the Tsar's ministers termed Napoleon "a giddy-head in regard to commerce". A year later Adams, himself a bitter Anglophobe, warned his French colleague at St. Petersburg that the Continental System was "instead of impairing her (England's) commerce, securing to her that of the whole world, and was pouring into her lap the means of continuing the war. . . . You will lay the world under the most grievous contributions for her benefit and advantage."

However much some of the Continental countries may originally have welcomed the French on political and social grounds, there was soon a widespread conspiracy to defeat Napoleon's measures, and this turned to the profit of Britain. She controlled the products of the Tropics and she was mistress of the seas, so, as she alone could import what was in so great demand, she could charge her clandestine customers what she pleased: there was no competition. The result was soon visible in a sudden rise of prices throughout France, Germany, and Italy. Raw cotton fetched 10 to 11 francs, sugar 6 to 7 francs, coffee 8 francs, and indigo 21 francs a pound. Smuggling was everywhere rife, and great ingenuity was displayed in connection with it. The number of funerals, for example, in a suburb of Hamburg came to assume enormous proportions, until the French authorities, their inquisitiveness aroused, looked into the hearses, and found them stuffed with bales of British merchandise. On another occasion large quantities of sand were brought under some pretence or another from the seashore, but some curious official found that it came from the West Indies.

Sugar was smuggled from London into Germany by way of Salonika, for that was almost the only neutral port open to British commerce. From there it was taken in panniers on the backs of mules over the Balkans to Belgrade, where it was transferred to barges, and sent up the Danube. Another illicit trade route was from the shores of Dalmatia through Hungary. The writer of a contemporary pamphlet stated that his firm then employed five hundred horses on and near that coast in carrying British goods into Central Europe, and that the cost of getting them into France was "about £20 per cwt., or more than fifty times the present freight to Calcutta". In effect, the result of the French Emperor's economic experiments may be summed up in the statement of Chaptal that the general run of prices in France was higher by one-third than it had been before the Revolution.

There was, however, another side to the picture, and Napoleon's decrees were by no means without effect in Britain. While Ministers were congratulating themselves upon the elasticity of the revenue, which rose from £103,000,000 in 1805 to £162,000,000 in 1814, a widespread depression began to make itself felt in consequence of the closing of the Continental market for manufactured articles. The glamour of Wellington's victories in the Peninsula cannot disguise the fact that there was very real distress in many quarters at home while they were being won. What principally enabled Britain to defeat Napoleon's attempt to strangle her was the wealth of the West Indies, so that it is no exaggeration to say that during these critical years the British Isles were saved by the British Empire.

Such was the economic background against which the wars and diplomacy of the Napoleonic era were set.

The early months of the year 1808 witnessed the beginning of what can only be described as the next round in the contest between the French Emperor and his British foe. The plans made at Tilsit had miscarried, and the attempt to put a stop to Britain's commerce with the mainland of Europe was proving none too successful, so Napoleon, fertile as ever in alternative schemes, decided to attack his rival in another quarter. If he could gain possession of Spain, and, better still, of Spanish America, not only would he be able to deal a severe blow at British commerce in the Atlantic, but he would also be in a position to threaten the route to the East round the Cape of Good Hope.

To carry out such a project he was admirably situated. In the first place, the Treaty of Fontainebleau had, from a military point of view, left Spain at the mercy of the French. In the second, the Spanish Royal Family was a house divided against itself, and Charles IV actually applied to Napoleon to arbitrate upon his differences with his son Ferdinand, Prince of Asturias. Finally, the French Emperor summoned both men to Bayonne, where they were forced to resign their rights to the Spanish throne. Thereupon he presented the Spaniards with a new sovereign in the person of his own brother, Joseph, hitherto King of Naples— soon to be known to his unwilling subjects as *Pepe Botellas*, from his alleged liking for the bottle.

The British government, or at any rate the Foreign Secretary, was not slow to realize the threat to the national interests which was involved in the establishment of the Bonaparte at Madrid, but for the moment there was nothing to be done. Britain might be mistress of the seas, but her fleet could not sail across the Pyrenees, and Napoleon was incontestably master of the Continent. Nevertheless, Canning was determined that if the French obtained Spain, it should at any rate be Spain without the Indies. Great Britain, without an ally on the mainland of Europe, could not stop the passage of French armies across the Continent, but she could stop the passage of French fleets across the Atlantic, and with the Danish and Portuguese navies in his pocket Canning was in a position to take full advantage of the growing discontent with Spanish rule which was beginning to manifest itself in the Americas. The area of the war was being extended with every year that passed, and the French invasion of the Peninsula was destined to have the most far-reaching consequences both in the Old World and in the New.

The idea of stirring up revolt in the Spanish colonies was not original, nor was it intended as a mere tit-for-tat for the action of Charles III during the War of American Independence. As long ago as 1790 Pitt had been in touch with Francisco de Miranda— the *Precursor*, as he is known in Latin-American history. At that time Great Britain appeared to be on the eve of war with Spain over the question of Nootka Sound, and in view of the information which was reaching him with regard to the growing unrest in the Spanish colonies, the British Prime Minister welcomed Miranda as a possible ally against Madrid. The two men met on several occasions, and had not the progress of the French Revolution prevented Louis XVI from coming to the aid of Spain, it is more than likely that the first risings in Spanish America would have been made with British support. Relations between Pitt and Miranda were renewed in 1804, and it was through the former that Canning met the Venezuelan patriots.

British prestige was none too high in the Americas, in view of the recent failure to take Buenos Aires and the enforced surrender of Monte Video. This circumstance, together with the advice of Miranda, induced Canning to favour Venezuela as the spot where the most telling blow might be struck against the supremacy of Spain in the New World. It was within easy reach of Jamaica and Trinidad, and there was already considerable discontent at the course of events in the Peninsula. The influence of Miranda was, indeed, so powerful that it had been decided to send large British forces to Venezuela under the command of Sir Arthur Wellesley when events in Spain itself completely changed the international situation. These efforts of Canning to foster the revolutionary movement in Spanish America could not, of course, be continued when Great Britain and Spain were in alliance, but they mark the origin of the policy which he was to pursue when he returned to the Foreign Office in 1822. No British government could prevent France, whether it was the France of Napoleon or of Louis XVIII, from conquering Spain, but it could prevent Paris from including Spanish America in the sphere of operations, and that was what Canning was preparing to do in 1808, and was what he actually did fourteen years later.

The events in the Peninsula which deranged the Foreign Secretary's plans were nothing less than the uprising of the Spanish people against the invader, which began in Madrid on May 2nd, and for Napoleon it was the writing on the wall. Hitherto, as we have seen, popular sentiment throughout Europe had generally favoured the French, but the rigours of the Continental System, combined with the increasing harshness of Napoleon's despotic rule, had produced a reaction, and of this the proud and independent Spaniards were the protagonists. It was in reality the beginning of the end, though the end itself was to be postponed for another six years.

The first thought of the Spanish patriots was to turn for help to the unyielding foe of France, namely Great Britain. The British government was not slow to realize the importance of what was taking place, so peace was made with Spain, and it was decided to send to the Peninsula the expeditionary force that had originally been intended for Venezuela. In consequence of a British victory at Vimeiro, overtures for an armistice were received from Junot, and the Convention of Cintra was concluded. By this agreement the French army was to surrender Lisbon and the other Portuguese fortresses intact, but was to be allowed to return to France with its arms and baggage at the expense of Great Britain.

The Convention roused in England the most violent resentment, which was shared by Canning, who had been absent from the meeting of the Cabinet when it was approved. The Portuguese, too, were far from being enamoured of an arrangement which allowed the invaders to deport unmolested with the loot of Lisbon in their knapsacks, and it was upon the Foreign Office that there fell the burden of answering their remonstrances. Indeed, the whole transaction brings out very clearly the difficulties that confront a British Foreign Secretary in time of war. He is responsible for the smooth working of the arrangements with his country's allies, and yet military decisions are continually being taken upon which he is often not consulted, with the result that he is left to explain away as best he can a *fait accompli* to indignant allied diplomats. On the other hand, there was much to be said for the Convention of Cintra, which, incidentally, was condemned by the French Emperor as roundly as by Canning, though with considerably more justification. In compelling the French to evacuate Portugal it struck a very severe blow at the whole Napoleonic system, for it opened the Portuguese ports to British shipping, and it rendered more remote than ever the hope of striking effectively at British maritime supremacy.

In October of the same year, 1808, there took place, at Erfurt, what was destined to be the last meeting between the French Emperor and the Tsar. As Algernon Cecil has well put it, "To all appearance . . . the sun of Austerlitz rode high as ever in the heavens. As Napoleon held high court with Alexander in those early autumn days of 1808 in the old Hanseatic town, whilst kings and sages bent before him, there seemed no end to his greatness. The Spanish insurrection seemed but as the rumbling of a distant volcano; the *malaise* of Austria no more than a cloud upon the horizon; to the east the sky remained rich with promise, and he tried once more to bewitch Alexander with the magic of the gorgeous vision." The scene was magnificently staged, but there was one notable absentee, Great Britain, and her absence meant more than the presence of all the other Powers. Erfurt was the apogee of Napoleon, but already the shrewdest brain in Europe, Talleyrand, had come to the conclusion that the tide was on the turn, and was making his preparations accordingly.

In spite of the Corsican's efforts to dazzle the Tsar it soon became clear that he was not in so complacent a mood as he had been at Tilsit. Alexander refused to be a party to any threats to Austria, while Napoleon retaliated by insisting upon the postponement of the partition of the Ottoman Empire. Outwardly, however, the alliance between France and Russia was preserved, and a secret convention was drawn up which assigned Finland and the Danubian Principalities to Russia in return for the Tsar's recognition of Joseph Bonaparte as King of Spain, and a promise of help to France in case she were attacked by Austria. The last act of the two monarchs was to send a note to George III summoning him to make peace, with the intention of thereby placing upon Great Britain the responsibility for the continuance of the war.

To this message Canning replied expressing the government's desire to open negotiations, provided that all parties were included, but added that Great Britain could not treat unless her Spanish allies were admitted to the conference. Napoleon retorted that the Spaniards were rebels, and that he could not recognize them. In these circumstances it was clear that the issue could be settled by the sword alone, and the British Foreign Secretary wrote to the Tsar expressing George's regret that Alexander should have sanctioned "an usurpation unparalleled in the history of the world".

The spring of the following year, 1809, was to provide further evidence of the lack of co-ordination which still characterized the enemies of France, and to give point to the observation of General Sarrail to Clemenceau over a century later, "Since I have seen alliances at work, I have lost something of my admiration for Napoleon". What happened was that Austria once more took the field against the French Emperor. There were several reasons for this action. Napoleon had foolishly neglected the advice of Frederick the Great never to "maltreat an enemy by halves", while the British successes in the Peninsula, combined with the growth of national feeling in Germany, seemed to render the moment opportune. Nevertheless, there was little previous negotiation between Vienna and London, and Austria and Britain were nominally at war. When, however, Francis drew the sword, the British government did all it could to help him. The cost of the war in the Peninsula was a serious drain upon the Exchequer, but Canning managed to send £250,000 in silver bars to Trieste. George III, not unreasonably, insisted that, before any actual help was given, peace should be formally made, and the ensuing delay prevented any real co-operation. Napoleon, too, was still invincible on the field of battle, and by the beginning of July the resistance of Austria was at an end: Vienna had fallen and Wagram had been fought, so that when, on July 29th, Canning acknowledged the receipt of the Austrian ratification of peace with Great Britain it was "accompanied by the afflicting intelligence of the armistice concluded on the 12th instance between the Austrian and French armies".

There was no maltreatment by halves about the Treaty of Schönbrunn, which was signed in October, 1809. Austria had to make considerable concessions of territory to France and Bavaria in Upper Austria, Carniola and Carinthia; parts of Galicia were ceded to Russia and Saxony; and Francis was not allowed to maintain an army of more than 150,000 men. Next year the Austrian Emperor was compelled to drain the cup to the dregs when his daughter was married to the Corsican, and so came to reign over the country which had sent her aunt to the guillotine. Metternich saw the political blessings which might be made to flow from this match, but it was generally regarded as a further humiliation for the House of Habsburg.

For the next two years the *façade* of the French Empire seemed as imposing as ever, though, to the observant, Talleyrand appeared to have much justification for his belief that in reality the tide had turned. The enforcement of the Continental System meant a progressive dissipation of French strength, while the system itself was goading the subject nations, particularly Germany, to revolt. Even Napoleon's own brother, Louis, King of Holland, refused to enforce it, but retribution was swift, for Holland was annexed to France, and Louis consequently lost his throne. In the same year, 1810, the French dominion over the North Sea coast was extended by the annexation of a corner of Germany, and as a result the Duchy of Oldenburg, which belonged to a branch of the Russian Imperial family, ceased to exist.

The prospect of war between France and Russia was, in fact, gradually becoming more certain, and it was definitely hastened when, in January, 1811, the Tsar declared Russian ports open to all vessels sailing under a neutral flag, and imposed duties on many French products. This was to effect a breach in the Continental System which Napoleon could not be expected to tolerate for long. Yet neither side was in any hurry to precipitate the crisis which both were coming to believe was inevitable, and seventeen months were still to elapse before hostilities actually began. One reason for the delay was that both France and Russia had certain commitments of which it was advisable to be quit before coming to grips with one another. The Tsar was at war with the Turks, and it was not until 1812 that he was able, largely through the good offices of Great Britain, to make peace with them by the Treaty of Bucharest, when Russia obtained possession of Bessarabia. The Tsar had thus protected his rear and flank. Napoleon was not so fortunate, for the British bull-dog had a firm hold of his coat-tails, and he was quite unable to shake the animal off, though why he made no effort to put an end to the Peninsular War, which he could easily have done at this time had he assumed command of the French armies himself, is one of the mysteries of history.

The other Continental Powers were more apprehensive than expectant. They had seen so many coalitions go down before Napoleon that they had no mind to try their fortunes again until they saw some sign that France was weakening. Prussia at one moment did endeavour to assert herself, but she was forced to come to heel when the French whip was cracked, and the final conditions imposed upon her were humiliating in the extreme. She was compelled to supply Napoleon with 20,000 men to serve as part of the French army, and she promised not to raise any other levies without the Emperor's consent. Prussia was also to afford a free passage, and to provide food and forage, for the French troops, and payment for this was to be made at a later date. All that Berlin received in return was a reduction in the war indemnity imposed after Jena. As for Austria, she was in no position to resist. The memory of Wagram was too fresh, while she was practically bankrupt, with government paper at a discount of ninety per cent.

In August, 1811, the threatened war was brought a step nearer. Napoleon indulged at the expense of the Russian ambassador in one of those calculated outbursts of fury such as had preceded the rupture with Britain eight years before, and he also withdrew 60,000 of his best troops from the Peninsula. It was, however, too late that year to commence a campaign against such a country as Russia, and so hostilities were once more postponed. Yet they had become inevitable unless the Tsar gave way, and of his doing this there was not the slightest indication. Napoleon's system depended for its very existence upon the adherence of every Continental nation, and if Russia would not co-operate willingly, then the only alternative was force. The French Emperor believed, of course, that the war was imposed upon him in defence of France, and it was in the name of security that he finally marched to Moscow.

Throughout the winter of 1811–1812 the whole of Europe rang with the preparations for the coming struggle, and both sides looked round for possible allies. Napoleon, as has been shown, had no great difficulty in compelling Prussia to obey his orders, but Austria was able, chiefly owing to her geographical position and also on account of the dynastic connection, to secure better terms. She was to provide an army of 30,000 men to guard the French flank in Volhynia, while in return Napoleon guaranteed the integrity of Turkey, and promised the restoration of the Illyrian provinces in exchange for Galicia, which was to form part of a reconstituted Poland. Sweden, on the other hand, although Marshal Bernadotte was heir to her throne, with the Baltic between her and the *grande armée*, resisted the blandishments of France, and concluded an alliance with the Tsar. Finally, in April, 1812, Napoleon made overtures to Britain, and offered to evacuate Spain and to recognize the House of Braganza in Portugal and the Bourbons in Sicily if the British Government would accept the "actual dynasty" in Spain and Murat in Naples. The phrase was ambiguous, and Castlereagh, now Foreign Secretary, refused to recognize Joseph, but declared his readiness to discuss the proposed basis if by "actual dynasty" was meant Ferdinand VII. No answer was received from Paris, and Napoleon told the French people that Britain had rejected his offer of peace.

Russia in her turn had to come to terms with Turkey, Sweden, Persia, and Great Britain. Her negotiations with the first two have already been discussed; with Persia no settlement proved possible; and, after some haggling, the British government promised financial aid, while the Tsar, as evidence of good faith, handed over his Baltic fleet to Britain for safe-keeping. In spite of appearances to the contrary, Russia was really in a stronger position than France in the matter of alliances, for her allies were devoted to her cause, since their interests and hers were identical, whereas it was fear alone that bound Prussia and Austria to Napoleon.

What followed is too well known to require elaboration in detail. On June 24th, 1812, Napoleon crossed the Niemen at the head of 630,000 men; on September 7th he defeated the Russians at Borodino; and on September 15th he was at Moscow; but by the end of December the French army was back in Poland only 20,000 strong, while the Prussian and Austrian auxiliaries were practically unscathed.

While these events were taking place in central and eastern Europe, the United States and Great Britain had drifted into war, largely in consequence of the repercussions of the Orders in Council. The two grievances which were specially resented by the Americans were the constant search of their ships for deserters, and the refusal of the British authorities to recognize their custom-house arrangements. As the law then stood a British subject could not get rid of his nationality, but the United States was full of English and Irish emigrants, as well as of deserters from British ships, and these facts caused many complications: American warships were continually being stopped and searched, and more often than not some of the crew were detained. The purely economic issue was somewhat complicated. It was a breach of inter-

national law for neutrals to trade between the colony of a belligerent and the mother country, but they might do so, for their own
supply, with the colony. Furthermore, if they imported from the
colony, or colonies, more than they wanted, they might re-export
even to the mother country, and the proof of a *bona fide* interrupted voyage was the payment of the custom-house dues in the
ports of the neutral. In the United States, however, these dues
were not paid in money, but in bonds, which were cancelled when
the goods were re-exported. The payment was thus fictitious, and
the British officials refused to recognize the arrangement.

In 1807 Jefferson secured the passage of Acts of Non-Inter-
course and Embargo, of which the object was to induce Great
Britain and France to modify their policy towards American
trade. Nominally these measures applied equally to both belligerents, but in practice they only affected Great Britain, for her
rival was debarred from direct trade with the United States by
the British command of the sea.

Relations between London and Washington continued to be
subject to an ever-increasing strain until war broke out in 1812,
only five days before the Orders in Council which caused it, were
revoked. This was a tragic error on both sides. It involved the
United States in a struggle with her best customer, and eventually
brought about the loss of the very trade which she had taken up
arms to increase. In actual fact the hands of the American government were forced by the Anglophobe party, which was thinking
a good deal more about Canada than about the Orders in Council. As for the British government, it was, as the saying goes, bit-
ing off its nose to spite its face by the rigid enforcement of the
Orders, for there was a great shortage of corn in Britain, and the
army in the Peninsula was largely fed from the United States.
Moreover, naval and military forces were at a critical moment
diverted from the main theatre of war where they were greatly
needed. During the conflict, for example, the United States sent
out 515 privateers, and thus a heavy demand was made upon the
Admiralty for the smaller fighting vessels, while it was a severe
blow to British pride that no fewer than 16,000 Englishmen are
said to have been serving on board the American fleet, for the
industrial depression at home had driven them from their own
country.

The actual campaign reflected little credit upon either side.
The American attempts upon Canada failed, while the British

generals relapsed into all the old errors of the War of American Independence, and military operations were reduced to the level of piratical excursions. The Americans perpetrated many barbarities on the Canadian frontier, to which their adversaries replied by loosing the Indians on them, and by burning all the public buildings in Washington when that city fell into their hands. The conflict dragged on until the end of 1814, and almost its last incident was the repulse of a British attack upon New Orleans. Peace was finally signed at Ghent, though it represented little more than a compromise, for the real points at issue were scarcely touched, and the question of boundaries was left for future negotiation.

When this settlement was reached Napoleon was an exile at Elba. Fifteen months had passed since the remnants of the Grand Army reeled back into Poland, but France had not been defeated without a great deal more fighting. Had Russia been in a condition to follow up her victory and carry the war into her enemy's territory, it is possible that Europe might have been spared the misery and bloodshed of the next two years, but for the moment her strength and resources were exhausted. Moreover, the magnitude of Napoleon's defeat was not at first appreciated in any country. Europe had been for so long under the spell of French invincibility when the Corsican himself was in the field that it was not easily broken. Time and time again the nations of the Continent had gone down before him, so it was hardly surprising that they should be slow to realize that at long last the master of Europe was in serious difficulties. On the part of France herself there was no hesitation: she rallied to Napoleon in the hour of defeat even more fiercely than she had done in that of victory. The doubts and hesitations only came later. There might be reluctance to serve in the Dutch and German provinces of the Empire, and in Royalist Brittany, but there was no slackening of effort or enthusiasm in France proper.

As for Napoleon himself, his optimism at this crisis of his fate was unbounded. To those who counselled him to make peace he turned a deaf ear. He was determined to carry on the war from the Tagus to the Vistula, to support Joseph in Spain, and to keep his garrisons as far east as Danzig. Russia and Prussia, he argued, had at least as much need of peace as France, while if he began by giving up towns it would not be long before his enemies would be demanding provinces; if he stood firm, they would be intimidated. Apart from the situation in Spain there was, superficially, much to justify such an attitude. Great Britain was weakened by the war with the United States, and in Central Europe the French position was still strong. Nearly all the places of strategic importance were in Napoleon's hands, and although the Grand Army had suffered grievous loss, not all the casualties had been French, for many a Pole, German, and Italian had also fallen. Furthermore, the brains of the army were intact. The "old coalition machines" Napoleon despised, for a single victory would undo "*ce noeud mal assorti*". What had happened after Marengo, Austerlitz, and Friedland would happen again.

The French Emperor did not realize that circumstances had changed, and to this he owed his downfall. At last, taught by himself, his enemies had realized that in union alone lay safety. As late as 1806 Fox had declared that "the project of combining the whole of Europe against France is to the last degree chimerical", and he was right. The Austro-Prussian league of 1792 was proved a failure owing to the preoccupation of the two Powers with the partition of Poland and the cynical neutrality of Russia. In 1798 and in 1805 the selfish conduct of Berlin had played into the hands of France, and had enabled Napoleon to crush Prussia in his own time. During the campaign of Jena and Friedland the Austrians had sulked in their tents, and they were thus left to face the enemy alone in 1809. When the attack on Russia took place both Austria and Prussia marched with Napoleon as his vassals. At long last the lesson had been learnt.

A new factor, too, had made its appearance. No longer was it only the kings and governments who were against Napoleon, for now the people were rising too: France had to face a Europe animated by that spirit of nationality to which she had herself given birth. The Russians followed the remnants of the Grand Army across Poland, while Prussia changed sides and the Hohenzollerns put themselves at the head of the German national movement. Austria, for a time, remained neutral, but Sweden joined the Allies. Nevertheless, the tide did not turn at once, and at Lützen and Bautzen the Corsican defeated his enemies, but at Pleswitz he had to agree to an armistice, though this was more necessary to them than to him.

Everything now depended on Austria, and she, under the guidance of Metternich and mindful of former disasters, was the personification of prudence. Napoleon thought that because

Francis was his father-in-law he could count upon the Austrian monarch's support, but sentiment played no part in Metternich's public life. On June 17th, 1813, a fortnight after the armistice at Pleswitz, the rulers of Austria, Prussia, and Russia signed the Treaty of Reichenbach, by which Austria assumed the position of a mediator, and promised to declare war on France if the conditions of peace were refused. These were that the actual territory of that Power should be confined within the limits of the Rhine, the Alps, the Pyrenees, and the sea; that Napoleon should restore the Bourbons to their Spanish throne and should evacuate Holland; and that he should abandon his position as Protector of the Confederation of the Rhine, and should allow the Pope, whom he held in captivity in France, to return to Rome. On the other hand, Murat, whom Napoleon had placed on the throne of Naples, was to remain there, as was Jerome Bonaparte in Westphalia.

Metternich took these terms in person to Napoleon, and there was a stormy discussion between the two men. After one outburst from the Emperor, the Austrian Chancellor replied, "In all that your Majesty has just said to me, I see a proof that Europe and your Majesty cannot come to an understanding. Your peace is no more than a truce. Misfortune, like success, hurries you to war. The moment has arrived when you and Europe will exchange challenges; you will pick up the gauntlet, and Europe as well; and it will not be Europe that will be defeated." Finally, Napoleon rejected the offer with the threat, "It may cost me my throne, but I will bury the world beneath its ruins". As Metternich got into his carriage he murmured to Berthier, *"C'est un homme perdu"*. He saw the Emperor once again, but it was useless, and on the night of August 10th the Austrian forces began to pour through the passes of the Riesengebirge.

Two months later occurred the slaughter of Leipsic, when the military power of France met with overwhelming disaster. Then was seen the danger of the great dispersal of force consequent upon the attempt to hold down the whole Continent, for when Napoleon most wanted troops he was unable to concentrate them. The battle of Leipsic was the signal for Germany to rise, and everywhere the French detachments and garrisons were cut off. The Dutch, too, rose in rebellion, and the Prince of Orange returned to his own country, to which was also sent a British force which reduced the few fortresses that the patriots were unable to take. Insurrection broke out in Italy, and British troops from Sicily

I

were landed at Genoa to encourage the insurgents, while an Austrian army entered the country from the north and won a decisive victory at Valsarno. Meanwhile, far away to the south, the French had been driven back across the Pyrenees, and by the end of the year Wellington was on the soil of France.

Such was the situation when, on December 31st, 1813, the British Foreign Secretary, in a pair of red breeches and jockey boots, sailed from Harwich on his way to the Allied Headquarters at Bâle. Castlereagh went with the widest powers given to a British statesman, for they were "to negotiate and conclude of his own authority, and without further consultation with the Government all conventions or treaties, either for the prosecution of war or for the restoration of peace". It was, indeed, high time that this step should be taken, for, as Lord Aberdeen wrote, "The enemy is, in my view, a source of danger much less to be dreaded than what arises among ourselves".

The fact was that the three Continental Powers in arms against France were by no means agreed as to the policy to be adopted towards that country now that victory seemed assured. The Tsar had been converted from a humble disciple and admirer of Napoleon into an inveterate foe, but he equally had no love for the Bourbons, since Louis XVIII had never made any great secret of his belief that the Romanoffs were *parvenus*. Accordingly, Alexander was inclined to favour the elevation of Bernadotte to the French throne as the best solution after the overthrow of Napoleon. Prussia, on the other hand, had two objects clearly in view, namely the reduction of France to the position of a second-rate Power, and the establishment of her own hegemony in Germany; for the rest, Berlin followed the lead of St. Petersburg, as she was to follow it for many years to come. Lastly, there was Austria, by which was to be understood Metternich. The object of the Austrian Chancellor was, then as always, to preserve a balance in Europe, and neither the somewhat nebulous fancies of the Tsar nor the frightfulness of the Prussians made any appeal to him. On the contrary, he was prepared to leave Napoleon in France as a check on Prussia and Russia, and he made several approaches to the French Emperor with this end in view during the autumn of 1813, but without success.

Castlereagh knew exactly what he wanted. It was to convert the loose and divided confederacy into a proper alliance with a definite policy and war aims, and to prevent at all costs the con-

clusion of a premature peace. In this task he enjoyed certain personal assets, of which the experience gained in handling the Irish
borough-mongers, when he was Chief Secretary at the time of the
Union, was by no means the least. Then there were the British
subsidies, without which the war would have come to a standstill;
Wellington's victories in the Peninsula; and the possession of captured French colonies. Castlereagh made full use of all these
advantages, and he rendered himself so agreeable to his Austrian
colleague that Metternich was soon declaring that "Castlereagh
behaves like an angel".

The Foreign Secretary was greatly aided by the course of
events, and no one knew better how to combine arms and diplomacy. The opening months of 1814 witnessed a series of French
successes. The Prussian invaders were practically destroyed; Austria was reduced to asking for an armistice; and proposals were
made for the evacuation of France. Castlereagh saw his chance.
He was living very simply at Chaumont, where he and his staff
worked, dined, and slept in a single room. From there he did not
hesitate even to direct military operations, and it was his insistence
upon the despatch of two Swedish corps to reinforce Blücher that
stemmed the tide. Actually Napoleon's victories strengthened
Castlereagh's position, for they encouraged the Emperor to demand terms which the Allies could not possibly grant, while they
served to prove to his foes that all danger from him was by no
means at an end. On both scores, therefore, Castlereagh found
that his task of creating a united front had been rendered easier
by the course which the war had taken.

On March 1st, 1814, was concluded the Treaty of Chaumont,
which was destined to keep the Allies together until after the fall
of Napoleon, and to form the basis of the final settlement at
Vienna. By this agreement Great Britain, Russia, Austria, and
Prussia concluded an offensive and defensive alliance which had
as its object the confinement of France to her old boundaries.
Each member of the alliance was pledged to maintain 150,000
men in the field, while Great Britain promised, in addition to paying her own contingent and maintaining her navy, to provide an
annual subsidy of five million pounds to be divided equally between the other three contracting parties. On the conclusion of
peace each of the Powers was to furnish a contingent of 60,000
men if any one of them was attacked.

As for the resettlement of Europe, it was to be effected upon these bases: the German Empire was to be restored as a federal union; Holland and Belgium were to be united into a monarchy under the House of Orange; the Bourbons were to be restored in Spain; Italy was again to be divided into independent states; and the neutrality of Switzerland was to be guaranteed by all the Great Powers. The agreement was a notable triumph for Castlereagh, who was fully justified in referring to it as "my treaty", and it had the immediate effect of concentrating the whole attention of the Allies upon their main objective, namely the overthrow of Napoleon.

The Treaty of Chaumont soon began to have important results. Napoleon attempted one last stroke at the Allies' communications, but it failed to stop the march of his enemies upon Paris, and on March 30th the French capital surrendered. The Emperor was himself ready to continue the struggle, but his Marshals were not, and still less by now were the French people. All the proposals for a Bernadotte dynasty, or for a regency on behalf of the infant King of Rome, were proved to have no basis in reality. Under the guiding of Talleyrand the French sought salvation in the return of their old Royal Family, and on April 6th the Senate "called to the throne the head of the House of Bourbon", while at Fontainebleau the fallen Emperor signed his abdication. On the 28th Napoleon sailed from Frejus for Elba, and on May 3rd, preceded by a few vague promises, Louis XVIII of France and Navarre entered, amid the cheers of the crowd, the capital which had sent his brother to the guillotine.

CHAPTER X

THE CONGRESS OF VIENNA, 1814–1815

THE Treaty of Chaumont united the Allies on the bases of peace, and no time was lost in dealing with their late adversary. Hardly had Napoleon abdicated than Castlereagh arrived in the French capital, and on April 11th the first definite step was taken towards the liquidation of the past. This was the provisional Treaty of Paris, which was made between the fallen Emperor, through his plenipotentiaries, and the Allies. It was in no sense a treaty with France, for Louis XVIII had not yet returned from exile. By this agreement Napoleon renounced for himself and his descendants the Empire of France and the Kingdom of Italy, and in return he was allowed to retain the title of Emperor, while the island of Elba was erected into an independent principality for him, and an annual income of £180,000 was guaranteed by the Allies. The Duchies of Parma and Piacenza were secured in full sovereignty to the Empress Marie Louise, and on her death to the King of Rome, while the divorced Empress Josephine was given £40,000 a year.

It now remained to deal with France, and Talleyrand neglected no opportunity of impressing upon the Allies that there was a great deal of difference between France and Napoleon, for he saw that in this lay the only possible hope of securing reasonable terms for his country. Relief at the cessation of the long war was as widespread among the French people in 1814 as it had been in 1713, and Paris gave its conquerors as cordial a welcome as it had accorded to Bolingbroke a century before—indeed, they might have been its guests. Talleyrand encouraged this attitude for the reasons already mentioned, and it was thus in a distinctly festive atmosphere that the work of peace-making began. The Allies were quite willing to draw a distinction between France and her late master, as had been already shown in a proclamation by Wellington to the effect that the war was being fought for the security of Europe, and that no interference was intended in the free decision of the French people with regard to their internal government. Alexander told the Senate that he imputed the faults of the French "to their chief alone", and the Autocrat of All the

Russias went on to advise his hearers to give France "institutions, at once strong and liberal, with which she cannot dispense in the advanced state of civilization" to which she had attained.

In such an atmosphere no great difficulty was experienced in drawing up the first Treaty of Paris, which Louis XVIII signed on May 30th. This document stipulated that France should return to the boundaries of 1792, which thus secured to her the original annexations of the Revolution, of which the most important were Avignon and several districts in Alsace. France also received Chambéry and part of Savoy, with certain frontier rectifications in the north-east and in the neighbourhood of Geneva. All the former French colonies, with the exception of Mauritius, Tobago, and Saint Lucia, were restored, while with regard to the general resettlement of Europe the provisions of the Treaty of Chaumont were recapitulated. This treaty was signed by the representatives of Great Britain, Russia, Austria, Prussia, Sweden, Spain, and Portugal. France was thus treated very generously, and it is to be noted that no indemnity was imposed.

In Article 32 of the treaty it was agreed that "all the Powers engaged on either side in the present war shall, within the space of two months, send plenipotentiaries to Vienna for the purpose of regulating in General Congress the arrangements which are to complete the provision of the present treaty", but the victors nevertheless thought it as well to come to a preliminary private agreement among themselves. This dealt principally with the future distribution of the territories on the left bank of the Rhine, which had been in French hands for the past twenty years, and it was decided that these provinces should go to Prussia, while by way of compensation Austria was to receive the whole of Lombardy, and Sardinia was to acquire Geneva. With the settlement with France completed, and these preliminaries over, the stage was set for the Congress of Vienna.

At Utrecht no real business had, as we have seen, been transacted, and negotiations had been carried on direct between Bolingbroke and Torcy. Vienna, on the other hand, was the centre of diplomatic activity, but by the time the Congress met in September the ground had been well prepared. Before the fighting was over the Allies had come to an agreement among themselves at Chaumont; then they had settled with the late ruler of France; and lastly they had made a treaty with their defeated enemy which they followed by a further arrangement between themselves. Above all, the interval of several months gave time for tempers to cool.

In one respect there was a comparison with the Utrecht settlement, namely in the relative youth of the leading negotiators. Talleyrand, it is true, was sixty, but the Tsar was only thirty-seven; Metternich was forty-one; Frederick William III was forty-four; Castlereagh was forty-five; while Nesselrode was but thirty-four. Their cosmopolitanism was as marked as their youth. The presiding genius was naturally Metternich, but although he was the Austrian Chancellor, he had been born in Coblence a subject of the Archbishop of Trèves, and to the day of her death he always corresponded with his mother in French: few statesmen in history have known so much of men as individuals and so little of them in the mass. The Prussian representative was Hardenberg, a Hanoverian who had originally been in the Elector's service: he was no match for Metternich, who was thereby enabled, not only to filch from Berlin many of the fruits of victory, but also to make the Prussian government a willing accomplice in his policy. From Russia there came Nesselrode, born in Portugal, a German by origin and education, an Anglican by baptism, and a Russian by adoption. The British delegate, Castlereagh, was an Ulsterman who had put an end to his own country's legislature. Of Talleyrand it may be said that from being at first hardly tolerated at Vienna he soon became one of the leading personages at the Congress.

With the statesmen came the monarchs, and these were by no means all figure-heads. Above them towered that paradoxical figure, the Tsar. An autocrat with liberal views, a legitimist who owed his throne to regicide, he has baffled posterity as he puzzled contemporaries, and it was only in keeping with his whole career that his death should have been as mysterious as his life. The Austrian Emperor had developed into a typical Viennese, and was probably more popular among his subjects than any other Habsburg ruler. In a moment of rash generosity he had offered to defray the delegates' expenses, and before long Austria was finding that peace was almost as costly as war. As for the King of Prussia, he had woken up to find himself famous, and at the head of a German national movement; in so far as he understood this he mistrusted it, but he was prepared to take advantage of any opportunity to add to his dominions, and there was a real chance of carrying out the plans of Frederick the Great with regard to Saxony, whose King had been slower than the other Central European rulers in leaving the sinking ship of Napoleon. The only notable Royal absentee was the Prince Regent of Great Britain.

In all this brilliant company Castlereagh possessed the inestimable advantage of long experience in the art of manipulating committees and assemblies, while he had by his side Wellington, the only soldier who had never been beaten by the French. The Secretary to the Congress was Gentz, whose pen had done so much to unite Germany against Napoleon.

From the beginning there was no intention that the Congress as a whole should have the last word, or indeed much say at all, in the settlement of Europe, and the effective members were meant to be the Powers which had signed the treaty with France. Yet even this number was found to be too large, and was reduced to Great Britain, Russia, Austria, and Prussia. When Talleyrand arrived at Vienna he found that the intention was to treat France as a pariah, and the most important development during the autumn of 1814 was his success in securing for his country a position of equality with the other Great Powers. He bided his time, and by the end of the year his patience had been rewarded. Great Britain and Austria had differed sharply from Prussia and Russia over the future of Saxony, and so Castlereagh and Metternich decided to associate France with them in order to outweigh the influence of St. Petersburg and Berlin. When the British and Austrian statesmen proposed the admission of France on an equal footing, Nesselrode and Hardenburg were consequently far from pleased, but the suggestion could not be decently opposed. After all, France was no longer an enemy, and she was indubitably a Great Power; moreover, Talleyrand was threatening to rouse the lesser states to a sense of their importance unless his own country obtained what she wanted. In these circumstances Russia and Prussia gave way, and on Christmas Eve, 1814, the Committee of Four was transformed into one of Five.

The question of Saxony was certainly very contentious. By the Treaty of Kalisch on February 28th, 1813, one of the many conventions made among the Allies during the war in order to satisfy one another, the extension of Prussian territory in North Germany had been promised, while Russia, by implication, was accorded a free hand in the disposal of Poland. Alexander and Frederick William interpreted this to mean that Saxony was to go to Prussia and Poland to Russia, a view which was far from being held by Castlereagh and Metternich. "I have 200,000 soldiers in the Duchy of Warsaw", said the Tsar. "Let them try and drive them from it. I have given Saxony to Prussia." Such was the position when the Committee of Four became one of Five, and the Russians and Prussians at once tried to win France to their side with a most tempting bribe. This was nothing less than the establishment on the left branch of the Rhine of an entirely new state with the Saxon dynasty on the throne. It was to include the territory of the Duchy of Luxembourg, and a portion of that of the Archbishopric of Trèves, as well as the Abbeys of Prüm, Stavelot, and Malmédy.

Metternich and Castlereagh both opposed this suggestion very strongly indeed. The former had no desire to see Prussia strengthened by the absorption of the whole of Saxony, while the latter feared that the new state would become a mere appanage of France. Yet had the proposal been adopted many of the troubles of the next hundred years might have been avoided, for the new kingdom would have had a Roman Catholic population with French tendencies, while the dynasty could, in view of the loss of Saxony, have been relied upon to be anti-Prussian for many a long year. In short, an admirable buffer would have been erected between France and the most aggressive of the German tribes. From the first, however, it was clear that Britain and Austria would fight sooner than accept the suggestion, and Talleyrand preferred to adopt the standpoint of London and Vienna rather than incur the risk of a fresh war. Accordingly he signed a treaty of alliance, which Castlereagh copied out with his own hand to ensure secrecy, on January 3rd, 1815, by which each of the three Powers promised to provide 150,000 men in the event of hostilities being provoked by Russia and Prussia. Thus did Talleyrand turn the differences between the Allies to the advantage of his own country, and France became the associate of her foes of less than a year before. "Now, Sire," he wrote to Louis, "the coalition is dissolved, and for ever."

This treaty remained secret until Napoleon found the French King's copy in the archives at Paris during the Hundred Days, and published it, but the suspicion that some such agreement was in being induced Russia and Prussia to compromise, and two days after the treaty was signed Castlereagh wrote to Liverpool, "I have every reason to hope that the alarm of war is over". In the end Saxony lost two-fifths of her territory to Prussia, who also obtained the greater part of the Rhineland, to which Castlereagh made no objection, as it coincided with his policy of placing strong states on the borders of France. The future of Poland was a hardly less difficult problem. Napoleon, after Tilsit, had created a Grand Duchy of Warsaw out of the central provinces of Prussian Poland, and to this he added, after the overthrow of Austria in 1809, western Galicia and Cracow. The King of Saxony was made Grand Duke, but the Duchy was run by, and in the interests of, the French. This settlement was rejected at Vienna. Austria regained Galicia, and Prussia much of what she had obtained by the Partitions: Warsaw and the central portion of the old Polish state was erected into the Congress-Kingdom of which the King was to be the Russian Tsar, while Cracow was left as an independent republic.

Some of the other problems were not so difficult to settle. Belgium was united to Holland under the House of Orange, as had been arranged at Chaumont, and in this way it was hoped to constitute an effective barrier to possible French aggression in the north. Switzerland assumed the form which she has since retained, and the provisions relating to that country proved to be the most durable part of the work of the Congress. Less happy was the settlement of Scandinavia. The Danes had not been very fortunate in their experiences during the war, and, like the Saxons, they stuck to Napoleon to the end. For this they were punished by being deprived of Norway, which was given to Sweden, who, in her turn, ceded Finland to Russia. This was far from being an ideal solution, but it lasted until the opening years of the twentieth century.

The future of Italy was far less easily resolved, and discussions, at once tedious and acrimonious, were taking place on this subject when the Congress was electrified by the news, first that Napoleon had escaped from Elba, and then that he had reached Paris. If he looked for success in the divisions among the Allies he was, like Alberoni, to be disappointed, for they were prepared to fight for the settlement upon which they had decided. At once their differences were composed, and it was resolved to put into force the relevant clauses of the Treaty of Chaumont. Three large armies were to converge on France, but it was destined that only two of them should be actually required.

As soon as Waterloo had been won the question arose as to

the punishment to be inflicted upon France for this fresh act of aggression. The Prussians at once demanded the most extreme measures. They wished Napoleon to be shot, and Blücher was only prevented by the intervention of Castlereagh and Wellington from exacting a contribution of a hundred million francs from the inhabitants of Paris alone. They were also making preparations to blow up the Pont de Jéna, of which the name had so many bitter memories for them, when Louis XVIII threatened to take his stand on the bridge, and be destroyed with it. Nor was this all, for Berlin further proposed to detach Alsace-Lorraine and French Flanders, if not the whole of Picardy, and to reduce France to her limits before the conquests of Louis XIV. These suggestions met with no support from Castlereagh and Metternich, who drew a clear distinction between the punishment of France and the further aggrandisement of Prussia. On the other hand, the reception accorded to Napoleon during the Hundred Days made it impossible any longer to differentiate between him and the French people, and common prudence thus dictated the exaction of securities for the future.

The result was the second Treaty of Paris, which was signed on November 20th, 1815. By this France lost all the gains of the earlier arrangement, except Avignon and the Venaissin, and was reduced to the frontier of 1789. Chambéry and the part of Savoy previously ceded to France were restored to the King of Sardinia, the districts in the neighbourhood of Geneva were returned to that canton, and the fortress of Huningen on the frontiers of Switzerland was to be dismantled; and various rectifications on the eastern and north-eastern borders were no longer sanctioned. Furthermore, a war indemnity of several hundred million francs was exacted, and in addition France had to maintain for five years, at the cost of another quarter of a million francs, an army of occupation of 150,000 men in her principal fortresses. Finally the victors decided that the numerous pictures and works of art, which had been collected in Paris from all parts of Europe during the wars of the Revolution and the Empire, should be restored to their former owners. Such was the price which France had to pay for the Hundred Days, and it would have been infinitely higher had the Prussians been able to obtain the support of the Tsar for their drastic proposals.

Although the Congress of Vienna had been interrupted by the return of Napoleon from Elba it had not suspended its activities, and the spring of 1815 saw a settlement of the thorny problem of Italy. There had been many changes in the peninsula during the Revolutionary and Napoleonic Wars, and the smaller states had disappeared. During the later years of the French Empire the boundaries of France itself had been extended until they marched with the frontier of the kingdom of Naples, over which Murat reigned, while Sicily was still ruled by the Bourbons, who had been displaced on the mainland. To the east lay the kingdom of Italy, which included the Milanese, the former territory of Venice, and the duchies of Parma and Modena. The position had been still further complicated by the fact that in January, 1814, Murat had been guaranteed the throne of Naples in return for his support against Napoleon. During the Hundred Days, however, he had rallied to his old master, and had thus forfeited his rights so far as the Allies were concerned.

Accordingly, the old dynasties and the Pope were all restored, though the republics of Genoa and Venice were not revived. Austria received compensation for the loss of the Low Countries by the annexation of the ancient possessions of the Republic of St. Mark, which, together with the Milanese, was erected into the Lombardo-Venetian Kingdom of which the Emperor Francis was King. Genoa went to Sardinia, and the Bourbons were restored to the whole Kingdom of the Two Sicilies, while the provision made in the agreement with Napoleon for the reversion of the Duchies of Parma and Piacenza to his son was annulled. Of the overseas possessions of Venice the islands of Corfu, Zante, Santa Maura, Cephalonia, Cerigo, Ithaca, and Paxo were, by a special treaty, constituted "a single Free and Independent State" under "the immediate and exclusive protection" of Great Britain, who also obtained Malta.

Two other very important matters were also broached, namely the problem of the great European rivers and the Slave Trade. A general "open" system was laid down for international waterways, and it was that from the point at which each river becomes navigable to its mouth the navigation was to be entirely free to all people, subject only to police regulations and necessary tolls, which latter were in no case to exceed those already in existence. In this way the Powers broke with the policy which had, to the ruin of Antwerp, kept the Scheldt closed to navigation from the sea ever since the middle of the seventeenth century. The Slave Trade was lucrative, and was therefore less easily regulated. Great Britain had abolished the trade, though not slavery, in 1807, and she was anxious that the rest of the world should follow her example, partly for reasons of philanthropy and partly for those of self-interest. All, however, that she was able to effect at Vienna was a pronouncement by the Eight Powers that the universal abolition of the Slave Trade was "a measure particularly worthy of their attention", but even this pious advice was subject to the reservation that "this general Declaration cannot prejudge the period that each particular Power may consider as most advisable for the definite abolition of the Slave Trade".

Most important of all was the settlement of Germany. There was no attempt to restore the Holy Roman Empire or to reconstitute the three hundred states whose princes had been mediatized during the years which had elapsed since 1789. Instead there was set up a Germanic Confederation which included thirty-five sovereigns and four Free Cities, with a Federal Diet over which the Austrian representative presided. It was not a very satisfactory solution, for Germany was left without a head, and already signs were not wanting that one day Austria and Prussia would struggle for hegemony. Centripetal forces, based upon an incipient nationalism born of the struggle against the French, had been unloosed, and the Habsburgs, with their millions of non-German subjects, were ere long to become objects of suspicion to an increasing number of Germans. Indeed, it is not too much to say that the settlement of 1815 looked forward to that of 1866, and further to the Hohenzollern Empire and the Third Reich. The men who re-made Germany after the fall of Napoleon certainly wrought more than they knew.

The final general Act of the Congress of Vienna was signed on June 8th, and as the second Treaty of Paris was concluded in the middle of November, by the end of 1815 Europe was once more at peace.

To whatever other criticisms they might be subject, the statesmen who made the Treaty of Vienna could at any rate claim that they did what they set out to do. They did not go to the Austrian capital to create a new heaven and earth, but to produce order out of chaos. The primary object of the Congress, as stated in the secret clauses of the first Treaty of Paris, was to establish "a system of real and permanent Balance of Power in Europe", and this was surely achieved, at any rate for a period

of more than fifty years. The men who negotiated this settlement were realists, and so it was based, like the Treaty of Utrecht
a century earlier, upon a frank acceptance of existing facts and
of the position of the defeated foe, who was treated with a justice
which was tempered with equity and commonsense; no attempt
was made to reduce France to the level of a second-rate Power,
but every care was taken to strengthen her neighbours so that
she could not with impunity resume her career of aggression.
It has been charged against the statesmen who assembled at
Vienna that they ignored the principle of nationalism, but they
can surely be forgiven in view of the use to which that principle
had been put by their late enemy.

The war had been won, and peace had been restored, but it
was felt, in view of the Hundred Days, that the alliance which
had defeated Napoleon should be kept in being in case he, or his
relations, or his fellow-countrymen gave any further trouble.
Accordingly, on the same day that the second Treaty of Paris was
signed, the principles laid down at Chaumont were solemnly
re-asserted in a Quadruple Alliance between Great Britain,
Russia, Austria, and Prussia. By this the contracting parties
agreed to maintain the settlement reached with France; to
come to the aid, with 60,000 men, of any of the signatories who
might be attacked by the French, and "to renew their meetings
at fixed periods, either under the immediate auspices of the
sovereigns themselves, or by their respective ministers, for the
purpose of consulting upon their common interests, and for the
consideration of those measures which at each of those periods
shall be considered the most salutary for the repose and prosperity
of nations, and for the maintenance of the peace of Europe".
These proposals were eminently sane, definite, and businesslike,
and the commitments under them were limited in scope. In
short, they provided for collective security against any renewal
of French aggression, and for the establishment of the Concert of
Europe. For seven years the attempt was to be made to govern
European relations, and the affairs of individual states, by common
action concerted in European conclave.

The outstanding event during the years which immediately
followed the Vienna settlement was the recovery of France, in
spite of the army of occupation and of the indemnities which
she had to pay by the terms of the second Treaty of Paris. The
fact is that Louis XVIII was a far shrewder and more capable

nonarch than either contemporaries or posterity, with the
ignificant exception of Gambetta, have been prepared to admit,
ind in Baron Louis he had an extremely competent Minister of
Finance. In these circumstances Castlereagh was not surprised
when, in June, 1818, he received a suggestion from Metternich
hat there should be a meeting of the Allies to take into considera--
:ion the state of France, and particularly to discuss whether it
vas necessary any longer to retain an army of occupation in that
:ountry. Accordingly, the signatories of the Quadruple Alliance
ind France decided to send representatives to Aix-la-Chapelle
n September, and to render agreement easier it was arranged that
:here should be no other item on the Agenda than the liquidation
of the second Treaty of Paris.

The position was that France had paid off eight instalments
of the indemnity, that is to say 368,000,000 francs, and there
vere still another 332,000,000 to be paid, but she had until the
end of November, 1820, to do this without being called upon for
nterest. The Duc de Richelieu, the French Prime Minister,
10w offered to clear off the rest of the indemnity by paying a
ium of 265,000,000 francs. Of this 100,000,000 francs were to be
n the form of Rentes inscribed in the Great Book of the Public
Debt of France, while interest was to be paid in nine (a figure
which was subsequently changed to twelve) instalments through
:he agency of two English financial houses, Messrs. Hope and
Messrs. Baring. In return the army of occupation was to be
withdrawn from French territory by November 30th, though
:he Government of Louis XVIII was prepared to continue to
provide for its pay, equipment, and clothing until that date.

This offer was accepted by the Allies, and it was embodied in
a treaty signed at Aix-la-Chapelle on October 8th, 1818, between
Great Britain, Austria, Russia, and Prussia on the one part, and
France on the other. This treaty was followed by a collective
note addressed by the four Allied Powers to France, stating that
'they regard this solemn act as the final completion of the General
Peace", and they ended by inviting His Most Christian Majesty
'to unite henceforth his councils and his efforts" to theirs in the
nterests of mankind and of France. This invitation was, needless
:o say, at once accepted by the French Government.

The Congress of Aix-la-Chapelle was thus highly successful.
The Allied Powers finally liquidated the Revolutionary and
Napoleonic Wars only three years after their termination; they

settled all claims against their late enemy; and they admitted her to the Concert of Europe as an equal, with the result that this body henceforth consisted not of four Powers but of five. It is true that as a purely precautionary measure the Allies secretly renewed among themselves the old Quadruple Alliance, but it remained a dead letter, and France soon asserted her influence on the same footing as that of the other Great Powers.

CHAPTER XI

THE EARLY YEARS OF THE HOLY ALLIANCE,

1815–1822

THE formation of the Quadruple Alliance had not gone far enough for the Tsar, who, before the Congress of Vienna had finished its labours, had exchanged his earlier devotion to Napoleon for a similar sentiment towards Barbe-Julie de Krüdener, and of this was born the Holy Alliance. The lady was the daughter of a Baltic baron, and her life had been characterized by adventures of many kinds before religion claimed her: thereafter she became convinced that she was a woman with a mission, and she began to make prophecies. In May, 1815, she contrived to meet Alexander, and within a very short time she was exercising a dominant influence over him.

The Tsar persuaded Madame de Krüdener to accompany him to Paris, and on alternate nights from ten till two he prayed and read the Sciptures with her. At first there was only mild amusement among the statesmen assembled in the French capital, and the whole affair was regarded as further evidence of the traditional Romanoff eccentricity: when, however, it was realized that the Tsar was serious there was general alarm at the possible consequences. Such alarm was more than justified, for if the old Alexander had been difficult, the new promised to be intolerable. "Scold me well," said the Tsar to his companion; "by the grace of God I will carry out all your instructions." The upshot was the Holy Alliance, though the basic idea had been in Alexander's mind for at least ten years. The Tsar expounded his proposals to the Allies. Castlereagh described the scheme as "a piece of sublime mysticism and nonsense", and wrote to Liverpool that Wellington had been with him on this occasion, "and it was not without difficulty that we went through the interview with becoming dignity". Metternich was hardly more complimentary, for he viewed the project with "great repugnance", and denounced it as "a loud-sounding nothing", but he soon saw that it might be made to serve Austrian interests, and so he became its partisan. Prussia followed obediently in the footsteps of the Tsar.

The text of the Holy Alliance was revised by Madame de

K   129

Krüdener in person, and it was contained in a Declaration consisting of a preamble and three articles. The preamble stated that the Emperors of Russia and Austria, and the King of Prussia, had, in consequence of the events of the previous three years (the Declaration was issued in September, 1815), acquired the intimate conviction of the necessity of conducting their mutual relations "according to the sublime truths contained in the eternal religion of Christ our Saviour", and they solemnly declared that this Declaration had no other object than to publish this fixed resolution in the face of the whole world. In the first article the three monarchs promised to consider each other as fellow-countrymen and to lend each other aid on all occasions; in the second they earnestly recommended their subjects to strengthen themselves daily in the principles and exercise of the duties which the Divine Saviour had taught to mankind; and in the third there was a general invitation to all the Powers to associate themselves with the project, the only exceptions being the Pope, with whom neither Alexander nor Frederick William desired to have any relations, and the Sultan of Turkey, to whom it was felt that "the sublime truths contained in the eternal religion of Christ our Saviour" were not calculated to make any great appeal.

All the Continental Powers to whom invitations were sent agreed to co-operate, some with their tongues in their cheeks, and others out of a desire not to offend the three powerful monarchs who were sponsoring the scheme. The Prince Regent of Great Britain was, of course, invited, but he replied that the provisions of the British Constitution would not allow him to accept, and from the beginning the Holy Alliance was regarded with disfavour both by Parliament and the public, owing to the innate British mistrust of vague generalities, above all in the field of foreign affairs. Castlereagh made his government's position perfectly clear:

> We shall be found in our place when actual danger menaces the system of Europe, but this country cannot and will not act upon abstract and speculative principles of precaution. The alliance which exists had no such purpose in view in its original formation. It was never so explained to Parliament, and it would be a breach of faith to Parliament now to extend it.

Time soon proved that the British government was, from its own point of view, wise to hold aloof. The Holy Alliance was, as has so often been pointed out, not very holy nor much of an alliance, but in its origin it was inspired by some not ignoble motives. "This great and noble brotherhood", wrote Metternich to Nesselrode in 1817, "is of far more value than all the treaties, and will ensure for a considerable time what the good Abbé de St. Pierre wished to establish for ever." Now, the Abbé de St. Pierre was a subject of Louis XIV and a disciple of Descartes who in 1713 had produced a plan for maintaining perpetual peace, but it is doubtful whether he would have recognized it among the aims of the Holy Alliance, which both men and events were converting into an organization for the perpetuation of the *status quo*. Austria had no interest in further changes in Europe, from which she could hardly benefit but could easily lose; the Tsar, long separated from Madame de Krüdener, had forgotten his Liberal and regicidal youth, and only remembered that he was Autocrat of All the Russias; and Frederick William was always content to follow the lead of St. Petersburg.

The groundswell of the revolutionary storm was still considerable, and especially was this the case in Germany. Just before the Congress of Aix-la-Chapelle there had been a meeting of students at the Wartburg festival to celebrate the third centenary of the Reformation and the fourth anniversary of the battle of Leipsic. This assembly proved somewhat disorderly, and ended with a bonfire of books in favour of the *ancien régime*. In March of the following year occurred the murder of the dramatist Kotzebue, who was a friend and agent of the Tsar. These events alarmed the Powers of the Holy Alliance, and in August, 1819, Metternich convoked a conference of all the German states at Carlsbad, when the most drastic measures were adopted. Every university was to have a curator, whose task it was to supervise the political significance of the teaching given, and who was to be appointed by the ruler in whose dominions the university was situated. All unauthorized student societies were to be dissolved, and a censorship of the Press was to be instituted. Finally, a commission was to be set up at Mayence to enquire into the origin of revolutionary movements; its labours were to be retrospective, and the different states were to arrest, even on mere suspicion, all individuals designated by the commission. Such were the Carlsbad Decrees, and they were duly converted into Federal laws by the Diet.

Alexander was by no means pleased at this strengthening of the Austrian position in Germany, but events soon occurred which frightened him into a closer relationship with Metternich. It proved, as usual, by no means difficult to coerce the German Reich into docility, but in 1820 revolution broke out in Spain, and it was not long in spreading to Italy, while in February of that year the ultimate heir to the French throne, the Duke of Berry, was murdered at the Paris Opera House. At Aix-la-Chapelle it had been decided to hold another congress, this time at Troppau, for a consideration of the affairs of Europe, and the Holy Alliance determined to utilize the occasion for the suppression of the movements which they regarded with such suspicion.

Castlereagh saw at once what was intended, and he refused to allow Great Britain to be drawn into support of any such policy, which was contrary both to her interests and to her feelings. The British government, he said, was prepared to fulfil all treaty obligations, but if it were desired "to extend the Alliance so as to include all objects present and future, foreseen and unforeseen, it would change its character to such an extent and carry us so far, that we should see in it an additional motive for adhering to our course at the risk of seeing the Alliance move away from us, without our having quitted it". Accordingly, although the Austrian, Prussian, and Russian monarchs appeared at Troppau in October, 1820, in person, Great Britain was represented only by the ambassador at Vienna, who happened to be the brother of the Foreign Secretary. In fact, Britain and her old associates of the Quadruple Alliance were approaching the parting of the ways. France, too, although her policy was less clearly defined, gave no plenary powers to her representatives.

Metternich took every advantage of his opportunity to associate the Tsar more closely with Austrian policy, and he found him in an extremely amenable mood. "I deplore", confessed Alexander, "all that I said and did between the years 1815 and 1818. I regret the time lost; we must study to retrieve it. You have correctly judged the condition of things. Tell me what you want and what you want of me, and I will do it." Accordingly, the Powers of the Holy Alliance passed a vote in favour of Austrian intervention in Naples, where Ferdinand I had been forced by his subjects to grant a constitution. The British representative refused to vote regarding the fate of an independent state, and he wrote to his brother, "The first acts of Troppau framed an alliance between the Three Courts which placed them in a new attitude from us, and they have now, I consider, hermetically sealed their treaty before Europe".

Nor was this all, for the Powers of the Holy Alliance proceeded to define the general principles upon which, in future, they proposed to act. In a series of conferences from which the representatives of Great Britain and France were excluded on the ground that they were present only to report and not to decide, they drew up a protocol which ran, "States which have undergone a change of government due to revolution, the results of which threaten other states, *ipso facto* cease to be members of the European alliance, and remain excluded from it until their situation gives guarantees for legal order and stability. If, owing to such alterations, immediate danger threatens other states, the Powers bind themselves, by peaceful means, or if need be by arms, to bring back the guilty state into the bosom of the Great Alliance."

Meanwhile the Congress had adjourned to Laibach, where it met in January, 1821, and where there was a further widening of the rift between Great Britain and her old allies. The discussions were at times acrimonious, and might have developed into a permanent breach had it not been for the sobering effect of the news of the Greek revolt, which tended at first to draw together the two Powers, namely Great Britain and Austria, most interested in the preservation of the integrity of the Ottoman Empire.

The position of the British government was not, indeed, an easy one. Castlereagh was far from approving of the policy embodied in the Carlsbad Decrees and elaborated at Troppau and Laibach, but it was not to the interest of Great Britain, as it was certainly beyond her power, to interfere. Nor did he wish to imperil the European equilibrium, so painfully re-established only a few years before, by encouraging movements which he knew to be doomed to failure, and with which he was in any case fundamentally out of sympathy. Furthermore, he realized that Austria had special rights in Italy, and her intervention in Naples was covered by an agreement of June, 1815, between her and the Neapolitan government, according to which the latter promised not to introduce constitutional changes other than those allowed in the Austrian dominions in Italy. At the same time he was quite firmly resolved that he would not give even a tacit consent to the employment of the same methods in respect of the Spanish revolt. Finally, Castlereagh believed in the congress system, since it provided an opportunity for the statesmen of Europe to come into personal contact, and he was reluctant to take any step which might accelerate the end of that system.

There was, however, soon to be a change at the Foreign

Office, for in August, 1822, Castlereagh died by his own hand, and he was succeeded by Canning. There was no such breach between the policies of the two men as is often alleged. Canning was by nature more downright than Castlereagh, and he was likely sometimes to read "England" where the other had read "Europe", but the difference was in pace rather than in direction. In any event, it is always easier for a new minister than for an old one to lead his country along a fresh path in international matters. Old friends and associates among the representatives of foreign Powers inevitably exercise a restraining influence, and even the most determined of men finds it difficult to turn his back upon those with whom he has been associated in good fortune and ill for a number of years. So it was with Castlereagh. He might entertain few illusions concerning the policy of Alexander or of Metternich, but he had worked with them, first of all to defeat Napoleon, and then to re-cast the map of Europe at Vienna. However much he might disapprove of their later conduct, it was in these circumstances but natural that he should tarry for a space at the parting of the ways, even if he had no doubt in his own mind that further co-operation was neither possible nor desirable.

For Canning the situation was very different. He saw in Alexander merely Napoleon's accomplice at Tilsit, and there was little in the memory of those days to recommend the Tsar in his eyes. With Metternich he had not had any earlier relations, so he was under no special obligation to consider the Austrian statesman's feelings. In effect, all that Canning did during his first few months at the Foreign Office was to pursue rather more vigorously the policy of detachment from the Holy Alliance which had been initiated by Castlereagh at Troppau and Laibach. To speak of any violent breach is to ignore the fact that there had been no change of government in Great Britain, and that Canning was not a dictator, but a minister in the Liverpool administration. "Our business is to preserve," he said, "so far as may be, the peace of the world, and therewith the independence of the several nations which compose it." That is not a definition to which his predecessor would have taken exception, and the difference between their conduct of affairs was dictated by changing circumstances rather than by any fundamental conflict of principle.

The first problem with which the new Foreign Secretary was confronted was the attitude to be adopted at the coming congress at Verona. The situation in Spain had gone from bad to worse, and Ferdinand VII was now little better than a prisoner in the hands of the revolutionaries. The Duke of Wellington was selected as the British representative, and his instructions were those which Castlereagh had, with the approval of the King and the Cabinet, drawn up for his own guidance.

The main subjects to be discussed were three—namely, the Eastern Question, Spain and her colonies, and the affairs of Italy. In respect of the last of these, the duty of the British representative was merely to keep himself informed, and to see that nothing was done "inconsistent with the European system and the treaties". So far as the Eastern Question was concerned, the successes of the Greeks and "the progress made by them toward the formation of a government, together with the total paralysis of the Ottoman naval power in the Levant", pointed to the fact that sooner or later Great Britain would be forced to recognize the Greek insurgents as belligerents. In the matter of Spain, which was clearly to be the chief topic at the congress, there was to be "a rigid abstinence from any interference in the internal affairs of that country". As for the Spanish colonies, they had, as will be shown, already been in part recognized by Great Britain *de facto*, and Wellington was to draw attention to British commerce with them, which it was impossible to interrupt. On the other hand, there was no immediate hurry to give *de jure* recognition "so as to create a certain impediment to the assertion of the rights of the former occupant".

The French government had already decided to intervene in the Peninsula; indeed, it was the only course open if even greater perils were to be avoided. The Tsar had already expressed a wish to send his Cossacks against the Spanish revolutionaries, and as Great Britain controlled the seas, the only route from Russia to Madrid lay through France. Louis had little love for Alexander, while his subjects had too lively a memory of the habits of Cossacks ever to wish to see them in France again either as friends or foes; thus it did not take the French government long to make up its mind that if intervention was to take place in the Peninsula it should be effected exclusively by French troops. In short, the only way of keeping a Russian army out of France was to send a French army into Spain. Furthermore, the evident differences between Great Britain and the Holy Alliance on the whole subject of intervention gave every hope that France would recover entire liberty of action, and the Duc de Montmorency, the French Foreign

Minister, thus went to Verona with some very strong cards indeed in his hand.

If these considerations of public policy induced the French government to regard intervention in Spain in a favourable light, Louis himself had reasons of his own for being by no means opposed to it. In the first place, although his personal opinion of Ferdinand was none of the highest, yet he had no wish to see revolution triumph at his very door, or a democratic Spain become the refuge of every opponent of the French monarchy. More important still, in his opinion, was the need for securing a military triumph under the *drapeau blanc*. The army was steeped in Napoleonic traditions, and was generally considered to be none too loyal to the Bourbons; but a success in the very country where Napoleon had met with disaster would inevitably produce a reaction, and would thus constitute an important victory for that policy of national consolidation which Louis had pursued unflinchingly ever since he ascended the throne. Above all, he knew that he had no time to lose. He was an old man, and he was under no illusions as to the mistakes which his brother and heir would make when he inherited the crown. The one hope of Louis was to establish the throne so securely that it would survive Monsieur's reign, for he had every reason to suppose that his nephew, the Duc d'Angoulême, would follow in his own footsteps. Such being the case, it is hardly surprising that the French King should have come to the conclusion that the interests both of France and of the monarchy would be best served by sending an army into Spain with the Duc d'Angoulême at its head.

The Congress of Verona met at the beginning of October, 1822, and of the principal European monarchs only the Kings of England and France were absent. Montmorency opened the proceedings by asking for a definition of the attitude which the other Powers would adopt if France found herself compelled to intervene in Spain. To this Austria, Prussia, and Russia replied that they would support such action by withdrawing their representatives from Madrid, but they hesitated to promise any material aid, which suited Montmorency's purpose very well indeed, as that was the last thing he wanted. Wellington, however, took the opposite line, and gave it as his opinion that there was no chance of the revolutionary movement in Spain spreading to other countries. He declared that the British government would not be committed in advance to approval of the attitude of any other Power, and before it could express an opinion it must know "the exact ground of complaint and the exact cause of war". This attitude, of which Canning highly approved, convinced both Paris and the Holy Alliance that nothing was to be hoped for from Great Britain, and when Wellington further declared that the British minister at Madrid would confine himself to allaying the ferment which the communications of the other Powers must inevitably excite, they excluded the Duke from their more private deliberations. Finally, the Holy Alliance gave France a free hand in Spain, of which she was not slow to avail herself. A large army under the Duc d'Angoulême swept through the country, and within a brief space the revolution was crushed.

These events represented a notable triumph for Louis and his ministers: seven years before their country had lain prostrate at the feet of its enemies; now, with the approval of the leading Continental Powers, its armies had triumphed in the very land where the great Napoleon had met with disaster. This approval, too, had removed all possibility of such a threat on the Rhine, while the French armies were fighting elsewhere, as was to paralyse the action of Napoleon III in Italy a generation later. On the other hand, Great Britain had proved powerless to prevent the invasion of Spain, and in these circumstances it would be difficult to deny that Canning displayed remarkable skill in saving his country from a serious diplomatic reverse which would have lowered her prestige in the eyes of the whole world. A lesser man would have made Europe ring with his denunciations of French villainy, but in that case he would soon have been confronted with the alternative of giving way or fighting: as Britain had neither the means nor the will to adopt the latter course, the former would have been inevitable, and that would, in its turn, have isolated her in Europe, since it would automatically have thrown France into the arms of the Holy Alliance. Instead, Canning allowed Metternich, who continued to work for the preservation of the old system of alliances at all costs, to paper over the cracks in the wall of European solidarity. Decisions were therefore reached at Verona on such matters as the Slave Trade, Latin America, Greece, and Italy that allowed a semblance of unity to be maintained, and it was thus made to appear that Great Britain had separated herself from the other Powers on the question of Spain alone.

What Canning really thought he was one day to tell the House of Commons:

It would be disingenuous, indeed, not to admit that the entry of the French army into Spain was, in a certain sense, a disparagement—an affront to the pride—a blow to the feelings of England: and it can hardly be supposed that the Government did not sympathize, on that occasion, with the feelings of the people. But I deny that, questionable or censurable as the act might be, it was one which necessarily called for our direct and hostile opposition.

Was nothing then to be done? Was there no other mode of resistance than by a direct attack upon France, or by a war to be undertaken upon the soil of Spain? What, if the possession of Spain might be rendered harmless in rival hands —harmless as regarded us—and valueless to the possessors? Might not compensation for disparagement be obtained by means better adapted to the present time? If France occupied Spain, was it necessary, in order to avoid the consequences of that occupation, that we should blockade Cadiz. No. I looked another way: I sought materials for compensation in another hemisphere. Contemplating Spain, such as our ancestors had known her, I resolved that if France had Spain, it should not be Spain with the Indies. I called the New World into existence to redress the balance of the Old.

In short, he reverted to his policy of sixteen years earlier.

Canning recognized the fact, unpleasant though it was, that England had neither means or interests to intervene in Continental affairs.

CHAPTER XII

THE INDEPENDENCE OF LATIN AMERICA,

1822–1825

THE relations between Pitt and the Spanish colonists in the person of Miranda have already been noticed, and it has been shown how only the Spanish rising against Napoleon prevented the dispatch of a British force to Venezuela under the command of the future Duke of Wellington. Two years later, in 1810, Bolivar had himself come to London in the hope of enlisting the support of the British government, but although he was received by Lord Wellesley, then Foreign Secretary, he was told that nothing could be done, in view of the alliance between Great Britain and Spain, but that consideration would be given to the just complaints and aspirations of Venezuela. The overthrow of Napoleon, and the manifest inability of Ferdinand VII to reduce his American subjects to obedience modified the situation, and Castlereagh was able to pursue an independent policy. When, for example, in 1816 the Spanish government attempted to play upon British suspicions of the United States, he told Ferdinand's ambassador that "a long perseverance on the part of Spain in false notions of imposing by force a restrictive and exclusive system upon that country (*i.e.*, Spanish America) had already alienated the minds of the people from her rule", and "the only chance she had of success was to lose no time . . . to put her system there upon a national footing".

Spanish America was not Castlereagh's pre-occupation, and, if he could possibly avoid it, he was determined not to allow the progress of events there to constitute yet another difference between Britain and the Holy Alliance. At first he had hoped to steer a middle course by encouraging the establishment, with or without the consent of Spain, of independent monarchies in the New World. Such a result would have served the double purpose of preventing the spread of republican principles—and this would appeal strongly to the Powers of the Holy Alliance—and of making British influence predominate over that of the United States. In 1818 San Martín, no lover of republics, had written to him suggesting that a representative monarchy should be set up in

Buenos Aires, and two years later he told the Colombian representative that the British government would at once recognize any colony that adopted monarchical institutions.

Circumstances, however, began to force his hands, for in June, 1822, the Colombian minister was formally received by the President of the United States. Furthermore, there was the increasing strength of British public opinion in favour of recognition based mainly upon commercial arguments. In the eyes of Spain all South American vessels and all vessels which traded with South America were nothing else than pirates, and British merchants were not prepared any longer to tolerate such a state of affairs in respect of what had become one of the most important parts of their foreign trade. Castlereagh determined, therefore, to divide the commercial from the political problem. Commercial recognition must be given at once; political recognition could wait on circumstances, and if possible could be used as a means of encouraging monarchical rather than republican institutions in South America.

This policy was rendered the easier to effect owing to a recent change in the official British attitude towards colonial trade. Until 1815 the monopoly of the Mother Country, where colonies were concerned, had been maintained quite as rigorously as in the case of Spain, but more liberal ideas had lately begun to prevail. The Government was actually preparing the legislation necessary to admit the vessels of other nations to this trade, and to allow them to use British ports much more freely than before. It is not clear who first devised the scheme of extending the provisions of this measure to the vessels of the Spanish colonies, and of thus giving them a definite status. The Cabinet accepted it without demur on the proposal of the Foreign Secretary, and thus, in the summer of 1822, the Spanish colonial flags secured recognition.

A breathing-space had now been obtained, and the way was clear for a cautious approach to the thorny question of political recognition. At the end of July there was a debate on the subject in the House of Commons when the Opposition urged full recognition. Castlereagh would not agree, but he declared that "the whole was purely a British question, uninfluenced by foreign Powers and resting only upon the law of nations, and the character of generosity and prudence, which he trusted this country would ever maintain". He obviously intended that the solution should be found at the forthcoming Congress of Verona, and in the instructions which he drew up, to which allusion has already been made, he wrote, "It will be the duty of the British Plenipotentiary to enter into discussion with the Allied Cabinets, endeavouring, as far as possible, to bring them to the adoption of common sentiments, but taking care, in every alternative, to leave to the British government an independent discretion to act according to circumstances".

It is, indeed, by no means improbable that had Castlereagh lived recognition might have come more quickly than Canning was able to bring it about, for Castlereagh would not have been hampered, as his successor was to be, by the hostility of George IV and the suspicion of many of his colleagues in the government. As Professor Webster has well said, "It would have been more clear to posterity that the independence of the Spanish colonies had been won and maintained by the enterprise and heroism of the South Americans themselves".

Such was the situation when Canning succeeded Castlereagh at the Foreign Office, and it was not rendered any easier by the nature of the war which was taking place in Latin America. It is a mistake to assume that Bolivar and his colleagues were leading a national revolt, in which all classes of the population joined, against an alien and inefficient regime at Madrid. On the contrary, the conflict was very definitely a civil war, and the number of Spanish troops engaged was extremely small, for the bulk of the Royalist forces was composed of local volunteers. As for the Indians, they either held aloof from the contest altogether or fought on the Spanish side. There was no national uprising against Spain, but rather a fratricidal war which had for its counterpart the struggle that was going on in the Mother Country between Ferdinand and the Liberals: in America those who held the views of the latter advocated independence because previous experience had taught them that liberty was out of the question so long as Spanish rule continued. There was, however, a large body of opinion which was favourable to absolutism, and so supported the Spanish connection; and, with a few exceptions, the clergy remained loyal to Madrid. In view of her weakness at home, the wonder is not that Spain lost her American colonies so soon, but that she retained them for so long, and the explanation is that there was a large body of opinion in her favour among the colonists themselves.

Of the Powers, apart from Great Britain and Spain, which

were interested in these developments, France pursued the policy that is the least easy to follow, and it is by no means improbable that Louis and his ministers were not of one mind on the subject. They were certainly not aiming, as is sometimes alleged, at placing French princes upon American thrones, for there were none available except the Duke of Orleans, and he, to whom even the title of Royal Highness was denied, was the very last man whom Louis wished to see upon any throne, European or American. What is more probable is that the French government wished Ferdinand to adopt the scheme that Aranda had suggested to his grandfather forty years before, namely that the Vice-Royalties should become kingdoms with Infantes to rule them, while the King of Spain should himself take the title of Emperor. Colour is lent to this supposition by the fact that in 1820 the French government was in negotiation both with Madrid and Buenos Aires for the establishment of the Duke of Lucca, who had been temporarily dispossessed of Parma in favour of Napoleon's widow, upon the throne of Argentina: a step against which Castlereagh protested vigorously. It is unlikely that Louis contemplated the use of force to achieve this object, though three years later it was suggested from Paris to Angoulême that he might spare a few troops, as well as some ships, to establish principalities in America, but he replied that he must first complete his work in the Peninsula itself.

At the same time there was nothing in the nature either of Louis or of the then Prime Minister, Villèle, to suggest that they were capable of such a gamble as that which prompted the Mexican expedition of Napoleon III. They had just scored a remarkable success in Spain, and were most unlikely to risk the loss of this prestige for the mere sake of placing Bourbon princes upon shaky thrones on the other side of the world. In these circumstances there was probably a good deal of bluff in the French threat of interference in the Americas, as well as a determination not to become too dependent either upon Great Britain or the Holy Alliance.

So far as the United States was concerned, the situation was also complex, for her policy was governed by several considerations. She was too weak to undertake any considerable military operations, though she was extremely advantageously placed to intervene with effect in the affairs of the old Vice-Royalty of Mexico, if she could raise the necessary men and money. In effect, the attitude of Washington was influenced by three main factors, namely the desire for expansion to the west, the wish to sever all connection between the Spanish and Portuguese colonies on the one hand and their Mother Countries on the other, and the determination to turn to the best possible account the commercial potentialities of the new Latin American market. These aspirations call for closer examination.

The growth of the United States had been rapid. It was only twenty years since its western boundary was the Mississippi, and although Napoleon had sold Louisiana in 1803, what was later to be known as the Middle West was still practically an unknown land. To the south, Florida had been in Spanish hands until 1819, while to the west of the Red River there stretched away to the Pacific a vast territory that until yesterday had been the Vice-Royalty of Mexico. Such being the case, it behoved Washington to walk warily, and President Monroe proved equal to the occasion. The anarchy in Mexico which had followed the over-throw of Spanish rule in that country had tempted some citizens of the United States to urge intervention, but Monroe set his face firmly against any policy likely to displease Ferdinand until the sale of Florida had been completed. Once that had taken place Washington began to regard the insurgent Spanish colonists with a much more favourable eye, and the first steps were taken along the road which twenty years later led to the annexation of Texas and the war with Mexico.

In reality, the independence of Latin America was an un-expected piece of good fortune for the United States. Instead of being, as at the beginning of the century, hemmed in on all sides by the colonial possessions of Spain, France, and Great Britain, she was now in a fair way to becoming the mistress of the northern part of the American continent. The necessity of Napoleon and Ferdinand had proved to be her opportunity to acquire Louisiana and Florida, and now the Spanish colonies had followed her example by severing the cord which bound them to Europe. As soon, therefore, as the sale of Florida had been completed, it became a cardinal point of policy at Washington that the revolted colonies must be prevented from returning to their former status; while if, in addition, they could be prevailed upon to adopt republican constitutions, so much the better, for they would in that case be more likely to rely upon the State Department than upon the Foreign Office.

Above all, there were the almost limitless possibilities that were opened up now that the shackles imposed on Latin American trade by the Council of the Indies had been removed. These advantages would, of course, come to an end if Spanish rule were restored, while there was always the danger that if the new states came within the British orbit their trade would go to Great Britain. In this circumstance Monroe and Adams, the latter his Secretary of State, decided to lose no time, and as soon as they had Florida safely in their pockets they proceeded to grant official recognition to the now independent republics. The advantages of this step were considerable, for it provided the State Department with a direct channel of communication that was denied to the Foreign Office, while the appointment of consuls was a very great help indeed to the advancement of trade. On the other hand, the United States was not really in a position to reap the full harvest of her policy of recognition, for it was clear that one of the first needs of every Latin American country would be a loan, and she was far too poor to lend any money; while her naval and military strength was quite inadequate for any armed intervention in support of her policy. The position of the United States was thus that she was the first Power to stake out a claim in the former Spanish colonies, but it was uncertain whether she would be able to effect much in the way of its development.

Russia, through her possession of Alaska, was at this time an American Power, and that Alexander was determined to exploit the fact was proved by a decree which he issued in 1821 forbidding all save Russian subjects to fish, trade, or navigate over an enormous area lying between Siberia and North America. There were also rumours that the Tsar was endeavouring to induce Haiti to cede him the Isle des Vaches, and Russian agents were reported in Colombia, but Canning took little notice of all this, for he held that it was only with French aid that Russia could intervene effectively in Latin America. In the United States, on the other hand, Russian pretensions were taken much more seriously, and Adams conceived a personal distrust of the Tsar's representative at Washington that went far to promote the formulation of the Monroe Doctrine, though the President himself never regarded the threats of the Holy Alliance as serious, and he took the view that the prevention of their translation into practice would be a task for Great Britain rather than for the United States.

From the very first Canning took the line that the old Spanish colonies must either come again under the rule of the Mother Country, or they must become independent; in no circumstances could Great Britain tolerate their annexation, in whole or in part, by any other state. Having come to this decision, he made up his mind that he would not be a party to the holding of any conference that had for its end any interference in the affairs of the New World. A congress would provide an excuse for intervention to those who were in favour of such a policy, and the precedent of Verona was a warning. In effect, Canning had come to the conclusion that the right course for his country was to hold the ring. If Ferdinand could subdue his rebels by himself, well and good; if not, then Great Britain would proceed to recognize their independence as soon as they had established some form of stable polity. The British mastery of the seas rendered the pursuit of such a policy eminently practicable, and it is in consequence not too much to say that for some time to come the destiny of the whole American continent lay in the hands of the British government.

The question was not, however, by any means purely an academic one. For Austria and Prussia all that was at stake was the principle of legitimacy, and Russia, in spite of her possession of Alaska, was in much the same position. France, in view of her commitments in the West Indies and of French Guiana, was more directly interested in the progress of events in the old Spanish colonies, but even she was not concerned to the same extent as Great Britain, whose trade was at stake. Canning had not been long at the Foreign Office before he was besought by the commercial interests, especially in his own constituency of Liverpool, to place them upon a more favourable footing. Spain was no longer able to give protection to the British merchant throughout vast areas of what were still nominally her colonies, and in the new states that were rising on the ruins of her empire he had no official *locus standi* at all. Furthermore, the sympathetic attitude towards the colonies adopted by Washington was enabling the citizens of the United States to obtain commercial advantages of which it would be very difficult to deprive them in years to come. In effect, the City wanted Canning to recognize the independence of the Latin American states, and thus to enable British commerce to steal a march on its rivals in the new market. Among those who urged this view was a young pamphleteer of twenty-one, Benjamin Disraeli, who declared that if the leaders of the revolt against Spain were "not pure and practical patriots, we know not what

L

names should be inscribed on the illustrious scroll of national gratitude".

There can be no doubt that to the end of his life Canning distrusted and disliked the United States, and he was determined that she should not obtain control of her southern neighbours. In one Cabinet memorandum he expressed the opinion that "sooner or later we shall probably have to contend with the combined maritime power of France and the United States", and in another he referred to "my apprehension of the ambition and ascendancy of the United States of America". His feelings of mistrust were far from being unreciprocated. Richard Rush, the United States Minister in London, wrote of him, "Mr. Canning never liked the United States nor their institutions, and never will. . . . He will watch all our steps with sharper and more active jealousy than perhaps any other English statesman living. Of all their public men, we have the least to expect from him". When Canning died, Adams noted, "May this event, in the order of Providence, avert the evils which he would, if permitted, have drawn down upon us!"

As has been seen, one of Castlereagh's last acts had been to recognize the Spanish colonial flags, and Canning determined to utilize this precedent. Meanwhile, the capture of Quito by the insurgents strengthened his hands against those who, like the King, and some of his colleagues in the Cabinet, wished to refrain from taking any action at all. At the same time reports were continually arriving in London of the damage done to British shipping by pirates who used Cuba as their base, and even the most convinced opponents of a forward policy were reluctantly forced to agree that the existing situation could not be allowed to continue. Accordingly, the British squadron in the West Indies was strengthened with the avowed intention of attacking the pirates on Spanish territory if necessary, while in December, 1822, Canning drew up a list of consuls for the chief towns in Latin America.

The result of the Congress of Verona, and the French invasion of Spain, caused the British Government to suspend any definite action for a time, but when it became clear that the Duc d'Angoulême would soon have the whole kingdom at his mercy, Canning felt that the moment had arrived to give effect to his determination that the Spanish colonies should not share the fate of the Mother Country, and pass under the control of Paris. While, therefore, the French armies were occupying Cadiz, the British

Foreign Secretary took three very important steps: he accredited the consuls, he sent a commission to Mexico and Colombia to report on the question of their recognition by Great Britain, and he asked the French ambassador, Prince Jules de Polignac, for the views of his government upon the American situation.

The discussions in October, 1823, with Polignac lasted several days, and the Frenchman strongly urged the convocation of a congress to deal with the whole question of Latin America. This was exactly what Canning did not want, so he outflanked Polignac by observing that he could not understand how a congress could discuss Spanish American affairs "without calling to their counsels a Power so eminently interested as the United States of America, while Austria, Russia, and Prussia, Powers so much less concerned in the subject, were in consultation upon it". This observation was, of course, the merest bluff, for Canning knew perfectly well that nothing would induce the United States to participate in a European conference, but the suggestion that an invitation should be sent to republican Washington would be sufficient to render the whole idea of a congress unpalatable to the Holy Alliance. Finally, Canning obtained from the ambassador an avowal that the French government considered the recovery by Spain of her colonies to be out of the question, while he disclaimed any intention on the part of his master to undertake armed intervention in America or to annex any territory there.

This admission cleared the air considerably, and represented a definite success for Canning. It ensured that there would be no repetition of the events of the previous year when a European congress had authorized France to interfere in the internal affairs of another country, and it definitely separated the French government from the Holy Alliance. On the other hand, the Foreign Secretary still had to face one difficulty, by which his predecessor in office would never have been confronted, namely the opposition of the King and of some of his Cabinet colleagues. Wellington, for example, declared, "We pass in Europe for a Jacobin Club", and Canning could never have got his own way but for the support of public opinion and the confidence which Bolivar reposed in him.

Canning and Bolivar never met, but from their first political contacts the two men developed a liking and admiration for one another, and the Latin American leader took every opportunity of expressing the feelings he entertained towards Britain. "We must look to England for relief," he declared, "we have no other resource. . . . I would infinitely sooner be indebted to England for its always generous and liberal assistance than to any other country." Bolivar also sought Canning's views upon his own political problems, for in 1827 the United States' representative is found writing to Henry Clay that the "Liberator President himself told me that he was expecting advices from Mr. Canning relative to the opinion the British Cabinet formed of the constitution he had framed" for Bolivia. Canning and Bolivar had, indeed, two things in common—they were both distrustful alike of the United States and of democracy. The Foreign Secretary's relations with San Martín, it may be added, were equally cordial, but Argentina did not present such difficult problems as did Peru, New Granada, and Venezuela, save, perhaps, where the Banda Oriental was concerned.

In December, 1823, came the news of President Monroe's message to Congress, and the situation was thereby rendered the more acute. The question to what extent Canning was responsible for the formulation of the Monroe Doctrine is not easy to answer, but the policy which he adopted towards France and the Holy Alliance in the early autumn of 1823 undoubtedly encouraged Monroe and Adams to make a stand which would not have been possible without the certainty of British support, given the weakness of the United States at the time. There had been several discussions between Canning and Rush before the President's message, but it was not long before it became apparent that although the two men agreed upon the main issue, there were differences between them in matters of detail. Rush was willing to sign a joint declaration provided that Canning would pledge himself to the immediate recognition of the colonies. Now, this was what he could not do, in view of the attitude of the King and his critics in the Cabinet; while, in addition, he still hoped that the new states would adopt monarchical constitutions, and this possibility would become very remote if Great Britain were to recognize their existing republican regimes. In these circumstances it is hardly surprising that the negotiations with Rush did not lead to any decisive result, but they showed the State Department where Britain stood, and so precipitated action on the part of the United States.

There can be little doubt but that in these negotiations Canning was thinking not so much of initiating a policy of Anglo-

American friendship as of making use of the United States in the game he was playing with the Continental Powers. Accordingly, he wished to be quite sure of her attitude towards the whole question of the Spanish colonies before he communicated with Polignac. Rush's comments convinced him that she was not prepared, to use a phrase of Adams, "to come in as a cock-boat in the wake of the British man-of-war", but he found that the two Anglo-Saxon countries were sufficiently agreed for it to be safe for him to spike the guns of the Holy Alliance by insisting upon the admission of the United States to any proposed congress. That Rush suspected this is shown by his letter to Clay, already quoted, and Adams certainly took the same view, and if Canning made use of the United States in his negotiations with Polignac, Adams used his knowledge of the British attitude in the formulation of the Monroe Doctrine, for which he was more responsible than the President whose name it bore. In effect, both Canning and Adams were trying to turn the other to his own uses.

The ultimate implications of Monroe's message were more important than the immediate, but the latter unquestionably strengthened the Foreign Secretary's hands against the Holy Alliance. At the time that Monroe spoke there were no illusions in the mind of himself, Adams, or Canning that the doctrine which he was formulating depended on the British Navy, and it is not surprising that the first thought of the chancelleries should have been that it was the result of an Anglo-American agreement. Canning was not slow to grasp the advantage of this from his point of view, and he wrote to Bagot, "the effect of the ultra-liberalism of our Yankee co-operators, or the ultra-despotism of Aix-la-Chapelle Allies, gives me just the balance that I wanted".

The year 1824 saw the international situation, at any rate so far as Latin America was concerned, still dominated by the British Foreign Secretary, but it took the whole twelve months to bring his opponents at home to agree to recognition. Wearisome as this task undoubtedly was, Canning possessed one great advantage, in that it was not possible for his opponents to rely upon the arguments which were influencing the conduct of the Holy Alliance. Alexander and Metternich based their refusal to recognize the independence of the Spanish colonies on the ground that the origin of the new states was revolutionary, though in actual fact the Austrian Chancellor did not believe in legitimism, while the Tsar had ascended the throne over the body of his murdered father. Such an excuse could hardly be put forward by the man who owed his crown to the Revolution of 1688, so George IV, and those who thought with him, were forced back upon the argument of expediency, and in that connection events were decidedly favouring Canning.

In the first place, the position of the Spanish forces was precarious in the extreme save in Peru, where Ayacucho had not yet been fought; elsewhere, the island of Chiloe, off the Chilean coast, and the castle of San Juan de Ulloa, which dominated the Mexican port of Vera Cruz, were practically the only places in America, apart from Cuba and Puerto Rico, that still held out for Ferdinand. Nor was this all, for there was grave danger that further delay in according recognition would play into the hands of the United States.

In the spring of 1824 Canning made a final effort to negotiate with Spain. He declined the suggestion of Madrid that Britain should participate in a conference on American affairs, but he offered to guarantee Cuba to Spain if the Spanish government would agree to a peaceful separation with the colonies on the mainland. This offer was refused, and the British representative at Madrid was then instructed to inform the Spanish Government that "His Majesty reserves to himself the right of taking, at His own time, such steps as His Majesty may think proper, in respect to the several states of Spanish America, without further reference to the Court of Madrid".

Meanwhile Canning's hands were strengthened by the reports of the commissioners that he had sent to Mexico and Colombia, and by the evident desire of the commercial interests in England that recognition should not be delayed any longer. The commissioners reported very favourably on the prospects both of Colombia and Mexico, while in Argentina the rule of Spain had not been effective for above a decade. On the other hand, the Foreign Secretary was disappointed to hear that his agents had not been able to find any great evidence of monarchical sentiments, for he had no wish to see Spanish America become wholly republican, and for a time he seems to have believed that Itúrbide would be able to establish himself upon the Mexican throne. In spite, however, of his own views, he was prepared to bow to the inevitable. In June, Sir James Mackintosh presented a petition, which bore the names of such City magnates as Baring and Montefiore, asking for the immediate recognition of such of the Spanish colonies as had established independent governments, and in particular Colombia, Argentina, and Chile. This step, it may be observed, was by no means unwelcome to Canning.

At this point the Prime Minister, Lord Liverpool, took action, and in the middle of December he and Canning laid a Minute before the Cabinet recommending the recognition of the three republics, and they announced their intention to resign if the proposal was not adopted. In the face of this threat the opposition at Court and in the government died away, and on the last day of 1824 the decision to recognize the new states was communicated to Spain: on January 1st, 1825, the same notification was made to the other Powers. The Holy Alliance expressed, in reply, deep regret at the British action, "since it gave a final blow to the interests of Spain in the New World, and tended to encourage the revolutionary spirit which it had been found so difficult to restrain in Europe". Canning's own views, in a letter to his friend Hookham Frere, are worth quoting as illustrative both of his hopes and fears :—

> The thing is done . . . an act which will make a change in the face of the world almost as great as that of the discovery of the continent now set free. The Yankees will shout in triumph, but it is they who lose most by our decision. The great danger of the time, a danger which the European system would have fostered, was the division of the world into European and American, Republican and Monarchical, a league of worn-out governments on the one hand, and of youthful and stirring states, with the United States, on the other. We slip in between and plant ourselves in Mexico. The United States have got the start of us in vain; and we link once more America to Europe. Six months more, and the mischief would have been done.

It would be an exaggeration to say that the British recognition of the Latin American republics marked the end either of the Holy Alliance or of the congress system, for the real dissolvent of both, as will be shown in the next chapter, was the Eastern Question, but it undoubtedly went a long way towards hastening their demise. On the other hand, it certainly provided an ingenious and complete answer to the Monroe Doctrine, and it effectively prevented the new nations from turning towards their northern neighbour.

Spanish America, however, was not alone in creating complications for the world's statesmen to solve, for events in Brazil were also pregnant with danger. The Prince Regent of Portugal, who, as we have seen, left Lisbon in 1807 when the French were on the point of entering the city, had ascended the throne in 1816 as John VI, but without leaving Rio de Janeiro. Five years later he was persuaded to return to Europe, but before he left he appointed his eldest son, Pedro, Viceroy of Brazil, with secret instructions to proclaim himself Emperor if he found it impossible to maintain the Portuguese connection. Pedro lost no time in taking advantage of his father's advice, and in October, 1822, the Empire of Brazil came into existence with himself as its first monarch.

At once there developed a situation which found Britain and the Holy Alliance in opposite camps. Canning welcomed the new Brazilian Empire because it introduced the monarchical element into Latin America, while in Vienna, St. Peterburg, and Berlin there was some uncertainty as to the course to be pursued in view of the circumstances. Alexander, curiously forgetful of the events attendant upon his own accession to the throne, fulminated against Pedro, but Metternich was more circumspect. For the Holy Alliance, too, the position was not made any easier by the fact that both Pedro and John proceeded to grant their subjects constitutions, a proceeding which rendered father and son equally obnoxious in the eyes of the Tsar and of the Austrian Chancellor.

All this placed Canning in a much more advantageous situation than had been the case with regard to Spanish America, quite apart from the fact that Great Britain possessed treaty rights in respect of Portugal which she did not enjoy so far as Spain and her colonies were concerned. It is true that John and his Portuguese ministers by no means relished Pedro's precipitate act, but Canning knew that their acceptance of the inevitable was only a question of time. Accordingly, he watched with considerable satisfaction the progress of the campaign during which Lord Cochrane established the new throne, first by capturing the various Portuguese posts in the country, and then by suppressing a republican movement. When this had been done Great Britain concluded a commercial treaty with Brazil. The Portuguese government was momentarily exasperated, but Canning began to exert all his influence to secure Lisbon's acknowledgment of Brazilian independence, just as he had worked unsuccessfully to secure a peaceful separation of the Spanish colonies from Spain. In this case he was more fortunate, and in August, 1825, Portugal officially recognized the independence of Brazil.

CHAPTER XIII

THE STRUGGLE FOR GREEK INDEPENDENCE,

1821–1833

F OR three centuries after the fall of Constantinople in 1453 Greece and the Greeks hardly entered into the calculations of European statesmen; indeed, so completely had Hellas become part of the Ottoman Empire with its Oriental associations that men talked of going from Greece "into Europe". The only foreign Power with whom the Greeks came in contact during this period was Venice, which for a time held some of the Greek islands and part of the mainland, but with her they had nothing in common either in point of race or, what was of greater importance, of religion: they were certainly not prepared to take up arms against the Porte for the sake of the Republic of St. Mark. The accession of Catherine II to the Russian throne in 1762, however, marked the beginning of a new era, and henceforth Russia, rather than Venice, was the foreign Power that loomed most largely in the eyes of the Greeks. With her they shared a common religion, and the Tsarina did all she could to win their support in the hope of one day reviving the Eastern Empire. She formed a corps of Greek cadets, she caused her younger grandson to be christened Constantine, and during her first war with Turkey she sent into the Mediterranean in 1770 a fleet which actually landed Russian sailors in the Morea. It is true that only a few Greeks joined them, but the incident ushered in a new phase of the Eastern Question.

The next fifty years witnessed the steady growth of Russian influence in the Levant, and, as has been shown, the efforts of the Younger Pitt to check it were unavailing owing to lack of support at home. By the Treaty of Kutchuk-Kainardji in 1774 the Tsarina not only obtained considerable territorial gains, but also a pretext for claiming protective rights over members of the Greek Church living in the Sultan's dominions—a concession which might mean much or little, according to the policy of St. Petersburg from time to time. The Treaty of Bucharest in 1812 gave fresh sanction to this provision, and it advanced the Russian frontier to the Pruth, thereby bringing the Tsar very much closer than before to those whose interests he claimed the right to protect.

In these circumstances it was not so surprising as might otherwise appear that the first blow for Greek independence should have been struck by an officer in the Russian service and an aide-de-camp to Alexander I, namely Prince Alexander Ypsilanti. In March, 1821, accompanied by a number of Greeks in the Tsar's army, he raised the standard of revolt in Moldavia, and called on the people to rise against the Sultan. The appeal met with no response from the Vlach peasantry, who hated the Greeks worse than the Turks, and the attempt ended in disaster, but it was the signal for a rising in the Morea on April 2nd of the same year. The War of Greek Independence had begun.

From the beginning the fighting was characterized by atrocities on both sides before which those that were being committed in Latin America paled into comparative insignificance, and it was the hanging of the Orthodox Patriarch in Constantinople, by order of Mahmud II, outside the gate of his own palace that did much to rivet the attention of Western Europe upon the struggle in Greece; though it is an interesting commentary upon Near Eastern politics that at least one of the Christian bodies in Constantinople sang a *Te Deum* to celebrate the death of the heretical ecclesiastic. Nevertheless, the anger roused by this savage act soon died away, or rather was damped down, since it did not at the moment suit the policy of any Power to exploit it.

The attitude of Metternich towards the Greeks was the same as that which he was adopting towards the risings in the Iberian and Italian Peninsulas and in Latin America. To him, in effect, the Greeks were merely rebels against their ruler, the Sultan. It is true that the Austrian Emperor was considerably affected by the death of the Patriarch, but the record of recent Austrian campaigns against the Turks was not encouraging, and in any case Vienna could hardly ally itself with those who were not only rebels against constituted authority, but schismatics as well. Metternich, therefore, was resolved upon a policy of strict neutrality so far as Austria was concerned, and he was also determined to enforce it upon the other members of the Holy Alliance. He was under no illusions as to the threat to the whole European system contained in the Greek rising; Prussia, having no interests at stake in the Near East, could be safely ignored, but the Tsar would obviously require very careful handling.

For Alexander the situation was very different from that which confronted him with regard to the insurrectionary movements elsewhere. His subjects had no ties with those concerned in them, and he could afford to indulge his absolutist opinions as he wished, but this was far from being the case in the matter of Greece. His own Russians and the insurgents were members of the same Church, and a wave of indignation had swept across his dominions when the death of the Patriarch became known. Nor was this all: ever since the Treaty of Kutchuk-Kainardji the policy of St. Petersburg had been to protect the Orthodox Christians in the Ottoman Empire, and if the Tsar now stood aside Russian prestige would be bound to suffer. Fortune favoured Metternich, in that Alexander was not in Russia but in Germany when the news of the Patriarch's death reached him, so that Russian public opinion exercised little or no influence over him. Metternich was therefore the better able to play upon the Tsar's dislike of revolution to cure him of any sympathy he might have felt for his co-religionists, and after a moment of hesitation Alexander adopted the point of view of the Austrian Chancellor. The Russian representative at Constantinople was instructed to make a vigorous protest, and to withdraw, but hostilities were not to follow, Metternich could breathe freely, the more so since neither France nor England showed any disposition to stir.

Louis XVIII was the last man in Europe to be affected by a series of massacres in the Levant, quite apart from the fact that friendship with the Porte had been the traditional French policy since the days of Francis I. France had no interests of any kind to consider in Greece, and so long as it was Orthodox, not Roman Catholic, Christians who were being slaughtered, the concern was none of the Most Christian King or of his ministers. Great Britain, too, was at first only remotely interested; Castlereagh was the disciple of Pitt, and the government was more interested in keeping in the good graces of the Sultan than in interfering on behalf of the Greeks. After all, there had been insurrections in plenty in the Ottoman Empire before, and they had come to nothing, so it was but natural for Castlereagh to fall in with Metternich's view that the Greeks were but another European complication which it would be wiser to leave alone. Indeed, so strongly was the British Foreign Secretary of this opinion that a proposal for a joint demonstration of the Powers at Constantinople, for the protection of Christians in the Sultan's dominions, failed owing to the strenuous opposition of the British ambassador. So far as French and British public opinion was concerned, it as yet took little interest in the Greeks and their cause, for news travelled slowly, and there were problems of far greater importance much nearer home to attract the attention of the ordinary citizen.

Such being the case it is hardly remarkable that the Greek delegates were not received at the Congress of Verona, where Metternich succeeded in imposing his own views upon the other Powers. Nevertheless, it was not long before two events took place which forced the Eastern Question upon the attention of Europe; one was the British recognition of the Greeks as belligerents, and the other was the arrival of Lord Byron at the seat of war.

The act of recognition took place in March, 1823, and was inspired by exactly the same motives, namely a care for British commerce, that were influencing Canning in his attitude towards the Spanish colonies. The Turks, like the Spaniards, were no longer able to protect British subjects and their goods throughout wide areas of land and sea over which they nominally ruled. The Ottoman fleet had taken shelter in the Dardanelles, and the Greek naval commanders were increasingly resorting to frank piracy, taking into Nauplia as prizes of war the ships of all nations impartially. It was useless to hold the Sultan responsible for a state of affairs which he was powerless to control, and so the responsibility had to be fastened upon the *de facto* Government of Greece. "The recognition of the belligerent character of the Greeks", wrote Canning, "was necessitated by the impossibility of treating as pirates a population of a million souls, and of bringing within the bounds of civilized war a contest which had been marked at the outset on both sides by disgusting barbarities." To Metternich's vehement protests Canning replied that he could only treat the Greeks as pirates or belligerents, and as they had acquired "a certain degree of force and stability", the latter course appeared preferable. The Austrian Chancellor was not converted by such reasoning, especially in view of the fact that much of the Turkish commerce was carried in Austrian ships. At the same time Canning was careful not to proceed any further than circumstances rendered necessary, and he persuaded the Admiralty and the War Office to strike off the active list all military and naval officers who were serving with the Greek forces.

Byron's action, and his death at Missolonghi in April, 1824, made the Greek cause popular in Western Europe. In an age

when to be educated was synonymous with an acquaintance with
the classics, Philhellenism was assured in advance of many
supporters, quite apart from the fact that Englishmen had not
yet learnt by bitter experience to be somewhat suspicious of
nations struggling to be free. In these circumstances the poet's
death came as a call to action, and Greek loans, with the most
doubtful security, were subscribed as soon as they were floated.
This demonstration of popular feeling was by no means lost upon
Canning, but he had not been President of the Board of Control
for four years without realizing the danger there would be of
arousing Moslem fanaticism in India if Great Britain gave open
support to the enemies of the Commander of the Faithful. For the
present, therefore, Canning was not prepared to depart from his
policy of neutrality, and he was confirmed in this attitude by the
obvious inability of the Turks to suppress the Greek rising, which
led him to expect that the independence of Greece was only a
matter of time, and of no long time at that.

For these reasons, as well as on account of his general dislike
of conferences, Canning refused throughout the year 1824 to
participate in any congress on the subject of Greece, and he
maintained this attitude in spite of the pleadings of Alexander
and Metternich. Both the Russian and the Austrian desired a
conference, though for very different reasons. The Tsar hoped
that he would be authorized to intervene in the Ottoman Empire,
just as France at Verona had been given a mandate to invade
Spain, for he was becoming impressed by the volume of opinion
in Russia in favour of the Greeks. Metternich, on the other
hand, thought that at another congress he would be able to
reaffirm his influence over Alexander, and prevent any departure
by the Powers from the policy of complete neutrality.

While these negotiations were in progress the news arrived
that the Sultan had called in the aid of Mehemet Ali, the Pasha
of Egypt, and in February, 1825, the latter's son, Ibrahim,
landed in the Morea. Before his arms the Greeks had to give
way, and his methods of warfare were marked by further atrocities; indeed, he was credited with the intention of depopulating
the Morea, and of re-peopling it with *fellaheen* from his father's
pashalic. This intelligence was too much for a Europe permeated
with Philhellenistic ideas, and it was clear that action of some
sort by the Powers was inevitable in the immediate future.

Alexander therefore called a conference at St. Petersburg,

at which the British government finally refused to be represented merely "as a buffer between the colliding interests of Russia and Austria", and which was consequently attended only by the delegates of the Holy Alliance and France. This congress had not long been sitting before it became clear that the points of view of Austria and Russia were not only incompatible, but actually irreconcilable, and by May its sessions were suspended altogether. A conference that fails to agree nearly always leaves a situation worse than it found it, and so it was in this case. The Tsar took umbrage at the opposition of Austria to his plans, and when it came to his ears that Metternich had openly boasted of his ascendancy over him, his anger knew no bounds. In August he wrote to his representatives abroad that he would work with Metternich no longer, and the Holy Alliance was at an end.

The residuary legatee proved to be Great Britain. By his adroit diplomacy Canning had avoided taking sides either with Russia or with Austria, and now that they had quarrelled he knew that before long one or other of them would seek British support. At the same time he was under no illusions that Britain alone could enforce a settlement of the Greek problem. Ever since she had been a Great Power it had been proved that she was powerless on the Continent unless she had a reliable ally on the mainland of Europe, and the events of the War of American Independence had provided added confirmation of this. In Asia and America it was different, for in that case sea-power came into play, as was being shown at that very moment in connection with the Spanish colonies; but Canning knew that he could no more prevent a Russian army crossing the Pruth, or an Austrian one marching down the Danube, than he had been able to stop the Duc d'Angoulême from invading Spain: if, therefore, Russian or Austrian armies must march, it was in every way desirable that they should do so in support of a policy agreeable to the British Government rather than of one to which the latter was opposed.

Such was the situation when, in the summer of 1825, Stratford Canning, later to be Lord Stratford de Redcliffe, arrived at St. Petersburg on a mission with instructions to suggest to the Tsar a joint intervention of the Powers, but with the stipulation that no coercion should be used against the Sultan. This did not go far enough for the Russian government, which replied that "intervention, once begun, must continue till its end is gained". All the same, Prince Lieven, the Russian ambassador in London, was instructed to listen to any "confidential communications" which Canning might make on the subject, and to draw him on by hinting that, if Great Britain finally refused to consider the use of force, Russia might be compelled to act alone. Each party now knew where the other stood, and at Seaford the outlines of the new policy were discussed.

An interruption to the negotiations was caused by the death, or disappearance, of Alexander on December 1st, and by the disturbances which took place in Russia before his brother, Nicholas I, was established on the throne. Canning realized that the new Tsar would be desirous of distracting the attention of his subjects from domestic to foreign affairs, and he determined to take advantage of the opportunity. With this end in view the Duke of Wellington was sent to St. Petersburg to congratulate the new Tsar on his accession, and to come to an understanding with him in respect of the Eastern Question. "I hope", wrote Canning, "to save Greece through the agency of the Russian name upon the fears of Turkey without a war." Nicholas and Wellington were admirably suited to one another, and the Tsar was in any event, as on a subsequent and more fatal occasion, anxious for a separate understanding with Great Britain. Negotiations were thus easy, and on April 4th, 1826, the Protocol of St. Petersburg was signed.

This document stipulated that mediation should be offered to the Porte in respect of Greece. If the Sultan accepted, Greece was to become a dependency of the Ottoman Empire, and was to pay tribute, though she was to enjoy liberty in all that concerned religion and commerce, while certain of her officials were still to be nominated by the Sultan. It was further agreed that the first effort at mediation was to be made by Great Britain alone, and it was only if this failed that the two Powers were to co-operate to bring pressure on the Porte, though the actual conduct of subsequent negotiations, and the delimitation of the boundaries of Greece, were to be undertaken by them jointly. Lastly, both Great Britain and Russia disclaimed any territorial or commercial designs upon the integrity of the Ottoman dominions, and they invited Austria, France, and Prussia to accede to the Protocol. The Tsar, indeed, went so far as to ask them to guarantee any settlement that might be reached, but the British government, which would not give such a pledge itself, naturally refrained from requesting others to do so.

The terms of the Protocol were thus such that they could be claimed as a victory either for London or for St. Petersburg. The Tsar congratulated himself that he had prevented British action in the Morea, and that he had committed Great Britain to a Turcophobe policy of which several members of the Cabinet, including the Duke of Wellington, most assuredly did not approve. To some extent this was certainly true, but Canning had merely allowed himself to be pushed along a road on which he was only too willing to travel in any event. He had no desire to take armed action of any sort in the Mediterranean, and by refusing to give a guarantee he had minimized the risk of becoming involved in hostilities. Furthermore, he had pledged the Tsar not to annex any Turkish territory, and in view of his fear that Nicholas had designs upon the greater part of the Ottoman dominions in Europe, this was a distinct gain. Although he had not got all he could have desired, nevertheless the continued separation of Russia from Austria was worth a few concessions.

The policy of moderating the Russian appetite for Ottoman vilayets by becoming the ally of Russia was a new departure in British diplomacy. The Younger Pitt had, unsuccessfully, endeavoured to achieve the same end by frontal opposition, and later British governments reverted to his methods rather than to those of Canning; the Crimean War and the crisis of 1877-1878 were the consequence. It was not until the shadow of the Germany of William II fell across Europe in the early years of the following century that Sir Edward Grey reverted to Canning's policy, and later still there were to be further deviations from it. Furthermore, it is not without interest to note that while Canning kept the nation practically united behind him, Disraeli alienated a large section of British public opinion.

It soon became clear that although the Greeks, chastened by the reverses they had sustained at the hands of Ibrahim, were willing to accept the terms of the Protocol, the Porte was not, and so even Canning was compelled to envisage the possibility of having to use force. In September of the same year, 1826, therefore, he paid a visit to Paris for the purpose of sounding Charles X, who had succeeded his brother two years before, upon the whole problem of the Near East.

French pride had been severely wounded by the signature of the Protocol, and Paris did not consider that the request that France should associate herself with Great Britain and Russia made up for the original affront. At the same time, the French government fully realized that if it merely continued to sulk there was a real danger of isolation, for the final decision of Austria and Prussia was not yet known, and there was thus still a chance that they might come into line with London and St. Petersburg. Villèle, too, had nothing like a free hand in the matter. His ministry was by no means so strong as it had been, while Romanticism, which was undermining the throne, was creating a great volume of Philhellenic sentiment throughout France. The country had to a large extent recovered from the war, it had been flattered by the success of the national arms in Spain, and it was in a mood for adventures, so that it would have been decidedly unsafe for so weak an administration as that of Villèle to swim against the current. There was also the attitude of the King himself to be considered. Charles X lacked the caution of his predecessor, and he was as impetuous in his old age as he had been in his youth, when he besought Louis XVI to let him fight in the War of American Independence, and when he had taken part in the siege of Gibraltar. In these circumstances it is hardly remarkable that he should have come under the spell of Philhellenistic ideas, while his piety spurred him on to complete the task of Saint Louis. Many factors, therefore, were at work to range France by the side of Great Britain and Russia, provided that this could be accomplished without any loss of prestige.

Canning returned to London not only thoroughly conversant with the trend of opinion in France, but, on the whole, by no means dissatisfied with it. He realized, however, that concessions would have to be made, for the French government had given him clearly to understand that it would not sign the Protocol, as if it were bound to follow the bidding of Great Britain and Russia, but would require a definite treaty to be drawn up, and ratified by the Powers on an equal footing. Canning would have preferred something less definite, but his cousin, Stratford, at Constantinople, where he was now ambassador, was informing him that force alone would bring the Porte to its senses, and it was very important that Metternich should be isolated in his opposition to the Protocol, for although he had the support of Prussia the attitude of Berlin was a matter of no importance in what related to the Near East.

In actual fact, some months elapsed before the French demands were met and the Treaty of London, which embodied them,

M

was signed. The delay was in no small measure due to Canning's succession to the Premiership, for the intrigues which preceded that event had distracted his attention from even the most pressing problems of foreign policy. Before the Treaty of London was concluded Canning had been succeeded at the Foreign Office by Lord Dudley, but the document was in reality the work of the new Prime Minister, and formed a fitting conclusion to his four and a half years as Foreign Secretary.

In its final form, the Treaty did not mention the Protocol in the preamble, and so saved the face of Villèle, whose ministry was by this time tottering to its fall. Article 1 required the immediate assent both of the Sultan and of the Greeks to an armistice. Article 2 put Greece under the suzerainty of the Porte, made her liable to pay a fixed tribute annually, but allowed her freedom in the matter of internal administration subject to Ottoman control. The Treaty, however, did not contain any clause about freedom of religion and commerce, but it provided for the expropriation of the Turkish landowners after compensation had been paid. Article 4 pledged the Powers to open negotiations with the Porte at once. Article 5 was an avowal of mutual disinterestedness. Article 6 contained an optional guarantee of the settlement. Article 7 provided for the ratification of the Treaty. There was also a secret clause pledging the three Powers, if the Porte did not accept the armistice, to accredit consuls to Greece, and to interpose between the Turkish and Greek forces with a view to the prevention of any further hostilities. The Treaty was signed on July 6th, 1827, by Dudley, Lieven, and Polignac.

The freedom of Greece was not, however, to be achieved without the two events which Canning had been most anxious to avoid, namely the use of force by the signatories to the Treaty of London and a Russo-Turkish War. In October, 1827, the Battle of Navarino occurred as a result of an attempt to carry out the last stipulation in the secret clause, and a new phase in the Eastern Question had begun. This was obvious to all Europe, save to the British government, over which Wellington now presided, and in the King's Speech at the opening of Parliament in January, 1828, the battle was referred to as an "untoward event", which it was hoped would not disturb the harmonious relations existing between His Majesty's Government and the Sultan. Mahmud II not unnaturally took a less detached view of the destruction of his fleet, and he proceeded to measures which rendered a clash with Russia inevitable: these were a *hatti-sherif* denouncing the cruelty and treachery of the Christian Powers and calling the faithful to a holy war against the infidel, and a declaration that the recently concluded Treaty of Akkerman was null and void.

From this moment Russia was mistress of the situation, while Great Britain pursued a vacillating and hesitant course. The latter Power would have done better to have adopted the suggestion of the French government, and prevented isolated action on the part of the Tsar by joining with him in following up the victory of Navarino, but neither Castlereagh nor Canning was at the Foreign Office. The Duke of Wellington was too honourable a man to go back on the Treaty of London, but he equally disliked the policy implicit in it, and the lead consequently passed from London to St. Petersburg. Thus the Treaty of London became the instrument for producing the very situation which it had been devised to prevent. Great Britain could hardly, in the circumstances, deny the right of Russia to make war; while the Tsar, so long as he adhered to the Treaty, was under no necessity to fear the intervention of the other Powers.

Russia certainly had a strong case against the Porte. The Treaty of Akkerman had been signed as recently as October, 1826, and, *inter alia*, it stipulated for the evacuation of the Principalities of Moldavia and Wallachia by the Turks; the formal repudiation of obligations so recently contracted was such a flagrant violation of international law that no objection could be taken to Russian action to enforce respect for treaties. The Tsar showed every desire to co-operate with any other Power that was willing to work with him, and he ordered the Russian admiral in the Mediterranean to exercise his belligerent rights "provisionally and moderately": later, he renounced them altogether. Nevertheless, it was not so much the restraint of Nicholas as the unexpectedly strong resistance of the Turks that prevented Russia from dominating south-east Europe in the war which began in May, 1828.

The French government, anxious to cover its waning reputation at home by military successes abroad, now suggested that it should be allowed to send a force to secure the evacuation of the Morea, and to this Wellington raised no objection, since he regarded it as the most effective counter-move to the Russian declaration of war. Actually, there was nothing for the French to do in Greece when they did arrive, for Ibrahim had already decided to evacuate the Morea.

The Russo-Turkish war dragged on until the summer of 1829, when General Diebitsch crossed the Balkans, and appeared at the gates of Constantinople. Mahmud bowed to the inevitable, and in September the Treaty of Adrianople was signed. Once more Nicholas displayed his moderation by refraining from any territorial acquisitions in Europe. The cession of Onapi and Poti, however, marked a further stage in the Russian advance in Asia, and alarm was expressed in London concerning the possible control of the Euphrates valley route to India. In addition, the Danubian Principalities were erected into what were practically independent states. Thereafter there were lengthy discussions between the Powers as to the form which independent Greece should assume, and as to her frontiers; and these discussions were retarded by the events of 1830. Such being the case, it was not until 1832 that the new kingdom finally came into existence, with the Arta-Volo line as its frontier; not, however, as had once been suggested, under the guarantee of the Concert of Europe, but under that of Great Britain, France, and Russia; and at the end of January of the following year the seventeen-year-old Bavarian King, Otto, landed at Nauplia.

From the death of Canning the leading part had been played by Russia, and she was the principal gainer in prestige by the establishment of the new state. It is difficult to know which to admire the more, the Tsar's firmness or his moderation, and he reaped the reward of his consistency. France was too obviously interested in glory alone for her position in the Near East to be enhanced by the line she had taken. As for Great Britain, she ended by pleasing nobody: the Sultan could not forgive Navarino, while the Greeks could not forget Wellington's efforts to place their state under the suzerainty of the Porte. The attitude adopted by the Powers in the Levant during the years which immediately followed Canning's death was not without its influence upon the progress of events in the Near East during the rest of the nineteenth century.

Greece independent; Danubian principalities practically autonomous and under Russian influence — England cordially hated by all.

CHAPTER XIV

THE RISORGIMENTO IN ITALY, 1815–1870

IN so far as its international repercussions are concerned, the *Risorgimento* falls into two clearly defined periods; the first extends up to the year 1848, when Italy was endeavouring to free and to unite herself by her own unaided resources; the second dates from the failure of the revolution of that year, and ends in 1870, when Rome became the capital of the new Italian kingdom. In the first period the interest in the struggle was largely local, while in the second it was world-wide, and for more than a decade the Italian Question was one of the major European problems.

Nevertheless, from the date of the Treaty of Vienna it had an international aspect which could not be ignored, and which became more accentuated as the years passed. It was all very well for Metternich to say that Italy was only a geographical expression, but that was a half-truth—if as much. The Austrian Emperor ruled the Lombardo–Venetian Kingdom, and thus Italy was brought definitely within the orbit of central European politics. Moreover, members of the House of Habsburg reigned in Florence, Modena, and, for a time, in Parma, while Bourbon princes sat on the thrones of Naples and Lucca. Above all, across the centre of Italy stretched the States of the Church, the greatest international organization of that, or any other, day. Such being the case, it was out of the power of the statesmen of Europe, whatever may have been their wishes, to isolate the problem of Italy.

There is also the spirit of the age to be taken into account. Fortunately or unfortunately, the world outside the chancelleries was beginning to make its voice heard. It was the backing of public opinion which had enabled Canning to defeat the Holy Alliance in the matter of Latin America, while the important part played by Byron and Philhellenism in the achievement of the independence of Greece has been recorded in the previous chapter. Before long Italy, too, was to grip the attention and excite the emotions of a large part of Western Europe, and that to a far greater extent than had been the case in respect of the Spanish colonies or of the Greeks. Not, indeed, that opinion outside Italy was by any means unanimous. If there were large numbers of liberals and Protestants to whom Mazzini and Garibaldi were heroes, there were not a few Legitimists and Catholics to whom their names were a synonym for the Evil One; indeed, the activities of the Secret Societies during the earlier period alienated many foreigners who later acclaimed Victor Emmanuel II and Cavour. For one reason or another, therefore, there was from the beginning a potential interest abroad in the affairs of Italy, and in due course passions were aroused which can hardly fail to strike a later age as remarkable. Such was the international background against which the *Risorgimento* was set.

From 1815 to 1848 the dominant foreign Power in Italy was Austria. France had not, indeed, entirely renounced her ambitions in the peninsula, but circumstances were not conducive to their pursuit; all the same she did on occasion intervene in the affairs of the States of the Church, and Ancona was held by French troops from 1832 to 1838. The British government approved of this occupation, because the further that London drifted from Vienna the less did the Foreign Office relish the increasing hold of Austria on Italy, and the more it welcomed a counterweight. As the century advanced the Italian Question became increasingly entangled in French domestic politics, and the despatch of the army which in 1849 overthrew the Roman Republic was regarded as conclusive evidence that the existing regime in France, namely the Second Republic, had definitely moved to the Right. French interference, however, was on the whole very slight, and Metternich was the only effective foreign factor in Italian politics until his fall in 1848. Until then every attempt at revolution was foredoomed to failure, since it was only a question of time when it would be suppressed by Austrian arms.

By the summer of 1849 certain facts were clear. The first was that Italy could never, as Mazzini and his supporters had hoped, achieve her own unity and independence, even with the Piedmontese forces thrown into the scale. From this it followed that the assistance of some foreign Power was essential, and that Power could only be France, for Austria was the enemy, while the active interest of Great Britain in Continental questions had diminished during the past two decades save for occasional outbursts of Lord Palmerston. To gain French support it was above all necessary not to alarm the *bourgeoisie* by revolutionary violence in word or deed, for the French middle-class had had enough of both immediately after the fall of the July Monarchy, and they were now rallying to Louis Napoleon as the saviour of society. In effect, the only solution was the House of Savoy, and when, in 1850, Cavour became Prime Minister of Sardinia there began a new phase in the Italian Question.

Difficult as was his position in many ways on the morrow of Austria's triumph, he possessed one great asset, namely that the traditional foreign policy of the House of Savoy was opportunism. From the far-off days when its rulers were petty Alpine potentates they had—for a price—opened the passes to this party or to that; in the contests between France and Spain, and then between France and Austria, they had sold their support to the highest bidder, and in so doing they had gradually increased the territory under their rule. In marriage, too, they had not been unfortunate, and so the once insignificant Dukes of Savoy had become Kings of Sardinia, nor was there any reason to suppose that their ambition stopped at this point. In short, the traditional policy of the House of Savoy, as, indeed, of all the Italian states, was to throw its weight first into this scale and then into that, with self-preservation as the immediate, and territorial acquisitions as the ultimate, goal. Too weak to stand alone, the House of Savoy could only achieve its purpose by being always on the winning side in the international controversies of the time. Cavour understood this perfectly, and by his skilful application of the old policy he brought about the unification of Italy under Victor Emmanuel II. His successors followed in his footsteps and succeeded in creating the impression that Italy was a Great Power in fact as well as in name, until one of them, deluded by his own exaggerations, acted as if this was really the case, and attempted to complete the work of Cavour by the establishment of an Italian Empire.

In 1854, as will be described in a later chapter, war broke out between Great Britain and France on the one hand, and Russia on the other. The points at issue had nothing whatever to do with Italy, but Cavour at once realized that if Sardinia threw in her lot with the Western Powers not only would she thereby earn a great deal of valuable good-will in Great Britain and France, but that at the ensuing peace conference she would be able to raise the problems in which she was specially interested. Accordingly, in January, 1855, the alliance between Great Britain and France was joined by Sardinia, and a contingent of Piedmontese troops was sent to the Crimea, where they acquitted themselves well, particularly on the Chernaya. At the Congress of Paris the Sardinian Prime Minister was able to bring up the Italian Question, and

with outstretched finger he pointed to Austria as the author of all
Italy's woes. He may not have been able to effect much, and he
was himself more than a little disappointed, but he had prepared
the way, better than he knew, for what was to follow.

The merit of Cavour, like that of all great statesmen, lay in his
ability to adapt to his own purpose any circumstances that might
arise: he himself admitted that if he had done for his own benefit
the things he did for his country he would have been a great
criminal, and the observation was entirely just. Yet never was his
diplomatic skill put to so grave a test as when, in January, 1858,
Orsini attempted the life of Napoleon III. For the moment this
outrage all but upset the friendly relations between Turin and
Paris, and had the French throne been occupied by any less
enigmatical figure than Louis Napoleon such would certainly have
been the case, but the Emperor respected the sincerity of the man
who had attempted to murder him, although he sent him to the
scaffold, and decided that he must "do something for Italy",
even if only to prevent a repetition of Orsini's conspiracy.

Cavour naturally encouraged Napoleon in this view, and in
June, 1858, the French Emperor invited Cavour to a secret con-
ference at Plombières, where three main points were settled: these
were, war with Austria, the marriage of the Prince Napoleon (the
Emperor's cousin and at this time his heir), and the cession of
Savoy to France in return for the latter's aid.

Circumstances had become favourable to Cavour and his designs by the time that this meeting took place. Relations between
Paris and London had deteriorated since the Crimean War, and
as the Conservative government in England inclined towards
Austria so did Napoleon tend to lean the other way. Then, although he had created himself a hereditary monarch, Louis Napoleon was in fact a dictator, and, as such, he dared not let France
become bored; excitement must always be kept at a high level.
Nor was this all, for public opinion in western Europe was becoming horrified at the methods of repression which were the
order of the day all over Italy beyond the frontiers of the House
of Savoy. These horrors were no doubt greatly exaggerated, not
least by Cavour, and they do not appear in retrospect too terrible
to a generation which has experienced something very much
worse; but they were too much for the stomachs of the average
mid-nineteenth century Englishman and Frenchman. In this way
there was created, in respect of Italy, just that sentimental atmo-

sphere in Western Europe which had proved invaluable to the Spanish colonists and to the Greeks.

The first signs of the coming storm were noticed on New Year's Day, 1859, when Napoleon, after the manner of his uncle on the eve of the rupture of the Treaty of Amiens, bluntly observed to the Austrian ambassador, "I regret that our relations are not as satisfactory as formerly". Victor Emmanuel followed this up by a speech to his Parliament ten days later in which he said, "With all our respect for treaties, we are not insensible to the cry of pain which rises towards us from so many parts of Italy". This was all very well, but from Cavour's point of view it was essential that Austria must be made the aggressor; otherwise there was always the risk that Napoleon would go back on his promise, or, worse still, that Germany might feel herself threatened by the ambitions of France, and might range herself with Austria. Cavour, therefore, used all his endeavours to produce such a situation as must necessarily compel Vienna to resort to force.

He spent several anxious weeks before this was effected. Napoleon came, for a time, under anti-Italian influences, and adopted a Russian suggestion that the affairs of Italy should be settled by a conference. To this the Austrian government agreed on condition that Sardinia should disarm, and that her representatives should not be admitted to the conference. Lord Malmesbury, then British Foreign Secretary, urged Cavour to consent, but the latter refused, and insisted that Sardinia should be represented on the same footing as the other Powers. Neither Vienna nor Turin would give way, so the idea of a conference had to be abandoned. Lord Malmesbury then came forward with the proposal that Austria, France, and Sardinia should all demobilize, and that, as at Troppau and Laibach, the various Italian states should plead their case before the Great Powers. This proposition was equally distasteful to Cavour, but as it recommended itself to the vacillating French Emperor there was nothing he could do but embrace it, however reluctantly. At this moment he was saved by the precipitate action of the Austrian government. The war party at Vienna was in the ascendant, and it persuaded the Emperor Francis Joseph to consent to the dispatch of an ultimatum to Sardinia, demanding immediate demobilization under threat of invasion. It was the same mistake that Austria was to make again in the case of Serbia in 1914. This false move played straight into Cavour's hands, for it made Vienna appear the aggressor in the eyes of the world, and it deprived Napoleon of all excuse for further delay.

War began on April 19th, 1859, and thereafter for a time all went well for Cavour. The French, with Sardinian help, won the battles of Magenta and Solferino, with the result that the Austrians had to abandon the Milanese, the Duchies of Parma and Modena, and the northern part of the States of the Church. In the rest of central Italy the revolutionary movement spread rapidly, for Italy is pre-eminently a country where nothing succeeds like success, since the mass of the people is politically apathetic, and everywhere there were unmistakable signs of a desire for unity under the House of Savoy.

Napoleon had not entered the war for the unification of Italy, which was diametrically opposed to the interests of France, though Thiers remarked, "*Ce fou va établir une autre Prusse au-delà des Alpes*", and the more he saw of the way in which the situation was developing the less he liked it. The States of the Church were seething with unrest, and as there was still a French garrison in Rome it would be extremely difficult for France not to become implicated if revolution broke out: this, in its turn, would be followed by serious complications in France itself which might easily endanger the Imperial throne. On the Rhine the signs of danger were equally clear and even more ominous.

In Germany opinion on the war was much divided. In the south the population ardently espoused the cause of Austria, urged their rulers to assemble troops on the Rhine, and clamoured to be led against the hereditary foe. In the North, however, feeling was very different, and in Prussia Olmütz (see Chapter XVIII) had not been forgotten, while the cause of Italian independence inspired no little sympathy. The Prussian government pursued a somewhat hesitant course: it took the line that the Italian quarrels of Austria did not concern Germany in the sense that they must necessarily be fought out on the Rhine, or solved by a direct attack upon France, yet any serious defeat of Austria in Italy would endanger the German position. The spring and summer of 1859 were therefore spent in mobilization, and after the Austrian defeats at Magenta and Solferino the Prussian government prepared to offer armed mediation to the belligerents. This proposal was equally displeasing to Paris and Vienna. Napoleon had no desire for a war on two fronts, while to Austria the possibility that, after her own failure, Prussia, by winning brilliant victories, might gain a supremacy which would place her once for all at the head of a united Germany, was even more distasteful.

The first move for peace came from Napoleon, who, on July 6th, without any preliminary understanding with Victor Emmanuel, submitted to Francis Joseph proposals for an armistice, and then for a conference at Villafranca. Five days later the two Emperors met, and agreed that Lombardy (exclusive of Mantua and Peschiera) should be ceded to France, and that France should transfer this territory to the King of Sardinia; that Venice should remain Austrian; and that the Grand Duke of Tuscany, and the Dukes of Modena and Parma, should be restored to their thrones on condition of granting an amnesty to their subjects. Cavour angrily resigned sooner than associate himself with such terms, but Victor Emmanuel, more wisely, was content with what he could get, and signed the Treaty of Zurich which followed on the Preliminaries of Villafranca.

In the months that followed Napoleon was brought to realize that he had started a movement which it was beyond his power to halt: first Tuscany, Modena, and Parma threw in their lot with Sardinia, then the States of the Church with the exception of Rome and the Patrimonio di San Pietro, and finally the Kingdom of the Two Sicilies. All that France obtained in return for the creation of a new Power on her frontier was Nice, which, in consequence of a very dubious plebiscite, was given to her in exchange for the incorporation of the Duchies in the new Italian State, Savoy having been promised at Plombières. Napoleon did not even earn the good-will of the Italians for what he had done; his repeated hesitancies, his negotiations with Francis Joseph at Villafranca, and his protection of Francis II of Naples at Gaeta, effaced the memory of Magenta and Solferino. On the other hand, Great Britain, which in the earlier stages of the struggle had been on the side of Austria, and in the later had done little for Italy but encourage her with fair words, very considerably enhanced her reputation in the new kingdom, which she was one of the first Powers to recognize. Cavour, in short, had made Italy with French aid at a very low price.

The great Italian statesman—for, whatever opinion may be held of the methods which he pursued, Cavour's claim to greatness cannot be denied—died in 1861, and it was not until five years later that the international situation again provided Italy with the opportunity for a further advance, and this lay in the approach of war between Austria and Prussia. On this occasion, however, Italian statesmen had to deal with Bismarck, a very different person from the vacillating and impressionable Emperor of the French.

The negotiations between Prussia and Italy were protracted, and they more than once nearly broke down. The treaty of offensive and defensive alliance was finally concluded in April, 1866, and it represented a definite triumph for Bismarck, since he induced Italy to accept obligations without receiving any corresponding rights. If the Prussian proposals for the reform of the German Confederation were rejected by Austria, and Prussia in consequence declared war on Austria, then Italy was to attack Austria immediately she was notified of the Prussian declaration. Peace was only to be concluded by mutual consent, but the Berlin government was not to withhold its consent when Vienna expressed readiness to cede Venetia to Italy and to afford Prussia equivalent territorial compensation. Furthermore, Prussia was to decide the moment for the outbreak of hostilities within the limit of the three months during which the treaty remained in force.

Certain considerations arise from this agreement. There was, for example, no mention of Prussia going to the aid of Italy if Austria should attack the latter while remaining at peace with Prussia. Moreover, Prussia could always prevent the conclusion of peace merely by declaring that the territorial compensation offered to her was inadequate, so that even if Austria were ready to cede Venetia, the Italian government would be compelled to continue the war until the claims of Prussia had been met. Bismarck had made a careful study of the negotiations between Cavour and Napoleon III, and he had drawn his own conclusions. To quote a recent historian, he "had harnessed the Italian horse to the Prussian war-chariot: he did not intend that it should bolt with it".

Although this agreement was meant to remain secret, news of it soon leaked out, and Austria made a formal offer of Venetia to Italy as the price of neutrality. This was refused by the Italian government on the ground that it would be equivalent to the betrayal of Prussia, and in June, 1866, Italy declared war on Austria. In spite of the enthusiasm which was evoked throughout the peninsula, the Italians were defeated both on land and sea, and it was only the Prussian victory at Sadowa that enabled the new kingdom to acquire Venetia. By the Treaty of Vienna in October

he Austrian government ceded Venetia to France, which, in her
urn, passed the province on to the King of Italy. There was thus
ittle in the events of the year 1866 of which a patriotic Italian
could be proud, and it is thus in no way remarkable that a period
of intense moral depression should have followed the incorpora-
ion of Venetia in the dominions of Victor Emmanuel II.

Meanwhile the relations between Italy and France were
steadily deteriorating after an interval of improvement. In 1864
Napoleon had concluded a convention with the Italian government by which he undertook to withdraw his troops from Rome
within two years in return for a promise on the part of Victor
Emmanuel not to attack what was left of the dominions of the
Holy See. The followers of Garibaldi, however, did not consider
hemselves bound by any such undertaking, and in November,
1867, they came into conflict with Papal troops at Mentana.
Shortly before, when the disturbances threatened, French soldiers
had returned to Rome, and they arrived on the battle-field in
ime to turn the day against Garibaldi. This shedding of Italian
blood would in itself have created a good deal of ill-feeling, but
he situation was rendered far worse by the provocative utterances
of French politicians and generals; de Failly, for example, boasted
of the "marvels worked by the *chassepots*", while Rouher, for the
purpose of pleasing the clericals, declared that the Italians would
"never" enter Rome. These unfortunate remarks were not soon
forgotten, and the memory of them was destined to affect Franco-
talian relations for many a long year.

In 1870 there came yet another chance for Italy to benefit by
nternational complications. The outbreak of the Franco-Prussian
War, and the French defeats by which the campaign was soon
marked, left Rome at the mercy of the first comer. The country
s a whole was insistent upon a policy of neutrality as between
belligerents from both of whom it had received substantial bene-
its, but it demanded the occupation of Rome: in the middle of
August the French troops abandoned Pontifical territory for the
ast time, and on September 20th the Italian forces entered Rome
through a breach in the walls at Porta Pia. The unification of
taly was complete. Whether the new state had been made too
asily and too quickly; whether there had been too much reliance
upon the aid of the foreigner and too little upon the efforts of the
talians themselves; the history of the next seventy-three years
was to show.

CHAPTER XV

FRANCE AND EUROPE, 1815–1870

SUPERFICIALLY, the most significant fact about the history of France in the nineteenth century is the repeated change of regime; actually, this did not prove to be of very great importance. From the return of Louis XVIII to his capital after the defeat of Napoleon I at Waterloo until the overthrow of Napoleon III on the morrow of Sedan, that is to say in a space of less than two generations, France was governed by two different types of monarchy, one empire which was really a dictatorship, and one republic. Nevertheless, these attempts to achieve the ideal in the matter of government had little effect upon French foreign policy, which continued to be governed by traditional influences and by the relative position of France in the world. A revolution, like a flood, may for a time seem to obliterate the old familiar features, but ere long they reappear, though possibly in a slightly different form. No nation can change its geographical position, its climate, or its economic resources, and it is upon these that its foreign policy must in the long run be based: what can and does change is the ability to put this policy into execution. It was, in short, not the repeated revolutions in which France indulged in the nineteenth century that affected her achievements in the field of foreign affairs, but her exhaustion after the Revolutionary and Napoleonic Wars—an exhaustion from which she was destined never to recover.

France after 1815 was not what she had been before 1789, and this was the case for a variety of reasons. In the first place, the policy of the Allies at Vienna of placing strong states upon her frontiers succeeded even better than they could have imagined, more particularly after the unification of Italy and Germany. Indeed, for twenty years after her defeat in 1870 France was hemmed in by hostile neighbours to the same extent that she had been when Louis XIV ascended the throne, and this situation might have continued for a great deal longer had the successor of Bismarck possessed his ability. Then, again, her traditional allies in the east of Europe were no longer of any service to her. Sweden had sunk to the position of a second-rate Power, and was only interested in Scandinavian and Baltic affairs; Poland had ceased to exist; and the awe-inspiring Ottoman had become the Sick Man of Europe. Nor was it possible to practise any longer in Italy or Germany the *divide et impera* policy of Louis XIV: Italy was, as we have seen, under the domination of Austria after 1815, and although Germany was divided between the partisans of Prussia and those of Austria, there were very few Germans who were prepared to look to Paris; the funest diplomacy of Napoleon I prevented that. Above all, France herself was exhausted: while her neighbours were growing stronger, she, at the best, remained stationary, which is to say that she was really growing relatively weaker.

It was long before the rest of the world realized what was taking place. The memory of the last years of the First Empire took a great deal of forgetting, and the spectacle of Napoleon again and again driving back the armies of united Europe lingered on until the overthrow of his nephew at Sedan, during which time it exercised a profound influence upon international diplomacy. Had Guizot and Napoleon III been more shrewd, and had the character of the French people been different, it is by no means improbable that the legend of a strong France might have survived even longer, and the collapse been postponed until a later date. For France had risen before, after the Hundred Years' War, after the Wars of Religion, and after the Fronde: the wars of Louis XIV, it was argued, had not prevented another outbreak of French aggression eighty years after his death, and what had happened before might well happen again, for the real position was hidden from the keen eyes in the chancelleries. The decline of a Great Power is always a matter of scepticism to the world at large. Cromwell was not alone in thinking that the Spain of Philip IV was the Spain of Philip II, so, two hundred years later, the France of Napoleon III was generally mistaken for that of Napoleon I. It is only in the light of these various considerations that the relations of France and the other Powers between 1815 and 1870 can be understood.

The earlier governments of the Restoration were, as has been shown, primarily concerned with securing for their country a position of equality with her conquerors, and then with obtaining liberty of action in the affairs of the world. In both they were successful, and French diplomacy was seen at its most resourceful during the reign of Louis XVIII. A careful distinction was drawn between France and Napoleon, and the effect of this was not wholly dissipated even by The Hundred Days; then by a prudent internal policy the Allies were in 1818 induced to withdraw the armies of occupation and to reach a financial settlement with their late enemy; lastly, with the blessing of the Holy Alliance a force crossed the Pyrenees, and overthrew a regime whose continuance might well have proved a threat to the existing order in France. This last, it should be noted, was effected without a breach with Great Britain. Thus the first ten years of the restored monarchy were marked by a steady revival of the prestige of France: she inclined, it is true, towards the Holy Alliance, but she never subordinated her interests to those of the Powers that composed it. and she preserved a balance in her foreign policy.

With the accession of Charles X a more aggressive tone began to be characteristic of French diplomacy, and not only where the Far East was concerned. This development was bound to bring France into conflict with Great Britain, but Charles and Polignac, who had now become Minister for Foreign Affairs, thought they were strong enough to face British hostility. The Holy Alliance was dissolved, but its constituent Powers were, largely for ideological reasons, favourably inclined to the new King, who early displayed his dislike of constitutional government, while Russia and Great Britain had drifted apart since the death of Canning. The opportunity appeared to be provided by the situation in Belgium, where resistance to Dutch rule was rapidly coming to a head.

Throughout 1829 plans for the annexation both of Belgium and the Rhenish Provinces were discussed in France. The Tsar had proposed that Russia and France should come to an understanding as to the territorial changes that should follow the defeat of Turkey which his armies were at that moment accomplishing, and with this encouragement Polignac drew up a scheme for a general re-settlement of Europe. In particular the Belgian provinces between the Meuse, the estuary of the Scheldt, and the North Sea were to be separated from Holland, and incorporated with France. North Brabant, Luxembourg, and Landau were also to be French possessions. The Dutch territory on the right bank of the Rhine was to be ceded to Prussia, and on the expulsion of the Turks from Europe the King of the Netherlands was to reign at Constantinople as the ruler of Greece. It was anticipated that Great Britain would resist these territorial changes, but an attempt was to be made to obtain her consent by an offer of the

Dutch colonies. If she refused this arrangement, as was most probable, she was to be confronted by a coalition of Continental Powers, which would leave her isolated, and with no alternative but to agree or face a general war.

This ambitious scheme received the approval of the Council of State in spite of the opposition of the Dauphin, but it came to nothing owing to the conclusion of the Treaty of Adrianople. Nevertheless, its mere conception created a breach between Great Britain and France, and it rendered London extremely suspicious of French intentions with regard to Belgium until 1870. Nor was the hope of obtaining that country entirely abandoned by Charles and Polignac, and it was the presence of so many regular troops on the Belgian frontier, as well as in North Africa, that made possible the success of the July Revolution.

Foiled in their European schemes, Charles and his ministers turned to Africa, where, just before they themselves were overthrown, they succeeded in planting the French flag in Algeria. To Great Britain this was a further cause of offence, for she had no desire to see France create a new colonial empire in the nineteenth century to replace the old one which she had been at such pains to destroy in the eighteenth. On every ground, therefore, there was considerable satisfaction in London at the disappearance of the elder branch of the House of Bourbon from the international scene.

If the Restoration inclined towards Austria and Russia, the July Monarchy leant on Great Britain, and for a few years there was a closer understanding between London and Paris than there had been since the third decade of the previous century. It was only natural that this should be the case. The throne of Louis Philippe was based upon principles which were acceptable in England, but which were anathema to Metternich and the Tsar, so that, as was later to be proved, France must either work in conjunction with Great Britain or stand alone, and, although she did not realize it, the latter course was beyond her power.

The first problem with which the new regime had to deal was that caused by the Belgian revolt against Dutch rule, and here the French government had to walk extremely warily in view of the suspicions which had been roused across the Channel by the schemes of Polignac. Important issues were involved. The kingdom of the Netherlands had been created at Vienna as a bulwark against French ambition, and King William I called

N

upon the Powers of the Quadruple Alliance to assist him by force
of arms. This they were by no means willing to do, for there was
now no danger from the side of France, and instead there was held
in London a conference of the plenipotentiaries of Austria,
France, Great Britain, Prussia, and Russia to discuss the situation.
From the beginning the lead was taken by the British and French
governments, not because the other Powers were wanting in
interest, but because they were pre-occupied with the Polish rising
which took place in November, 1830. It is no exaggeration to say
that the Belgians owed their independence, like the French the
success of their revolution forty years before, to the action of the
Poles.

Towards the end of December the Conference, having previously arranged an armistice, accepted in principle the independence of Belgium and the dissolution of the kingdom of the
Netherlands. It also drew up two protocols which defined the
frontiers of the two states, settled the proportions of the debt
which each was to bear, and declared that no King of the Belgians
should be recognized unless he agreed to the conditions set out in
the protocols and was in other ways acceptable to the Powers.

These decisions pleased neither the Belgians nor the Dutch,
and the former endeavoured to secure their own ends by driving
in a wedge between Paris and London: at Brussels particular
exception was taken to the assignment of Luxembourg to William
II, and it was felt that the elevation of a younger son of Louis
Philippe, in the person of the Duc de Nemours, to the Belgian
throne might persuade the King of the French to make a stand for
wider territories for the new state. The French monarch, however, was not prepared to risk his good understanding with Britain
for any such reason, and after somewhat lengthy negotiations
Prince Leopold of Saxe-Coburg, uncle of the heiress-presumptive
to the English throne, was chosen as King of the Belgians. At the
same time important concessions were made to Belgium both in
respect of her portion of the debt of the old kingdom, and with
regard to Luxembourg and Maestricht, which questions were to
be reopened and dealt with separately. On July 21st, 1831, King
Leopold I took the oath to the constitution in the Place Royale in
Brussels amid scenes of great enthusiasm. Not long afterwards he
strengthened his position internationally by marrying Louis
Philippe's daughter.

William, however, was not prepared to lose his Belgian provinces so easily, and he was resolved to convince Europe that the Dutch nation was quite capable of maintaining its rights by its own efforts. Accordingly, he sent his son, the Prince of Orange, to re-assert his authority with a force which soon beat down all opposition. The Powers were not prepared to see their authority flouted in this way, and with their sanction, a strong French army entered Belgium: the Dutch withdrew before it, and re-crossed the frontier, but William, hoping to gain better terms, refused to evacuate Antwerp. Once again the Powers took action, and to Great Britain and France was deputed the task of driving the Dutch from Belgian territory. This was accomplished by a naval blockade and the siege of Antwerp, and by the Convention of London in May, 1833, it was agreed that, pending the conclusion of a definitive treaty, there should be no renewal of hostilities between Holland and Belgium, and that navigation on the Scheldt and Meuse should be entirely free and open. William nevertheless still refused to recognize Belgian independence, so that the Convention of London was in reality nothing more than the maintenance of the *status quo*; Belgium, it is to be noted, remained in possession of Luxembourg, except for the fortress which was a German Federal stronghold, and of Limburg without Maestricht.

It was not until 1839 that a final settlement was reached, not without some misgivings on the part of the Belgians, who had to make territorial concessions in Luxembourg and Limburg. In May of that year the kingdom of Belgium finally took its place, under the guarantee of the five Great Powers, as an independent but neutral state in Europe.

The negotiations leading up to the recognition of Belgian independence had shown what could be effected by French diplomacy in collaboration with Great Britain: a few years later, in connection with the ambitions of Mehemet Ali, it was equally clearly proved that the days of Louis XIV and Napoleon I were passed, and that independent action on the part of France was fraught with danger.

It was not long before Mahmud II had cause to regret his appeal to the Pasha of Egypt to help him against the Greeks, and in 1833 he had owed the preservation of his throne against Mehemet Ali very largely to Russian support. In 1839 the struggle had been renewed, and when Mahmud died in July the Ottoman Empire appeared to be at its last gasp; the road to Constantinople lay open

to Ibrahim, while the Turkish fleet had been handed over to the
Egyptians by its own admiral. In these circumstances the advisers
of the new Sultan, Abd-ul-Mejid, recommended a direct approach
to Mehemet Ali with the offer of generous terms. To these overtures Mehemet Ali returned a diplomatic reply, for he was well
aware that he must ultimately depend upon the support of one of
the Powers, and that this could only be gained by an appearance
of moderation. Meanwhile, the Powers were themselves by no
means agreed as to the course which was to be pursued, though
they did unite in a somewhat vague note to the Porte urging it "to
suspend all definite decision made without their concurrence,
pending the effect of their interest in its welfare".

Both public and official opinion in France favoured the Pasha
of Egypt. The mantle of Napoleon seemed to have descended
upon him, and if he was to be the dominant factor in the Near East,
there seemed more than a possibility that an alliance with Egypt
might take the place of that with Turkey which had been so
profitable ever since the days of Francis I. Moreover, the military
strength of Mehemet Ali was grossly exaggerated, and it was not
believed in Paris that he could be easily dispossessed of Syria,
while French troops would in the last resort come to his assistance.
In these circumstances, it was the object of the French government to secure for Mehemet Ali the maximum concessions that
could be wrung from the Sultan, even if this meant the imposition
of a severe strain upon the interpretation of the joint note.

Lord Palmerston, who was then British Foreign Secretary,
wished to co-operate with France if this was at all possible, but
this policy was not easy of fulfilment, partly owing to the situation
in Paris, and partly because the Tsar, always ready to work with
Britain whenever he could, was much more conciliatory than the
French government. In September, 1839, Nicholas informed
Palmerston that if Ibrahim's army advanced any nearer to
Constantinople a Russian fleet would enter the Bosphorus, remaining, however, at the disposal of the Powers. He was prepared, he
said, to act in concert with Great Britain and France, but he would
prefer to co-operate with the former alone. When the French
government was informed of the naval suggestion it replied that
if a Russian fleet entered the Bosphorus a French squadron would
also appear off Constantinople. Palmerston saw that this would
mean war between Russia and France, and having secured
Russian consent to a proposal that Anglo-French naval forces

should also have authority to enter the Dardanelles, he informed Paris that the British government would agree to act with Austria, Prussia, and Russia "whether France joins or not, but that on every account we should deeply regret that France should not be a party to the proceedings".

Events were clearly moving to a crisis, and France showed no sign of giving way. Louis Philippe and his advisers did not believe that Great Britain and Russia could ever come to an understanding; they over-estimated the strength of Mehemet Ali; and they hoped to detach Austria from the coalition of Powers. Above all, French opinion and the Paris Press were strongly in favour of the Pasha of Egypt, and they constituted a force which the regime could not afford to disregard. The winter of 1839–1840, therefore, saw France still adamant; Thiers became Prime Minister, and Guizot was appointed to the London Embassy. The lists were set.

French reliance upon Austria was not fundamentally unreasonable. Metternich was always inclined to view the schemes of Nicholas with suspicion, and it was only in defence of the established order against revolutionary attack that Vienna and St. Petersburg were prepared to co-operate at all cordially. On the other hand, no Austrian purpose was to be served by insisting upon the retention of Syria by Mehemet Ali, and it might well be that Austria would find herself pulling French chestnuts out of the fire at the cost of a war with Great Britain and Russia. In these circumstances Metternich displayed no great enthusiasm for the overtures of Thiers, which certainly did nothing to dissipate his inbred suspicion of the July Monarchy. However, neither the co-operation of Russia and Britain, nor the coldness of Austria, daunted Thiers, who thought that he was on the eve of triumph. Separate negotiations were being conducted at Constantinople, under the auspices of the French Ambassador, between Mehemet Ali and the Porte, and at any moment Thiers expected to hear of their successful conclusion, when he looked forward to confronting Palmerston and Nesselrode with a *fait accompli*.

He was speedily undeceived. As soon as the British Foreign Secretary realized what was afoot, he easily persuaded the representatives of Austria, Prussia, and Russia to sign, in July, 1840, a Four-Power Treaty, to which Turkey was also a party. This document provided for the settlement of the dispute between the Sultan and Mehemet Ali on condition of the assignment of the hereditary pashalic of Egypt to the latter, together with Acre and Southern Syria for life. The offer of Southern Syria was to hold good for ten days, and that of Egypt alone for twenty days. If pressure were required to be put on Mehemet Ali, the Powers agreed to unite in a blockade, while if he advanced upon Constantinople they would co-operate with Abd-ul-Mejid in the defence of his capital. A further article maintained, "the ancient rule of the Ottoman Empire to keep the Dardanelles closed to foreign ships of war when the Porte was at peace".

The news of this treaty was greeted with a storm of indignation in France. Thiers, indeed, admitted that the French government would not have signed, but it felt insulted at not being invited to sign. Indeed, nothing could disguise the reverse which the diplomacy of France had sustained. "No wonder", wrote Palmerston, "Guizot has been looking as cross as the devil for the last few days". Nor was French anger in any way assuaged by the ease with which Mehemet Ali, who had refused to comply with the demands made upon him, was driven out of his conquests. For a space war appeared inevitable, and the Tsar on his own initiative offered to send a squadron to the aid of Great Britain if she was attacked. Thiers talked of reviving the glories of 1793, of placing France at the head of the revolutionary movement in Europe, and of advancing the French frontiers to the Rhine. Military preparations were hurried forward as the only possible reply to what was felt to be a return to the Treaty of Chaumont. The French Prime Minister even prepared a speech from the Throne which threw down the gauntlet to the whole of Europe. "France," it declared, "which has not been the first to expose the world to the fortune of arms, must hold herself ready to act on the day when she believes the balance of the world to be seriously menaced."

More pacific counsels, however, soon prevailed. Mehemet Ali had been defeated, and armed intervention on his behalf could only serve to precipitate his ruin, while France would be left to face the other Powers unaided. Above all, Louis Philippe fully realized the danger of pushing matters to extremes, and, as he said himself, "*parler de faire la guerre, et faire la guerre, sont deux choses bien différentes*". Palmerston, too, was most willing to leave the door open for a settlement, and at the beginning of October, 1841, he wrote to the British ambassador in Paris, "If France makes us a friendly communication tending to lead to an amicable discussion of the present state of affairs, we shall receive it, and deal with it in the spirit in which it is made". On October 21st, the Thiers administration resigned, and the crisis was at an end.

In due course France was invited to associate herself with the other Powers "on the invitation and according to the wish of His Highness the Sultan". Accordingly, on July 13th, 1841, two treaties were signed: the first definitely established peace between the Sultan and Mehemet Ali, and confirmed the latter in the hereditary pashalic of Egypt; the second, known as the Convention of the Straits, re-enacted "the ancient rule of the Ottoman Empire" as defined by the Four Power Treaty of the previous year.

The crisis occasioned by the ambitions of Mehemet Ali had brought into prominence several important considerations, though not all of them received at the hands of contemporary statesmen the attention for which they called. In the first place, it had been conclusively proved that France was too weak to play the dominant part in Europe which had for so long been hers: unfortunately this fact was not appreciated in Paris, with the result that France was condemned to a series of crises and wars which culminated in the disaster of Sedan. Secondly, the progressive decline of the Ottoman Empire was further stressed, and it was clear to all who wished to see that the precedent set by the Greeks and Mehemet Ali would ere long be followed elsewhere. Once more, too, confirmation had been given to the old truth that Great Britain can only intervene decisively on the Continent when she has a powerful ally there. Palmerston was in many ways far from an ideal Foreign Secretary, but he handled the Egyptian phase of the Eastern Question in a manner reminiscent, and according to the methods, of Canning. The Tsar, as in the case of Greece, had shown every desire to work with Britain, and Palmerston had gone half-way to meet him. Last, but by no means least, the settlement had been a triumph for the Concert of Europe, which in the final resort had been ready to enforce its decisions by arms.

The differences over Mehemet Ali had weakened the friendship between France and Great Britain which had existed since the accession of the July Monarchy, but there were too many influences at work to allow it to be seriously impaired. Louis Philippe was by no means the least important of these, and he was strongly supported by Queen Victoria and Prince Albert, while among the statesmen Guizot and Aberdeen were strong partisans of an Anglo-French understanding. Above all, there was Leopold I of the

Belgians, who was not only closely related to the French and British Royal Families, but the security of whose subjects seemed to depend upon the existence of friendly relations between London and Paris. All the same, there were repeated differences between the two countries which more than once brought them to the verge of war.

One of these concerned the island of Tahiti. Since 1797 the London Missionary Society had been working there, and the Society Islands, of which Tahiti was one, were ruled by a Christian, Queen Pomare. She was an admirer of Britain, and in 1826 asked for her dominions to be placed under British protection; a request which Canning refused, though he assured her that George IV would "be happy to afford . . . all such protection as H.M. can grant to a friendly Power at so great a distance from his own kingdoms". The trouble with France began in 1836 when two French missionary priests were refused admittance to the islands. A similar event took place in the following year, and in 1838 the French government sent a squadron to demand an apology and an indemnity. Both were given, but in 1842 the admiral in command of the French Pacific Fleet exceeded his instructions by obtaining, under threat of bombardment, Queen Pomare's recognition of the Protectorate of France.

When this news reached England there was an outburst of indignation. The missionary societies and all the Evangelical interest, at that time very strong indeed, were roused; public meetings of protest were held at which Protestant feeling was stirred up as in the case of Jenkins' ear over a hundred years before; and deputations were sent to the Foreign Secretary, Lord Aberdeen, and to the French ambassador. On the other side of the Channel there was no less excitement, and the government was given to understand that the Chamber would never allow the French flag to be hauled down. At this point fresh fuel was added to the fire of the controversy by the action of the French admiral in annexing Tahiti (November, 1843), and by the arrest, and subsequent deportation, of the ex-British consul, one George Pritchard. That this latter step was to some extent justified was not likely to be remarked by Englishmen in their existing attitude of mind.

Once again France and Great Britain appeared to be on the eve of war. In June, 1844, the British Prime Minister, Sir Robert Peel, declared in the House of Commons that a gross outrage, accompanied with gross indignity, had been committed upon Pritchard, and that, if the statements received were correct, it must be presumed that "the French government will at once make that reparation which this country has a right to require". The international atmosphere was further disturbed by what in many British circles was regarded as fresh evidence of French aggression, namely the naval bombardment of Tangier. Guizot by no means approved of all that had been done, but he dared not suggest to the Chamber that the government should retract. Nevertheless the influences working for peace carried the day in the end, and the dispute was settled directly between Guizot and Aberdeen. The former expressed regret for the affront to Pritchard, and agreed to pay indemnity. The Chamber was far from approving of this arrangement, and Louis Philippe had to pay the indemnity out of his own pocket. In September, 1844, Peel stated that the affair had been satisfactorily settled, but Queen Pomare, who had been banished by the French, was not restored under their Protectorate until three years later. France formally annexed the islands in 1880.

France took Tahiti as a protectorate from under British influence, 1844. But had to pay an indemnity to do so.

CHAPTER XVI

FRANCE AND EUROPE, 1815-1870 (*continued*)

THE Tahiti crisis, following so soon after that caused by Mehemet Ali, made it clear that Franco-British friendship, the key-note of the foreign policy of the July Monarchy, was subject to a strain which it might well not be able permanently to withstand. As in the case of the collaboration of the two Powers in the years which followed the death of Louis XIV, the co-operation was purely political; the two nations entertained to the full their old distrust of one another, and there was no common danger from without, as at the beginning of the following century, to bring them together. In these circumstances it was easy to see that at any moment a situation might arise when the government of one country or the other would find itself compelled by public opinion to adopt an attitude on some question which must necessarily bring the *entente* to an end. The House of Hanover had reigned in England for a hundred and thirty years; the House of Orleans had been on the throne for fourteen years; thus it seemed probable that the events producing such a situation would occur in France rather than in Britain. Louis Philippe was a pacific and moderate man, if, like all the members of the House of Orleans, entirely devoid of principle; in his international outlook he resembled Louis XVIII, who had done so much to restore the reputation of France. Where they differed in effectiveness was that Louis XVIII ruled by the grace of God, and Louis Philippe by the will of the people; and the latter are a far harder taskmaster, at any rate on this side of the grave.

The final clash between Great Britain and the July Monarchy arose over the affair of the Spanish Marriages.

Ferdinand VII of Spain had died in 1833, and he had been succeeded, at the price of the First Carlist War, by his daughter, Isabella, under the regency of his widow, Maria Cristina of Naples. By the early forties Isabella, together with her younger sister, Luisa, was of an age to marry. The Regent, in default of a suitable Austrian Archduke, wished both girls to marry French Princes. From the beginning, however, this suggestion was strongly opposed by the British government, which took the line that the Treaty of Utrecht was still in force, and that it could not tolerate

a union between the crowns of France and Spain, even though
both were at that time in possession of monarchs whose thrones
were not based upon the principle of legitimacy. It was, thus,
clear to the French government that any attempt to carry out the
wishes of the Spanish Regent would meet with the most violent
resistance on the part of Great Britain; on the other hand, the
chances were that on this occasion England would stand alone, as
the other Powers had not the same interest in Spain that they
possessed in respect of the Near East.

At first the matter was discussed between the British and
French governments, and between Queen Victoria and Louis
Philippe personally. Aberdeen, always desirous of a close understanding with France, made it clear that Great Britain would not
raise any objection to the marriage of Isabella with a descendant
of Philip V, and would refrain from pressing any other candidate;
moreover, in the event of the Queen having children the British
government would not see any objection to a union between the
Duke of Montpensier, a younger son of the King of the French,
and the Infanta Luisa. On this basis an agreement was reached
between London and Paris in 1843. While these negotiations were
in progress, however, the marriage of Isabella became a party
question in Spain. One section suggested that she should marry
her cousin, the Carlist claimant to the throne, and, in the light of
later events, it is perhaps to be regretted that this solution was not
adopted; another, with the support of the Queen-Mother, by now
no longer Regent, favoured Isabella's maternal uncle, the Count
of Trapani. Finally, the choice was limited to two of the Queen's
cousins, namely Francis, Duke of Cadiz, and his brother Henry,
Duke of Seville. Isabella herself preferred the latter, but he was
obnoxious to her mother on account of his advanced political
views.

Cristina wished to secure a French match for both her daughters, and she made no scruple of creating a breach between Paris
and London if she could thereby achieve her ends. At this stage
the candidature of Prince Leopold of Saxe-Coburg was much discussed, and for a time Cristina appeared not to reject it, in order
to put pressure on the French government to defy the British
lightning and comply with her own wishes. Louis Philippe and
Guizot were under no illusions as to the danger of going back on
their agreement with Britain, but the internal situation in France
was disquieting, and another apparent concession to British views,

following on the Mehemet Ali and Tahiti affairs, might well be disastrous. It was thus decided to take the risk, and on Cristina giving her consent, the marriage of Isabella to the Duke of Cadiz, and of her sister to the Duke of Montpensier, was celebrated in October, 1846. In defence of this action it was stated that the British government had violated the agreement of 1843 by secretly favouring the Coburg candidature, an accusation which may, indeed, have been made in good faith, but which was nevertheless untrue.

By the time that the marriages took place Aberdeen had been succeeded at the Foreign Office by Palmerston, and he was certainly not the man to lie down under treatment of this nature. It was generally believed that the Duke of Cadiz was impotent, in which case Luisa and her French husband would come to the throne: indeed, it was these considerations which had prompted Aberdeen to insist that Isabella should have children before the British Government would consent to her sister's union with Montpensier. For the next fourteen months Palmerston devoted all his energies to thwarting French diplomacy, wherever he came into contact with it, and to assist the opponents of Louis Philippe at home. His success was considerable, and this was not to be the last occasion on which Spanish politics were to be the indirect cause of the overthrow of a French regime.

During the Second Republic and the Second Empire the influence of French domestic politics upon French foreign policy was very marked. The leading, one could hardly say dominant, personality was Louis Napoleon, and whether as Prince-President or as Emperor his influence was decisive. By nature he was undecided, and circumstances compelled him to walk delicately. As the nephew of the great Corsican he was the heir of the Revolution, and the French people expected him to revive the glories associated with the name of his uncle. "*La France s'ennuyait*" Lamartine had remarked during the reign of Louis Philippe, and that boredom had resulted in revolution. France wanted glory abroad and the satisfaction of its national vanity. On the other hand, Napoleon III was also the saviour of society from the Red peril, and in this capacity he was strongly supported by the French Church and by the *bourgeoisie*, neither of whom would at all approve of him embarking upon a crusade in favour of revolution and oppressed nationalities. A greater man might have been able to co-ordinate these conflicting factors, but Napoleon III was unable to do so; accordingly, while he was at the helm the foreign policy of France was continually vacillating, and he himself became the instrument and the dupe of those who, like Cavour and Bismarck, were both stronger and knew what they wanted.

The events leading up to the Crimean War will be discussed in a subsequent chapter, and it has already been shown how French intervention in Italy, originally undertaken to conciliate the Left, had had the most unexpected and undesired results. Roumania, Syria, and China afforded fresh outlets for French energy, but in the case of the first little was effected save the union of Moldavia and Wallachia; intervention in Syria re-affirmed the position of France as protector of the Catholics in the Near East; and the Chinese campaign, undertaken in conjunction with Great Britain, served to show that France was a world Power. None of these events, however, stirred the public imagination to the extent which Napoleon knew to be necessary for the maintenance of his throne. Indeed, by the end of 1863 he had largely lost the prestige which had been his at the end of the Crimean War. He had alienated the new kingdom of Italy without gaining over the Holy See; remonstrances to Russia on the Polish question had estranged the Powers that were interested in Poland; and in England suspicion of French motives had caused the Volunteer movement, a suspicion which was by no means allayed by the conclusion of Cobden's commercial treaty with France in 1860. As Napoleon surveyed the scene it appeared to him that in Mexico his lost prestige could most easily and most completely be restored.

Since that country had achieved its independence forty years before it had, in addition to suffering defeat at the hands of the United States, been rent by civil war: more recently there had been the added complication of a default on the foreign loans. In these circumstances France, Great Britain, and Spain decided to take armed action to enforce the claims of their nationals, but it soon became clear that Napoleon's ambitions went a good deal further than the mere collecting of debts. Civil war was breaking out in the United States, and there was thus no risk of any application of the Monroe Doctrine to prevent the establishment of a great Catholic and Latin Empire in Mexico. With the Emperor's imagination busy with such schemes it is not remarkable that there should soon have been differences of opinion between the allies; the British troops re-embarked, the Spaniards ere long followed their example, and by March, 1862, only the French remained in Mexico. Napoleon was now free to pursue what had become the great idea of his reign.

Unfortunately the essential elements for the constitution of such a regime as he had in mind did not exist: Conservatives and Clericals there were in plenty, but not many of them were prepared to co-operate with a foreign invader. On the other hand, Benito Juarez in the North, and Porfirio Diaz in the South, were leading the resistance, and theirs soon became the national and patriotic party. In June, 1863, the French entered Mexico City, where they proclaimed as Emperor the Archduke Maximilian of Austria, a brother of Francis Joseph and the son-in-law of the King of the Belgians. Napoleon was now definitely committed to the support of the Mexican monarchy, and that at the cost of fourteen million francs a month and an army of occupation of 40,000 men.

The end of the story is soon told. By 1866 Maximilian was wholly dependent on the French troops, while Bazaine, who was in command of them, was intriguing against him with a view to taking his place. Napoleon now had to make up his mind whether to abandon Maximilian, which would be ruinous to his prestige, or to send reinforcements, which would probably lead to war with the United States, and this at a moment when hostilities were on the eve of breaking out between Prussia and Austria. The former course was decided upon, the French troops were withdrawn, and in June, 1867, Maximilian was shot without mercy at Queretaro. It was the end of the glory of the Empire, and from that moment its twilight began to deepen into night.

While Napoleon was wasting the resources of France in over-seas expeditions the balance of power in Europe was being upset. Bismarck was preparing for war with Austria, and it was most important that his intended victim should first of all be isolated. There was always the danger that the French Emperor might realize where his true interests lay, and make an agreement with Austria by which, in return for his help against Prussia, he would receive compensation on the left bank of the Rhine. In October, 1865, Bismarck and Napoleon met at Biarritz, and the Prussian persuaded the Frenchman to sign the death-warrant of the Second Empire. The Emperor not only promised his neutrality in the event of war between Prussia and Austria, but undertook to persuade Italy to align herself with the former. In adopting this policy he hoped to place France as arbiter at the end of what he believed would be a long struggle between the two Germanic Powers in the course of which both would be considerably weakened; then he would be able to claim compensation either on the Rhine or in Belgium. Bismarck, on the contrary, relied upon being able to overthrow Austria before Napoleon could interfere, and then upon tricking France of her anticipated booty; which was exactly what happened.

After the Prussian victory at Sadowa the French Emperor realized that his opportunities were passing away, and he instructed Benedetti, his ambassador, to demand Mayence and the left bank of the Rhine. Bismarck, now sure of his position in central Europe, bluntly refused, and declared that if the suggestion was pressed it would mean war, and war with a united Germany. For such a conflict France, in process of withdrawing from Mexico, was not ready, while the Prussian army was still mobilized, and was flushed with its recent victory over Austria. Napoleon, therefore, was forced to give way. It was at this time, too, that he drew up the draft of a secret convention between France and Prussia, by which the latter agreed to the incorporation of Luxembourg with France, and promised her armed assistance should circumstances compel Napoleon "to invade or conquer Belgium". Bismarck totally rejected this proposal when it was made to him in August, 1866, but he kept the draft for future use.

In spite of this rebuff Napoleon was not prepared to abandon his expansionist ambitions, and in 1867 he returned to the possible acquisition of Luxembourg. The Dutch, who had obtained the province from the Belgians in 1839, were willing to sell it to France, on condition that the German garrison was withdrawn. At this point Bismarck contrived to let the negotiations become known, and the result was a wave of nationalist feeling in Germany which effectually prevented the accomplishment of the Emperor's scheme. On this occasion, however, French diplomacy was sufficiently skilful to disguise the reverse which it had suffered. The subject was referred to a conference of the Great Powers in London, and the issue of their deliberations was that Luxembourg was to be a sovereign and independent Grand Duchy, with its neutrality guaranteed by the Powers. France abandoned her designs, and the German troops were withdrawn from the fortress.

Napoleon now began to realize that France was isolated, and he feverishly sought for allies. During the whole of the year 1869 there were negotiations between France, Austria, and Italy, but in the end they came to nothing. The French Emperor at the same time insisted upon seeking an agreement with Prussia, and in consequence merely caused further suspicion in the minds of all with whom he was dealing. Nor was this all, for he antagonized Italy by retaining his troops in Rome, while he quarrelled with the Church over the refusal of Pius IX to invite the French ambassador to the Oecumenical Council.

Such was the position when the affairs of Europe were, for the third time, complicated by the question of the succession to the Spanish throne. In 1868 Isabella II left Spain in consequence of a successful revolt against her, and as her son was unacceptable to the dominant faction, the Spanish crown was hawked round Europe. Finally it was offered to Prince Leopold of Hohenzollern-Sigmaringen, a relative of William I of Prussia: neither the Prussian monarch nor the young man's father wished him to accept what they felt to be a dangerous offer, but they were over-persuaded by Bismarck. A Hohenzollern at Berlin and another at Madrid would revive that Germanic encirclement of France which it had been the life-work of Louis XIV to bring to an end. The Hohenzollerns had replaced the Habsburgs in the German Reich; why should they not also pursue the policy of Charles V? So, with considerable reluctance, William I on June 21st, 1870, agreed to Prince Leopold's candidature.

The possibility of a Hohenzollern at Madrid filled France with alarm, and Napoleon found himself compelled to take immediate action. Benedetti was sent to Ems, where the King of Prussia was taking the waters, to demand the withdrawal of Leopold's acceptance, and William, in the absence of his masterful Chancellor, gave way. The French Emperor had gained his point, and had humiliated the Hohenzollerns in the eyes of all Europe. Such was the moment chosen by the Duc de Grammont, the French Foreign Minister, without previous consultation with his master or the Cabinet, to order Benedetti to demand from the Prussian monarch an assurance that he would never give his consent to any renewal of the Hohenzollern candidature. William felt this to be a reflection upon his personal honour, and he refused the assurance. Later, he sent an aide-de-camp to Benedetti to say that as Leopold had withdrawn he had nothing to add. He also gave orders for an account of his interview with the French ambassador, and of his subsequent message to him, to be telegraphed to Bismarck in Berlin, with an accompanying instruction that he left it to his

Prime Minister to decide whether the news of the fresh French demand and its rejection should be made public.

This gave Bismarck the opportunity of which he was not slow to take advantage. He emended William's account of his interview with Benedetti in such a way as to create the impression that the Prussian monarch had refused to give the required assurance, thereby revealing, as the French felt, Hohenzollern perfidy to the world, and had insulted France through her ambassador by refusing to receive him and by sending him a message through an aide-de-camp. For a brief space the French government thought of a congress, but pressure of public opinion decided it in favour of war. On July 15th this decision was endorsed by the Chamber with only ten dissentient votes: outside the *Marseillaise* was being sung in the streets, and the mob was crying "*A Berlin*".

Within two months the fate of France had been decided upon the field of battle, but before that took place the diplomacy of Bismarck had struck a further blow at the moribund Second Empire. On July 25th he caused to be published in *The Times* the draft of the French proposal of 1866 regarding Belgium: at the same time he informed the British government that Prussia was ready to join with Great Britain in a new and special guarantee of Belgian integrity. Memories of Polignac's proposal were revived across the Channel, sympathy with Prussia grew, and long before his overthrow at Sedan on September 3rd, Napoleon was isolated.

So fell the Second Empire, and with it France, after creating, in antagonism to French interests, United Italy and United Germany. An epoch in French history had come to an end, while Europe had exchanged a mistress for a master.

CHAPTER XVII

THE FOREIGN POLICY OF NICHOLAS I,

1825–1856

THE expansion of Russia was very considerable during the reign of Alexander I. Catherine II had left to her successor, Paul, a realm eighteen million square kilometres in extent and peopled by thirty-three million inhabitants: by 1815 the area was twenty million square kilometres and the population was forty-five million. Russia had definitely established her western frontier, and she had considerably extended her limits towards the east and south. In addition, she had acquired a very strong position in the councils of Europe, where she played an increasingly important part in the years which followed the overthrow of Napoleon I. The decade which elapsed between the Congress of Vienna and the death of Alexander I was not, it is true, marked by as striking territorial acquisitions as was the earlier period, but it saw Russia one of the leading, if not the leading, Power on the Continent. Alexander's policy was often tortuous, not infrequently contradictory, and sometimes vacillating, but it could never be ignored. In effect, Russia was a far greater force in the world at his death than she had been at his accession.

Nicholas I was heir, not only to the assets which his brother had built up, but also to the liabilities which he had incurred, and not the least important of these latter were in the Near East, where, as has been shown, the Turks were engaged in a losing fight with the Greeks at the time of his accession. The Greek Question, which has been discussed in an earlier chapter, was, however, only one of the problems at issue between the Tsar and the Porte, and the future of the Ottoman Empire obtruded itself upon Nicholas throughout the whole of his reign.

In the late seventeenth, and early eighteenth, century Russia had been on the defensive against the Turks, and her diplomatic relations with them were governed by this fact. Thus by the Peace of Falczi in 1711 Peter the Great had been compelled to purchase the safety of himself and his army by restoring Azov to the Porte, and it was not until the Treaty of Kutchuk-Kainardji in 1774 that Russia finally became the more important of the two Powers. There was something of victorious arrogance in the recital that it was made "in the tent of the Commander-in-Chief, Field Marshal Count de Roumanzow, near the village of Kutchuk-Kainardji, upon the right bank of the Danube", and it began by making a clean sweep of all previous treaties between Russia and the Porte. The territorial clauses marked a definite step in the Russian advance to the south and south-west, for the Black Sea ceased to be an Ottoman lake, and the Sultan's European dominions were bounded by the Bug. Even more important were the establishment of a permanent Russian embassy at Constantinople and the erection of a new Greek church at Galata, which was to be under the protection of Russia, and on behalf of which and its clergy the Russian ambassador had at all times the right to make representations to the Porte: this clause was soon interpreted so as to give St. Petersburg an excuse for interference on behalf of the Greek Church generally. Lastly, the Tsarina exacted promises for the better administration of Moldavia and Wallachia, and reserved the right of remonstrance if these promises were not kept.

Such in its main outlines was the Treaty of Kutchuk-Kainardji which formed the basis of the conduct of Russo-Turkish relations until the Crimean War. The aims of St. Petersburg never varied during this period, and they were the aggrandisement of Russia at the expense of the Ottoman Empire. The attempts to attain them varied from time to time, but the Treaty of Kutchuk-Kainardji remained as their starting-point and their justification.

The next milestone is the Treaty of Jassy in 1792. This advanced the Russian frontier to the Dniester, and restored Moldavia to the Sultan on condition that he carried out the terms settled at Kutchuk-Kainardji. In 1812 there was another treaty, this time at Bucharest, concluded under the auspices of the British government, which wished to free the Russian armies for the struggle with Napoleon. Bessarabia was now ceded to the Tsar, and this fixed the Russo-Turkish frontier in Europe at the Pruth: it also confirmed the provisions of the treaties of 1774 and 1792. A new departure, however, was a reference to Serbia, for Article 8 recited that "there can be no doubt that the Porte, in accordance with its principles, will show kindness to the Serbians, as a people long subject and tributary to it", but it went on to state that it had nevertheless been thought proper, "in consideration of the share which the Serbians have taken in the war, to make a solemn agreement for their safety". The Porte therefore promised that while it would continue to garrison the strong places it would allow the Serbs "such liberties as are enjoyed by the islands of the Archipelago; and, as a token of its generosity, will leave to them the administration of their internal affairs".

Such was the position when Nicholas I ascended the throne. Russia had been, over a period of years, taking advantage of the decline of the Ottoman Empire to acquire one province after another, and at the same time she was coming forward as the champion of the Christian subjects of the Porte, who were beginning to regain their national consciousness. During the latter part of Alexander's reign there had, it is true, been a marked cessation of Russian activity in the Levant, due to the influence of Metternich, who wished at all costs to avoid a clash between the interests of the Tsar and those of his own master, but Alexander and the Austrian Chancellor quarrelled in the summer of 1825, and the restraining influence of Vienna was removed.

That Nicholas was determined to continue the policy of his predecessors was soon apparent, for on March 17th, 1826, while Wellington was still in St. Petersburg, and before the Protocol had been signed, he sent an ultimatum to the Porte demanding the evacuation of the Principalities, the release of certain Serb deputies, and the immediate despatch to the frontier of plenipotentiaries for the purpose of arranging a final settlement. At first the Sultan showed a disposition to fight, but the mutiny of the Janissaries in June left him defenceless, and at the beginning of October he was compelled to sign the Treaty of Akkerman, of which mention has already been made. Its object was "to determine the manner of putting in force all the articles of the Treaty of Bucharest which have not been executed by the Porte since 1812", and it proceeds to describe how this was to be effected. The Treaty of Akkerman, however, was not, as we have seen, destined to be operative for long, and at the conclusion of the Russo-Turkish War of 1828–1829 it was replaced by the Treaty of Adrianople.

The general implications of this agreement have been discussed in an earlier chapter, but by no means the least significant aspect was the interest displayed by the Tsar in the Christian nationalities under Turkish rule. The Hospodars of Wallachia and Moldavia were in future to be elected, not for seven years, but for life, and were to have full liberty in the conduct of the internal affairs of the Principalities, in which, moreover, no Mohammedan was to be allowed to reside. As regards Serbia, the relevant clauses of the Treaty of Bucharest were to be put into effect by the Porte. The provisions for freedom of commerce contained, in addition to the usual stipulations for navigation of the Black Sea and the Dardanelles, promises to the effect that Russian merchants should be under the exclusive jurisdiction of their own consuls, and that their ships should not be liable to visitation by Ottoman authorities even when they were lying in Turkish harbours. The Treaty of Adrianople was signed on September 14th, 1829, and it was described by that strong Turcophil, the Duke of Wellington, "as the death-blow to the independence of the Ottoman Porte, and the forerunner of the dissolution and extinction of its power".

In actual fact the Treaty of Adrianople was followed by a change in the attitude of Russia towards Turkey. Nicholas and his Chancellor, Nesselrode, were far from being Pan-Slav chauvi- nists, and they showed at every turn their desire to co-operate with the other Powers, always provided that what they considered to be the vital interests of their own country were adequately safeguarded. By the end of the third decade of the nineteenth century the world was a great deal smaller than it had been even a generation before, and it was clear that the rest of Europe would not stand idly by to watch Russia annexing one Turkish province after another, as in the days of Catherine II and Alexander I. When Nicholas first came to the throne he took the view that provided he did nothing to offend British susceptibilities he could rely upon enjoying a relatively free hand in the Near East, but he soon discovered that Britain was an uncertain ally on account of the ever-changing political scene at Westminster. Then, in 1830, came the Polish rising and the recrudescence of revolution in many parts of Europe: this at once brought St. Petersburg and Vienna together again in defence of the established order, but it also estranged them somewhat from the Western Powers. Such being the case, the Tsar could not afford to offend Metternich by the pursuit of his immediate predecessor's aggressive policy in respect of Turkey.

In these circumstances the alternatives seemed to be war with the other Powers or partition with them. The Tsar chose a third course, namely the preservation of the Ottoman Empire as a weak state dependent as far as possible upon the support of Russia. This policy appeared to ensure all the advantages of a more adventurous one without any of the risks. In effect, the attitude of Russia towards Turkey in the nineteenth century is reminiscent of that towards Poland in the eighteenth, and it was governed by much the same factors. In the present instance the progress of events favoured Nicholas, for the prowess of Mehemet Ali made Mahmud dependent upon the Tsar. By the beginning of February, 1833, Ibrahim had over-run Anatolia, and the Sultan was at his last gasp. "A drowning man", said the Seraskier Pasha, "clings to a serpent", and the Tsar was not slow to take advantage of his opportunity. By the middle of April the Sea of Marmora was crowded with Russian men-of-war, while Russian troops to the number of some thirteen thousand were encamped on the Asiatic shore of the Bosphorus. On April 27th the curious spectacle was witnessed of the Padishah reviewing on Turkish soil a Russian army which had come to protect him against his own subject, the Pasha of Egypt. Times had indeed changed since Mahmud had sent that same Pasha's son to uphold Ottoman power in Greece, and since he had signed the Treaty of Adrianople with his present protector. Nevertheless, there was a price to be paid for such help, and on July 8th, 1833, there was signed the Treaty of Unkiar Skelessi.

The public articles of this agreement provided for nothing more than mutual aid and succour between the contracting parties in case of need, but by an additional clause it was arranged that Russia should waive her rights to assistance in men and money under the treaty in return for an undertaking by the Porte to close the Dardanelles to the warships of all nations *au besoin*. The British ambassador was not slow in securing a copy of the complete treaty, and the Seraskier Pasha, who had no love for Russia, explained that *au besoin* could best be translated "at the demand of the Tsar". Both Great Britain and France protested against the treaty, but Nicholas, still under the influence of the Polish rising, was in no mood to listen to them.

Indeed, pressure of events had revived, albeit in a modified form, the old Holy Alliance. In March, 1832, the Tsar had proposed to Prussia a league of the three Eastern monarchies for the support of Divine Right against the two Powers which had "the courage to profess aloud rebellion and the overthrow of all stability". In September of the following year Nicholas, Ferdinand of Austria, and the Crown Prince of Prussia met at Münchengrätz, and their deliberations there were embodied in a formal Convention. It was agreed that the three Powers should combine, not to partition, but to maintain the integrity of, the Ottoman Empire;

while by separate articles the contracting parties undertook to oppose any combination threatening the sovereign power of the Sultan, either by a change of dynasty or by an extension of the rule of Mehemet Ali. Finally—and ominously reminiscent of the fate of Poland—Austria and Russia agreed, in the event of the failure of their efforts to preserve the Sultan's heritage intact, to act in perfect harmony in any settlement of the reversion. Metternich advised that the terms of this transaction should be communicated to London and Paris, but Nicholas preferred to follow the tradition of mystery inherent in Russian diplomacy rather than disclose the Convention to the two Powers whom he chose to regard as for the present outside the European Concert.

Relations between Great Britain and Russia, so good during the latter part of Canning's life, had, indeed, much deteriorated. There were two main reasons for this. One lay in the differences between the two countries in Asia. Both Powers were expanding, and men were beginning to ask what would happen when the advancing tides met. In 1835, for example, obstacles were placed by the Porte in the way of a British attempt to establish a new mail-route to India by steamers on the Euphrates, and three years later Persia made an attack upon Herat: in both cases it was believed in London that Russia was behind what had taken place, and that she was moving in the direction of India. To this latter rumour Nicholas thought it worth while to give a personal denial: Russia, he stated, had no other aim than to secure her legitimate share of the trade of Central Asia, hitherto monopolized by England, while she might, in her turn, justly complain of the intrigues of British agents in the border khanates and of the presence of a British force on Persian soil. Out of these conflicting suspicions developed the First Afghan War, which was to end so disastrously for Britain.

The second cause of estrangement lay in the Tsar's distrust of the political movements in contemporary England. He declared that William IV, by giving his consent to the Reform Bill of 1832, had "thrown his crown into the gutter", and he had no confidence in the Whigs. In time his fears subsided, but they were sufficiently lively for some years to prevent, when taken in conjunction with the rivalry between the two Powers in Central Asia, any improvement in Anglo-Russian relations. Such being the case, Thiers had good reason for his belief that St. Petersburg and London were unlikely to unite in opposition to French schemes in the Near East.

This conviction was belied by the course of events 1839-1840, and Nicholas, reassured by the Conservative victory at the General Election of 1841, returned to his old policy of co-operation with Great Britain in the Near East. In 1844 he came to England, when Aberdeen was Foreign Secretary in Sir Robert Peel's administration, and the two men had a frank and confidential talk as to the attitude which their two countries should adopt in the event of the demise of the "Sick Man of Europe", as the Tsar termed the Ottoman Empire. Nicholas believed that he and Aberdeen were thinking along the same lines, for the Foreign Secretary did not dissent from what was suggested to him. The Tsar, on his return to St. Petersburg, caused Nesselrode to embody the substance of these conversations in a memorandum which he duly sent to Aberdeen, who received it without protest, and deposited it in the archives of the Foreign Office, where it remained undisturbed for a decade. This misunderstanding was, unfortunately, typical of the irresolute diplomacy which ranged Britain in opposition to Russia in the Crimean War. First of all, however, it is necessary to see how the crisis of 1854 arose.

In the middle of the eighteenth century Louis XV had obtained for France a treaty right to the custody of the Holy Places in or near Jerusalem which were objects of veneration and pilgrimage to all Christendom, whether of the Latin or the Orthodox rite. For more than a hundred years, however, France had done little or nothing to carry out the duties thus entrusted to her, while the Greek Church, backed by the growing might of Russia, had repaired the shrines which France was permitting to fall into decay, and it had even obtained permits from the Porte authorizing it to do so. In 1850, however, a new situation arose, for Louis Napoleon, at that time Prince-President, was anxious for Catholic support in France, and he renewed the French claim to the custody of the Holy Places; after lengthy negotiations the Porte accepted the French contentions on a number of points, but only to find that it had thereby aroused the wrath of the Tsar. Fresh fuel was heaped on this fire when the Second Republic became the Second Empire: Nicholas despised the new Emperor of the French, and he marked his displeasure by addressing Napoleon III in a letter not as "Brother" but as "Friend". Whatever may have been his personal inclinations, the new master of France was in too insecure a position not to resent publicly so marked an affront.

These were the circumstances in which the Tsar, at the

beginning of January, 1853, opened his mind to Sir Hamilton
Seymour, the British ambassador in St. Petersburg. He used much
the same language as he had employed nine years before, and as
Lord Aberdeen had recently become Prime Minister, the Tsar
felt that he had chosen an opportune moment to re-open negotiations. The Turk, he said, was very ill, and it would be a grave
misfortune if no provision were made for the contingency of his
demise. He did not wish to see Constantinople in the possession
of Russia or of any other Great Power; at the same time he would
not consent to the restoration of the old Byzantine Empire, to the
extension of the boundaries of Greece, or to the partition of the
Ottoman Empire into a number of small states. The Principalities
already enjoyed independence under the protection of Russia, and
he saw no reason why Serbia, Bulgaria, and the other Turkish
provinces should not be given a similar status. As for Great Britain,
she might safeguard her communications with India by the
occupation of Egypt and Crete. To these proposals the British
government turned a deaf ear: it did not believe that the Sick
Man was so ill as the Tsar thought, and in the event of his death it
considered that the disposal of his inheritance could best be
effected by a congress of the Powers.

Convinced in his own mind that Turkey could not survive,
Nicholas proceeded to act in such a way as to precipitate a crisis.
He sent Prince Menshikoff to Constantinople to demand that the
Orthodox Church in the Ottoman Empire should be placed under
Russian protection; this demand was, in fact, the logical outcome
of the Treaty of Kutchuk-Kainardji and the various Russo-
Turkish settlements which had succeeded it. The Porte was in a
panic, but on the advice of Lord Stratford de Redcliffe, the
British ambassador, it rejected the Russian proposal, and Prince
Menshikoff left Constantinople in May. Lord Stratford had
acted on his own responsibility, and he had completely altered the
situation. Great Britain, who had originally been no party to the
dispute concerning the Holy Places, at once became a principal to
the quarrel, and this was emphasized by the appearance of an
Anglo-French squadron at the entrance to the Dardanelles. Lord
Stratford had brought war considerably nearer.

At this point Austrian diplomacy became extremely active in
its efforts to prevent a rupture, and on more than one occasion it
appeared likely to be successful. Nevertheless it proved impossible
to get Turkey and Russia to agree without some reservations, while

there can be no doubt that Lord Stratford persuaded the Porte to adopt a much more intransigent attitude than it would otherwise have done, and he must bear a large part of the responsibility for what subsequently took place. With his approval the Sultan, in October, 1853, called upon Russia to evacuate the Principalities, which she had occupied on the failure of Prince Menshikoff's mission, within fifteen days, and added that a refusal would be considered as tantamount to a declaration of war : in pursuance of this threat a Turkish army crossed the Danube. Once more Vienna attempted to keep the peace, and Austria, France, Great Britain, and Prussia offered to mediate between the combatants. It was too late, for the Russians had not been slow to retaliate, and on the last day of November a Turkish squadron on its way from the Bosphorus to Batum was attacked at Sinope by the Russian fleet, and destroyed. The "massacre" of Sinope, as the incident was at once termed in London and Paris, inflamed popular feeling in both capitals, and made the participation of the Western Powers practically inevitable, although, given the circumstances, it is difficult to resist the conclusion that the Russians had very considerable justification for their action : fighting had already begun in the Principalities, while the junction of the Allied and Turkish fleets was only a question of time.

The situation thus produced was in no small measure due to differences within the British government. There can be little doubt but that, for reasons of internal policy, the French Emperor was by no means averse from war; Lord Stratford in the last resort was prepared to fight rather than see the Ottoman Empire a Russian protectorate; but it was the vacillation in Downing Street which really made the preservation of peace impossible. As the late Sir Spencer Walpole wrote, "Lord Aberdeen thought that peace could be preserved by endeavouring to meet what was reasonable in the demands of Russia. Lord Palmerston thought, on the contrary, that peace was to be secured by convincing Russia that, if war broke out, she would have to deal with other Powers besides Turkey. If Lord Aberdeen had stood alone, he might have averted the war by conciliation. If Lord Palmerston had stood alone, he might have averted war by action. But Lord Palmerston's action robbed Lord Aberdeen's conciliation of its grace; and Lord Aberdeen's conciliation took the strength out of Lord Palmerston's action."

So Great Britain, in the wake of France, drifted into war

against the one Power in Europe most desirous of co-operating
with her. At the beginning of January, 1854, the Allied fleets
entered the Black Sea with orders to compel all Russian warships
to return to the harbour of Sevastopol, and at the end of the same
month the French Emperor, with the approval of the British
Government, sent an autograph letter to the Tsar suggesting that
the Russians should withdraw from the Principalities, the Allies
from the Black Sea, and there should be direct negotiations
between St. Petersburg and Constantinople. There was, however,
a sting in the tail of this epistle, for it concluded, "If, from a motive
difficult to understand, Your Majesty should refuse this proposal,
then France as well as England will be compelled to leave to the
fate of arms and the chances of war that which might now be
decided by reason and justice". Nicholas replied that "Russia
would prove herself in 1854 what she had been in 1812", and the
ambassadors on both sides were withdrawn. On February 27th a
Franco-British ultimatum was presented to the Tsar, who refused
to answer it, and at the end of March the Western Powers declared
war.

Nicholas I died on March 2nd, 1855, in the middle of a war
which reflected more credit upon the soldiers in the field than
upon the governments which had sent them there. His failure
appeared to be complete, for Great Britain had spurned his
advances, and the Russian winter had failed him, yet if his shade
was conscious of what was happening upon earth it must have
derived some satisfaction from the fact that, after slaughter upon
a scale which he never contemplated, the territorial position in
the Near East was seventy years later settled on lines very similar
to those which he had in 1853 suggested to Lord Aberdeen.

During the progress of the Crimean War a change came over
those who were engaged in it. Napoleon developed satisfaction
at the successes of the French arms and consciousness of the strain
which the struggle was imposing upon his finances, so that in due
course he became an advocate of peace. The war had served his
turn, and he wanted to put an end to it. Great Britain, on the
other hand, had, as usual, started badly, and public opinion was
anxious that the British Army should acquire fresh laurels before
peace was made. As for Russia, the new Tsar, Alexander II, was
by no means indisposed to terminate a struggle which was now
turning against him, and in which there was no inconsiderable
danger of fresh enemies participating. Accordingly, after a

preliminary failure to effect a settlement at Vienna in 1855, the Congress of Paris opened at the end of February in the following year.

The participants were the Allied Powers, namely France, Great Britain, Sardinia, and Turkey; Russia; and one neutral, Austria. Their task proved easier than might have been anticipated, and the Treaty of Paris was concluded on March 30th, 1856. By this agreement the Black Sea was neutralized, and the Russian and Turkish governments undertook "not to establish or to maintain upon that coast any military-maritime arsenal". So far as the lot of the Christians in the Ottoman Empire was concerned, the Sultan had, four days before the Congress opened, issued a *hatti-houmayoum* promising them complete religious equality before the law, and the Contracting Powers recognized "the high value of this communication", though they were careful to add that "it cannot, in any case, give to the said Powers the right to interfere, either collectively or separately, in the relation of His Majesty the Sultan with his subjects, nor in the internal administration of his Empire". The Danubian Principalities were granted entire independence under the suzerainty of the Porte, and "no exclusive protection shall be exercised over them by any of the Guaranteeing Powers"; there was also to be "no separate right of interference in their internal affairs", while Russia was compelled to cede a strip of Bessarabia to Moldavia. For the rest, the navigation of the Danube was opened to all nations, and an international commission of the riparian states set up to give effect to this provision; the Russo-Turkish frontier in Asia was restored to its position before the war; there was to be no armed intervention in Serbia "without previous agreement between the High Contracting Powers"; and Austria, France, and Great Britain pledged themselves severally and collectively to regard any infraction of any part of the treaty as a cause of war.

It is easy to be cynical with regard to the Treaty of Paris. The decree, under which the Sultan promised religious liberty and equality to his subjects, was never carried into effect; the neutrality of the Black Sea was only maintained until 1870; the strip of Bessarabia ceded by Russia was restored twenty-two years later; and none of the Great Powers, when the integrity of the Ottoman Empire was assailed in 1878, intervened in its defence. These observations are true, but they overlook the fact that the treaty did achieve the object for which the Crimean War had been fought. Russia was compelled to renounce the privileged position within the Sultan's dominions, which she had built up over a period of years by a series of agreements commencing with the Treaty of Kutchuk-Kainardji. It is the fashion to speak of the Crimean War as a political blunder, but in the circumstances it can hardly be denied that the Treaty of Paris was a complete diplomatic success for the victors.

Although the affairs of the Ottoman Empire played a large part in the foreign policy of Nicholas I, they were far from being his only concern in that field. When he ascended the throne the Holy Alliance had recently been denounced by his predecessor, but in spite of this there always existed one bond between St. Petersburg, Vienna, and Berlin, namely Poland. The common interest of the three Powers in keeping the Poles in subjection always brought them together, however much other issues might tend to force them apart, and this state of affairs may be said to have continued until the fall of Bismarck. The new Tsar had not long succeeded his brother when the Polish rising of 1830 afforded an admirable example of this community of interest.

The Polish revolutionary party at once appealed for support to the signatories of the Treaty of Vienna against the determination of Nicholas to liquidate the Congress-Kingdom, but without any success. Prussia, from the very beginning, took the most drastic action to prevent any assistance reaching the insurgents from Posen; nor was this all, for she departed from neutrality not only by hindering the Poles from communicating with western Europe, but also by supplying provisions and ammunition to the Russian forces, and by allowing them to cross Prussian territory. Austria played a somewhat deeper game, at any rate until the result of the struggle was certain, for Metternich held secret conferences with the Polish envoy, and the Poles were deluded by the prospect of an Archduke for their ruler; yet at the same time Nicholas was kept informed of their projects. The conduct of France was hardly less equivocal, for although, in the early weeks of 1831, La Fayette made spirited appeals in the Chamber on behalf of the Poles, the French government was intercepting the correspondence of the Polish envoy in Paris, and communicating its contents to Nicholas, in the hope of thereby inclining him favourably towards the July Monarchy. In England there was a good deal of vague sympathy for the Poles, but that was all: the

Reform Bill and the affairs of the Low Countries were absorbing the attention of government and people alike.

In actual fact there was very little that the Western Powers could have done, once Russia had decided to infringe the provisions of the Treaty of Vienna, and Austria and Prussia had assented. The days had long gone by when France could intervene effectively in eastern Europe, and Britain was powerless without an ally on the spot. So Poland was crushed once more, though in the process Belgium was given a chance to establish her independence. Such being the case, it would probably have been better had the British and French governments kept silent, but under pressure of public opinion they made representations to St. Petersburg after the insurrection had been crushed. To a despatch from Palmerston at the end of 1831 Nesselrode denied the right of England to interfere in Russo-Polish affairs, and there the matter had perforce to rest.

This revelation of the weakness of the Western Powers in lands where they had no allies and where their navies could not operate was not lost upon the rest of the world, and when the dispute over the Spanish Marriages had estranged London and Paris, it was clear that this feebleness was enhanced. Accordingly, in November, 1846, Austria, Prussia, and Russia, without consulting either France or Great Britain, decided to suppress the Free Republic of Cracow, and to authorize its absorption into the Habsburg dominions. Palmerston protested, and the grounds upon which he did so were perfectly sound: he urged that if there was a case for the revision of the Vienna settlement it should be discussed by all the signatories, and in any event it was highly improper for the Power which so stoutly championed the *status quo* on the Rhine and the Po to violate it so flagrantly on the Vistula. Both the Foreign Secretary's arguments and his sarcasm went unheeded, for Metternich was secure in the support of the Tsar, and the Republic of Cracow perished unaided.

This was neither the last nor the most notable occasion on which Nicholas gave a helping-hand to Austria. He has been described as "a straightforward, honourable gentleman, an affectionate husband and father, a loyal brother, a sincere friend, and a brave enemy"; these personal characteristics have to be taken into account in connection with the assistance which he gave to Francis Joseph in 1849 to suppress the Hungarian revolt under Kossuth. There was undoubtedly an impulse of chivalry behind his attitude at this time, though it is true that there were also other factors at work, apart from the fact that Kossuth and his colleagues were desirous of promoting trouble in Poland. Nicholas had a great fear of revolution reaching Russia, and he believed that the best way to prevent this was to crush it before it reached his frontier; in view of what happened two generations after his death, his policy is the more understandable. In the present instance his forces restored Hungary to the Habsburgs, but when the Crimean War came five years later Austria stood aside—an attitude which was never forgiven either by Nicholas I or by Alexander II, and which far away at Frankfurt was being noted with satisfaction by the Prussian delegate to the German Diet, Otto von Bismarck.

CHAPTER XVIII

THE UNIFICATION OF GERMANY, 1815–1871

T HE nineteenth century, like the sixteenth, was particularly fertile in important events and movements which were to leave their mark upon future generations, but none has proved so momentous in its consequences as the unification of Germany. Moreover, unlike the similar development in Italy, it possessed an international aspect from the very beginning, for before there could be a united Reich the question of supremacy had to be fought out between Austria and Prussia, and this struggle had very wide repercussions, some of which have already been discussed. For the rest, the history of the unification of Germany falls into two periods, of which the second is by far the more important, and the dividing-line is the appointment of Bismarck as Premier and Foreign Minister of Prussia on September 23rd, 1862.

The conflict between Austria and Prussia might have come earlier had it not been for the skilful diplomacy of Metternich in the former, and for the lack of statesmanship in the latter. Even as late as 1856, the King of Prussia was not invited, as was the Austrian Emperor, to send a representative to participate in the deliberations of the Congress of Paris, but merely to sign the treaty which crowned its work. In foreign policy Prussia was greatly under the influence of Russia, and its attitude towards Austria often depended in no small measure upon the relations existing between St. Petersburg and Vienna. Prussia was the Cinderella among the Great Powers. In these circumstances it is hardly remarkable that no decided lead was given by Berlin, though the Zollverein did much to strengthen the Prussian position. In the last resort Prussian statesmen were usually brought to heel by the crack of the Austrian whip, and when Frederick William IV refused the Imperial Crown, offered to him by the National Parliament at Frankfurt in 1849, one of the motives which most influenced him was fear of offending Austria.

Nor was this state of affairs materially affected by the fall of Metternich and the revelation of Austrian weakness in face of the Hungarian rebellion, as was proved by the crisis over Hesse-Cassel in 1850. The exact causes of the dispute concern German domestic politics, and it will suffice to say that Austria and Prussia took opposite sides in a quarrel between the Elector and his subjects, thus coming within an ace of war; indeed, five Austrian riflemen and one Prussian horse were actually wounded. The upshot of the controversy was that Prussia gave way at a conference held at Olmütz, and throughout the country there was a widespread feeling of humiliation. This was not without its effect nine years later, when Austria was being defeated by France, though Prussian resentment did not go so far as to allow the national enemy a free hand.

This somewhat confused period came to an end in 1862 with the advent to power in Prussia of Bismarck, probably the greatest figure in the nineteenth century, with the doubtful exception of Napoleon I. He was born in 1815 in the Old March of Brandenburg, and after being for some years a member of the Prussian Diet he was sent to represent his King at Frankfurt. Not that Frederick William IV by any means approved of Bismarck, for he wrote beside his name on a list of suggested ministers, "A red reactionary thirsting for blood. Only to be employed when the day comes for using bayonets mercilessly." At Frankfurt the future Imperial Chancellor had an unrivalled opportunity of obtaining a first-hand knowledge of German problems, and by 1856 he had made up his mind as to what the future held in store: "I am convinced", he wrote, "that in a short time we shall have to fight for our very existence against Austria, and that we are incapable of avoiding this fight, because the course of events in Germany permits of no other development."

Bismarck's next appointment, at the age of forty-three, was to be Prussian minister at St. Petersburg, and his residence there was to exercise a very great influence upon Europe as a whole. He had studied with extreme care the history of Russo-Prussian relations during the previous century, and he had come to certain conclusions. With a friendly Russia there was very little that Prussia could not effect, but a hostile Russia would spell her ruin, for in that case she would be faced with a war upon two fronts: therefore there must be no breach between St. Petersburg and Berlin. During the four years that he spent in the Russian capital Bismarck prepared the ground for the policy which he was to pursue until his dismissal by William II in 1890, and in this he was aided by the fact that Alexander II was the nephew of the Prince Regent of Prussia, soon to be William I.

P

Nevertheless, it was the internal situation which actually brought Bismarck to power. Prussia was in the middle of a constitutional crisis, and the question at issue was whether the army was to be answerable to King or Parliament. If the Liberal majority in the Lower House succeeded in its endeavour to establish Parliamentary control by means of an annual revision of the army estimates, Prussia would be transformed overnight from an autocratic to a constitutional monarchy of the British type. To prevent this William I summoned Bismarck to take office, and the new Prime Minister's first words gave the clue to his policy both at home and abroad. "The great issues of the day", he told the Prussian legislators, "will not be decided by speeches and majority resolutions . . . . but by blood and iron."

The fundamental considerations which governed Bismarck's foreign policy, first as Prime Minister and then as Imperial Chancellor, were, firstly, good relations with Russia; secondly, the prevention of the formation of groups of Powers which might be opposed to his projects; and, thirdly, the isolation of any potential enemy. Not long after his accession to office fortune gave him a chance to unite Berlin and St. Petersburg more closely than ever.

This was the insurrection which broke out in Russian Poland in January, 1863, and its leaders at once called upon the Prussian and Austrian Poles to help them. Within little more than a fortnight General von Alvensleben, on the instructions of Bismarck, concluded an agreement with the Russian government to set up a military cordon along the Russo-Prussian frontier to prevent any fugitives from escaping from Russian into Prussian Poland. The Alvensleben Convention served several Prussian purposes. It prevented the rising from spreading across the frontier; it enormously aided the Tsar in the suppression of the rebellion, while, as a recent biographer of Bismarck, Mr. Morrow, has well said, "The merciless crushing of the revolt by the firing-squad, the knout, and banishment to Siberia, would be an object-lesson for Prussian Poles in the dangers of insurrection"; and it established a claim upon Russian gratitude which would be extremely useful in the future. For the moral indignation of the rest of the world Bismarck cared nothing.

This was not, however, the only service which he was able to render the Tsar in connection with Poland. Great Britain, France, and Austria invited the adherence of Prussia to a protest which they were presenting to the Russian government against the treatment of the Polish insurgents. Bismarck bluntly refused to be associated with the protest, thus enabling the Tsar to reject it on the ground that the fate of the Poles was a domestic Russian concern. The upshot of the Polish rising was thus to widen the breach between St. Petersburg and Vienna, and to prove that in the last resort Great Britain and France were either unable or unwilling to back their threats by force. Neither of these lessons was lost upon Bismarck.

Later in the same year he proved to Austria that Prussia was no longer what she had been at Olmütz. In August the Austrian Emperor visited William I at Bad Gastein and informed him of his intention to summon a congress of the German Princes and Free Cities to discuss the reform of the Reich constitution, and among other proposals was one for a federal directory composed of Austria, Prussia, and Bavaria, and three other members chosen in rotation from the lesser states. Bismarck saw at once that this would mean that Prussia would find herself in a permanent minority of one, for the South German states could be relied upon to follow the lead of Vienna; nevertheless it was only under the threat of his resignation that he could persuade the King not to attend the congress, which, in the absence of Prussia, broke up. A severe blow had been dealt at Austrian prestige, and Germany had been shown that its problems could only be solved with the consent of Berlin.

Nor was this all, for Bismarck followed up his success by a circular note to the German states in which he insisted upon the inseparable identity of Prussian and German interests, and declared that a German Parliament worth the name must be representative of the whole German people and elected by it. This document was a subtle appeal to range German national feeling on the side of Prussia in her struggle with Austria, and it was highly successful. Bismarck had thus scored two notable diplomatic victories before he was confronted by the first great international crisis of his career, namely the problem of Schleswig-Holstein.

This was one of the most complicated questions with which European diplomacy had to deal: only three persons, according to Lord Palmerston, really understood it; one was the Prince Consort, who was dead, the second was a Danish professor, who was in a lunatic asylum, and the third was himself, who had forgotten it. The relations of the duchies with the kingdom of

Denmark had undergone many changes which there is no need to notice here, and the Congress of Vienna had left Schleswig outside the Germanic Confederation while Holstein and Lauenburg were included in it. When Christian VIII succeeded his father, Frederick VI, in 1839, the elder male line of the House of Oldenburg was obviously on the point of extinction, since the new monarch's only son and heir had no children. At once the question of the succession was raised, and there were two views as to what should be done. The German attitude was that as female heirs could succeed to the crown of Denmark, while the Salic law applied to the duchies, the succession to the latter should pass to the Dukes of Augustenburg. The Danes, on the other hand, claimed that the monarchy was indivisible.

In the revolutionary year 1848 matters came to a head. Frederick VII, who had by then succeeded Christian VIII, promulgated a constitution under which Schleswig, while retaining its local autonomy, became an integral part of Denmark. On this a rising took place in the duchies, and Prussian troops marched in on the grounds that they were independent states and that their union was indissoluble. The other Powers, however, were not prepared to see the dismemberment of the Danish monarchy, and after lengthy negotiations there was signed in 1852 the Treaty of London by the five Great Powers as well as by Denmark and Sweden. This treaty was based on the following terms: Germany gave up the political union between the duchies, while Denmark abandoned the incorporation of Schleswig with the Danish kingdom, and at the same time promised not to attempt this at any future date. The extreme views on both sides having been thus eliminated, it was hoped that peace would be maintained. It was further agreed that the heir both to Denmark and the duchies was Prince Christian of Glücksburg.

For eleven years there was a somewhat uneasy peace, until in March, 1863, the Danish government, without any previous consultation with the estates of Schleswig-Holstein, issued a patent which foreshadowed the separation of Schleswig from Holstein and its incorporation in Denmark. Feeling soon began to run high in Germany, and the Federal Diet, although it was not a party to the Treaty of London, ordered the Danish government to restore the historic *status quo*. The reply of Copenhagen was at once to give the patent the force of law, whereupon the Diet ordered a Federal Execution in Holstein. By this time Frederick

VII had been succeeded by Christian IX, but the German Diet went back on the settlement of 1852, and it was in the name of the Duke of Augustenburg that Saxon and Hanoverian troops occupied Holstein: by the first days of 1864 the duchy was in their hands.

Both parties had now put themselves in the wrong: the Danes by the incorporation of Schleswig in Denmark, and the Federal Diet by its recognition of the claims of the Duke of Augustenburg. It was clear that the next step lay with the Great Powers, and of these Prussia was the most intimately concerned. Bismarck had already made up his mind, and he was determined that the duchies should pass into Prussian hands. For him it was not "an affair of right and wrong, but of force—and we have it". The geographic and strategic position of the duchies was extremely important to Prussia; they constituted a back-door through which she could be attacked, while they contained potential naval bases that could be of the greatest use. Accordingly, Bismarck opened his diplomatic campaign by taking his stand upon the inviolability of treaties; when it came to annexing the duchies he would prefer to do so from a foreign monarch rather than from a German Prince. For the moment this decision won him great unpopularity with the German chauvinists, but it went a long way towards blinding the Powers as to his real intentions.

The first step was to secure the co-operation of Austria, for if she championed the cause of the Diet the position of Prussia inside Germany would become very difficult. Bismarck argued, therefore, that the two countries should take their stand on the treaty of 1852, though if the Danes refused to give way Prussia and Austria would themselves be entitled to disregard it. The line of argument carried conviction at Vienna, and the two German Powers agreed to send an ultimatum to Denmark. This was, as Bismarck knew would be the case, rejected, and by February, 1864, Austrian and Prussian troops were pouring into Schleswig.

Meanwhile the position of the Germanic Federation and its Diet had become truly Gilbertian. It refused to associate itself with the measures of Berlin and Vienna, so that a somewhat puzzled world witnessed the spectacle of a Federal occupation of Holstein to upset the settlement of 1852, while Austrian and Prussian armies were invading Schleswig for the purpose of upholding that same settlement. In short, the Diet had made itself ridiculous, which fitted in very well indeed with the plans of Bismarck. It was the rallying-point of Liberal opinion in Germany, and the Prime Minister of Prussia was the foe of Liberalism both within and without his own country. The progress of the Schleswig-Holstein dispute thus enabled him to strike an effective blow at Liberalism in Prussia by making it a laughing-stock at Frankfurt. The Federal troops withdrew, and the way was clear for the application of more drastic methods.

The efficacy of these was soon seen. The obstinacy of the Danes had provided Bismarck with an excuse for war, but by the beginning of 1864 the aggressive attitude of Prussia and Austria had swung a large section of European opinion over to the Danish side. Such being the case, the hope of the Danes lay in protracting the war, and in tiring out the Germans by attacks upon their commerce, all in the belief that the other Powers would come to their aid. In particular they relied upon Great Britain, and there were several reasons why this should be the case: hostility to the dismemberment of Denmark was universal; the Prince of Wales had recently married a Danish princess; and, above all, as recently as the previous July the Prime Minister, Lord Palmerston, had declared in Parliament that in case of an attack upon the integrity of the Danish monarchy, Denmark would not stand alone. The hopes of a prolonged resistance were, however, dashed by the progress of the Austro-Prussian armies, and before the end of April, 1864, Denmark was at her last gasp. Danish sea-power was unable by itself to redress the balance, and was, in fact, on the point of being challenged by an Austrian squadron from the Adriatic which had got as far as Deal.

At this point hostilities were suspended by an armistice while the Conference of London took place between the parties to the settlement of 1852. From the beginning Bismarck was master of the situation. Trusting to the obstinacy of the Danes, he advanced the most conciliatory proposals in order to prejudice his enemy in the eyes of all Europe by the refusal of them. He demanded, as the price of victory, the union of the duchies as independent states under the sovereignty of Denmark, and the admission of Schleswig to the German Confederation so as to ensure its safety from any future Danish encroachments. At the same time he secretly abetted the agitation in favour of the total severance of the duchies from Denmark, and in London he pointed to this excitement in Germany as ominous of revolution if some concession was not made. His calculations were correct, and the Danes, relying upon British and French support, refused the German demands, with the result that the conference broke up at the end of June.

The Danish government was not long in realizing the mistake it had made. The flower of the French army was far away in Mexico, and Napoleon was unwilling to take any action because he always believed that any alteration in the *status quo* might somehow be made to suit his own ends; moreover, his relations with London were none too good, and the prospects of an Anglo-French understanding were extremely remote, as Bismarck well knew. In Britain neither government nor people was willing to fight in the last resort, and Lord Palmerston's policy of non-intervention was approved by both Houses in the course of a debate in which even the Opposition leaders were careful to deprecate the conclusion that they advocated a recourse to arms. The Prime Minister, it may be noted, laid particular stress on this occasion upon the fact that in his opinion British prestige abroad stood as high as ever, and to assert the contrary was a gratuitous libel upon the country: he then, in words, which, to quote the late Sir A. W. Ward, "took away the breath of all who heard" them, rested the defence of his administration on what, during its five years in office, it had done for the national prosperity. In these circumstances there is much to be said for the quip that Palmerston commenced his official career as member of a government which stood up to Napoleon, and ended it as head of one which went down on its knees to Bismarck. The Prussian statesman himself remarked contemptuously, "I wasted several years of my life by taking it for granted that England was a great nation".

Further armed resistance on the part of the Danes was now out of the question, and on August 1st, 1864, Schleswig-Holstein and Lauenburg, that is to say nearly two-fifths of the Danish kingdom, were handed over to Austria and Prussia. This meant the transfer of about a quarter of a million Danes to German rule. As for the views of the inhabitants of the ceded territory, a British envoy had reported earlier in the crisis that Holstein was for the Duke of Augustenburg from end to end, and that the same attitude was to be noticed among the urban middle-class in Schleswig: the one solution which was nowhere advocated was an Austro-Prussian occupation.

On the morrow of this triumph Bismarck declared, "We confront the question of the duchies like two guests before a succulent dish. One has no appetite and will not eat. Nevertheless he refuses to allow the other who is hungry to devour the food." His foreign policy for the next eighteen months was directed towards the creation of a state of affairs in which Prussia could go to war with Austria in the reasonable certainty that no other Great Power would intervene. To bring this situation about he had to ensure that both European and German opinion should consider Austria to be in the wrong.

Once more his opponent played into his hands, as Austria ever did into the hands of her enemies. The campaign against Denmark had not redounded to her credit, for the commander-in-chief had been a Prussian. In an attempt to retrieve the situation Vienna placed itself at the head of the Augustenburg movement, and demanded Prussian recognition of the Duke as ruler of Schleswig-Holstein. Bismarck had foreseen this move, and had fortified himself against it. Unknown to Austria, he had already offered the throne to the Duke on conditions which would have made him little more than a Prussian provincial governor, and the offer had been refused. Bismarck now informed the Austrian government that he would join in the installation of the Duke upon conditions, which proved to be those already rejected. This action placed Austria in a difficult position: if she agreed she consented to the transformation of the duchies into what would be virtually a Prussian province, while if she refused she would appear to be wrecking a settlement of which the main point was the installation of the Duke of Augustenburg. To escape from the dilemma the Austrian government put pressure on the Diet to demand immediate and unconditional installation on the part of Berlin: Bismarck thereupon told the Diet to mind its own business, and informed Austria that he regarded her action as a breach of the arrangement of 1864, in the spirit if not in the letter.

All the same Bismarck's position was far from being as strong as it appeared, for he had to deal not only with a refractory Parliament but also with a monarch who had by no means been persuaded of the inevitability of war with Austria. William, however, was extremely annoyed when the suggestion was made, even if unofficially, that Prussia might be willing to exchange Silesia for Holstein: at once the shade of Frederick the Great rose between the Hohenzollerns and the Habsburgs, and William grew suspicious of Vienna. Finally, on August 14th, 1865, a settlement was reached. Austria came to terms with Prussia, and by the Convention of Gastein acquired Schleswig while Prussia took Holstein. The two states were to enjoy equal rights in the harbour of Kiel, which it was agreed that Prussia might fortify, while she was also to have the right to construct a canal between the North and Baltic Seas. No mention whatever was made of the claims of the Duke of Augustenburg, and the two Powers destroyed that historic unity of the duchies which they had nominally fought Denmark to maintain. It was little wonder that Bismarck said, "I could never have believed that I would find an Austrian diplomatist who would have signed such a document".

The ensuing eight months were spent, as has been shown, in diplomatic preparation for war with Austria: for the army Roon and Moltke could already answer. In October, 1865, Napoleon promised his neutrality, and on April 8th, 1866, the alliance with Italy was signed. All that was now lacking was a plausible *casus belli* which would make Austria appear to be in the wrong.

On the day following the signature of the Italo-Prussian alliance Bismarck brought forward a motion for Federal reform: a new constitution was to be drawn up by a German national Parliament elected by universal suffrage but in consultation with the Princes. Austria did not, however, reject the proposal, as Bismarck had hoped, but had it referred to a special committee for examination. In spite of its caution on this occasion the Vienna government had decided to bring matters to a head, and at the end of April it repudiated the Convention of Gastein by declaring that the future of the duchies should be settled by the Confederation and the estates of Schleswig-Holstein. By this means Austria hoped to force Prussia into the open, and to find such a pretext for war as would rally the lesser German states to her side. Bismarck retaliated by ordering Prussian troops into Holstein, and by introducing into the Diet a scheme of reform which would exclude all Austrian participation in German affairs. To this Vienna replied by securing the passage in the Diet, by nine votes to six, of a motion ordering a Federal Execution in Prussia on the ground that the latter had violated the Convention of Gastein: furthermore, the Austrian government announced that this motion was tantamount to a declaration of war against Prussia. This was exactly what Bismarck wanted, because it enabled him to persuade his King and his fellow-countrymen that the war had been forced upon them. On June 20th, 1866, it was declared at

Berlin, and on July 3rd it was virtually at an end with the Austrian defeat at Sadowa.

The completeness of Bismarck's success cannot blind us to the risks which he ran. Until the very last moment the prospect of war was extremely unpopular, and there was always the chance that William, yielding to popular clamour and his own instincts, might take him at his word and accept his resignation. Again, had the war gone badly, or had the issue remained for long in doubt, Napoleon would have exerted pressure on the Rhine, and Prussia, greatly weakened, would have been compelled to fight on two fronts with the certainty of disaster. In that event Bismarck would have gone down to history as the man who ruined his country, and who conspired with the national enemy behind the back of his own monarch. That this did not happen was because his faith in the Prussian sword was not misplaced. Once more it was proved how much diplomacy can achieve with force at its disposal, and how little when that condition is not fulfilled.

Bismarck had, however, one more victory to win, and that was over that section of Prussian military opinion which desired the humiliation of Austria. On the night of Sadowa he had remarked, "The struggle is decided. The next thing to do is to regain Austria's friendship." He had his way, as was to be seen in the Preliminaries of Nikolsburg (July) and the Treaty of Prague (August). Austria did not lose an acre of her German territory, and she managed to preserve Saxony intact, but her other allies were severely punished: the kingdom of Hanover, the electorate of Hesse-Cassel, part of Hesse-Darmstadt, Nassau, and the Free City of Frankfurt, as well as Schleswig-Holstein and Lauenburg, were incorporated in Prussia. The Germanic Confederation was dissolved, and in its place there was set up a North German Confederation, with its boundary at the Main.

This settlement marked the end of one epoch in the history of central Europe, and the beginning of another. The Habsburgs were driven out of the Reich, and compelled to seek compensation in a policy in the Near East which fifty-two years later was to prove their undoing. The North German Confederation meant the Prussianization of Northern Germany, while the secret offensive and defensive alliances which Bismarck at once concluded with the South German states closed the road by which French armies had so often penetrated into Germany. The epoch which ended at Prague had begun with the Thirty Years' War and Louis

XIV; that which commenced in 1866 was to include the Four Years' War and the ambitions of Adolf Hitler. In a sentence, the political centre of gravity in central Europe had shifted from Vienna to Berlin.

The course of events between Sadowa and Sedan has been related on an earlier page. The German Empire came into existence at Versailles in January, 1871, and on May 10th of the same year the Treaty of Frankfurt was signed between France and Germany by which the former ceded Alsace-Lorraine and paid an indemnity of two hundred million pounds. Bismarck had thus in nine years achieved German unity under the leadership of Prussia, and had made Germany the dominant Power on the mainland of Europe. All this he had been able to effect because he knew so well how to co-ordinate arms and diplomacy, and because he carefully avoided a breach with Great Britain or Russia.

CHAPTER XIX

THE DECLINE OF TURKEY, 1856-1878

THE Treaty of Paris did much to ease Russian pressure upon the Ottoman Empire, but it could not stay the latter's disintegration, for the real weakness of Turkey was internal. "I did not condemn the Crimean War", Lord Salisbury wrote, "because our grounds for fighting were insufficient, but because it was not our interest to undertake the championship of a Power so clearly moribund as Turkey." The years which followed that conflict saw no improvement in Turkish methods of government, and the Christian populations, especially in the European provinces, became ever more ready to revolt. Although no important changes took place for nearly two decades, there were certain events which indicated what lay ahead. In 1866, for example, Carol I ascended the throne of Roumania; in the following year the Turkish garrison was withdrawn from Belgrade; and in 1870 the Sultan, desirous of sowing dissension among his Christian subjects signed a firman creating the Bulgarian Exarchate. In 1870, too, Russia took the opportunity of the overthrow of France and the weakness of Britain to announce that she no longer considered herself bound by those clauses of the Treaty of Paris which restricted her sovereignty in the Black Sea. There was thus foreshadowed the rise of the Balkan States and yet another trial of strength between Russia and Turkey.

In 1875 matters came to a head with a rising in Herzegovina, which the Turks proved unable to suppress, and in the following year Serbia and Montenegro declared war on the Sultan. By this time the revolt had spread to Bulgaria, where the Turkish reprisals were of such a nature as to earn the execration of the whole civilized world: it was the story of Ibrahim in the Morea over again. In England the lead was taken by Mr. Gladstone, who, with his pen and voice alike, declaimed against Turkish rule in Bulgaria. "Let the Turks", he wrote in words which were to become famous, "now carry away their abuses in the only possible manner, namely by carrying off themselves. Their Zaptiehs and their Mudirs, their Bimbashis and their Yuzbashis, their Kaimakams and their Pashas, one and all, bag and baggage, shall, I hope, clear out of the province they have desolated and profaned."

Lord Derby, then Foreign Secretary in Lord Beaconsfield's administration, telegraphed to Constantinople that "any renewal of the outrages would be more fatal to the Porte than the loss of a battle". A further complication was caused by a series of palace revolutions in the Turkish capital, and after two Sultans had been deposed in the space of three months Abdul Hamid II ascended the throne.

The Turks had little difficulty in crushing the revolt in Bulgaria, and when this had been accomplished it soon became clear that a like fate threatened Serbia in the very near future. The Powers, however, were in no mind to tolerate any further atrocities, and under a threat of war by Russia the Porte agreed to an armistice at the beginning of November, 1876, while there was a meeting at Constantinople of the representatives of the Concert at the suggestion of the British government. This conference drew up proposals for the rectification of the Montenegrin frontier, and for the autonomy of Bulgaria, Bosnia, and Herzegovina under governors-general to be nominated by the Porte with the consent of the Powers. The Turks rejected these suggestions, and also refused to give any assurances in the matter of reforms. Lord Derby, it should be noted, left the Porte under no illusions as to the British attitude, and he warned the Turkish ambassador that if his country found itself at war with Russia the British government would not lift a finger to help her. That eventuality soon occurred, for on April 27th, 1877, Russian forces crossed both the European and Asiatic frontiers of the Ottoman Empire.

As in the war of 1828–1829, the Russian campaign did not open so auspiciously as St. Petersburg had hoped, and Osman Pasha's defence of Plevna so seriously upset the Tsar's plans that Alexander had to avail himself of Roumanian assistance. The siege of Plevna, which lasted from July to December, afforded the Powers a breathing-space during which they were able to take stock of the situation.

Austria was particularly interested in the course which events were likely to follow. She had never been indifferent to what took place in South-East Europe, but since her defeat by Prussia eleven years before that part of the Continent had become of even greater concern. At the beginning of July, 1876, the Emperor Francis Joseph had met the Tsar at Reichstadt, and had promised his neutrality in a Russo-Turkish war at the price of the occupation of Bosnia and Herzegovina. Now that the anticipated conflict had already begun, however, the Austrian government was by no means certain that this promise would be fulfilled, for Pan-Slav influences were in the ascendant at St. Petersburg. Accordingly, Vienna and London drew together, and on July 26th, 1877, they came to an agreement by which they declared their opposition to the exclusive protectorate by any Power over the Christian population in the Balkans; Russia was not to be allowed acquisitions of territory on the right bank of the Danube or to occupy Constantinople; the existing arrangements as to the Dardanelles were to be maintained; and no great Slav state was to be established in the Balkans to the prejudice of its neighbours. When Bismarck heard of this arrangement, he expressed his complete approval.

In Great Britain opinion was divided. The administration was Conservative, and for many years that party had tended to favour the Turk. On the other hand, the Bulgarian atrocities, and Gladstone's attitude towards them, had created a strong body of opposition to any policy that tended to end in a repetition of the Crimean War. Early in the conflict the British government had declared its intention to remain neutral so long as the interests held to be vital to Great Britain were respected. These were stated to be the maintenance of complete freedom of communication between Europe and the East through the Suez Canal, which had been opened eight years before; the exclusion of Egypt from the sphere of military operations; and the recognition by Russia of the inviolability of Constantinople and the navigation of the Bosphorus and the Dardanelles. Gortchakoff, the Russian Chancellor, furnished assurances on all these points, and, as we have seen, they were further safeguarded by the agreement with Austria. All the same, British opinion, both official and unofficial, followed the progress of events on the battle-fronts with a considerable amount of misgiving.

As for Bismarck, although he did not believe the Balkans to be worth the bones of a Pomeranian grenadier, he realized from the beginning that the war must not be allowed to spread if vital German interests were not to be adversely affected. If Britain was drawn into the conflict it was clear that Austria would go with her: now the basis of Bismarck's policy was friendship with both Vienna and St. Petersburg, and he had no desire to be forced into a position where he would have to choose between them. Nor was this all, for if the war became general it might not be possible to continue that isolation of France, which was another great objective of the Iron Chancellor. Unlike some of his successors, Bismarck knew where to stop, and he knew that no German interest was to be served by a general disturbance of the existing order; the war, in short, must be localized.

The other Great Powers, that is to say France and Italy, were not in a position to exercise any decisive influence, for the one was still busy licking her wounds, and the other was a Great Power in name alone.

Such was the attitude of Europe when Plevna fell at the beginning of December, 1877; thereafter Turkish resistance collapsed rapidly, and on January 20th, 1878, Russian troops occupied Adrianople for the second time in half a century. At once there was an outburst of fury in Britain, and a large section of opinion, headed by the Queen, became intensely Russophobe; music-halls and public-houses echoed with denunciations of the Tsar, and with songs to the effect that the Russians should not have Constantinople. At the cost of the resignation of the Colonial Secretary a British squadron lay off the island of Prinkipo; a few miles away, at San Stefano, the Grand Duke Nicholas had his headquarters. With the forces of the two Powers so close to one another hostilities seemed inevitable, and for several weeks war between Britain and Russia seemed to hang upon a thread. To complicate the situation the Greeks, who had long been eager to enter the fray, threatened to throw in their lot with the victors, and it was largely by British pressure and promises that they were restrained.

On March 3rd, 1878, there was signed between Russia and Turkey the Treaty of San Stefano. This document provided, in the first place, for the creation of that "great" Bulgaria which has ever since been the goal of the statesmen of Sofia. The principality was to have a frontage on both the Black Sea and the Aegean, while its northern frontier was to be the Danube, and it was to include the lakes of Prespa and Ochrida. Serbia and Montenegro were also enlarged to such an extent that their boundaries almost met. As for Russia herself, she took Ardahan, Kars, Bayazid, and Batum, while Roumania, who had done so much to make the Russian victory possible, had to cede to Russia the southern part of Bessarabia, and received the Dobrudja in exchange. There were also stipulations regarding the treatment of the Sultan's Christian subjects.

The Treaty of San Stefano was the Slav settlement of a problem which also concerned other races. It would have given the final blow to the Ottoman Empire in Europe by cutting the remaining Turkish territory into two parts, and by imposing a Bulgarian barrier between the two chief cities of European Turkey, while it was carefully calculated to aggrandise Bulgaria at the expense of Greece. Hardly was the ink dry before protests began to be made in every quarter, and appeals were addressed to the British government to interfere. The Greeks expressed disapproval of the disregard of their claims; the Mohammedans appealed to Queen Victoria as the ruler of a hundred million Moslem subjects; the Lozes begged for British protection to prevent the cession of Batum; and the Serbs were indignant at the inclusion of Serbian districts in Bulgaria. The Roumanians went so far as to promise to go to war with their late allies if Great Britain would take the lead, and even the Albanians formed a league to resist to the death any attempt upon the inviolability of their land.

The Great Powers were no less perturbed by the treaty. In British eyes the "big Bulgaria" of San Stefano would be merely a Russian province, a constant menace to Constantinople, and a base for any future Muscovite attack upon the Ottoman Empire. Austria likewise had no relish for so purely Slav a solution of a problem which concerned her so vitally, and London and Vienna began to draw even more closely together. The choice lay between war and a conference, and it was at this moment that Bismarck came forward as the "honest broker". He announced that he was willing to support any terms of settlement which Britain might think necessary for her own security, provided that they were acceptable to Russia, for he would do nothing to imperil the relations of Berlin and St. Petersburg. As Lord Salisbury wrote at this time, "He holds an exceptional position in this matter, not so much on account of his military strength, which is not likely to come into play in this question, as because he is credited with always knowing his own mind and sometimes saying it".

There were, however, still to be some anxious moments before the statesmen of Europe were gathered round the conference-table in Berlin. The British government demanded that the Treaty of San Stefano as a whole should be discussed, while Russia was only prepared to allow certain clauses, selected by herself, to appear upon the agenda. On this Lord Beaconsfield passed

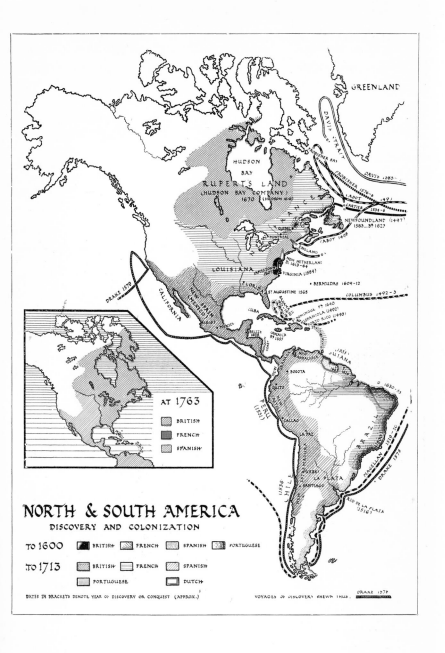

NORTH & SOUTH AMERICA
DISCOVERY AND COLONIZATION

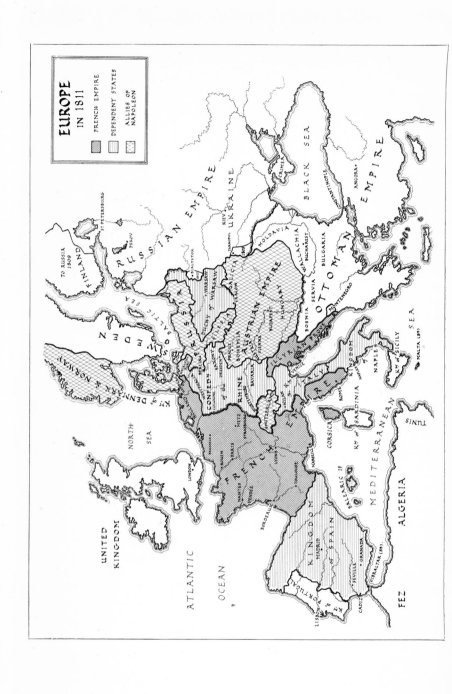

from words to deeds; the reserves were called out, and Indian troops were sent to Malta. These measures proved, however, too bellicose for Lord Derby, who resigned, and was succeeded at the Foreign Office by Lord Salisbury. Austria also mobilized, and before these threats the Tsar began to hesitate, more especially because it was clear that too intransigent an attitude would not commend itself to Bismarck. Lord Beaconsfield was thus success-ful in the exercise of pressure in a quarter where the British Navy could not by itself be effective because he had enlisted the support of a sufficiently powerful Continental Power. The old law govern-ing British intervention on the mainland of Europe had operated once again.

Accordingly, an agreement between Great Britain and Russia was reached before the Congress of Berlin opened, and it was negotiated by Lord Salisbury and Count Schouvaloff, the Tsar's ambassador in London. The Russian government undertook not to offer final opposition to a division of the proposed Bulgaria into two provinces, of which the northern alone was to receive com-plete autonomy, nor to a withdrawal of its frontiers altogether from the coast of the Aegean. The British claim to an equal right of consultation upon the reforms to be introduced in other parts of the Ottoman Empire was placed in the same category, and Salisbury in return promised a similarly limited resistance to certain clauses of the Treaty of San Stefano. With regard to Asia, the Russian government solemnly repudiated any intention of extending the frontiers further in the future, but it was warned by the Foreign Secretary that should it, after full discussion at the congress, persist in retaining its latest acquisitions, Great Britain would regard herself as being thereby placed under a special obligation to safeguard the Ottoman Empire in those regions. Upon all these issues, as well as upon a long list of sub-sidiary points concerning which no rupture was feared, both parties reserved to themselves full liberty to secure, if they could, more favourable terms by process of diplomatic bargaining at the forthcoming Congress. Such process would only be effected by the agreement in that neither side would be able to extort by threats concessions for which it had frankly admitted that it was not prepared to fight.

This agreement was, of course, never intended for publication, but owing to the dishonesty of a copying-clerk at the Foreign Office a summary appeared in a London evening newspaper, and

Q

the Foreign Secretary was in consequence attacked in several quarters, but he refused to answer any questions likely to prejudice subsequent negotiations.

The Congress of Berlin thus opened on June 13th, 1878, with the air cleared of the threat of an immediate outbreak of war. The quality of the participants was high, and recalled Vienna in 1814 rather than Paris in 1856. Great Britain was represented by Beaconsfield and Salisbury; Russia by Gortchakoff and Schouvaloff; Austria-Hungary by Andrassy and Haymerle; France by Waddington; Italy by Corti; and, above all, Germany by Bismarck, who was elected President of the Congress. If cosmopolitanism was less in evidence than had been the case at Vienna, the Sultan at any rate remained true to tradition, for he sent as his representatives to plead the cause of the Commander of the Faithful a Greek and a German. The British delegation urged the presence of envoys from the kingdom of Greece, on the same footing as those from the Great Powers, but to no purpose, for it was decided that the representatives of Greece and Roumania should be admitted merely to state their views, but without the right of voting. The Congress was thus effectively limited to the European Great Powers.

So competent a chairman was the Iron Chancellor that at the end of a month the Congress had completed its work. On the whole the proceedings had been harmonious, though there was one moment when Lord Beaconsfield ordered his train, and it took all Bismarck's diplomatic skill to prevent the departure of the British delegation at a critical stage of the negotiations. The result of this Congress was the Treaty of Berlin, which severely modified that of San Stefano. The "big Bulgaria" disappeared, and in its place were set up two states; the first was a small "autonomous and tributary principality under the suzerainty of the Sultan" which was bounded by the Danube, the Balkans, the Serbian frontier, and the Black Sea, with its harbour at Varna; the second was a province south of the Balkans to be known as Eastern Roumelia, and it was placed "under the direct political and military authority of the Sultan", but administered by a Christian Governor-General "named by the Porte, with the assent of the Powers, for a term of five years". It was further provided that the Prince of Bulgaria should be "freely elected by the population and confirmed by the Porte, with the consent of the Powers", and that no member of any reigning dynasty should be eligible.

In pursuance of the Reichstadt agreement, and on the proposal of the British delegation, Bosnia and Herzegovina were to be "occupied and administered by Austria-Hungary", which also received "the right of keeping garrisons and having military and commercial roads" in the Sanjak of Novibazar. A further step was thus taken along the road which was leading the Habsburgs to the East: in 1866 they had been driven out of Germany; in the following year they took Hungary into equal partnership with Austria; and now they became entangled in the web of Slav hatreds and desires. The consequences were to be momentous both for them and for the world. As for Serbia and Montenegro, they had to be content with much less than would have been theirs had the Treaty of San Stefano been implemented. Serbia obtained formal recognition of her independence, and she received a considerable accession of territory, some of which, however, was inhabited by Bulgarians, while she was cut off from any direct contact with Montenegro. For the rest, the frontiers of Roumania remained as they had been settled at San Stefano, except that she received more of the Dobrudja; she was thus denied Bessarabia, which was historically and ethnographically Roumanian, and was given the Dobrudja, a desolate waste largely peopled by Turks and Bulgars. In Asia the arrangements of San Stefano stood, except that the Sultan retained Bayazid, and undertook "to carry out, without further delay, the ameliorations and reforms demanded in the provinces inhabited by the Armenians, and to guarantee their security against the Circassians and Kurds".

While the Congress of Berlin was still in session it learnt with no little astonishment that a few days before it began its labours the Cyprus Convention had been made between Great Britain and Turkey. By this England promised to join the Sultan in the defence of his Asiatic dominions against any further Russian attack, while he undertook in return "to introduce necessary reforms" there in consultation with his ally. In order the better to enable Britain to carry out her promises, the Porte agreed to assign to her the island of Cyprus as "a place of arms" in the Levant, on payment of an annual tribute and on the understanding that the British would evacuate the island when the Russians restored Batum and Kars to the Sultan. The Cyprus Convention caused the enemies of Britain to observe that Beaconsfield had consolidated the Ottoman Empire by assigning the administration of Bosnia and Herzegovina to Austria-Hungary, and that of

Cyprus to England, with which its only historical connection had been its conquest by Richard I nearly seven centuries earlier.

The cynic can, indeed, find as much cause for merriment in the Treaty of Berlin as in that of its predecessor of Paris in 1856. It contained many contradictions, and the years which followed its conclusion were marked by repeated modifications of its provisions. All this is profoundly true, but there is much to be said on the other side. It marked a definite advance in the disposal of the Sick Man's inheritance, and whatever the theorists may say the Austrian occupation of Bosnia and Herzegovina, which may be compared with British control in Egypt and the French protectorate of Tunis, converted two wild Turkish provinces into a pattern Balkan state. Lastly, it endured in its main outlines for thirty-four years until a new cycle of wars began to transform the balance of power in the Near East.

CHAPTER XX

BISMARCK AND HIS NEIGHBOURS, 1871–1890

THE foreign policy of Bismarck as Imperial Chancellor was fundamentally the same as that which he had pursued when he was only Prime Minister of Prussia, namely to prevent the formation of any such coalition as might threaten his country. This aim he pursued steadily during the remaining nineteen years of his official life, and after 1871 he added another, namely the isolation of France. That Power had not accepted defeat, and Bismarck knew very well that she would be on his back the moment he got involved in war with any of his other neighbours. This was not, however, the only reason why the victor in three conflicts laboured hard to keep the peace. Germany was "satisfied", and Bismarck realized that further adventures might well cause her to lose what she had gained. In this respect Germany was in marked contrast to her predecessor in the hegemony of continental Europe, namely France. Every French regime after 1815 sought to overthrow the Vienna settlement, and in consequence French policy was restless and aggressive, culminating in the sheer opportunism which marked the reign of Napoleon III. Imperial Germany, on the other hand, displayed no inclination to embark on any adventures so long as Bismarck remained at the helm, save possibly in 1875, when there was nearly a renewal of the war with France.

For this reason Great Britain found it much easier to co-operate with Germany than she had done with France. Bismarck himself said, "The German Empire in alliance with Austria would not lack the support of England", and he was right. As has been shown, there was collaboration between London and Paris on occasion both during the July Monarchy and the Second Empire, but it was an uneasy partnership, for in the main Britain supported the Vienna settlement, which it was the object of France to destroy. With Germany the position was very different, for after 1871 it was to her advantage to maintain an order which she had done so much to establish. In short, Anglo-German interests were largely complementary, and they nowhere clashed; so London welcomed the supremacy of Germany on the mainland of Europe, and it was not until, after the fall of Bismarck, different counsels began to prevail in Berlin that the two countries drifted apart.

The Iron Chancellor was greatly assisted in his foreign policy by the weakness of France. When he first took office her population amounted to 37,400,000, while that of Prussia was only 19,100,000; after the Treaty of Frankfurt the figures were 41,100,000 for Germany and 36,100,000 for France, and the disproportion steadily grew. Nor was this all, for France became a prey to internal disorders and scandals such as subsequently heralded her second downfall seventy years later. Nevertheless, Bismarck was not taking any chances, and he neglected no opportunity of keeping France weak. In particular he favoured the establishment of a republican regime as contributing to that end. So early as December, 1872, he wrote, "It is certainly no task of ours to render France powerful by the consolidation of her internal relations and the restoration of a settled monarchy, and thus to make her capable of entering into alliances with those Powers that have hitherto been our friends. The hostility of France compels us to desire that she may remain weak". In consequence he preferred a republic for France, although everywhere else in the world he was a firm advocate of monarchical institutions. When Count von Arnim, the German ambassador in Paris, showed sympathy for the Comte de Chambord he was broken without mercy.

In 1875 there was much talk of a preventive war on the part of Germany, and both Great Britain and Russia let it be known that they would not stand idly by while France was struck down again. At the same time it is exceedingly doubtful whether Bismarck ever really intended to do more than frighten the French; what is more than likely is that he was engaged in a piece of terrorism, or what a later generation would have termed a war of nerves.

Meanwhile the early years of the Second Reich had witnessed something in the nature of a revival of the Holy Alliance. "The foreign policy of the German Empire since 1871", Bismarck later told the Emperor Frederick, "has been the maintenance of peace and the prevention of anti-German coalitions, and the pivot of this policy is Russia." The friendly relations which had so long existed between Berlin and St. Petersburg continued unabated for some time after the war of 1870, and Austria-Hungary became more reconciled to her late antagonist as Bismarck put into practice the policy which he had forecast on the night of

Sadowa. In 1872 both the Tsar and the Emperor Francis Joseph came to Berlin, so that there was every justification for the German Chancellor's boast that he had "thrown a bridge across to Vienna, without breaking down that older one to St. Petersburg". From this meeting dated the so-called *Dreikaiserbund*, though there was no written agreement, and it was rather an informal understanding between the three Powers to take counsel together upon all matters of mutual interest. This grouping was further strengthened by a visit to Berlin from the King of Italy in the following year, while in 1874 the British ambassador was able to report that "our relations with Germany were never better, more cordial, or more satisfactory than at present".

The crisis in the Near East in 1877–1878 put a severe strain upon the *Dreikaiserbund*. Although Bismarck prevented war he incurred great unpopularity in Russia by his attitude at the Congress of Berlin, when he was considered to have taken a line far too friendly to Great Britain and Austria-Hungary. For his part he told Gortchakoff, "Do not compel me to choose between Austria and you": nevertheless, the tension grew, and in 1879 he made his choice; it was in favour of Austria. No other decision was, in fact, possible. German security demanded that the Danubian lands should be under German control, and this was ensured by the presence of the Habsburgs at Vienna. The central European balance of power was stabilized, and Pan-Slavism was checked. Had Bismarck chosen Russia rather than Austria he would have alarmed Great Britain, and Germany would have been involved in Russian designs in Asia without acquiring any compensating advantages. In that case Austria, France, Great Britain, and Italy might have come together. Above all, Bismarck knew that in the last resort he could control Vienna as he could not control St. Petersburg.

All the same, the Chancellor had very considerable difficulty in persuading his master to agree to an alliance with Austria, for the old Emperor entertained to the full the traditional Hohenzollern dislike of the Habsburgs and sympathy for the Romanoffs, but the agreement which created the Dual Alliance was ratified in October, 1879. The treaty itself opened with the usual pacific preamble that the "intimate co-operation of Germany and Austria menaces no one", and went on to promise that the two Powers would never "allow their purely defensive agreement to develop an aggressive tendency". It went on to say that should "one of the two Empires be attacked by Russia the other is bound to assist and only to conclude peace in common". Another clause provided that "should one of the two be attacked by another Power, the other will observe at least benevolent neutrality; should, however, the attacking party be supported by Russia, either by active co-operation or by military measures which constitute a menace, the other shall aid". The conclusion of the treaty was immediately followed by the signature of a joint memorandum in which the two Powers declared "their intention not to attack or menace Russia owing to differences arising out of the treaty".

The terms of this agreement were not made public until 1888, but the fact that it had been concluded was soon general knowledge. The British Government welcomed the new arrangement when Lord Salisbury declared, "The papers say a defensive alliance of Germany and Austria has been concluded: if true, it is good tidings of great joy". The King of Italy expressed his satisfaction, and even the French Prime Minister described it as a pledge of peace. Only in Russia was the formation of the Dual Alliance eyed askance, but even there it was not regarded as a menace.

Bismarck had no intention of becoming embroiled with Russia in consequence of the alliance with Austria, and no sooner was the latter concluded than he set to work to improve relations between Berlin and St. Petersburg. In this his task was facilitated by the accession, in 1881, of a new Tsar. Alexander III was a man of inferior intellectual calibre to his father, but he possessed greater steadiness of character; and although he opposed German influences at his own Court, he was far from desiring a rupture with the Reich, for he saw in the conservative empires of Germany and Austria welcome allies in the struggle against the forces of anarchy and irreligion to which his father had fallen a victim. Alike at Berlin, St. Petersburg, and Vienna it was fully realized in the eighties of the last century, as it was not appreciated in 1914, that war might well unleash the forces of revolution. This knowledge was a powerful factor in bringing the three states together, and so in preserving the peace of Europe.

The month of June, 1881, therefore witnessed a new affirmation of the *Dreikaiserbund* but in a far more definite form. The three Powers not only pledged themselves not to act except by common consent; they also defined their attitude upon a number of points at issue. Austria-Hungary reserved the right to annex

Bosnia and Herzegovina at whatever moment she might deem opportune, while all three Powers agreed not to oppose the eventual union of Bulgaria and Eastern Roumelia if this question should come up by force of circumstances. It may thus be safely affirmed that the *Dreikaiserbund* was an essentially pacific grouping, and that it represented a further triumph for Bismarck. Ever since 1871 his policy had been to safeguard the gains of his three wars, to keep on good terms with Britain and Russia, and to isolate France. Ten years after the Treaty of Frankfurt, he could point to an alliance with Austria-Hungary, a revived *Dreikaiserbund*, and a friendly England as proofs of his success.

The year 1881, however, was not to close without events which still further strengthened the position of the Iron Chancellor. For some time there had been considerable rivalry between France and Italy over the future of Tunis. That country nominally formed part of the Ottoman Empire, but it was ruled by a dynasty which had been in possession for two centuries. The Bey's finances were in disorder, and in 1869 there had been set up a Triple Financial Control consisting of British, French, and Italian representatives who worked unharmoniously together, and under which Great Britain secured most of the concessions for public works. When the news of the Cyprus Convention leaked out France was pacified by the suggestion that she might seek compensation in Tunis. "Waddington and I often discussed the events taking place in the Mediterranean", Salisbury reported. "With respect to Tunis I said that England was wholly disinterested, and had no intention to contest the influence which the geographical position of Algeria gave to France." In adopting this standpoint the Foreign Secretary was only emphasizing the views of his government in respect of the Mediterranean as announced during the previous year: all that really concerned Britain was the security of the sea-route to the Suez Canal. Once this was safeguarded the question of the ownership of the North African littoral was relatively unimportant.

Bismarck also offered no opposition to a French occupation of Tunis, though his reasons were somewhat different. He wished to distract the attention of France from Alsace-Lorraine to Africa, while he knew that the presence of the French in Tunisia would create a permanent breach between Paris and Rome. All happened exactly as he foresaw. The French made little secret of their intentions, and suggested to Italy that she should seek compensation in Tripoli. M. Freycinet even promised that Rome should have due notice of any French move, but his administration fell, and M. Ferry, who succeeded him, ignored the pledge. A border raid into Algeria gave France the excuse she needed, and her troops invaded Tunisia. The British Government offered mediation, but discouraged any move on the part of the Sultan to help the Bey, and merely exacted from France a confirmation of the treaties favouring British commerce and a promise not to fortify Bizerta. The difference in the attitude of London to the occupation of Algeria and of Tunis is the measure of the decline of France in the interval.

The Treaty of Bardo, in May, 1881, established a French Protectorate, and France undertook to defend the Bey against any danger to his person or dynasty, guaranteed existing treaties with the Powers, and assumed control of foreign relations. When the treaty came to be ratified Clemenceau voted against it on the ground that "it profoundly modified the European system and chilled precious friendships cemented on the field of battle". The reaction in Italy was violent, and, as Bismarck had foreseen, it drove that country for protection into the arms of Austria-Hungary and Germany. In May, 1882, the Triple Alliance came into being, in fact if not yet in name, after some hard bargaining. It was agreed that if Italy was attacked by France without provocation her partners would come to her assistance, while Italy in turn would help Germany against a French attack. If any of the allies were engaged in war with two or more Great Powers the *casus foederis* would arise for all, but if a single Great Power threatened the security of one of the allies, and that one was forced to make war, the others would observe benevolent neutrality, reserving the right to take part in the conflict if they should see fit. The pact was to last for five years, was to be kept secret, and at Italy's wish each of the signatories subscribed to an undertaking that the treaty could in no case be regarded as directed against Great Britain.

It will be seen at once that Italy gained considerably by this arrangement, and she obtained greater advantages than did Austria, for the latter was bound to aid her against a French attack, while she was not pledged to help her ally against a Russian onslaught. Moreover, by the very existence of the alliance Italy was protected against an Austrian attack. The treaty also brought solid advantages to the two Germanic Powers. Bismarck was not only freed from the remote fear that Italy might join France in an attack, but he secured an ally in resisting such aggression. Austria-Hungary, too, had no longer to fear a stab in the back if she was engaged in a struggle with Russia, while she could count on Italian assistance in repelling a Franco-Russian assault.

The *status quo* in Europe could thus be said to rest firmly upon the *Dreikaiserbund* and the Triple Alliance, but it was, to the German Chancellor's great satisfaction, further buttressed by complementary arrangements. Not the least important of these was the Austro-Serb Treaty signed in June, 1881, Serbia being then ruled by the Obrenovitch dynasty, which always inclined to Vienna just as their Karageorgevitch rivals looked to St. Petersburg. By this treaty the Serbs undertook not to tolerate any intrigues on their territory directed against the Dual Monarchy, and Austria-Hungary assumed the same obligation towards Serbia and the House of Obrenovitch. Serbia also obtained the leave of Vienna to expand southwards, except the Sanjak of Novibazar, and to become a kingdom, a privilege of which Prince Milan availed himself in the following year. In return Serbia placed her foreign policy under the control of Austria-Hungary.

If Serbia, traditionally Russophil, had been driven into the Austrian camp in consequence of Russian partiality for Bulgaria as shown by the Treaty of San Stefano, Roumania, ruled by a Hohenzollern and smarting under the insults heaped upon her by St. Petersburg, naturally gravitated in the same direction. At first she asked for too much, namely Transylvania and Bukovina, but she soon moderated her demands. In 1883, therefore, a secret alliance for five years was concluded between Vienna and Bucharest. If Roumania was attacked without provocation Austria-Hungary was to come to her assistance, while if the latter were attacked on the side of Russia, then Roumania assumed a similar obligation: if either state were threatened by aggression, military questions were to be determined by a convention. A treaty providing for the accession of Germany was signed on the same day, and both parties forthwith invited the Reich to adhere to the pact. Germany accepted the invitation, and five years later Italy was also included. The treaty was renewed at intervals, and it remained in force at the beginning of the Four Years' War.

Further south, the Mediterranean area was being brought into the Bismarckian network of alliances, conventions, and pacts to maintain the *status quo*. At the beginning of 1887 Great Britain and Italy came to an agreement to support the existing order in that inland sea in which both were so deeply interested, and if this proved impossible no modification was to take place except with their joint consent. The British position in Egypt was recognized, while Great Britain promised "in case of encroachments by a third Power to support the action of Italy at every other point of the North African coast, especially in Tripoli and Cyrenaica".

Before the end of that same year, 1887, Austria-Hungary, Great Britain, and Italy entered into another agreement which went somewhat further than the earlier arrangement between London and Rome. In addition to the maintenance of peace based upon the *status quo* the three Powers stated that the independence of Turkey was a vital interest, and that she "can neither cede nor delegate her suzerain rights over Bulgaria to any other Power": they went on to pledge themselves in the event of any threat to the Sultan to "agree on measures to procure respect for the independence and integrity of the Ottoman Empire". Rumours of the pact led to a question in Parliament, but the reply given was that the Government had not concluded any agreement which bound Great Britain to take military action. What has been described as "the Mediterranean insurance risk" was still further distributed by the inclusion of Spain, who promised not to lend herself in respect of France, in so far as North Africa was concerned, to any treaty or political arrangement aimed against Austria-Hungary, Germany, or Italy either severally or collectively.

In the meantime the Triple Alliance treaty was renewed in 1887 for a further period of five years, though with modifications in favour of Italy. Austria now recognized Italian interest in the Balkans and claim to compensation in the event of a partition of the Ottoman Empire, while Germany pledged herself to take part in offensive war should Italy's ambitions in North Africa demand such action.

Superficially it may well appear that Germany's position and the European *status quo* was adequately safeguarded by these various arrangements, but Bismarck was far from happy about his relations with Russia; the *Dreikaiserbund* had indeed been renewed in 1884, but Pan-Slav feeling was predominant in the Tsar's dominions, where it was ably voiced by Katkoff in the *Moscow Gazette*: the leading articles were written for the special benefit of Alexander III, and Katkoff was unquestionably the most powerful man in Russia after the Tsar. All this was bad enough from the point of view of the German Chancellor, but on his other frontier France was beginning to look back wistfully at her glorious past, and Boulanger was the hero of the hour. Now, a French attack would not necessarily bring Russia into the field, but a Russian onslaught would certainly cause an explosion in the West. Moreover, the hostility of France was incurable, while there was still hope of the Tsar, so once more Bismarck turned to St. Petersburg.

The result was the secret Treaty of Reinsurance of 1887 between Germany and Russia, of which the contents were not disclosed to Austria-Hungary at the request of the Tsar, who feared the opposition of the Pan-Slavs. By the first clause of this new agreement it was stipulated that if either signatory should find itself at war with a third Great Power, the other would maintain a benevolent neutrality, and would try to localize the conflict. This provision, however, was not to apply to a war against Austria or France as the result of an attack by one of the contracting parties. The second clause contained the recognition by Germany of the rights historically acquired by Russia in the Balkans, and especially the legitimacy of her preponderant and decisive influence in Bulgaria and Eastern Roumelia: there was to be no disturbance of the existing order save with the consent of the two Powers. Lastly, they affirmed the principle of the closing of the Straits to warships of any nation in the event of hostilities. It will thus be seen that there was nothing in this treaty which conflicted with Germany's other obligations, while it did serve the purpose of keeping open the wire from Berlin to St. Petersburg.

In spite, therefore, of those conflicts of interests in the Near East and in Africa to be related in subsequent chapters, Bismarck could claim, when his old master died in 1888, that his foreign policy had been successful. The German sword had been kept in the scabbard without any German interest being sacrificed, and France was still as isolated as she had been on the morrow of the Treaty of Frankfurt. Two years later Bismarck was dismissed by William II, and the relations of Germany with her neighbours began to undergo a change which led directly to the Four Years' War. Dr. Gooch has summed up this transformation in the words, "During the twenty-eight years of Bismarck's dictatorship the foreign policy of Prussia and the German Empire was directed by a single brain and will. . . . From 1890 onwards German policy was never again controlled by a single hand, and in the years immediately following it represented an unstable compromise between the views of the Emperor, the Chancellor, Marshall von Bieberstein, the Foreign Minister, and a mystery man in the Foreign Office."

CHAPTER XXI

THE GERMANY OF WILLIAM II, 1890–1904

T HE situation which began to develop in consequence of the fall of Bismarck was very well summed up by Sir Edward Grey in a statement to the Committee of Imperial Defence in the spring of 1911, when he said, "I must go back rather an alarming way to the time when I first became Under-Secretary at the Foreign Office in 1892. . . . The situation then, and for some years previously, had been this: that the two restless Powers in Europe were France and Russia. . . . The solid quiet group . . . was the Triple Alliance of Germany, Austria, and Italy. It had been the policy of Lord Salisbury before 1892, and it was the policy of Mr. Gladstone's Government of 1892, not to join the Triple Alliance or come under definite commitment to it, but generally in diplomacy to side with the Triple Alliance as being the stable Power in Europe, and the one which was securing the peace. . . . Soon after 1892 the situation began slowly to change."

There were several reasons for this quite apart from the dismissal of the Iron Chancellor; indeed, even if he had remained in office it is by no means certain that circumstances would have allowed him to pursue his old policy. To avoid difficulties with Great Britain he had abstained from the creation of such a navy as the position of Germany in the world might seem to warrant, and he had refrained from direct interference in the Near East for fear of snapping the links which still connected Berlin with St. Petersburg. Nevertheless, the German Empire had become a commercial and colonial Power of the first rank, and as such could hardly be expected to leave her shipping unprotected; while signs were by no means lacking that in the Near East a crisis of more than usual magnitude was impending, and that the German government would be forced to adopt a standpoint commensurate with its growing interests in that part of the world.

To some extent, of course, the impetuosity of the new Emperor contributed to the breach with Bismarckian traditions in foreign affairs; he was rash and tactless, and he did not realize the full implication of much that he said and did: nor did he know when to stop, though that, it must be admitted, is a knowledge with which singularly few monarchs and statesmen have been endowed.

At the same time, William II was throughout his life the sport, rather than the master, of circumstances, and if he was restless in the last decade of the nineteenth century, his subjects were becoming restless too. The generation which had been content to rest on its laurels after three victorious wars was passing away, and its successor was bent on winning triumphs of its own. Moreover, Bismarck had Prussianized the whole Reich, with the result that the German people as a whole were becoming imbued with that aggressive spirit which hitherto had chiefly characterized the subjects of the House of Hohenzollern; in a way, indeed, it is even true to say that Bismarck had himself rendered impossible the continuance of his own policy.

All this, however, does not necessarily mean that the changes to which Sir Edward Grey referred rendered the outbreak of the Four Years' War inevitable; on the contrary, there were many occasions between 1890 and 1914 when a different decision might have averted it, but that this was not the case was largely due to the absence of a single controlling hand in Berlin and to the growing aggressiveness of the German people.

On the purely material side the transformation of the international scene was accelerated by Austro-Russian differences in the Balkans, to be described in a later chapter, which led to the dissolution of the *Driekaiserbund*. It had become imperative that Germany should choose between Austria-Hungary and Russia; such being the case, her choice was inevitable; and this in its turn led to that very understanding between France and Russia, and the emergence of the former from her isolation, which Bismarck had struggled so hard to prevent.

Even before the death of the Iron Chancellor relations between Paris and St. Petersburg had become a little closer, though it was not easy for Alexander III to overcome his objections to a republican France. In 1888 there was negotiated the first French loan to Russia, and in the succeeding years it was followed by further financial transactions which strengthened the ties between the two countries. In 1890 the Russian Government placed an order for rifles in France, and gave an assurance that these would never fire upon Frenchmen. Nor was popular support lacking in either country for this new policy. *"L'empire des Tsars est à la mode"*, wrote one Belgian diplomat from Paris as early as 1888, and two years later a fellow-countryman reported that "the infatuation for Russia has gained all classes", while "the contrast between the institutions of the two countries is not felt in Paris". In Russia it was the same, and when a French squadron visited Cronstadt in 1891 the sailors were astonished at the enthusiasm with which they were received. The climax was reached when, after the French naval band had rendered the Russian national anthem, the Tsar ordered a Russian band to play the *Marseillaise*, hitherto forbidden in public places, and he himself heard it standing and uncovered.

With the ground thus prepared it became possible to go a little further, and before the end of that same year, 1891, a political agreement was reached between the two Powers, who declared that in future they would confer on every question of a nature to threaten the maintenance of peace, while if the latter were in actual danger, and especially if one of the two countries was menaced by aggression, the two governments agreed to concert measures. This was not yet an alliance, but one was clearly foreshadowed, particularly in view of the fact that the Russo-German Reinsurance treaty was not renewed, while on May 6th, 1891, the Triple Alliance was extended for another six years, with an extension for another six unless notice was given. It may be added that this renewal of the Triple Alliance met with the unconcealed sympathy of Great Britain.

Two more years elapsed before the final step was taken in Paris and St. Petersburg, and the military convention of December, 1893, was concluded. Briefly, this provided in various ways for the contingency of an attack by the Triple Alliance. If France were to be assailed by Germany, or by Italy with German support, then Russia was to attack Germany: similarly, in the event of an onslaught by Germany on Russia, or by Austria-Hungary with German backing, then France was to come to the aid of Russia. Various clauses defined the means by which the two Powers were to co-operate, and stipulated that they would not conclude a separate peace. That an alliance had been concluded was generally known, but it was not officially announced until the beginning of 1895, and in the following year the new Tsar, Nicholas II, visited Paris, where he received an ovation.

The German government was, with good reason, profoundly disturbed at the course which events had taken, and William II did everything in his power to point out to Nicholas the dangers of the policy his ministers had adopted, while Bismarck in his retirement angrily complained that by their attitude towards Russia his successors in office had cut the telegraph wire to St.

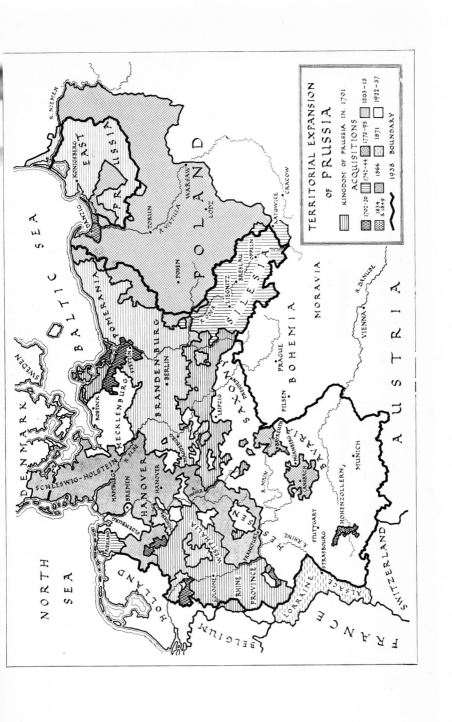

TERRITORIAL EXPANSION
of PRUSSIA

KINGDOM OF PRUSSIA IN 1701

ACQUISITIONS

1702-20   1742-44   1772-95   1803-15
1834   1866   1871   1922-37
&1849
1938 BOUNDARY

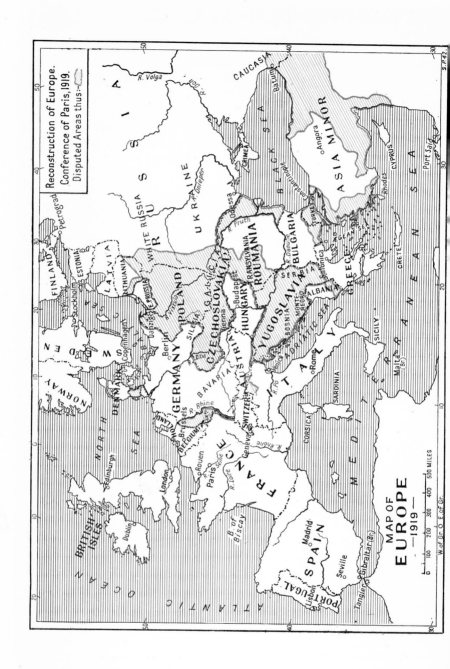

Reconstruction of Europe.
Conference of Paris, 1919.
Disputed Areas thus:—

MAP OF
EUROPE
— 1919 —

0   100   200   300   400   500 MILES

Petersburg. In London the Franco-Russian alliance met with equal disapproval; it was felt that both parties to it would become more aggressive, and trouble was in consequence apprehended in regard to questions arising out of the situation in Alsace-Lorraine and the Near East.

What contemporaries suspected, posterity knows, to be a fact, namely that a new era was beginning in international relations, German predominance on the mainland of Europe was no longer to go unquestioned, and the Powers were splitting into two groups. For France the conclusion of the alliance was a notable triumph; it meant that she had recovered sufficiently from the disaster of 1870 to be regarded as a desirable ally, and that her period of isolation was at an end. Russia, indeed, cared less about prestige than her new ally, but she had expensive ambitions in the Far East, for which she hoped the French investor would now pay. Actually, both Powers were a great deal weaker than appeared on the surface, as the events of the next ten years were to prove, and it was not until the weight of the British Empire was thrown into the scale that the new group was a match for its older rival. The brilliance of French diplomacy between 1870 and 1914, largely due to the skill of the Cambons in London and Berlin and of Barrère in Rome, cannot be allowed to blind us to the weakness of French arms during this period or to the putrefaction of French politics.

At the time any weakening of the ties between Berlin and London seemed very remote, for Anglo-German relations had rarely been more friendly than they were during the first seven years of the reign of William II. In June, 1890, an agreement was reached by which Great Britain obtained Uganda and a protectorate over Zanzibar in exchange for the cession to Germany of Heligoland, which she had conquered from Denmark in 1807. Both parties appeared to have equal cause for satisfaction: the construction of the Kiel Canal was already in progress, and for this reason the island had recently come to possess a considerable strategic importance; as for Britain, she had founded an East African Empire at the price of an outlying possession which in the opinion of her Prime Minister she could not defend in the event of war.

The sky began to darken in 1894, and Anglo-German relations were never again to be on the same friendly footing as during the opening years of the reign of William II. At first, however, the friction between London and Berlin was confined to relatively unimportant frontier questions in East and Central Africa, and at the opening of the Kiel Canal in 1895 the German Emperor went out of his way to flatter his British guests. Nevertheless, the clouds were gathering, and the recent substitution of Hohenlohe for Caprivi as Imperial Chancellor had done nothing to dispel them. Hohenlohe himself accepted the Bismarckian doctrine that Germany was a satisfied Power, and that *Weltpolitik* was not worth the risks which it involved; but Hohenlohe's opinions were of little practical importance, and at no period of his reign was William II so completely in control of German foreign policy as during the three years which elapsed between the fall of Caprivi and the appointment of Bülow. It was at this time that the final breach with the Bismarckian tradition took place and that a "forward" policy was adopted.

In this development a leading part was played by Baron von Holstein, whom King Edward VII described as "that infernal mischief-maker", and of whom his own master was to express a very low opinion in later years. Holstein was a professional diplomat, but he was merely a *Vortragender Rat* in the Political Department of the German Foreign Office: nevertheless he was the most powerful influence in the formation of German policy for the fifteen years which followed the fall of Bismarck. He was unknown to the outside world, and he scarcely ever met the Emperor, but his mysterious activities were legion. It was small wonder that he was called the *Reichsjesuit*. One of his closest colleagues, Baron von Echardstein, wrote of Holstein: "He belonged to the category of people who cannot see things under their nose. The more natural and obvious the thing appeared the greater was his suspicion. He would break off negotiations directly the other party was ready to adopt his wishes. He only desired a thing so long as the others did not." The influence of Holstein upon Anglo-German relations was as considerable as it was funest.

At this point something must be said of the attitude of the Prince of Wales, later King Edward VII. Controversy has raged most fiercely in respect of the line which he adopted in foreign affairs, a subject in which he was keenly interested and upon which he held decided views. In this matter there are two schools of thought. In Germany he has always been regarded as little better than a fiend in human guise, and Princess Blücher could write from Berlin after his death, "Popular hatred here is centred on the shade of King Edward VII; he is supposed to have been the moving spirit in forming the encirclement of Germany". In the Reichstag in August, 1915, the Imperial Chancellor, Herr von Bethmann-Hollweg, declared, "King Edward VII believed that his principal task was to isolate Germany. The encirclement by the Entente with openly hostile tendencies was drawn closer year by year. We were compelled to reply to this situation with the Greatest Armament Budget of 1913." On the other hand, there are those who maintain that neither as Prince of Wales nor as King did Edward the Peacemaker play any great part in international affairs, and that his influence upon them has been largely exaggerated. The point is no mere academic one, for it concerns British relations with Germany at a critical period of European history.

During the long years when he was Prince of Wales there were three influences which much affected the future King's attitude towards foreign Powers. First of all, there was in his extreme youth the Crimean War, and the close relations which for a time existed between the British Royal Family and Napoleon III; these had the effect of making him intensely pro-French and anti-Russian. Then there was his marriage to Princess Alexandra of Denmark, which was so soon followed by a German attack upon his wife's country; from that date the Prince was pronouncedly pro-Danish and anti-Prussian. Lastly, there occurred the long Premiership of Palmerston during his most impressionable years: this, in its turn, fixed in him a permanent leaning towards an active foreign policy. With such a background it is hardly surprising that there should have been an innate antipathy between such dissimilar characters as the German Emperor and his uncle, and by 1895 relations between them were extremely strained. The Prince regarded his nephew as a bounder, while William was jealous of the popularity and cosmopolitanism of his uncle. "The regatta (at Cowes) used to be a pleasant recreation for me," the Prince observed to a friend, "but now, since the Kaiser takes command, it is a bother"; while at dinner one night William referred to his uncle as "an old peacock".

Even in a so-called democratic age the personal relations of monarchs and statesmen have a greater influence upon policy than is commonly supposed: the consequences, therefore, of the antipathy between Edward and his nephew, which first became obvious in 1895, may often have been exaggerated, but it is impossible to resist the conclusion that the suspicion and dislike with which the Englishman was regarded by the Prussian had some influence upon German policy, and that this in its turn further estranged uncle and nephew until the vicious circle was complete.

In that same year, 1895, there was an interview at Cowes between the Kaiser and Lord Salisbury, who had newly returned to office, which revealed a fundamental difference of opinion between London and Berlin in regard to the Near East. Salisbury had by this time definitely turned his back upon the policy of the Crimean War period, which had also been that of Disraeli, and he despaired of any real reform in the Ottoman Empire: Germany, on the other hand, was beginning to play an increasingly important part in the politics of the Near East, and she was extremely desirous of standing well in the opinion of the Sultan. Deadlock in this matter was complete, and elsewhere, too, the clouds were gathering: in South Africa, in particular, there was acute rivalry between the two nations, and matters were brought to a head by the famous telegram from William to President Kruger on the morrow of the failure of the Jameson Raid in January, 1896—"I heartily congratulate you on the fact that you and your people, without appealing to the aid of friendly Powers, have succeeded by your unaided efforts in restoring peace and preserving the independence of the country against the armed bands which broke into your land".

The telegram was one of the most disastrous errors of the reign of William II. "The raid was folly," Salisbury remarked, "but the telegram was even more foolish." The Transvaal was not a sovereign state, and the Kaiser's action merely hastened its doom by increasing the determination of Great Britain to remain the paramount Power in South Africa, while it created an intense suspicion of Kruger as one who was intriguing with foreign nations contrary to his agreement with the British government. The British people, for their part, never forgot or forgave what they took for a wanton challenge to their position in South Africa, while the Germans were driven to fury by the British reaction to their ruler's telegram.

Causes of friction between the two Powers were everywhere multiplying. German industry was expanding rapidly, and its low-priced products were making their appearance in the British home market. In Asia and Africa, as well as in Europe, the interests of Britain and Germany were often found to clash. All this was ominous enough, but what was destined to widen the breach immeasurably was the Kaiser's determination that his country should become a naval Power. In April, 1898, the First German Navy Bill became law, and in September of the same year William uttered, in a speech at Danzig, the fateful words, "Our future lies on the water". There was all the difference between a satisfied Germany which was content with the military hegemony of the mainland of Europe and an aggressive Germany which aimed also at the mastery of the seas; with the former Great Britain could live on terms of friendship, but with the latter she was bound sooner or later to come into armed conflict.

This deterioration in Anglo-German relations was particularly disquieting to one member of the British government, namely Joseph Chamberlain. In the third Salisbury administration he was not merely Colonial Secretary, for he was also one of the leading men in the government, which was largely a triumvirate of himself, the Prime Minister, and Arthur Balfour. In this way he exercised very considerable influence upon general policy, especially in the field of foreign affairs, which also concerned him closely in his work at the Colonial Office. From the first he envisaged the situation somewhat differently from Lord Salisbury, who had come, not altogether justly, to be regarded as wedded to a policy of "splendid isolation". In this Chamberlain had never believed, and of late he had been advocating a foreign policy based on the closest collaboration with Germany and the United States: the Prime Minister was sceptical concerning the possibility of this, but he was prepared to allow his colleague a free hand.

It was at the beginning of 1898 that Chamberlain had his first interview with Hatzfeldt, the German ambassador in London, and he made no secret of his wish for a binding agreement between Great Britain and the Triple Alliance. The offer was a perfectly genuine one, and had Berlin replied in the same spirit an agreement might well have been reached. However, Prince von Bülow, who had succeeded Hohenlohe as Imperial Chancellor, doubtless under the inspiration of Holstein, argued that Chamberlain's policy was a sign of weakness, and convinced himself that "time is telling against England". He therefore plunged into a maze of tortuous diplomacy, and while Chamberlain was making public speeches in favour of an understanding with Germany, the Kaiser divulged his offer to the Tsar. At this moment there occurred the

Fashoda incident, and although this did not lead to a war between Great Britain and France, as had been eagerly anticipated in Berlin, it was generally assumed there that there was no chance of real agreement between London and Paris: for this reason the Kaiser and his advisers thought they were in a very strong position where Great Britain was concerned.

All the same, a settlement was reached in October, 1898, between the British and German governments of the vexed question of the future of the Portuguese colonies. The finances of Portugal were, as usual, in confusion, and the interest on her external debt was in arrears. In the expectation that Lisbon would soon require foreign assistance, and with the determination to forestall France, the two Powers agreed that they could only finance Portugal jointly, and that as security for a large loan the colonies should be pledged or ceded. A secret treaty was signed dividing the Portuguese possessions into spheres of influence, and by this Southern Mozambique, Northern Angola, Madeira, the Azores, and Cape Verde Islands fell to Great Britain, while the German share consisted of Southern Angola and Northern Mozambique. Partition, however, was only to be effected if Portugal desired to sell. This agreement, it may be added, remained a dead letter, for the Portuguese government managed to overcome its financial difficulties.

In November, 1899, the Kaiser was at Windsor, and the Colonial Secretary was invited there to meet him. After some conversation William asked Chamberlain to see Bülow, who was also the Queen's guest, and to discuss the whole question of Anglo-German relations with him. Chamberlain thereupon went to the Imperial Chancellor's room in the Castle, where he found him in his shirt-sleeves unpacking his luggage. The two men had a long talk, of which the outcome was they agreed it was very desirable that the differences between their two countries should be removed, but the difficulty was that both in Great Britain and Germany public opinion was unfavourable to more friendly relations. Bülow then asked Chamberlain to take the first step in order that when he himself spoke the atmosphere might be better. The Englishman replied that this was setting him no easy task, but that he had risked his fortunes more than once in what he believed to be a good cause, and he was prepared to do so again. He said that he would be speaking at Leicester in about a fortnight's time, and would deal with the matter there. Bülow declared this would suit him admirably, as he was going to speak in the Reichstag on foreign affairs a few days later, and Chamberlain's speech would give him the opportunity for a friendly reply which would carry matters forward.

Accordingly at Leicester the Colonial Secretary flew his kite:

> The natural alliance is between ourselves and the great German Empire. . . . We have had our differences with Germany. . . . I cannot conceive any point which can arise in the immediate future which would bring ourselves and the Germans into antagonism of interests. On the contrary, I can foresee many things in the future which must be a cause of anxiety to the statesmen of Europe, but in which our interests are clearly the same as the interests of Germany.

He proceeded to pour scorn on the French Press for its attitude towards Queen Victoria and the South African War, and he declared that this would "have serious consequences if our neighbours do not mend their manners". The German Press, no doubt, had been bad enough, but "it is not with German newspapers that we desire to have an understanding or alliance; it is with the German people". Chamberlain concluded:

> I may point out to you that at bottom, the character, the main character of the Teutonic race differs very slightly indeed from the character of the Anglo-Saxon . . . and if the union between England and America is a powerful factor in the cause of peace, a new Triple Alliance between the Teutonic race and the two great branches of the Anglo-Saxon race will be a still more potent influence in the future of the world.

The reception of the speech was equally unfavourable at home and abroad, and everything now turned on the attitude of the Imperial Chancellor, who promptly went back on his word. In his statement to the Reichstag he made no allusion to Chamberlain's remarks at Leicester, and he referred very coldly to Great Britain by comparison with his cordiality towards Russia, France, and the United States, while he indirectly satirized British envy as the bitterness of a declining Power towards a rising one. "As for England," he said, "we are ready and willing, on a basis of full reciprocity and mutual consideration, to live with her in peace and harmony. But just because the foreign situation is at present

favourable, we must utilize it to secure ourselves in the future."
The reason for Bülow's treachery was, of course, the ill-luck that
dogged Britain's early efforts in South Africa, for the German
government was being advised by its military experts that the
British forces would not reach Pretoria. Chamberlain's feelings
may be imagined, and he wrote to Eckardstein that he considered
it "advisable to drop every kind of further negotiations on the
alliance question which has been discussed between us".

The sequel was not unamusing. Chamberlain only met the
Kaiser once again, and that was at Sandringham. While they
were waiting to go to church, William came up to the Colonial
Secretary, and asked him what he thought of Bülow. Chamberlain replied, "Do you want my real opinion, sir?", and on receiving
an answer in the affirmative, said, "Well, I think that, as we say,
he is a bad man to go tiger-shooting with".

In spite of this setback the Cabinet agreed to let their colleague
try again, for Chamberlain realized, though he could not pardon,
the motives which had prompted the Imperial Chancellor to play
him false; so when the Boer armies were in flight, and the General
Election of 1900 had returned the government to power with an
unimpaired majority, the Colonial Secretary once more got in
touch with Eckardstein. In the very month that King Edward
came to the throne (January, 1901) Chamberlain told Eckardstein
that the moment had come for Great Britain to abandon her policy
of isolation and to link herself either with Germany or with Russia
and France. He said that he would himself prefer closer relations
with Germany, and in his opinion a beginning could best be made
by a secret agreement concerning Morocco. If the German government refused, Great Britain would be obliged to make a treaty
with Russia, even at the price of considerable sacrifices in China
and on the Persian Gulf.

Accordingly negotiations were resumed, and they dragged on
for some six months, but, warned by his previous experience,
Chamberlain left the principal part in the conduct of them to the
new Foreign Secretary, the Marquess of Lansdowne. Once again
Holstein was the chief factor in bringing them to nothing, for he
kept instilling into the Kaiser and Bülow the belief that Great
Britain had always pursued the policy of getting others to pick her
chestnuts out of the fire, and that this was why she wanted an
agreement with Germany. He did not believe that there was any
possibility of an understanding between London and Paris, and

therefore Germany was in a position to sell her friendship at a very high price.

Far from opposing this move on the part of his ministers, King Edward did everything that he could to second it. In August, 1901, he had a long interview with the Kaiser at Wilhelmshöhe; but the meeting proved a failure, for it left both upon the King and the British Government the impression that, to quote Sir Sidney Lee, "the Kaiser was insincere in his protestations for an alliance, and that the chauvinist tone of the German Press more correctly represented the attitude of Germany". Meanwhile Chamberlain was becoming increasingly restive, though Bülow remained deaf to warnings that the Colonial Secretary's attitude was changing. In the summer *The Times* openly advocated an understanding with Russia, and called attention to the growing strength of the German Navy. As the months passed an Anglo-German alliance was seen to be a mere dream, and the winter witnessed an exchange of polemics between Chamberlain and Bülow which marked the end of the attempt to arrive at an understanding with Berlin.

Chamberlain had now learned the lesson which was one day in even more tragic circumstances to be forced upon his younger son, namely the impossibility of coming to an understanding with Germany. Every concession was either regarded as weakness or was used as an excuse for making another demand. King Edward had probably reached this conclusion earlier, but, if so, it made no difference to his efforts to further his Government's policy of friendship with Berlin. This arch-conspirator of encirclement, as the Germans termed him, left no stone unturned to come to an arrangement with Germany, and when the Anglo-Japanese Alliance was concluded at the end of January, 1902, he insisted that the German government should be informed at once. So much for the legend that King Edward was always working against the Reich. On the contrary, the Franco-British Entente would never have been formed, and Great Britain would have become the ally of Germany, had it not been for the attitude of the Kaiser, the Imperial Chancellor, and, above all, Baron von Holstein.

A friend of some sort on the mainland of Europe, however, Britain must have. As at the time of the War of American Independence she was discovering that isolation could be the reverse of splendid, and that she could not exert her proper influence in the world unless she had an understanding with a Continental

Power. It is true that she had not, during the South African War, been in so great peril as in the War of American Independence, but that was partly because the European states were more divided in 1900 than in 1780, and partly because Lord Salisbury had paid far more attention to the Navy than did Lord North. All the same, the universal hostility to Britain which was evoked by the campaign against the Boers was a warning which no British government could afford to neglect.

It would be untrue to say that King Edward initiated, or even played the leading part in, the negotiations with France which then took place, but it is extremely doubtful whether they would have been successful without him. He created the atmosphere in which the statesmen of the two countries were able to collaborate. The turning-point was his visit to Paris in May, 1903. As Prince of Wales in the days of his youth he had been a favourite in the French capital, but since then Great Britain and France had more than once been on the verge of war, while French sympathy for the Boers was notorious. The visit to Paris was therefore one of the most critical episodes of the King's life, and as he drove down the Champs Elysées, on his way from the Bois de Boulogne station, the crowd was sullenly respectful, and few were the hats that were doffed; here and there, too, were heard cries of *"Vivent les Boers"*, *"Vive Marchand"*, and *"Vive Fashoda"*. "The French don't like us", somebody remarked to the King. "Why should they?" was the characteristic reply, and before the visit was over the scene was completely changed.

The King neglected no opportunity of impressing upon the French his desire to be their friend, and one incident will suffice to illustrate the scrupulous attention which he paid to detail. One evening, accompanied by his suite, he went to the Théâtre Français. The house was full, but the public were icy, so during the interval the King left his box with the intention of winning this hostile crowd to his side. In the lobby he saw an actress whom he had met in London. Holding out his hand, he said, "Oh, Mademoiselle, I remember how I applauded you in London. You personified there all the grace, all the *esprit* of France." Never had King Edward better displayed his ability to say and do the right thing: the remark spread like wildfire, and the ice was broken. The incident, moreover, was typical. In the streets and at official receptions, in public and in private he exerted all his tremendous powers of charm, with the result that when he left

Prince of Wales helped create necessary atmosphere for the Entente.

Paris the route was lined with a madly enthusiastic crowd, and where there had been cries of *"Vivent les Boers"* there were now shouts of *"Vive notre Roi"*. The visit was one of the greatest personal triumphs in recent history.

Some months elapsed before a settlement of all the points of issue between Great Britain and France was reached, and the principal part in the negotiations was played by Lansdowne and Delcassé. The result, in April, 1904, was a series of agreements which collectively initiated the Anglo-French Entente.

The first of these concerned Egypt and Morocco. Great Britain declared that she had no intention of altering the political status of Egypt, and France undertook not to obstruct British action by asking that a limit of time be fixed for the occupation or in any other way. France, in her turn, declared that she had no intention of altering the political status of Morocco, and Britain promised not to obstruct French action in that country. Both in Egypt and Morocco there was to be commercial liberty for at least thirty years, and no fortifications were to be erected on the Moorish coast opposite Gibraltar. For the rest, France was to come to an understanding with Spain concerning Morocco; the Egyptian government was given a freer hand in financial matters so long as the service of the debt was maintained; and the juridical position of the Suez Canal in time of war was settled in accordance with the wishes of France.

A second agreement removed a long-standing difference relating to the fishing rights off Newfoundland. The controversy dated from the Treaty of Utrecht which recognized that the island was in future to belong to Great Britain, but gave to the French "the right to catch and dry fish" on part of the coast henceforth known as the French shore. France now renounced these rights, which had given rise to endless disputes, and her fishermen were placed on the same footing as those of other nationalities. In return Great Britain agreed to certain territorial modifications in West Africa, in consequence of which France obtained 14,000 square miles and uninterrupted access from her territories on the Niger to those on Lake Chad.

A third document contained a declaration concerning Siam, Madagascar, and the New Hebrides. The two Powers agreed to refrain from armed intervention or the acquisition of special privileges in the basin of the Menam; France recognized that all Siamese possessions on the west of this neutral zone and of the

[handwritten marginalia:] England: free hand in Egypt; France: free hand in Morocco.

[handwritten marginalia:] France got 14,000 sq. miles in west africa, renounced "drying rights" in Newfoundland

Gulf of Siam, including the Malay Peninsula and the adjacent islands, should come under British influence; and Britain admitted French influence in all Siamese territory on the east and south-east of the zone. As regards Madagascar the British government abandoned the protest which had been maintained since 1896 against the tariff introduced after the annexation of the island. A special arrangement, it was decided, was necessary in the case of the New Hebrides, and in 1906 an Anglo-French condominium was duly established there.

Such was the inception of the Anglo-French Entente. It was far from being an alliance, and it did not profess to do more than settle the problems which had long been outstanding between the two Powers, but it prepared the way for a closer understanding when circumstances arose, and only a short time was to elapse before this happened.

CHAPTER XXII

IMPERIAL BRITAIN, 1815–1904

GREAT Britain played a much less prominent part in the politics of the mainland of Europe in the nineteenth century than had been the case in its predecessor or was to be the case in its successor. There were several reasons for this, of which two are outstanding. The accession of Queen Victoria in 1837 severed the link with Hanover which had existed ever since the death of Anne, and so obviated the necessity of definite action whenever a crisis arose in Germany: this was indeed fortunate from the British point of view, for had the association of Great Britain with Hanover continued into the Bismarckian era the consequences would have been very serious. Then, again, domestic and—later—Imperial affairs tended to absorb the attention of successive British administrations, not to mention that of the British public, so that in the main there was a gradual withdrawal from Europe save when the national interests were vitally affected.

To pass from the general to the particular, the foreign relations of Great Britain during the nineteenth century fall into four periods. The first of these lasted until the defeat of Napoleon at Waterloo, and was wholly concerned with the struggle against France. The second extended until the death of Canning in 1827, and was marked by the settlement of the problems arising out of the Revolutionary and Napoleonic Wars as well as by the definition of the British attitude towards the Greek and Latin American questions. These two periods have already been considered in some detail on an earlier page. Next came the decades in the middle of the century, from the death of Canning to the formation of Disraeli's second government in 1874, when Great Britain took a fitful, occasionally forceful, but not very consistent, interest in the problems of the rest of the world. Lastly, there was the period from 1874 to the conclusion of the Entente with France when Great Britain was influenced very largely by Imperial considerations.

Of the Foreign Secretaries during these hundred and four years it is difficult to resist the conclusion that only four were of the first rank, namely Castlereagh, Canning, Salisbury, and Lansdowne. It may be objected that Palmerston should be included in this select quartet, but it is not easy to admit the argument. He had, it is true, a genius for publicity which served to cover a multitude of sins with his contemporaries, but he had little sense of responsibility, and still less of relative values, as was shown when he tarnished the name of his country by bullying Greece in the interests of the worthless Don Pacifico. For some years he was able to appear in the *rôle* of a great statesman for there were few of the latter with whom he was called upon to compete, but when Bismarck rose to power the star of Palmerston paled before him, as that of Olivares had done before Richelieu. Of the rest, Aberdeen was well-meaning but weak, and was generally in poor health; Granville and Malmesbury were little better than nonentities; while Lord John Russell, who allowed his heart to rule his head, was placed by a later Foreign Secretary in the Chamber of Horrors of his predecessors. Of the men of second rank who were at the Foreign Office during this period it would seem that Clarendon was the most capable.

So much for the men. The policy which they pursued was in the main based upon the maintenance of the Vienna settlement, though modifications of this were accepted on more than one occasion, and in such a way as to give a very definite appearance of inconsistency. In the main, however, it was appreciated that Great Britain could not bring her full weight to bear upon the mainland of Europe without a Continental ally, and one was usually persuaded to appear as represented by Russia in the question of Greek independence, France at the time of the Belgian rising and of the Crimean War, and Austria in 1878. When Britain was isolated she could do nothing, as was proved on the occasion of the Schleswig-Holstein crisis, and might even be herself in danger, as in the War of American Independence and in the earlier days of the South African War. It was the realization of this fact which drove Salisbury and Chamberlain to attempt a renewal of the old understanding with Germany, and, when this proved impossible, to conclude the Entente with France.

As the years passed there arose another factor which by no means always received the attention it deserved, and that was the relative strength of armaments. In the eighteenth century Britain had been able to send overseas armies of a size sufficiently respectable to turn the scale in favour of herself and her allies, but with the passage of time the man-power required for the successful conduct of war increased, and the land establishment of Great Britain

[margin note: England needed an ally on the Continent to function efficiently.]

began to lag behind, though how far behind was not fully realized by her rulers until the Four Years' War. On the other hand the mistake was not made of reducing the naval forces, and in 1889 a two-power standard was adopted in consequence of which the British Navy was to be maintained on a footing equal to that of the combined fleets of France and Russia, for the German Navy was still negligible, and in any event a war with the Reich was deemed impossible. The British Army was not prepared for Continental, but for Indian and colonial, warfare, and its weight could not have been considerable if thrown into the European scale. Britain's chief assets as an ally by the end of the century were, therefore, her Navy and her purse, and this fact had to be taken into account by those responsible for the conduct of her foreign policy.

Neglectful as mid-Victorian statesmen might be of colonial considerations their attitude was very different where India was concerned. The steady Russian advance towards Afghanistan was always regarded with the gravest suspicion, and Russian control of the Straits was resisted because of the threat which it implied to the British line of communication with India and the Far East; especially was this the case during the years which elapsed between the opening of the Suez Canal in 1869 and the occupation of Egypt in 1882. Nor was this all, for Britain was a great Mohammedan Power, and any attacks upon the Ottoman Sultan had repercussions in India. It would, of course, be an exaggeration to say that British policy towards Russia and Turkey was solely influenced by such considerations, but they unquestionably played their part even in the era when British statesmen, misinterpreting the lesson of the American colonies, were forgetful of their Imperial heritage.

With the advent of Disraeli to power in 1874 there came a realization of the potentialities of the Empire, and for the next thirty years it had an important influence upon the foreign policy of successive administrations, more particularly after the assistance given by the Dominions in the South African War. Of this development Joseph Chamberlain was one of the protagonists, and it has already been shown how important a *rôle* he played in the Anglo-German negotiations at the turn of the century. One difficulty began to confront the national statesmen at this period, and it was that while a bad foreign policy may easily lose an election in modern England a good foreign policy rarely wins one. Beaconsfield was defeated in 1880 very largely because of what were considered to be his blunders in South Africa and Afghanistan; Gladstone was never forgiven for the death of Gordon, and the Near Eastern policy of Mr. Lloyd George was chiefly responsible for the overthrow of his administration in 1922. On the other hand, it is doubtful whether the brilliant diplomacy of Lansdowne was worth a single vote to Balfour in 1906, and the Locarno Pact certainly did nothing to prevent a Conservative disaster in 1929.

It was in Africa that these Imperial tendencies were most manifest, and events in that continent during the last years of the nineteenth, and the opening ones of the twentieth, century had the greatest influence upon the mutual relations of the Powers.

In 1860 the possessions of the European states were mere patches on the map, that is to say Algeria in the north, two British colonies thousands of miles to the south, with a few British, Spanish, and Portuguese settlements dotted along the west and east coasts. Forty years later Abyssinia and Liberia were the only portions of Africa not subject to European rule. The rapidity with which this change took place engendered friction, and Great Britain and France, in particular, were more than once on the verge of war.

Not for the first time in its history the state of Egypt provided an opening for foreign intrigues. In 1863 the Khedivial throne was ascended by Ismail, whose extravagance soon exhausted the country's finances, and drove her ruler to seek accommodation abroad. His Suez Canal shares were bought by the British government in 1875, but this did not suffice to avert bankruptcy, and in the following year the Caisse de la Dette was instituted with control by Great Britain, France, Germany, Austria-Hungary, and Italy over a large part of the revenue. The financial interests of the Powers, especially those of Great Britain and France, not unnaturally became entangled in the domestic politics of Egypt, which were dominated by the desire of the Khedive to govern absolutely; chaos ensued, and in 1879 the Sultan deposed him by telegraph, appointing Tewfik as his successor.

For two years all went well. An international Commission of Liquidation was appointed to arrange a composition with Egypt's creditors, and the British government insisted that it should deal not only with the debt but with the needs of the country. The creditors were accordingly divided into three classes, two-thirds of the revenue was mortgaged for their claims, interest was reduced to four per cent, and a limit was placed on national expenditure. In spite of many differences between London and Paris the Dual Control of Britain and France was not working badly when, in 1881, a strong Nationalist movement, headed by Arabi Pasha, began to sweep the country. Thereupon there ensued a period of divided counsels not only in Cairo, but also in London, Paris, and Constantinople. Gladstone wished to avoid strong action at all costs, but Egypt could not be ignored owing to her geographical position; the ephemeral Cabinets of the Third Republic blew hot and cold; while the Sultan feared that Egypt was going the same way as Tunis. In Berlin the Iron Chancellor was watching the course of events with grim satisfaction: Egypt, he declared, was the Schleswig-Holstein of the Western Powers, who would intervene together and quarrel over the spoils.

The crisis came in the summer of 1882. In June there was a rising in Alexandria in the course of which fifty Europeans were killed, and the situation became so threatening that even the pacific administration of Gladstone was finally driven to armed intervention. Alexandria was bombarded on July 11th, and two months later Arabi was crushed at Tel-el-Kebir. As Lord Granville, then Foreign Secretary, protested, this isolated action was by no means of British seeking, and never was a province acquired with greater reluctance than was Egypt by Gladstone. French co-operation had been sought from the beginning, but, on the motion of Clemenceau, the French Chamber refused its assent. Italy was then approached, but she, too, declined. Germany, on the other hand, gave the British government its full diplomatic support, and Bismarck declared that "the friendship of the British Empire is much more important for us than the fate of Egypt".

The British position was definitely anomalous, for Great Britain had not conquered Egypt, which still formed part of the Ottoman Empire. Accordingly, in January, 1883, a circular dispatch was sent to the Powers in which the attitude of the British Government was defined. "Though for the present a British force remains in Egypt for the preservation of public tranquillity, H.M. Government are desirous of withdrawing it as soon as the state of the country and the organization of proper means for the maintenance of the Khedive's authority will admit of it". The Suez Canal must be neutralized in time of war, and open equally to the commerce of all nations in time of peace. Among desirable reforms were the equal taxation of foreigners and natives, the

s

creation of a small but efficient army under foreign officers, and the substitution of an efficient *gendarmerie* for the native police. A British adviser was to supersede the Dual Control, and a representative assembly was foreshadowed. In September of the same year Sir Evelyn Baring, later Earl of Cromer, arrived in Cairo with the modest title of Consul-General and Diplomatic Agent, and there he was destined to remain as ruler of the country for twenty-three years. Egypt had become a British Protectorate in all but name.

Although France was responsible for the turn which events had taken she was far from appreciating it, and she did all in her power to render difficult the position of the British authorities until the conclusion of the Entente in 1904. In 1898, indeed, the hostility between the two Powers in the Nile valley came very close to involving them in war at the time of the "Fashoda incident".

The weakness of Egypt had resulted in the loss of the Sudan, which remained in the hands of the Mahdi, and of his successor, the Khalifa, until Kitchener's victory at Omdurman in 1898. This was in September, but two months earlier Marchand had arrived at Fashoda, five hundred miles south of Khartum, from the west, and it was clear that a crisis of the first magnitude had arisen. Kitchener and Marchand met on terms of perfect courtesy, but the latter refused to withdraw his force unless he received instructions from Paris to that effect. At first the French government, of whom the most important member was Delcassé, the Foreign Minister, declined to give way, and public opinion on both sides of the Channel was soon inflamed. The Liberal leader, Lord Rosebery, assured the government that behind it was "the united strength of the nation"; Sir Michael Hicks-Beach, the Chancellor of the Exchequer, bluntly declared, "there are worse evils than war, and we shall not shrink from anything that may come"; and the reserves were called up. The Press, for the most part was decidedly bellicose, and a cartoon in *Punch* well represented the popular attitude. "What will you give me if I go away?" asks the little organ-grinder: "I will give you something if you don't", replies a muscular John Bull with a menacing frown.

War seemed inevitable, but the French government realized its weakness at sea, and the impossibility of defending its overseas possessions. Delcassé, too, was in favour of moderation, and his influence was considerable. So, at the beginning of November, France gave way, and Marchand evacuated Fashoda, though he refused to return through Egypt and preferred the long route by way of Abyssinia. Great Britain had achieved her aim by the threat of war, and Anglo-French relations were in consequence still further embittered. The repercussions of the "Fashoda incident" upon German diplomacy have already been discussed.

To the south-east these years were also marked by a series of events which were fraught with momentous consequences in the future. Italy had sought compensation for Tunis by occupying Massowah on the Red Sea, where the Khedive had long maintained a garrison; since the early eighties this port had been isolated by the Dervishes, and the British government was glad to see it in friendly hands. From there the Italians advanced slowly towards the highlands of Abyssinia, but not without reverses, such as that at Dogali in 1887. Nevertheless, two years later there was concluded the Treaty of Uccialli by which the King of Italy was made the intermediary for Abyssinia's relations with foreign Powers, and Italy henceforth regarded the country as a Protectorate. In 1891 an Anglo-Italian agreement settled the boundaries of the two spheres of influence: Kassala was placed in the British zone, but Italy was allowed to occupy it for military reasons, while Abyssinia was definitely recognized by Great Britain as belonging to the Italian zone.

Meanwhile Menelek II, the Emperor of Abyssinia, rejected the Italian claim to a Protectorate over his country, but in spite of a recent success in the field he did not wish to push matters to extremes; he therefore contented himself with overtures for peace on the basis of an Italian withdrawal from territory recently occupied and a revision of the Treaty of Uccialli. The Italian commander-in-chief, General Baratieri, knowing that he was about to be superseded, rejected these proposals, and in March, 1896, attacked a greatly superior Abyssinian army at Adowa. The Italians were completely defeated, and in consequence they were compelled to agree to the cancellation of the Treaty of Uccialli and to recognize the complete independence of Abyssinia. The administration of Crispi, who was primarily responsible for this expansionist policy, fell from power, and another fifteen years elapsed before Italian public opinion took kindly to the idea of colonial adventures, and even then it was by no means united, for strong opposition developed in the Socialist ranks led by a young man called Benito Mussolini.

If the later decades of the nineteenth century were marked by

<!-- marginalia handwritten: 1896: Italy beaten in Ethiopia, decides to give up Empire dreams for a whilex -->

tension and strife in Egypt and in East Africa the situation in South Africa was no less complicated, and, as we have seen, was not without its influence upon Anglo-German relations. Disraeli had annexed the Transvaal to the British Crown, but the Boers continued restive, and at last rose in revolt under Kruger. They gained a victory at Majuba in 1881 over a British force, and Gladstone then agreed, by the Pretoria Convention, to evacuate the country, though the suzerainty of the Crown was to be retained. This settlement was regarded by the Boers as a triumph, and by many people in England as a piece of magnanimous statesmanship, but the British in South Africa and their friends at home denounced it as a betrayal of loyal subjects, both white and coloured, who were handed over to the tender mercies of their enemies, the Boers.

There was continual trouble between Boer and Briton in the years which followed the conclusion of the Pretoria Convention, but nothing more serious might have happened had it not been for the discovery of gold at Johannesburg and the election of Kruger as President of the Transvaal Republic. The first of these events resulted in the immigration of large numbers of British subjects, whom the Dutch termed Uitlanders, and the second placed supreme power in the hands of a man who was, although probably sincere, narrow-minded to the point of fanaticism. The Uitlanders were promised equal rights with the Dutch, but they never got them, although they provided nine-tenths of the revenue. Neither their persons nor their possessions were safe, for they were not allowed to carry arms to protect themselves or their women. When they demanded representation, they were mocked, and told "to come and fight for it". This was bad enough, but it was by no means all. Kruger sent out filibustering expeditions into Bechuanaland, Zululand, and Swaziland, territories which were no concern of his; he conscripted Englishmen to fight the natives with whom they had no quarrel; and he closed the Vaal River drifts, over which goods were sent by road to Johannesburg, in order to make the Uitlanders pay the exorbitant tariff exacted on his railway.

This was the situation which Chamberlain found when he went to the Colonial Office in 1895, and he was not the man to put up with it. He at once took a strong line with Kruger, and as the Dutchman was not yet ready to fight, he had to give way. The drifts were reopened, but this was not to be the end of the crisis.

Unable to procure redress for themselves, aware of the strained relations existing with the British government, and smarting bitterly under the consciousness of their inferior position, the Uitlanders came to the conclusion that something more drastic than constitutional agitation was required to redress the balance. Feelings such as these produced, at the end of 1895, the Jameson Raid.

The failure of this ill-considered exploit not only prompted the Kaiser to send Kruger the telegram of which the consequences have already been discussed, but it both strengthened the Dutchman's hands and increased his suspicions of Great Britain. Although the Transvaal was not a sovereign state he sent missions to Europe in order to obtain the support of the more Anglophobe Powers; he made a treaty with the Orange Free State, with whom the British government had no quarrel, by which that country promised to throw in its lot with the Transvaal; and he intrigued with the Dutch in Cape Colony for the formation of a united front against the British. Vast sums of money were spent on armaments. As for the Uitlanders, their position grew steadily worse. Kruger secured the passage of several laws which adversely affected the status of aliens, he harassed the mining and commercial population with increased taxation, and he made no effort to check the corruption which characterized the Boer administration.

For two and a half years the relations between London and Pretoria grew steadily more embittered. It is difficult to say which mistrusted the other more, Chamberlain or Kruger, and in spite of repeated negotiations they remained as far apart as ever. Not that it was impossible to obtain concessions from the Dutchman which appeared satisfactory, but it was quite another thing to get any that really were satisfactory when examined in the light of the grievances they were to remove; it was still more difficult to obtain guarantees, without which the concessions would be useless. "He dribbles out reforms", Chamberlain declared, "like water from a squeezed sponge."

With the coming of autumn in 1899 the storm burst. The President of the Orange Free State complained that British troops were massing on the frontier, and refused to hear the argument that this step was rendered necessary by the attitude of the Boers; he then caused his Volksraad to pass a declaration that there was no reason for war, that the responsibility would rest with Great Britain, and that the Orange Free State would act with the Transvaal. This caused the British government to reinforce, though to no great extent, the troops in South Africa, whereupon, on October 9th the Transvaal issued a forty-eight hours' ultimatum demanding that the forces on its border should be instantly withdrawn, that all the reinforcements which had arrived since June should be removed, and that the troops on the high seas should not be allowed to land. If the reply was not favourable "the Transvaal Government would be compelled to regard the action of Her Majesty's Government as a formal declaration of war". The ultimatum was, of course, rejected, and on October 12th the Boer commandos invaded Natal.

The influence of the South African War upon Britain's relations with her neighbours was very considerable, apart altogether from her own realization of the perils of isolation. The difficulty which her army experienced in overcoming the resistance of the Boers caused it to be rated extremely low by the General Staffs of the Continental Powers, and this depreciation continued until the Four Years' War. On the other hand it was the campaign in South Africa which led to those reforms in training and organization which enabled Sir John French's forces to save the day in 1914-1915. This was not realized abroad at the time, and Britain was despised as well as hated. "In this war I am on the side of England", the Austrian Emperor observed to the British ambassador at a diplomatic reception, but his attitude was exceptional. Elsewhere throughout the world Britain was regarded as a bully, and scorned as an incompetent one at that. In these circumstances it is hardly remarkable that the rally of the self-governing Dominions to the cause of the Mother Country, and the evidence of Imperial solidarity which this afforded, should have escaped the notice of foreign Powers, prophetic though it was of future developments.

In West Africa, as well as in other parts of the continent, the ambitions of Britain at this time led to complications with her neighbours, notably with the French. Since the occupation of Tunis the attention of more than one government in France had been directed towards Africa as the place where compensation might be found for a diminished prestige in Europe, and as the British began to press up into the interior from the coast, so the French were pressing down from the interior towards the coast. With the arrival of Joseph Chamberlain at the Colonial Office in 1895 there occurred a clash of personalities, as well as of national policies. At the Quai d'Orsay was Hanotaux, and the biographer of Richelieu was pursuing a policy of which the great Cardinal would most heartily have approved. This was the utmost expansion of France in Africa, and his aim was that directly or indirectly French rule should extend from the Mediterranean to the Congo, and from the Atlantic to the Red Sea. This did not in the least fit in with Chamberlain's ideas.

As the French columns began to penetrate into territory hitherto considered British, the Colonial Secretary decided that the time had come to act, whatever might be the consequences. He created a new military body, the West African Frontier Force, which soon proved itself the equal of the Senegalese forces in the service of France, and he gave the command of it to Colonel, later Lord, Lugard. For some months hostilities seemed inevitable, and on several occasions British and French troops confronted one another in some African village which was claimed both by Paris and London. France was in the middle of the Dreyfus *affaire*, and the British ambassador warned his government that a foreign war might prove an irresistible temptation in such circumstances. Salisbury was at one moment alarmed at the progress of events, and hinted at the advisability of making concessions, but Chamberlain insisted that these must not be unilateral. "I thought he was entirely with us", he wrote, "and now he is prepared to give away everything and get nothing. I am more than sorry to differ from him, but I cannot stand it."

With Chamberlain's full support and encouragement, Lugard proceeded to safeguard the British position on the Niger. All places where the tricolour was found flying and was guarded by men in uniform were to be avoided, but any territory upon which the Union Jack had once been planted was to be defended at all costs. In no circumstances were British troops to fire first, but if hostilities did break out the authority of Great Britain was to be asserted throughout the whole of Borgu. Both sides had considerable justification for what they were doing. The French argued that effective occupation conferred superior right, while the British held that title belonged to priority of treaties with native potentates, and that actual occupation of territory was not a matter of great importance. This state of suspended war lasted for nine months, and the wonder is that the guns did not go off by themselves.

Meanwhile negotiations for a settlement had been taking place in Paris, and they dragged on from the late autumn of 1897 to the summer of the following year without reaching a conclusion. The French first of all thought that Chamberlain was bluffing, and when this proved not to be the case they tried to exploit the known differences between him and the Prime Minister. This manoeuvre, too, failed, and on June 14th, 1898, the Anglo-French Convention was signed. Hanotaux declared that it united three great regions— Algeria and Tunis, Senegal and Niger, Lake Chad and the Congo, while Great Britain gained the bulk of the territory which had been in dispute during the two previous years.

A month later Marchand hoisted the tricolour over Fashoda, and Anglo-French relations were in the melting-pot once more; the situation was far more serious than it had been in West Africa for on the Niger there was room for territorial compromise, but there was none on the Nile. Even when the French Government gave instructions to Marchand to withdraw the wider issue still remained to be settled. In November, 1898, Chamberlain spoke out. After paying a high tribute to the French people he denounced a "policy of pinpricks", and declared, "Fashoda is only a symbol: the great issue is the control of the whole valley of the Nile". In this the Colonial Secretary was in deadly earnest, and in private conversation with Eckardstein he remarked, "We are a peaceful, commercial nation, but as soon as we are ready we shall present our bill to France, not only in Egypt, but all over the globe, and should she refuse to pay, then war". For a space the French hoped that Germany or Russia would come to their aid, or that Salisbury would over-rule Chamberlain. When neither of these hopes was fulfilled, they came to terms, and on March 21st, 1899, a second Anglo-French Convention was signed. By this the watershed between the Congo and the Nile became the line of political demarcation, and so Chamberlain gained his point on the Nile as on the Niger.

In view of these continuously strained relations between Great Britain and France as a result of their colonial rivalry it is perhaps understandable that Holstein refused to believe that the two nations would ever co-operate, and held that the history of the eighteenth century would repeat itself in that the differences which separated London and Paris overseas would prevent them from coming together in Europe. Had the policy of Bismarck been continued this conjecture might well have proved correct.

CHAPTER XXIII

THE FAR EAST, 1713-1905

As the nineteenth century drew to its close the problems of the Far East began to assume a world-wide importance which had not been theirs since those far-off days when the course of events in China more than once set forces in motion which eventually overturned empires in Europe. There is a regrettable tendency to regard international relations over too short a period, and the result of this has often been to obscure the fact that when the West came into contact with the East in the eighteenth and nineteenth centuries Asia was undergoing one of its periods of decline while Europe was in the ascendant. It had not always been so, and for several hundreds of years previously, the West had been on the defensive. Now, however, the Ottoman and Persian monarchies were decadent, and the great Moghul empires in India and China were in a similar condition. That this state of affairs might not be permanent, and represented but one cycle among many, never occurred to the statesmen of contemporary Europe; their successors have in consequence been compelled to learn the lesson in a hard school.

For many centuries the great nation of the Far East was, to the outside world, China, and it was in no way surprising that this should have been the case. In 1662 the last of the Ming Emperors committed suicide, and henceforth the destinies of the Middle Kingdom were in the hands of the conquering Manchus. The earlier monarchs of this dynasty were men of great force of character, perhaps the most noteworthy being K'ang Hsi (1662-1723) and Ch'ien Lung (1736-1796); with the death of the latter decay set in. The Manchus ruled not only over China proper, but also over vast territories which have long since passed into other hands. K'ang Hsi added Tibet to his possessions, and Ch'ien Lung annexed Ili and Turkestan. Manchu armies penetrated Burma, while Korea, Annam, and Siam paid tribute to the Son of Heaven in Pekin. During this period there were many contacts, both commercial and cultural, with Europe, and the influence of France, then at the zenith of her power, was felt in the Far East. Louis XIV took a personal interest in Oriental matters, and the splendour of Versailles can easily be traced among the ruins of the Summer

Palace. The Manchus reciprocated; the Jesuits were placed in charge of the bureau of astronomy; and K'ang Hsi issued what amounted to an edict of religious toleration.

With the passage of time these religious contacts became weaker, and commercial difficulties arose. First of all Europe, being in process of losing its own faith, no longer took any interest in those who were endeavouring to spread that faith elsewhere. Then the long Revolutionary and Napoleonic Wars absorbed the attention of the Western nations. At the same time commercial intercourse, encouraged by the beginnings of the Industrial Revolution, was growing in importance. The Portuguese were settled in Macao; by the middle of Ch'ien Lung's reign British trade, which was a monopoly of the East India Company, was more important than that of any other European country; and in 1784 there arrived in Chinese waters the first ship flying the flag of the United States. The complications to which these developments gave rise were largely due to the attitude of superiority affected by the Chinese in their dealings with the outside world: they refused to treat on any basis of equality, and regarded all foreign envoys as bearers of tribute. This had not mattered so much in the height of Manchu power, for the Manchus were foreigners themselves, and did not share all the prejudices of their subjects: Ch'ien Lung, for example, in 1793 treated Lord Macartney with perfect courtesy, but after his death the Manchu grip slackened, and an impossible state of affairs came into existence. By the beginning of the nineteenth century Canton was the only port open to merchants from abroad; Europeans were there confined to a small area, and were ordered to spend the quiet months at Macao. Nor was this all, for there were many other vexatious regulations, such as the absence of fixed tariff charges, the exactions of corrupt officials, the prohibition against a Chinese teaching a foreigner the language, and the subjection of Europeans to the jurisdiction of the Chinese courts.

These pretensions were not supported by any real military power, or capacity. The Chinese themselves were—and still are—a peace-loving people who hold soldiers in low esteem, and the Manchu garrisons, which had been placed in the principal cities, were far from being distinguished by that warlike spirit which had animated their ancestors two centuries earlier. Their arms were also markedly inferior to those of European troops. Furthermore, there was a want of cohesion about the provinces of China. The

Manchus had left them a considerable amount of autonomy, and particularism was the keynote of both civil and military administration. To quote a British representative at Pekin, "If the Governor-General of Canton got into difficulties with the English, if his forts were captured, his war-junks destroyed, and the city itself forced to pay a heavy ransom as the price of being spared an assault, his immediate neighbour, the Governor-General of Fuhkien, did not regard it as his duty to render assistance, or even to abstain from friendly relations with the English, and Cantonese willingly enrolled themselves to carry the scaling ladders for the English troops, which took by assault the forts at the mouth of the river that was the highway to Pekin".

Such being the case opportunities for aggression on one side, for obstruction on the other, and for misunderstanding on both, abounded, and a further complication was introduced in 1834 when the monopoly of the East India Company was terminated, and the Chinese had to deal with a direct representative of the British government. In 1839 the Cabinet came to the conclusion that steps must be taken to place relations with China on a more satisfactory footing, and a small force was sent to the Far East to give material support to this policy. Meanwhile, the Chinese government had seized a large quantity of opium belonging to British subjects who had accumulated it in the hope of its importation being legalized, and who were now demanding compensation for their loss. Not for the first, or the last, time in British history the force originally despatched proved to be inadequate for the purpose for which it was intended, and it had to be augmented. By the middle of August, 1841, the Chinese had been sufficiently beaten to be ready to make peace, and on the 29th of that month was concluded the Treaty of Nanking.

This agreement provided for the cession of Hongkong, and the payment of a war indemnity of twelve million dollars. There were also many regulations for the settlement of past, and the prevention of future, disputes, while it was provided that in addition to Canton the ports of Amoy, Foochow, Ningpo, and Shanghai should be open to foreign trade.

So far Great Britain had in recent times been the foreign Power most interested in China, but France now reappeared on the Far Eastern scene, and the United States began to make her influence felt. The years following the opening of the treaty ports were thus marked by a rapid development of relations between China and the outside world, and this in its turn gave rise to many a difficulty. Much of necessity had to be left to the men on the spot owing to the slowness of communications, and in passing judgment upon the actions of the European Powers it should be remembered that the usual time required for a report from China to arrive in Europe and for instructions to be returned, was at least ten months, up to 1846; after that the voyage one way was reduced to about fifty days, and in 1853 to about forty-four; but so late as 1870 the news of a massacre in Tientsin took thirty-five days to reach Europe. To remedy the abuses to which this state of affairs gave rise the Powers decided to establish permanent legations in the Chinese capital, and to put relations with the Celestial Empire upon a normal diplomatic footing for the protection of their nationals engaged in religious or commercial ventures.

The Chinese government by no means approved of this suggestion which meant that once and for all the representatives of foreign Powers would have to be received on a basis of equality, with a consequent loss of face to itself in the eyes of its people. Nevertheless it was, under pressure, compelled to agree by the Tientsin Treaties in 1858. These, however, were not carried out, for disputes at once arose as to the ceremonial with which the foreign representatives were to be received by the Emperor, and in 1860 an Anglo-French force began its march to Pekin. At this point a further complication supervened when the Chinese were found to have tortured to death a number of prisoners whom they had captured in spite of the flag of truce carried by the latter. For this outrage the allies destroyed the Summer Palace, the place where the victims had actually suffered, and the residence of the monarch who had offered monetary rewards for the heads of "barbarians". China was in addition compelled to pay an indemnity of two-and-a-half million pounds, and to add Tientsin to the number of treaty-ports. Even so, the British and French ambassadors were unable to present their credentials to the Emperor, as he, or his officials, refused to omit the ceremony of the *Ko-t'au*.

Legations were soon established in Pekin by all the leading Powers, and this betokened a changed attitude in their relations with China. Hitherto they had tended in the main to settle disputes with local officials by force of arms, but they now began to treat with the Imperial Government direct. This development, of course, implied that the Imperial Government could make its will effective throughout the whole Empire; this was certainly not the case, for ever since 1851 there had been in progress the Taiping Rebellion, which was in part organized banditry and in part a nationalist rising against the Manchus. The foreign Powers now proceeded to assist the Imperial Government to suppress the Taipings, and, largely owing to the strategy of Gordon, this was accomplished by the summer of 1864, but not before the richest provinces of the Empire had been devastated by civil war for upwards of a decade. As the nineteenth century drew to its close, therefore, everything pointed to the fact that China was on the eve of another of those periods of weakness which have occurred so often during her long history. The dynasty was in full decay; the country was weakened by internal strife; and the Imperial Government had lost prestige in consequence of the concessions which it had been compelled to make to foreign Powers. At this point another rival appeared upon the scene in the shape of Japan.

This is not the place for an account of the earlier Japanese relations with the outside world, for ever since 1638 these had been non-existent except for the fact that a few Dutch and Chinese traders had been tolerated, rather than encouraged, at Nagasaki. Japanese subjects, it may be added, were forbidden to travel or to trade abroad. The position was further complicated by the fact that for six-and-a-half centuries the legitimate sovereign, that is to say the Mikado, had been a mere figure-head: he kept entirely in the background, exercised no authority whatever, and was never seen by the people. He was surrounded by a sort of phantom Court, whose members bore administrative titles dating from the remote period when he was *de facto* as well as *de jure* ruler. All effective power was in the hands of the Shogun or Tycoon, who corresponded to the Merovingian Mayor of the Palace or to the Mahratta Peishwa.

More than once during the earlier years of the nineteenth century attempts had been made by the European Powers to persuade the Shogun to adopt a different attitude towards foreigners, but without success, and it was not until the arrival of the U.S. Commodore Perry with his squadron in 1853 that a new policy began to be adopted. Thereafter events moved rapidly: the Shogunate was overthrown in 1868, the Mikado resumed the powers of which he had been divested for centuries, and Japan appeared in due course with a constitution modelled on that of the Hohenzollern Reich. Needless to say, these developments were not uninfluenced by what was taking place in contemporary China. Japanese states-

men realized that whether the Orient liked it or not the Europeans
and Americans had come to stay, and the results of the obstruc-
tional policy of the Chinese government were not encouraging.
The Mikado and his advisers, therefore, decided to adopt quite
another line, and to allow their country to be westernized, at any
rate externally, in the hope that by this means she might not only
be able to retain her independence but also to take advantage of
the increasing embarrassments of her Chinese enemy and neighbour.

The affairs of Korea soon provided both an opportunity and
an excuse for Japanese expansion. That country held the anomalous position of being tributary to two separate Powers, China
and Japan, and so long ago as the seventeenth century it had got
into difficulty with the Chinese Emperor over the question of
suzerainty. By the end of the nineteenth century Korea was in a
state bordering upon anarchy, and Tokyo pressed for reforms of
which Pekin would not hear. When the Japanese took the matter
up with the Korean government direct China began to prepare
for war, and by the summer of 1894 hostilities had broken out. It
was universally assumed that China, with her vast resources,
would vanquish her tiny rival, and great was the astonishment
throughout the world when this did not prove to be the case. The
armies and fleets of the Celestial Empire went down to disaster
before those of Dai Nippon, and the consequences of this were seen
in the Treaty of Shimonoseki which was signed in April, 1895.
By this treaty the Chinese ceded to Japan the Liao-Tung peninsula,
the island of Formosa, and the Pescadores group, while there was
also an indemnity.

The balance of power in the Far East had shifted, and before
long this change was destined to have the most momentous consequences all over the world. It is difficult to decide whether the
Powers were more surprised or displeased. Russia had no desire
to have as a neighbour an aggressive Japan rather than a moribund
China; France was apprehensive of anything that might weaken
her Russian ally; while Germany did not want to see Russia turning to Europe in consequence of being thwarted in Asia. On the
other hand, if China was really so weak as she had proved herself
to be in the recent war then she was in no condition to resist any
demands which might be made upon her from other quarters.

With these considerations in mind the governments of France,
Germany, and Russia presented a collective note to Japan urging

her to forego the acquisition of the Liao-Tung peninsula on the ground that whoever possessed Port Arthur would dominate Pekin. The Japanese very wisely gave way, and secured a further monetary payment by way of recompense. This sum was lent to China by Germany and Russia, who thereby strengthened their hold over the Pekin government. With Japan thus out of the way the three Powers proceeded to put pressure upon the helpless Chinese. The result was all that could be desired. In 1897 Germany obtained one of the best ports in the Far East at Tsingtao, though she held it by courtesy of Great Britain and Japan. The following year saw Russia established in Port Arthur from which the Japanese had been requested to withdraw, while France demanded the port of Kwang Chow Wen, and accepted an assurance from the Chinese government that the *hinterland* would be recognized as being under French influence. In 1898, too, Great Britain obtained a lease of Wei-Hai-Wei, though this was not regarded by Japan as an unfriendly act, since the British Government had manifested its friendship for Tokyo four years before by the surrender of extra-territorial rights; it had also refused to be associated with the collective note of France, Germany, and Russia.

The attitude adopted by Russia at this time is understandable; her energies were concentrated on the Far East, and she was not prepared to tolerate a rival there, even if she had to fight. Germany, on the other hand, was not vitally affected by recent developments, and her deliberate alienation of Japan was all of a piece with that reckless giving of pledges to fortune which had marked her policy ever since the fall of Bismarck. Russia was no longer her friend, so it was an act of folly to antagonize Russia's potential enemy, Japan.

The Japanese government was far from forgetting the affront which it had received, but events in China for a time concentrated foreign attention upon the internal politics of that country. An attempt at reform under the auspices of the weak, but well-meaning Emperor Kwang Hsi was prevented by the Dowager Empress, who then endeavoured to distract attention from abuses at home by encouragement of the ultra-nationalist Boxers, whose Chinese name means "patriotic harmonious fists". This policy succeeded so well that before long the lives of foreigners were unsafe, and the legations in Pekin were besieged. An international force was despatched to the Far East in 1900, and the rivalries of the Powers were suspended while they came to the aid of their fellow-countrymen. When the Boxers had been crushed, China was called upon to pay the price, which proved to be no light one. Two Imperial princes were sentenced to death, three high officials were ordered to commit suicide, and three leading Mandarins were beheaded; in addition missions were sent to Berlin and Tokyo to present the Chinese Emperor's apologies for the murders of German and Japanese diplomats; lastly there was an indemnity of 450,000,000 *taels*. The result of the Boxer rising was thus to impose further burdens on China, while the terms of the Powers caused the dynasty to lose face to such an extent that its overthrow became a mere question of time.

This was in September, 1901, and in January of the following year the Anglo-Japanese Agreement, as it was called though it was really a defensive alliance, was concluded for a period of five years. Relations between the two Powers had, as we have seen, always been friendly, and both had recently experienced the dangers of isolation, so it was not unnatural that they should come together. By this agreement they recognized the independence of China and Korea; but they authorized each other to safeguard their special interests in those countries by intervention if they were threatened either by the aggression of another Power or by internal disturbances. If either Britain or Japan in the defence of such interests became involved in war the other would maintain strict neutrality; if, however, either were to be at war with two Powers, its partner would come to its assistance.

In the existing state of international politics this treaty afforded equal cause for satisfaction to both the parties to it. Great Britain, faced by the increasing naval strength of Germany, was able to leave the Pacific waters to the care of her ally, and herself to concentrate on the North Sea and the Atlantic. Her statesmen also hoped that in alliance with Japan they would be able to restrain her ambitions more easily than might otherwise have proved to be the case: in effect, they were guided by the precedent of Canning's, rather than Disraeli's, Russian policy. As for Japan, her prestige throughout the East was greatly enhanced by the fact that she was the first Oriental state in modern times to conclude an agreement with a European Power upon equal terms, while the substance of the treaty afforded her every assurance that when she had to fight Russia she would have a clear field.

That hour was clearly approaching. Russian influence was

penetrating northern China at an accelerated pace. Not only was St. Petersburg pouring troops into Manchuria, but she obtained permission from Pekin to make railways connecting Vladivostok and Port Arthur with the Siberian system. The winter of 1902-1903 was marked by fresh activities on the part of Russian subjects in north Korea, and by the movement of Russian troops towards the Yalu river under pretext of protecting nationals who were cutting timber there in right of a concession from the Chinese government. Japan had always been as sensitive concerning foreign interference in Korea as has Great Britain in respect of the position in the Low Countries, and for the same reason, so her government at once took alarm: lengthy negotiations between St. Petersburg and Tokyo then ensued, and they culminated in January, 1904, in the Japanese promise to regard Manchuria as outside Japan's sphere of influence if Russia would give a similar undertaking in respect of Korea. No reply was received within the period considered sufficient by the Japanese, that is to say three weeks, and diplomatic relations with Russia were promptly severed.

Once more it was generally assumed that Japan must inevitably be defeated. Her resources were vastly smaller than those of her antagonist, while Russian military prestige stood very high indeed. Above all, nearly four centuries had elapsed since an Oriental Power had defeated a Western, and the memory of Mohacs and the subsequent siege of Vienna had grown very dim. Yet again the unexpected happened; the Japanese captured Port Arthur and Mukden, and sank the Russian fleet at Tsushima. Perhaps the most apposite comment is that of Sir Frederick Maurice: "The success of Japan cannot be ascribed to the greater valour of her troops. Splendid as was the courage of the Japanese soldiery, the Russians, whom no glimmer of success had come to cheer, fought with a dogged determination which commands equal respect. . . . The national spirit of Russia had never fired her armies or her fleets, nor singleness of purpose inspired her leaders. Japan had been victorious because she had learnt from her German tutors that war is the business, not merely of the soldier or of the sailor, but of the nation as a whole."

If the Japanese knew how to make war they also knew when to make peace. The spring of 1905 found them, indeed, supreme in eastern waters, but the land-war had reached a stalemate, and in these circumstances there was always the possibility that the

T

vast resources of Russia might yet be brought into play in ti
to redress the balance. Such being the case the Japanese gover
ment gladly accepted the good offices of the President of t
United States, Mr. Theodore Roosevelt, and peace was conclud
at Portsmouth, U.S.A., in August, 1905. The victors showed the
selves surprisingly moderate. They waived all claim to an i
dcmnity, and contented themselves with the cession by Russia
the Liao-Tung peninsula and of the southern part of the island
Saghalin, together with the recognition by Russia of their spec
position in Korea.

From whatever angle it be regarded the Treaty of Portsmou
must appear as one of the great events of modern history, for
would be impossible to exaggerate its importance. Its effect up
the Tsarist regime in Russia was comparable with that of the Box
rising upon the Manchu dynasty in China; defeat in the field l
to rebellion at home, and although this was suppressed for a tin
the seeds had been sown of the revolution of 1917. The connectic
between the Treaty of Portsmouth and the establishment of B
shevism is much closer than has always been realized: moreover,
was the proved incompetence of the Tsarist regime which pr
duced both. If defeat had serious consequences within Russia
had the gravest repercussions outside the country. The Muscovi
colossus was proved to have feet of clay, and the fact was du
noted in Berlin. The balance of power was affected, and t
aggressive elements in Germany were led to the conclusion that
war on two fronts might not be such a formidable propositic
after all: even if Britain did join in, so it was argued, that wou
not make a great deal of difference in view of her ineptitude
the South African War. So the treaty which was concluded
August, 1905, had a direct bearing upon the course of events
another August nine years later.

In Asia the results were not less striking. An Eastern natic
had beaten a European in fair fight, and every Oriental felt th
the tide had turned at last. From the Treaty of Portsmouth dat
not only the belief by Japan of her destiny as the mistress of Asi
but the rise of nationalism in Turkey, Persia, India, and mar
another country. Some years, indeed, were to pass before the
developments were to make themselves felt in all their intensit
but when they did it was clearly seen that they had their orig
in the Treaty of Portsmouth.

CHAPTER XXIV

THE U.S.A. AS A WORLD POWER, 1783-1898

THE history of the United States from the achievement of independence at the Treaty of Versailles in 1783 until the conclusion of the war with Spain in 1898—and some would say until a much later date—is that of a country which was becoming a World Power without realizing, or even desiring, this change in its fate. In consequence, each step forward was followed by a recoil, and it is impossible to understand the relapse into isolation at the close of the Four Years' War unless it is realized that this was but the natural development in view of what had gone before. Like Great Britain in an earlier day, the United States did not deliberately set out to create an empire, and the implications of what was happening were the longer hidden from her because for the first century of her existence her territorial acquisitions were in her own continent. Thus it may be said that her expansion was natural, while her foreign policy was forced on her by circumstances which her citizens more often than not tried to ignore.

In its earlier stages the expansion of the United States did not lead to international complications; indeed it was definitely facilitated by other Powers. In 1803, for example, Napoleon, who had forced Spain to cede him Louisana three years before, sold the province to the United States for $15,000,000 in his desire to avoid complications in America in the war with Great Britain which was about to re-commence. No boundaries were assigned to Louisiana on the north, west, or south, but it was generally understood that it stretched from the Mississippi to the Rocky Mountains on the west, and from the boundary of the British possessions—itself as yet undefined—to the Gulf of Mexico, or, as was held in some quarters, even to the Rio Grande. In these circumstances disputes soon arose with Spain over the question of the frontier, and in particular whether Texas was included in the purchase. These differences were only settled in 1819, when the Spanish Government sold Florida to the United States for the sum of $4,500,000, and there was an abandonment by Washington of all claims to Texas.

Meanwhile the Stars and Stripes had been flown by American men-of-war in the Mediterranean as early as 1804 when an

expedition had been sent against the Barbary pirates, but unt
the revolution in Latin America began to make headway the rela
tions of the United States with the European Powers were chiefl
confined to frontier and maritime questions; it was one of thes
latter that led to the war with Great Britain in 1812–1814. Fc
the rest Jefferson's fellow-countrymen scrupulously observed h
warning against "entangling alliances".

The revolt of the Spanish colonies confronted the Unite
States with two sets of problems. The first of these was the attitud
to be adopted towards Spain and her former possessions, toward
the Holy Alliance, and towards Great Britain. The outcome wa
Monroe's Message to Congress in 1823, and both the backgroun
and the implications of this have been discussed in an earlie
place. The other set of problems arose from the breakdown c
authority on the frontier of the old Vice-Royalty of New Spair
and chiefly concerned Texas. As we have seen, the boundaries c
Louisana had from the beginning been ill-defined, and in additio
this was the age when the population was moving rapidly wes
"Go west, young man", was the slogan of the hour, and the youn
men who acted on this advice did not always pay much attentio
to national frontiers.

After Mexico had achieved its independence the province c
Texas for a time had a separate political organization, but in 182
the Constituent Congress of Mexico united it temporarily with th
State of Coahuila, at the same time giving an undertaking that i
should become a State of the Mexican Confederation as soon a
circumstances allowed. About this time, it may be noted, a larg
number of citizens of the United States were entering Texas, an
the character of the population was beginning to change in con
sequence. The abolition of slavery in Mexico in 1829, the exclu
sion of settlers from the United States in the following year, an
dislike of the military rule to which they were subjected cause
the Texans to request fulfilment of the promise that they shoul
be admitted as a State into the Mexican Confederation. Thi
request was refused, and Texas seceded from Mexico, not, how
ever, without a fight. In 1837 the independence of Texas wa
recognized by the United States, and subsequently by Belgium
France, and Great Britain.

In the same year the Texans made formal application fo
admission into the American union, and at once a difference c
opinion manifested itself in the United States. Eight State

entered a protest against the proposal, and both President Van Buren and his successor, Harrison, were opposed to it. Tyler, on the other hand, was an ardent annexationist, but Daniel Webster, his Secretary of State, did not share his views, and there was a further delay. By this time the question had become one of much public interest, and there was considerable discussion as to the constitutional aspect, while some questioned the wisdom of provoking a war with Mexico. Texas was one of the chief topics at the Presidential Election of 1844, when Polk was returned on a platform of "the re-annexation of Texas and the re-occupation of Oregon at the earliest possible moment". In due course Congress passed the necessary legislation, the Texan Congress did the same thing, and in December, 1845, Texas was formally admitted into the Union.

These events were not to pass unchallenged, and before Texas had become a member of the Union the United States and Mexico were at war, for the Mexican government had repeatedly warned Washington that the annexation of Texas would be a *casus belli*. War began in the summer of 1845, and it lasted until September, 1847, when United States troops occupied Mexico City. Peace was signed at Guadalupe Hidalgo in February, 1848, and it was a mirror of the North American victories. Mexico ceded New Mexico and Upper California to the United States; recognized the Rio Grande from its mouth to the southern limit of New Mexico as the boundary of Texas; received by way of compensation a sum of $15,000,000; and was released from the payment of certain claims which American citizens had against her. The United States thus came into possession of an immense area which included, in addition to Texas, the present States of California, New Mexico, Nevada, Arizona, Utah, with parts of Wyoming and Colorado.

The American people were in a bellicose spirit at that time, and Polk had been elected not only to solve the problem of Mexico but also that of Oregon. This territory had long been a bone of contention between Great Britain and the United States: the former based her rights on the Nootka Sound Convention which had been concluded by Pitt in 1790, but since then the American Fur Company had founded Astoria in 1811 and so had given the United States a claim by occupation. Russia, then in possession of Alaska, also had pretensions in this quarter, but she agreed to waive them south of 54° 40' north latitude. From 1818 Oregon

was occupied jointly by Great Britain and the United States, but
the situation had been modified by the movement of population
in the latter country, and in the Middle West at any rate there was
much support for a "fifty-four forty or fight" policy. In reality
neither party wanted war. Polk was on the eve of the Mexican
campaign, while Peel had just surmounted one difficulty with
France over Tahiti, and was in the middle of the complicated negotiations relating to the Spanish Marriages; the Foreign Secretary,
Aberdeen, was, moreover, the most pacific of statesmen. Accordingly, in June, 1846, an agreement was reached by which the
parallel of 40° north latitude, running from the summit of the
Rocky Mountains to the coast and continued down the Straits of
Juan de Fuca, was established as the northern boundary of Oregon,
thus leaving Vancouver Island in the possession of Great Britain.

By the middle of the nineteenth century, therefore, the United
States had by the sword, by cash, and by migration put into
execution the "manifest destiny" idea of territorial expansion to
the Pacific. It was a policy in all ways comparable with that pursued by European Powers, but its full implications, for reasons
already mentioned, long remained hidden from the majority of
American citizens, who came, in consequence, to imagine that
their expansion was less reprehensible than that of other nations.
It so happened, too, that the acquisition of these vast territories
exacerbated certain domestic differences, chiefly connected with
the problem of slavery, and some years elapsed before the United
States was in a position to resume her forward march. In the
interval she was at one time so weakened by internal strife as to
imperil what she had already gained, and to tempt a European
Power to defy the Monroe Doctrine.

Continental Europe, with the exception of France, was too
busy with its own affairs to pay much attention to the American
Civil War, but Great Britain, as a maritime Power, was from the
beginning closely concerned. British opinion was at once confused and divided, and it was not until the North raised the
slavery issue that the sentimental appeal began to make itself felt.
The great majority in the House of Commons was content to
leave the conduct of affairs in the hands of the government, and
whenever during the contest opinion was really tested the general
attitude was always found to be the same. On May 13th, 1861
Queen Victoria signed a proclamation of neutrality, thereby
recognizing the Confederacy as a belligerent, an act which aroused

anger in the North and joy in the South, but further than that the British government refused to go. At one moment, in the autumn of 1862, Gladstone, then Chancellor of the Exchequer, went so far as to declare that Jefferson Davis " had made an army, had made a navy, and, what was more, had made a nation", but the Prime Minister at once made it clear that his colleague was speaking for himself alone, and not for the Cabinet.

At the same time England was seriously affected by the interference with the cotton trade, which in one way or another concerned about a quarter of the population, and it was upon this fact that the South relied to compel the British government to recognize the Confederacy as a sovereign state. From 1862 onwards there was acute distress in Lancashire, but Palmerston refused to change his policy.

Once, indeed, it did look as if Britain might be involved, and that was at the beginning of the contest owing to the high-handed action of the Federal authorities. In November, 1861, Jefferson Davis sent two envoys, Mason and Slidell, to Europe. They embarked at Havana in a British mail steamer, the *Trent*, on the 8th of that month, and the following day the vessel was boarded by a Federal warship, commanded by one Wilkes, who took Mason and Slidell out of her, and carried them away as prisoners. The British government at once demanded their surrender as well as an ample apology for the insult to the British flag, and to give point to its remonstrances ordered a brigade of Guards to Canada. War appeared imminent, and it was only prevented by the intervention of the Prince Consort. He pointed out that the difficulty might be surmounted without any wound to the national pride of either country. If the Federal Government would declare that Wilkes had acted without instructions, Great Britain could be satisfied with the release of the prisoners. Both Palmerston and Lincoln agreed with this suggestion, Slidell and Mason were duly allowed to proceed on their way, and friendly relations between London and Washington were restored.

One cause of friction between the North and Great Britain was the blockade of the Southern ports which had been declared by Lincoln, but which it was not always possible to enforce effectively. This led to blockade-running, and privateering also was adopted on a considerable scale. It was in consequence of this latter activity that the British Government became involved in the exploits of the *Alabama*. In June, 1862, it was brought to the notice of the Foreign Office that this ship, which was being completed at Birkenhead, was intended for use as a Confederate privateer. Owing to some unfortunate delays several days elapsed before the case came before the Law Officers of the Crown. They then decided that there was sufficient evidence to show that a breach of the Foreign Enlistment Act was contemplated, and that the ship ought to be detained. By this time it was too late, for the *Alabama* had sailed, and for the next two years, with a crew of which a great part was British, she played havoc with the commerce of the North. Both during the Civil War and afterwards Washington continued to demand compensation for the damage done by the *Alabama* and other similar privateers, but tempers were hot on both sides of the Atlantic, and it was not until 1871 that the two governments agreed to submit the dispute to arbitration.

The *Alabama* case is not only of importance in the history of Anglo-American relations but it possesses a special interest as being the first occasion on which an international dispute was referred to the decision of a regular tribunal of lawyers and statesmen on the analogy of a private lawsuit in a court of justice. Five arbitrators were appointed respectively by Queen Victoria, the President of the United States, the King of Italy, the President of the Swiss Republic, and the Emperor of Brazil. This tribunal met at Geneva, and both parties to the dispute bound themselves in advance to abide by the decision of the majority. The outcome was that Great Britain had to pay £3,250,000 as against £9,500,000 claimed by the United States.

The cautious attitude adopted by the British government towards the Civil War was far from being imitated by Napoleon III who was only too ready to fish in the troubled waters of the New World. When he found that London was unresponsive to his suggestion of intervention in favour of the Confederacy he embarked on his Mexican adventure, to which Washington was strongly opposed as a challenge to the Monroe Doctrine. The United States refused to recognize Maximilian, and when the Civil War was at an end broad hints were given that before the army was demobilized it might be used to expel the French from Mexico. In face of this threat, and in view of the progress of events in Europe, Napoleon withdrew, as has been described on an earlier page.

Once peace had come the United States resumed her expansionist policy, of which during these years the protagonist was Seward, the Secretary of the State Department. In April, 1867, the Senate ratified a treaty for the purchase of Alaska from Russia for the sum of $7,200,000, though there was a good deal of opposition in many quarters to what was considered to be a waste of money. This step forward was followed by the inevitable recoil, and the proposal to buy the Danish West Indies had to be abandoned owing to the hostility which it roused. Similarly when Grant, in 1871, took the preliminary steps for the annexation of San Domingo he was compelled to drop the project by adverse majorities both in the Senate and the House of Representatives.

As the century drew to its close there was a revival of expansionist feeling which was to lead the United States to take one of the most momentous steps in its history, namely the acquisition of territory which did not lie in the Americas. The occasion of this was the disturbed condition of Cuba. Washington had already, in the seventies, complained of the continued anarchy in the island in a note to the Powers, but took no further action at that time. In 1895 another rebellion against Spanish rule broke out, and Martinez Campos was sent from Spain with an army to suppress it. He completely failed in this task, and was succeeded by General Weyler, who established a system of concentration camps, which offended the more sentimental section of opinion in the United States. In addition, American investments in Cuba were considerable, so that the financial interests were also concerned with what was taking place in the island. For these reasons it was becoming plain that it would require very little to precipitate war. It was not long before the clash came.

On the night of February 15th, 1898, the United States battleship *Maine*, which had been in Cuban waters for some months for the purpose of protecting American citizens, was destroyed by an explosion in the port of Havana, and 266 of her crew perished. This event roused excitement both in Spain and in the United States to the highest pitch. The American consul reported that the explosion was due to a mine, which the Spaniards denied, but offered to assist an enquiry into the causes of the disaster. The United States refused to participate, and its experts reported that the explosion took place outside the ship. The Spanish experts, on the other hand, declared that it had happened inside, through the ignition of the *Maine's* ammunition.

These events in themselves were serious enough, but it was the way in which they were treated in the North American Press that made war inevitable. In the prevailing temper in the United States all attempts at mediation were doomed to failure. On April 1st, President McKinley reported that the Spanish government had sent an unsatisfactory reply to his message which had demanded an armistice in Cuba, the abandonment of the system of concentration camps, and the proper distribution of relief funds subscribed in the United States. Ten days later he asked Congress for permission to use the army and navy to put an end to the war in Cuba, and these powers were duly granted. Congress declared the Cubans a free people, and called upon Spain to evacuate the island, but at the same time it disclaimed all intention of acquiring territorial rights. A state of war existed virtually from April 21st, though it was not formally declared by Spain until three days later.

The campaign which followed proved disastrous to the Spaniards both on land and sea, though they fought gallantly and by the middle of July peace had become a necessity to them. Spain had lost the last remains of her American empire, for the greater part of Puerto Rico, as well as Cuba, had passed into the possession of the United States. Sagasta, who was then the Spanish Prime Minister, accordingly opened negotiations for peace on the basis of an agreement as to the political status of Cuba. McKinley refused to consider any such limitation, and declared his terms to be the immediate evacuation of Cuba, the surrender of Puerto Rico in place of an indemnity, and the possession of Manila pending a settlement of the ownership of the Philippines. The Spanish government demurred at the last clause, but was finally forced to accept it, and on August 12th, 1898, the preliminaries were signed.

The commissioners to arrange the terms of peace met in Paris at the beginning of October, and the two disputed points were the Cuban debt and the sovereignty of the Philippines. With regard to the former the Spanish contention was that the debt was attached to the island, and that change of ownership did not affect the matter. As for Manila, it had been captured by the Americans after the signature of the preliminaries of peace, and Spain demanded possession of the city and the archipelago. Washington refused to consider these arguments, and the Spanish government was given the alternative of a surrender or a renewal of the war.

As Spain was in no position to fight again she had to give way, and the treaty was signed on November 28th: by this the United States paid a sum of $20,000,000 for the Philippine archipelago.

The victory over Spain marked the definite and final emergence of the United States as a World Power whether its citizens liked it or not, and many of them, possibly even the large majority, did not like it at all. Time and again they tried to get back to the shelter of isolation, but found that there was no return along that path, and on each occasion a larger number of them came to realize that they must shoulder the responsibilities which they could no longer escape. The conquest of the Philippines brought the United States into close contact with the problems of the Far East, and it was no mere coincidence that two years later its forces formed part of the international army which marched to Pekin at the time of the Boxer rising; indeed, the first step had been taken along the road which led to the clash with Japan in 1941. Equally the acquisition of Cuba, temporary though this proved to be, involved Washington more deeply than ever before in the affairs of Latin America, and this had consequences which were not always too happy.

One result of the emergence of the United States as a world Power was a steady improvement in relations between London and Washington. It would seem that the acquisition of Imperial responsibilities did much to make Americans understand the difficulties of the British; however this may be, the beginning of the twentieth century marked the growth of a friendship which was to develop one day into co-operation on the battle-field. This was in marked contrast with what had gone before, for there had been many acrimonious disputes between Great Britain and the United States in addition to those for which space has been found in the preceding pages. The two countries disagreed on such questions as the boundary of Venezuela, the Bering sea problem, fishing rights in waters off Canada, and the control over the Panama Canal. The Venezuelan dispute very nearly led to war in 1895, but resort was finally had to arbitration, and, as has been said, with the turn of the century an entirely different, and much better, spirit, began to prevail between the two countries.

CHAPTER XXV

TURKEY AND THE BALKANS, 1878–1908

THE Treaty of Berlin raised as many problems as it solved, and the settlement, or attempted settlement, of these latter occupied the attention of European statesmen for many a long year: chief among them was the establishment of the new state of Bulgaria, and its relations with its neighbours.

Bulgaria started on its independent career as a peasant community with a population of two millions, and for its ruler was chosen Prince Alexander of Battenberg, a nephew of the Tsar by marriage. His task from the beginning was no easy one, for the Russians ruled his country with a high hand, and they filled all the more important official positions. "I am devoted to the Tsar", wrote Alexander to Prince Carol of Roumania a few weeks after his arrival in Sofia, "and wish to do nothing that could be construed as anti-Russian, but unfortunately the Russian officials have behaved with great lack of consideration. Utter chaos exists in all Ministries. Every day I am confronted with the alternative of signing the Russian demands or being accused in Russia of ingratitude. My position is really frightful. I reject everything that is against my conscience, and every day I must write to the Tsar to anticipate the slanders of the Russian officials." A little later he remarked to an Austrian diplomat, "If the Russians go on like this, they will be the most hated people in Bulgaria in a few years. They take their orders from Milutin (the Russian Minister of War), not from me". The murder of the Tsar Alexander II in 1881 rendered the situation worse, for his successor made no pretence of sharing his father's affection for the Prince, and Bulgaria continued to be governed like a Russian province, and Russian generals were appointed to the Interior, War, and Justice; they took their orders not from Prince Alexander, but from St. Petersburg.

The final crisis came over the question of Eastern Roumelia. A movement there for union with Bulgaria had long been gaining ground: at first it had met with Russian support, but Alexander III ceased to desire a change which would strengthen what he considered to be an ungrateful satellite, and Prince Alexander was induced to promise that he had no intention of disturbing the *status quo*. In September, 1885, however, a revolution broke out in Eastern Roumelia, and the revolutionaries proclaimed union with Bulgaria. Prince Alexander hesitated between offending Russia and disappointing his own subjects, but he finally adopted the former course. Great Britain at once accorded her recognition of what had taken place, for Queen Victoria wished to support the brother-in-law of her favourite daughter, and Salisbury was in process of reversing the Turcophil policy of Disraeli. Germany was actuated solely by a desire not to antagonize Russia, and Austria-Hungary in the main followed the lead of Berlin. The Tsar was implacably hostile, but after he had in vain attempted to persuade the Sultan to slaughter Orthodox Slavs with the Moslem sword, he accepted the fact of union, but warned the Bulgarians "so long as you keep your present government expect from me nothing, nothing, nothing".

At this point a further complication was caused by a Serbian demand, not without the connivance of Vienna,[1] for compensation. Neither Germany nor Russia, however, was prepared to support Belgrade, and when, in November, 1885, King Milan put his claims to the arbitrament of the sword he was decisively beaten by the Bulgarians at the battle of Slivnitza; indeed, so rapidly did the situation change that Belgrade was only saved from Bulgarian occupation by Vienna intimating to Prince Alexander that if he advanced any further he would be confronted by Austrian troops. In consequence of the strength thus unexpectedly displayed by Bulgaria nothing more was heard of the reconquest of Eastern Roumelia, and the Powers duly recognized the Prince of Bulgaria as Governor-General of that province for five years. The omission of Prince Alexander by name was to meet the wishes of Russia, and was prophetic of what was to come.

The truth was that the Tsar was not to be offended lightly, and he was merely biding his time. In May, 1886, he announced that "circumstances might compel him to defend by arms the dignity of the Empire", and he was far from pleased when Prince Alexander summoned the representatives of his new province to Sofia. It was one of that luckless ruler's last acts as Prince of Bulgaria, for on the night of August 21st some discontented Bulgarian officers in the pay of Russia entered the palace, forced him at the point of the revolver to sign his abdication, and hustled him out of the country.

By this time the mass of the Bulgarian army and people was

[1] *Cf.* The Austro-Serbian Treaty of 1881.

overwhelmingly anti-Russian, and a counter-revolution besought the Prince to return to the throne. His nerve, however,
was broken by Russian threats, and although he did come back to
Sofia for a brief space, it was only to appoint a Regency, and to
hope that his successor would have better luck. Events soon
proved that Russia had over-reached herself by the kidnapping of
Prince Alexander. Queen Victoria wrote to the fallen monarch
of her indignation against "your barbaric, Asiatic, tyrannical
cousin"; Salisbury denounced the treachery of officers "debauched
by foreign gold"; and the Bulgarians themselves declined to obey
the orders of the general who had been sent by the Tsar to restore
Russian influence in their country. Not less important was the
declaration of Austria-Hungary that a military occupation of
Bulgaria would compel her to take action. Bulgarian politics had
provoked a European crisis of the first magnitude, and one that
was to call for all Bismarck's ability to solve without recourse to
arms.

It will be remembered that this was the time when the Iron
Chancellor was endeavouring to keep the peace of Europe by
means of the *Dreikaiserbund* and the Triple Alliance, and when the
Tsar was much under the influence of Katkoff and the Pan-Slavs.
In January, 1887, Bismarck made a speech in which he laid down
the policy of his country towards the crisis in the Balkans.

> We have no warlike needs, for we belong to what Metter-
> nich called saturated states. . . . We do not expect an attack
> or hostility from Russia. . . . We maintain the same friendly
> relations with the present as with the late ruler, and they will
> not be disturbed by us. Nor do I believe that Russia seeks
> alliances in order to attack us. . . . We shall not have
> troubles with Russia unless we go and seek them in Bulgaria,
> as our Opposition journals demand. . . .
>
> What is Bulgaria to us? It is all the same to us who rules
> there and what becomes of her. I reiterate my words about
> the bones of the Pomeranian grenadier. The Eastern Ques-
> tion is not a *casus belli* for us. We shall allow nobody to throw
> a noose round our neck and embroil us with Russia. The
> friendship of Russia is of much more value to us than that of
> Bulgaria.
>
> The difficulty is not to keep Germany and Russia, but
> Austria and Russia, at peace, and it is our duty to ingeminate

peace in both Cabinets. We risk being called pro-Russian in Austria and still more in Hungary, and pro-Austrian in Russia. That does not matter if we can keep the peace. . . . Our relations with Austria rest on the consciousness of each that the existence of the other as a Great Power is a necessity in the interests of European equilibrium, not on the notion that the one places its whole strength at the service of the other. That is impossible. There are special Austrian interests for which we cannot intervene. We do not ask Austria to take part in our quarrels with France, or in colonial difficulties with England, and in the like manner we have no interests in Constantinople.

Having thus made his position clear to Vienna, and having extended the hand of friendship to St. Petersburg, the German Chancellor concluded, that same summer, the Treaty of Reinsurance with Russia. What had in fact happened was that the long Bulgarian crisis had ended with the defeat of Russia, for Bismarck had played his game with matchless skill. Peace had been preserved; France and Russia had been kept apart; the Austrian alliance had remained intact; and a secret treaty kept open the line to St. Petersburg. "It was a complicated business", Bismarck was to confess. "The Emperor once said to me, 'You are like a rider who tosses five balls into the air and catches them every time. I should not care to change places with you.' "

Austria-Hungary, too, had, under the direction of Kalnoky, played a dangerous diplomatic game, which she had won, for she had succeeded in eliminating Russian influence from Bulgaria, since that country, for the next few years, continued, like Serbia, to lean upon Austria. It was not, indeed, until 1896 that there was a reconciliation between St. Petersburg and Sofia, and that was when the new ruler of Bulgaria, Ferdinand of Saxe-Coburg, broke his word by having his son, Boris, baptized in the Orthodox, rather than in the Roman Catholic, Church: the Tsar, by this time Nicholas II, congratulated the Prince on his "patriotic resolve", but Francis Joseph refused to receive him for several years, and thereafter until 1913 Bulgaria inclined towards Russia once more.

The affairs of Greece, as well as of Bulgaria, attracted the attention of Europe during the years which followed the Treaty of Berlin. Since she had established her independence fifty years before Greece had never ceased to demand, though with no success, better frontiers, and her territorial acquisitions had been limited to the Ionian Islands, ceded by Great Britain in 1864. Her representatives were admitted to the Congress of Berlin, and her case was supported there by Waddington, but Article 24 was extremely vague, for Turkey and Greece were merely exhorted to come to an agreement on the "rectification of frontiers", and to seek mediation in case of need. The frontier proposed by Waddington, assigning Thessaly and the larger part of Epirus to Greece, was inserted in the protocol but not in the treaty, and it soon became a bone of contention between Athens and Constantinople.

The Greeks took the view that the line suggested at Berlin was as good as theirs, and that the negotiations with the Porte were to be a mere formality: the Sultan, on the other hand, issued a memorandum condemning the pretensions of Greece, and emphasizing his rights over provinces "happy under the laws of the Empire". With these irreconcilable standpoints agreement was not easy, and for three weary years the Chancelleries of Europe were occupied with a dispute which at one moment looked like ending in a settlement and at another like resulting in war. Finally, the Powers imposed a compromise solution, in May, 1881, which pleased neither of the interested parties. By its terms Greece was allotted almost the whole of Thessaly, including Larissa and Volo, while the Sultan retained all Epirus except the district of Arta. Bismarck would have preferred the cession of Crete to that of Thessaly, but the Greeks would not hear of it; accordingly special arrangements were made for Crete, by which the island was to have a Governor-General, and a General Assembly consisting of Christians and Moslems in stated proportions; Greek was to be the official language of the Assembly and the ports; and there was to be a political amnesty.

The dove-cotes of European diplomacy were once more fluttered by the Greeks in 1885 when they demanded Epirus as compensation for the union of Bulgaria and Eastern Roumelia, and began to mobilize. The Powers, however, were unsympathetic, and ordered Greece to disarm, at the same time intimating in no uncertain terms that a naval attack would not be permitted. Delyannis, the Greek Premier and an uncompromising expansionist, returned an unsatisfactory reply, and it became necessary to employ coercion if the Powers were to maintain their authority. The Concert was not, it should be observed, entirely united, for

[margin note: Boundary dispute, Greece vs. Turkey]

Italy abstained, while the French government was unwilling to go to extremes, for which it was much criticized by the Opposition in Paris on the ground that such a policy tended to accentuate that isolation of France so much desired by Bismarck. Nevertheless, at the end of April, 1886, the fleets of Austria-Hungary, Germany, Great Britain, and Russia instituted a blockade of the Greek ports. On this George I of the Hellenes decided to save his subjects from themselves, and he ordered Delyannis to demobilize or resign. The Premier resigned, and Tricoupis, one of the greatest statesmen of modern Greece, took his place. The crisis was at an end.

In connection with Tricoupis, it is too often forgotten that he was the precursor of that Balkan League of which such use was to be made by his fellow-countryman Venizelos in later years. In 1891 he proposed to Belgrade and Sofia a joint campaign against the Turks, which was to be followed by the partition of Macedonia between the victors. These, however, were the years when Bulgaria was looking to Vienna and Constantinople, and her Prime Minister, Stombuloff, betrayed the scheme to the Porte. If this was the first, it was certainly not the last, time that a Bulgarian government set its face against united action on the part of the Balkan States, and preferred to seek support elsewhere in the hope of thereby furthering its national interests the more effectively. This attitude explains much of the history of the Balkan Peninsula during the early decades of the twentieth century.

For ten years Crete had remained in the background, but in 1889 elections in the island gave the Sultan an opportunity of interference, and thereafter the disturbances broke out afresh. Under pressure from the British government the Porte agreed to a settlement which, while preserving the suzerainty of Abdul Hamid, met the wishes of the more moderate Greeks. On paper the programme was satisfactory, but the will to carry it out was lacking, and the Moslems resisted the reforms. This time it was the turn of the Greek government to benefit from what was taking place. The annexation of the island to Greece was announced in a Note to the Powers in February, 1897; Prince George was rushed across to the island as his father's representative; and he was followed by contingents of Greek troops.

A very difficult situation had arisen, and it was not rendered any easier of solution by the fact that the sympathies of the Powers

U

were divided: on the one hand the Greek Queen was a Russian Grand Duchess, while Germany and Austria-Hungary, in their new-found sympathy for the Sultan, were for strong measures against Athens. The credit for the achievement of joint action in these circumstances must go to Salisbury, who, after Prince George had withdrawn from Crete under pressure, persuaded the Powers to present notes to both the Greek and Ottoman governments. King George I was informed that Crete could not be annexed to Greece, but would receive absolute autonomy. In return the Greek troops and ships were to be withdrawn from the island within six days, or they would be ejected by the Powers. The Note to the Porte demanded complete autonomy for Crete, and promised that it should not be transferred to Greece. The Sultan had no choice but to accept; the Greeks were not so amenable, and it was clear that their rifles were about to go off by themselves, for the King could not restrain his excitable subjects again.

Meanwhile both Greek and Turkish troops had massed on the frontier, and only the slightest incident was required to cause an explosion. This was the moment chosen by one hundred British Liberals to send a telegram of sympathy to the Greeks, and by Mr. Gladstone to commend them on their "marvellously gallant action"; in these circumstances little heed was paid to the warning of the Powers that whoever began hostilities would be held responsible, and would be allowed no advantages from victory. On April 8th, 1897, the Greeks crossed the frontier, and nine days later the Sultan declared war. In a month all was over; the Turkish armies were marching on Athens, the mob in the capital was threatening to overturn the monarchy, and the Greek government had appealed to the Powers to mediate between it and the victorious Sultan.

This was the moment for which Salisbury had been waiting, and he was assisted by the fact that, although Germany was desirous of doing nothing that would offend Abdul Hamid, the Sultan's demands were too high for even the Kaiser to stomach. In consequence peace was made on the basis of a slight frontier rectification in favour of Turkey, and of the payment of an indemnity. The Cretan settlement proved more difficult, more particularly as Germany and Austria-Hungary withdrew from the Concert when the time came to put pressure on the Porte, so the remaining Powers, that is to say France, Great Britain, Italy, and Russia, acted by themselves. The upshot, after the compulsory removal of the remaining Ottoman forces, was that Crete obtained autonomy with Prince George of Greece as High Commissioner under the suzerainty of the Sultan.

It may thus be said that although, during the first twenty years after the Treaty of Berlin, the Christian states in the Balkans were vigorous enough they showed little tendency to combine. At the same time the Turks were in no condition to take advantage of these centrifugal tendencies. As after the Treaty of Paris, so after that of Berlin, no serious effort was made by the Porte to set its house in order, and the Ottoman Empire continued to decay.

During these years there was a marked change in the attitude of the Powers individually towards the Near East and its problems. It has already been shown that Salisbury by no means shared Disraeli's Turcophil sentiments, and from 1885 onwards there was little difference in view between the two parties in Great Britain where international affairs were concerned; the result was that the period 1885–1914 was marked by much greater consistency in British foreign policy than had been the case since the death of Canning, and in the Near East it was consistently anti-Turk. Not the least important reason for this was that Turkey no longer played a vital part in the British line of communications with India, the Far East, and Australasia. The possession of Cyprus and Egypt had completely transformed the situation, and a strong Ottoman Empire was not an essential factor in the strategy of the British Empire; furthermore, Turkish methods of government had never commended themselves to the British public, and now that there was no need to wink at them for political reasons they aroused positive disgust.

The policy of Russia, too, underwent modification. Her experiences in Bulgaria in the eighties of the nineteenth century disgusted her with the affairs of south-east Europe, and her rulers' attention was increasingly attracted by the Far East, where another dying Empire—the Chinese—seemed to offer greater prizes. This dream, it is true, was shattered by the Treaty of Portsmouth, but after that St. Petersburg tended to be interested in the Middle, rather than in the Near, East; that is to say in Persia rather than in Turkey. For all these reasons the scene at Constantinople was changed. Ottoman rights were no longer fiercely challenged by Russia and hotly defended by Great Britain. For thirty-six years Osmanli and Muscovite did not cross swords, and when war once more broke out between them both found themselves in company which would have been inconceivable a generation before.

While the older combatants were withdrawing somewhat from the Near Eastern arena a new one had entered it in the shape of Germany. The successors of Bismarck did not echo his sentiments about the Pomeranian grenadier, nor did they realize that in the Balkans were to be found the causes of that Russo-German war which the old Chancellor had worked so hard to prevent. The Kaiser was determined that Germany should make her presence felt everywhere, and he was only too ready to take the place of Britain as the friend of the Turk. His intentions were first made manifest to the world at the time of the Armenian massacres.

The interest which the Powers had betrayed for the Armenians in the Treaty of Berlin proved a very mixed blessing for the objects of their solicitude. The Sultan's suspicions of their loyalty were aroused, and a leading Turk observed that the best way to get rid of the Armenian problem was to get rid of the Armenians. No reforms were carried out in Armenia any more than elsewhere, and as the prospect of foreign intervention receded the Sultan made up his mind that the country should not become another Bulgaria. Accordingly in 1894 there were widespread massacres in the Sasun district in the vilayet of Bitlis, which Abdul Hamid blandly defended on the grounds that "just as there are in other countries nihilists, socialists, and anarchists, endeavouring to obtain concessions of privileges which it is impossible to grant them, and just as steps have to be taken against them, so it is with the Armenians".

From the beginning the British government, whether headed by Rosebery or Salisbury, did all in its power both to bring those responsible for the atrocities to justice and to arrange for the better administration of Armenia in the future. In this policy London received only half-hearted support from Russia, and not even that from some of the other Powers. In these circumstances her menaces left the Sultan unaffected, for he knew that Britain stood alone. At the end of September, 1895, further massacres took place, and at Urfa three thousand men, women, and children were burnt in the cathedral. The consular reports left no doubt that the campaign had been carefully organized; that the slaughter often began and ended to the call of the bugle; that regular Turkish soldiers took part in the killing; that the authorities either instigated the tragedy or remained passive spectators of it; and that not a single foreigner was injured. Once more the British government tried to persuade the Concert to act, but the Powers contented themselves with sending warships through the Dardanelles for the protection of their nationals.

By this time the Armenians had themselves been driven to despair, and in August, 1896, a band of the more desperate of them seized the Ottoman Bank at Galata. The attempt to call Europe's attention to their plight by this means proved a fiasco, but it provided the Sultan with an excuse for further repressive measures. The more fanatical Moslems in Constantinople were armed by the government, and six to seven thousand Armenians were killed in broad daylight in the streets of the capital. This was too much for the Powers, who thereupon insisted that the massacre must cease, but the only manifestation of their displeasure which Abdul Hamid was called upon to experience was the refusal of the diplomatic corps to illuminate their houses on the occasion of his birthday a few days later.

The fact was that the Concert, with the exception of Great Britain, was not in the least interested in the fate of the Armenians. Russia, as we have seen, was looking to the Pacific rather than to the Bosphorus, and was by no means desirous of reopening the Near East question. Germany never pretended to care what became of the Christian subjects of the Sultan, for whose friendship she was in any case angling. France followed her Russian ally, and Italy did not count. The United States, indeed, was far from approving of what was taking place, but Washington was not a signatory of the Treaty of Berlin, and it was still a cardinal maxim of American policy to hold aloof from European complications. British anger was hot against Abdul Hamid, whom Gladstone denounced as "the Great Assassin", and whom William Watson cursed as "Immortally, beyond all mortals, damned"; but in the circumstances there was nothing that the British government could do. "Isolated action", Rosebery declared, "means a European war", and Salisbury was not prepared to risk that, so Britain, though very angry, remained impotent.

The result of the Armenian crisis thus was that Germany strengthened her position at Constantinople while Britain lost further ground there. Above all, London had been warned of her growing isolation in Europe, and this was prophetic of what was to occur three years later on the outbreak of the South African War.

For a short space the centre of interest in international matters was fixed elsewhere, but the twentieth century had hardly begun when Turkish misrule in Macedonia provoked another crisis. At first the Powers showed a disposition to act together, and in October, 1903, the Austrian and Russian governments agreed upon what was called Murzsteg programme of reforms, which provided for foreign officers for the *gendarmerie*, and for the division of Macedonia into zones each administered by one of the Powers. Once more there was gone through the weary round first of applying pressure to compel the Sultan to accept the reforms in theory, and then of trying to coerce him to apply them in fact. Some progress had, however, been made when, in January, 1908, the Austro-Hungarian government announced that it had obtained from the Porte permission to survey the route for a railway through the Sanjak of Novibazar: this was only in accordance with the Treaty of Berlin, but Russian suspicions were at once aroused, and such co-operation as there had been between St. Petersburg and Vienna in the affairs of the Balkans came to an end. In July of that same year, 1908, there occurred the Young Turk revolution, and the future of the Near East was again in the melting-pot.

CHAPTER XXVI

THE EVE OF WAR, 1904–1914

DURING the course of this work the problems of the Mediterranean have on many occasions been shown to have been the pre-occupation of the world's statesmen, but rarely has that great sea played so important a part in the history of mankind as during the decade which culminated in the outbreak of the Four Years' War. Morocco, Bosnia-Herzegovina, Tripoli, and the Balkan Peninsula, all lands whose shores are washed by its waters, are milestones on the road to that struggle which may yet prove to have been the Peloponnesian War of modern civilization, until at Serajevo the murder of the Archduke Francis Ferdinand gave the signal for the slaughter to begin.

It will be remembered that the Anglo-French Entente gave France a free hand in Morocco, but Delcassé made a serious blunder in not conciliating Germany in respect of that country. The goodwill of Italy had been bought by the recognition of her claims to Tripoli, and that of Spain by the hypothetical reversion of the northern littoral, but the French government omitted to take any precautions with the only one of its neighbours whom it had serious cause to fear. Bülow determined to make use of this opportunity partly to justify the German contention that Morocco was an international, not a French, concern, whatever London and Paris might arrange to the contrary, and partly to test the strength of the Entente. From his point of view the moment was particularly well-timed for Russia was being beaten by Japan, and was on the eve of revolution; France was torn with dissension over the problem of the separation of Church and State; while in Great Britain the Conservative administration of Balfour was plainly tottering to its fall.

The Kaiser somewhat unwillingly agreed with his Chancellor, and the Moroccan question in its new form may be said to have been opened in March, 1905, when William II landed at Tangier from his yacht, and made a speech to the German colony there in the course of which he said, "My visit is to show my resolve to do all in my power to safeguard German interests in Morocco. Considering the Sultan as absolutely free, I wish to discuss with him the means to secure these interests." This was plain enough, but to ensure that there should be no misunderstanding of the German position two introductory sentences were added in the official version of the Imperial speech: "It is to the Sultan in his capacity of independent sovereign that I pay my visit to-day. I hope that under his sovereignty a free Morocco will remain open to the peaceful competition of all nations, without monopoly or annexation, on a policy of absolute equality." Germany's case, in effect, was that, if she did not act, Morocco would become another Tunis, and would be closed to her commerce.

In the early days of April the Imperial Chancellor took the matter a stage further, and in a circular dispatch suggested a new conference of the signatories of the Treaty of Madrid in 1880, which followed the last international gathering held to discuss the affairs of Morocco. Hardly had this suggestion been made when, under pressure from Germany, the Sultan of Morocco, Abdul Aziz IV, refused to allow his troops to be trained on the French model, and invited the Powers who had signed the Treaty of Madrid to a conference at Tangier. Delcassé was strongly opposed to any such proceeding, but the German government passed from proposals to threats, and as his colleagues were not in the last resort prepared to fight the Foreign Minister resigned at the beginning of June. This was a notable triumph for Germany, though France did not even then at once give way, and it required the intervention of President Roosevelt before her consent to the conference was finally secured. "It looked like war", the President has left on record, "so I took active hold of the matter through Speck and Jusserand, and got things temporarily straightened up. I showed France the great danger of a war, and the little use England could be, and that a conference would not sanction any unjust attack on French interests. I would not accept the invitation unless France was willing, but, if I did, I would, if necessary, take a strong ground against any attitude of Germany which seemed to me unjust and unfair. At last France told me on June 23rd that she would agree."

The conference met at Algeciras in January, 1906, but before then there had been a change of government in London, where Campbell-Bannerman had succeeded Balfour as Prime Minister, and Grey had replaced Lansdowne at the Foreign Office. The substitution of a Liberal administration for a Conservative one, however, had no influence upon the country's foreign policy, and when the French government asked for consultations between their General Staff and the British permission was readily accorded. These military conversations, it may be noted in passing, continued at intervals until 1914, and there were similar, though unofficial, discussions between the British and Belgian Staffs.

The Conference of Algeciras lasted from January to April, 1906. The German case was a strong one, for the Treaty of Madrid ensured every signatory to that document most-favoured-nation treatment, and there was much to be said for the contention of Berlin that this principle extended beyond the economic sphere. What happened was that the German representatives, under the influence of Holstein, over-acted their part, and so alienated the other Powers, though when Bülow realized that Holstein's policy was leading straight to war he took the control out of his hands. A moderating influence was throughout exercised by President Roosevelt, and the Spanish delegates supported their French colleagues, while Austria-Hungary acted as a brake on the German wheel. As for the attitude of Great Britain, it was admirably summed up in the observation of King Edward to the French ambassador in London, "Tell us what you wish on each point, and we will support you without restriction or reserves".

This Franco-German duel resulted in a draw. It is true that France obtained the control of the police for herself and her Spanish ally, but Germany established her contention that the problem of Morocco was the concern of all the Powers. At the same time the conference strengthened the ties between Great Britain and France, while it brought the former into closer touch with Russia who steadily supported her French ally throughout the proceedings. As Professor Gooch has well said, "The process which Germans describe as encirclement, and Englishmen as insurance, had begun". For the rest, the part played by Roosevelt was evidence of the growing importance of the United States as a World Power.

The growing division of the Powers into two camps was, not long after the Conference of Algeciras, followed by the conclusion of an understanding between Great Britain and Russia. It was only natural that this should be the case, for what kept London and St. Petersburg apart was the memory of old rivalries, while the facts of the present, combined with their common alliance with France, were every day tending to bring them together. At the same time agreement was not easy, for there were many outstanding points of difference. In the first place there were British interests in the Persian Gulf which seemed to be threatened by Russia, whose emissaries, in one disguise or another, swarmed in that area. On the other hand Russian suspicions were roused by British activity in Tibet, and the arrival of the Younghusband Mission in that country in 1904 gave rise to considerable apprehension in St. Petersburg. The Russo-Japanese War was also productive of more than one incident between Great Britain and Russia, and war between the two Powers was very close in October, 1904, when the Russian men-of-war on their way to the Far East opened fire on the Hull fishing fleet on the Dogger Bank.

Nor was the situation rendered any easier by the vacillation of the weak, though well-meaning, Tsar, Nicholas II. In 1905 the Kaiser was hankering after a return to Bismarck's Russian policy, and he believed that an agreement with St. Petersburg would be the most effective reply to the Anglo-French Entente. Accordingly, in July, 1905, he persuaded the Tsar to sign a pact at Björko by which the two Powers agreed that if either of them was attacked by a third European state the other would come to its assistance. When Nicholas returned to his own country he was informed by his ministers that this agreement conflicted with the terms of the Franco-Russian alliance, and he was compelled to repudiate it. Shortly afterwards came the Conference of Algeciras, and after somewhat lengthy negotiations Sir Arthur Nicolson and Isvolsky signed, on August 31st, 1907, the Anglo-Russian Convention.

The three most important points in this document were those which concerned Persia, Afghanistan, and Tibet. The first of these countries represented yet another of the decaying empires of the Orient with which the West had come into contact, and British and Russian interests were continually clashing in that wide area which was still nominally subject to the Shah. It was now agreed to divide Persia into a large Russian and a small British sphere of influence, with a neutral zone between them in which the two Powers were to be on an equal footing. The Persian Gulf was not mentioned since it was only partly in the Shah's dominions, but Grey emphasized the intention of the British government to maintain the *status quo* in that quarter. So far as Afghanistan was concerned Great Britain declared that she had no intention of changing the political status of the country or of interfering in its internal concerns, and she promised neither herself to take, nor to encourage the Amir to take, any measures threatening Russia. The

Russian government, on its part, recognized Afghanistan as outside its sphere of influence, and promised that all its political relations with Kabul should be conducted through the British Foreign Office. In the matter of Tibet the two Powers agreed to respect its territorial integrity, and to abstain from all interference in its internal administration.

The reconciliation of Great Britain and Russia was confirmed by the conclusion of an understanding between their respective allies. In June, 1907, France and Japan had already agreed not to take any step contrary to the independence and integrity of China, and in the following month Russia and Japan signed a similar treaty, by which they agreed to maintain the *status quo*, and to secure respect for it by all pacific means at their disposal. Three months later they signed a further instrument which disposed of several problems left over from the Treaty of Portsmouth.

The conclusion of these arrangements did much to redress the balance which had been upset in Germany's favour by the Russo-Japanese War, though this fact was not appreciated in all circles in Berlin. Russia, having relinquished her ambitions in the Far East and having accepted her defeat by Japan, was now able once more to turn to the Balkans and the West. As for Japan, her hands were now completely free, and she set to work to build up that commanding position in Eastern Asia which was to be so prominent a feature of the years to come; a position to which she never could have attained had it not been that the quarrels of the European Powers on their own continent compelled them to relax that grip on the Orient which they had established during the previous century and a half. Tribute is certainly due to Grey for his courage in coming to an agreement with Russia, for, like Canning, he had to carry out his foreign policy in spite of a section of opinion in his own party, some Liberals, and a great many Socialists, being opposed to the particular type of autocracy which then existed in Russia. A few Conservatives, too, disapproved of the concessions which had been made in the Middle East: yet the Anglo-Russian Convention did much to save Europe seven years later, for it ensured that when Germany fought she should from the beginning have to do so on two fronts. In this respect the contrast with 1939 is instructive.

The Triple Entente had not long been in existence before the repercussions of the Young Turk revolution produced another international crisis. In retrospect we can now see that the Young

Turk movement was the prototype of that one party government which was adopted by so many countries later in the century, and the Committee of Union and Progress had not a little in common with German National Socialism and Italian Fascism. In 1908, however, it posed as a liberal and democratic movement, and one of the first acts of Enver Pasha and his colleagues was to convoke a Parliament of the whole Ottoman Empire. This action went a long way towards rallying support for the new regime in western Europe, but it raised the question of Bosnia and Herzegovina in an acute form.

It will be remembered that when the *Dreikaiserbund* was renewed in 1881 the Austro-Hungarian Government reserved the right to annex the two provinces whenever it should deem the moment opportune, but the attitude adopted by Russia towards the union of Eastern Roumelia with Bulgaria had shown that St. Petersburg had moved far from the position which she had adopted in 1881. In 1897 a proposal by Vienna to reaffirm the right of annexation provoked the cool reply from the Russian government that this would "require special scrutiny at the proper time". So matters might have continued for many years but for the action of the Young Turks. Austria-Hungary was only in occupation of Bosnia and Herzegovina; the two provinces still in theory formed part of the Ottoman Empire, and as such were entitled to send representatives to the new Turkish Parliament. Yet if this happened, and if Turkey under her new rulers really succeeded in putting her house in order, then there was considerable danger that Bosnia and Herzegovina might pass out of the keeping of Vienna altogether.

Nor was this all, for the relations between the Dual Monarchy and the Southern Slavs were becoming acute. The substitution at Belgrade in 1903 of the Russophil dynasty of Karageorgevitch for the Austrophil House of Obrenovitch meant that Vienna could no longer control her Slav subjects by means of a compliant King of Serbia, for under Peter I the more chauvinistic elements in that country were already looking forward to the union of all the Southern Slavs under the Serbian crown, and to a revival of the Serbian Empire of the Middle Ages. For more than one reason, therefore, it behoved Austria-Hungary to act before the situation got completely out of hand.

The Foreign Minister of the Dual Monarchy, Aehrenthal, realized that he could not move in the matter without Russian support, and to his surprise he found Isvolsky a great deal more friendly than he had supposed to be possible. The two statesmen met in Bohemia in September, 1908, but as the discussion between them took place without witnesses, as nothing was committed to paper, and as the participants subsequently put out conflicting versions of what had taken place, it is not easy to be certain what exactly occurred. In the main, however, it seems to have been agreed that Austria-Hungary should be allowed to annex Bosnia and Herzegovina in return for the opening of the Straits to Russian warships. Having, as he said, created a situation in which the Russian bear would growl but not bite, Aehrenthal proceeded to secure the support of Bulgaria, and Ferdinand, though not fully informed of what was afoot, was assured that Austria-Hungary would raise no objection if he were to proclaim his independence. Accordingly, on October 5th, 1908, Bulgaria was proclaimed at Tirnovo an independent kingdom, and on the following day Francis Joseph announced the annexation of Bosnia and Herzegovina to the Habsburg dominions.

The reaction of the Powers was an interesting commentary upon the international situation. Germany had neither suggested nor desired the annexation, and Bülow realized that it would not be too easy for him to reconcile Turkey to what had occurred: the duty and interest of the Reich to stand by her ally were, however, manifest, and the closeness of the ties which bound Vienna to Berlin was advertised by the Kaiser's appearance "in shining armour". Whether Bismarck would ever have allowed a situation to develop in which Germany had to follow the lead of Austria-Hungary is another matter. Clemenceau, then Prime Minister of France, was more indignant with Isvolsky for not consulting Russia's ally than with Aehrenthal for infringing the Treaty of Berlin, and French public opinion was not seriously alarmed. King Edward VII, on the other hand, made no secret of his annoyance, and Grey took his stand on the Berlin settlement. In these circumstances the Russian claim to compensation, which would also have constituted a violation of the Treaty of Berlin, received little support in London.

Yet if no Great Power was willing to make the annexation a *casus belli* the Serbs were prepared to fight. For them everything seemed to be at stake; if Bosnia and Herzegovina settled down under Habsburg rule then the very future of Serbia itself would be at stake, for the Dual Monarchy might become Triune, as it was already rumoured that the heir to the throne, the Archduke Francis Ferdinand, wished. Serbia, however, could not fight alone, and Aehrenthal's brilliant diplomacy was isolating her; Bulgaria had already been gained in advance, and the Porte was soon won over by the withdrawal of the Austrian garrisons in the Sanjak. Only Russia remained as a potential ally. Very skilfully Aehrenthal refrained from any hostile act towards Belgrade, while Germany exerted pressure on Russia. When he realized that this had been successful, for the reason that the Russian government was in no condition to fight, he announced that he was about to send an ultimatum to Belgrade. On this, as he had anticipated, the Triple Entente advised the Serbs to yield, and at the end of March, 1909, Serbia recognized that her rights were not infringed by the annexation of the two provinces, while she undertook to cease her attitude of protest and opposition, to modify her policy towards Vienna, and to live with the Dual Monarchy on neighbourly terms.

If the Conference of Algeciras had been in some measure a drawn battle between the Triple Alliance and its opponents the Near Eastern crisis of 1908–1909 had represented a triumph for what were so soon to be known as the Central Powers. Austria-Hungary had gained a considerable accession of territory, and had humiliated Serbia; Germany had supported her old ally in Vienna without alienating her new friend at Constantinople. Russia, and through her the Triple Alliance, had been challenged, and had given way sooner than submit to the arbitrament of war. Such being the case it is little wonder that Bülow wrote: "For the first time the Anglo-German alliance proved its strength in a grievous conflict. The group of Powers whose influence had been so much over-estimated at Algeciras fell to pieces when faced with the tough problems of Continental policy."

For the next two years there was a relaxation of international tension, though the Powers continued to pile up armaments upon an unprecedented scale, and, in particular, there was a close and ominous competition between the naval construction programme of Germany and Great Britain. In 1910 there died King Edward VII, the last British monarch to play a leading part in world politics, and during the years which followed there was much speculation whether had his life been spared, he would have been able to prevent or postpone the catastrophe which was so soon to overtake Western civilization. However this may be, the restless policy of Germany soon produced another crisis, and thereafter, with an ever-increasing momentum, the Powers slipped down to destruction.

The first conflict of interests was in Morocco once more. Berlin had taken full advantage of the acceptance of its contention that the affairs of the Sherefian Empire were the concern of the world, and German businessmen were encouraged to take part in the development of the country. The result was more than one clash between the Mannesmann and Krupp groups on the one hand and the Schneider and Creusot on the other. This was bad enough, but in addition there was the growing anarchy among the Moors. Abdul Aziz IV was overthrown in 1908 by his brother Mulai Hafid, but the new Sultan was hardly more secure on his throne than had been his predecessor. In 1909 the Riff tribesmen rose against Spain, who was obliged to send an army of 50,000 men to reduce them to submission. Two years later the tribes round Fez revolted, and the capital was besieged; in his despair Mulai Hafid called upon France to save him, and in accordance with his request French troops occupied Fez. The Spaniards, not to be outdone, landed a force at Larache.

German opinion, both official and public, was roused to fury by this news, and it was generally believed in the Reich that the French government was endeavouring to use the unrest in Morocco as an excuse for turning that country into another Tunis in violation of the Treaty of Algeciras. At the beginning of July, 1911, therefore, the German government decided to challenge the French position by sending the *Panther* to Agadir, and in justification of this step Berlin announced that the Treaty of Algeciras was dead. "Some German firms established in the south of Morocco, notably at Agadir and in the vicinity, have been alarmed by a certain ferment among the local tribes, due, it seems, to recent occurrences in other parts of the country. These firms have applied to the Imperial Government for protection of their lives and property. At their request the Government have decided to send a warship to Agadir to lend help in case of need to their subjects and *protegés* as well as to the considerable German interests in that territory. As soon as the state of affairs has resumed its normal tranquillity the ship will leave."

There is, it must be admitted, a good deal to be said for the German point of view, and the French had already been warned of the consequences of an occupation of Fez. Indeed, the repercussions of the arrival of the *Panther* at Agadir were more violent in London than in Paris, where they were followed by negotiations with the German government as to the compensation to be paid by France for a free hand in Morocco. Great Britain had no desire to see Germany established on the Moroccan coast, right athwart her own lines of communication, and she was prepared to go to any lengths to prevent this. Grey denounced the voyage of the *Panther* as an unprovoked attack on the *status quo*, and Lloyd George, then Chancellor of the Exchequer, made an extremely bellicose speech at the Mansion House, when he talked of a peace at a price that "would be a humiliation intolerable for a great country like ours to endure".

This speech brought war very close, it is true, but it also made Germany realize that in the event of hostilities Britain would stand by France, so that while it inflamed German opinion it resulted in a modification of German demands. The immediate crisis passed, though there was another in the middle of August in consequence of a deadlock in the Franco-German negotiations, but the Kaiser threw his weight into the scale in favour of peace, and a settlement was reached early in November. France obtained all she wanted politically in Morocco, and in 1912 she established her Protectorate; in the economic field she conceded the maintenance of tariff equality; and in return she ceded to Germany some hundred thousand square miles of the French Congo. By the end of the year British and German statesmen were making friendly references to one another, and the storm seemed to have subsided as quickly as it had arisen. Actually, it had left many a bitter memory and much suspicion behind it on both sides of the North Sea.

Before agreement had been reached there had been another change in the *status quo* in Africa due to the seizure of Tripoli by Italy. Her interests in that vilayet had long been recognized by the Powers, and in September, 1911, she declared war on Turkey on the somewhat inadequate pretext of ill-treatment of her nationals and interference with her trade. In actual fact the Italian government was becoming fearful that when France had consolidated her position in Morocco she might cast covetous eyes on Tripoli, while an easy conquest would prove popular with public opinion at home, and would go far to erase the memory of Adowa. The only serious domestic opposition came from the more extreme Socialists who looked to Mussolini, and the ease by which the conquest was effected in its earlier stages justified the hopes of

Rome. The Porte had no fleet which could compare with the Italian, and although Egypt was still nominally an Ottoman province the British government refused to allow the passage of Turkish troops through that country. Italy thus had Tripoli at her mercy from the start.

Internationally the repercussions of this war were significant, and there is not a little to be said for the standpoint that it marks a stage on the passage of Italy from the Triple Alliance to the Triple Entente. Certainly she did not consult the interests of her old associates. For Germany, in particular, a very difficult situation had been created by this war between two of her allies, and the Kaiser was more than a little annoyed at this disturbance of German plans to win the support of Moslem opinion. The Triple Entente, on the other hand, made no protest against the action of Italy, though in Great Britain at any rate there was general reprobation at this sudden and unprovoked attack. The government, however, was too wise to let its heart run away with its head, and Grey knew that any attempt at interference would merely drive Italy back into the arms of Germany without being of the least assistance to the Turks.

At the same time, the Powers insisted that the fighting should be confined within certain limits. Italy was allowed to capture the Dodecanese, but Austria-Hungary placed her veto upon any attack on European Turkey, and the Italians were not permitted to blockade the Dardanelles. In these circumstances the war dragged on for some time, and it might have continued even longer but for the formation of the Balkan League: the Turks were desirous of getting rid of the old enemy in view of the advent of a new one, and Italy did not wish to be placed on the same footing as the Balkan states. Peace was accordingly made at Ouchy in October, 1912; Turkey ceded Tripoli to Italy, who was in her turn to restore the Dodecanese to the Porte; this latter provision was not, however, to be immediately carried out, for the Turks were quite unable to protect the islands from seizure by the Greeks.

The events which caused the Porte to come to terms with Italy were the formation of the Balkan League and its victories in the field. The author of this alliance was the Bulgarian Prime Minister, Gueshoff, for he and his master had come to the conclusion that the aspirations of Bulgaria could only be satisfied in co-operation with the other Balkan states, and on this account they were prepared to sink, for the time being, their differences with Serbia.

x

With the full support of Russia, once more actively interested in
the affairs of south-east Europe, a treaty between Serbia and
Bulgaria was signed in March, 1912; in May the Greek government joined the alliance, a military convention following in September; and in August the adhesion of Montenegro was secured.
Ostensibly these documents provided for mutual support if one of
the Great Powers tried to annex or occupy any Balkan territory
under Turkish rule, but there was a secret annex which provided
for common action by the larger states, subject to the approval of
Russia, against the Porte in the event of disturbances or menace
of war in the Ottoman Empire. The Russian government, it may
be added, by no means kept its French ally fully informed of what
was afoot, and Poincaré, then Prime Minister, was far from pleased
when he came to learn the truth.

As the summer began to pass into autumn the tension grew
more tense: Turkish promises of reform for Albania evoked complaints of neglect from Sofia and Belgrade, and Montenegro commenced to mobilize. With the advent of October the progress of
events was accelerated. The Powers had for weeks been trying to
agree upon a common plan of action, and on October 7th Austria-
Hungary and Russia were authorized to inform the Balkan States
that the Concert condemned any steps likely to cause a breach with
the Porte, that it would itself take the reforms in hand, and that
no change in the *status quo*, as a result of war, would be allowed.
This declaration came too late, for on October 8th Montenegro
took up arms, and the other Christian states immediately followed
her example. Contrary to general expectation the Turks proved
no match for their foes, and on November 3rd, with the Bulgarians
threatening Constantinople itself, the Porte craved the intervention of the Powers.

The sweeping victories of the Balkan States were by no means
to the liking of the Triple Alliance. Germany saw her Turkish ally
weakened, and Russian policy triumphant, while Austria-Hungary
and Italy were firmly opposed to the acquisition by Serbia of a
port on the Adriatic. On the other side, Great Britain and France
were more concerned with preventing an extension of the struggle
than with any other aspect of the situation, and from December
1912, to March of the following year the danger of war between
Russia and Austria-Hungary was acute. There were, however,
strong moderating influences at work, and the Kaiser told the
Imperial Chancellor, Bethmann-Hollweg, that he would not march

on Paris or Warsaw for the sake of Albania, while Francis Joseph refused to listen to the counsels of the extremists in Vienna and Budapest, and he was strengthened in this attitude by the announcement that Austria-Hungary would only receive German support if she were the victim of aggression.

In these circumstances a conference of ambassadors of the Powers was called into being in London, where it sat from December, 1912, onwards under the chairmanship of the British Foreign Secretary, but before Vienna would consent to participate an assurance was given that the permanent establishment of Serbia on the Adriatic would be excluded from discussion. It may be added that throughout the conference Great Britain and Germany worked in perfect accord.

Meanwhile the situation in the Balkans was marked by the most violent changes of fortune. The representatives of the belligerents signed a treaty in London in December, 1912, but it was promptly repudiated in Constantinople, where the government was violently overthrown by Enver Pasha. When fighting was renewed Adrianople fell to the combined attack of the Bulgarians and Serbs, and the Greeks captured Jannina. At the end of May, 1913, therefore, the Porte was compelled to sign a treaty by which Greece obtained Salonika, southern Macedonia, and Crete; Serbia secured central and northern Macedonia; and to Bulgaria was assigned Thrace and the Aegean coast, though she had to surrender Silistria to Roumania: thus Bulgaria received once more that outlet to the Aegean which she had been promised at San Stefano but denied at Berlin. As for Turkey, she emerged from the settlement with nothing but a foothold in Eastern Thrace.

A month had hardly elapsed after the conclusion of this agreement before the Bulgarians fell on the Serbian forces in Macedonia, while another Bulgarian army made a dash for Salonika. Once more the Balkans appeared to be in the melting-pot, but it soon transpired that Ferdinand had taken on a task which was beyond his country's strength. The Serbs and Greeks held, while the Roumanian government, determined to prevent a Bulgarian hegemony, sent an army across the Danube; even the Turks plucked up enough courage to recapture Adrianople. The result was the Treaty of Bucharest in August, 1913, by which Bulgaria lost not only her access to the Aegean and her gains in Macedonia, but was also compelled to cede to Roumania territory with a population of 340,000. The Turks retained Adrianople. All that now remained was for the Powers to create that independent Albania which was the logical outcome of the refusal to allow Serbia an outlet to the Adriatic: by the end of the year 1913 this task had been accomplished, and the Balkans were, in theory at any rate, once more at peace.

The crisis had proved that a general war could be averted by co-operation between Great Britain and Germany, and by that alone: Russia and Austria-Hungary had partially mobilized in 1912, and had only been held back with the greatest difficulty. Yet in Germany the strength of militarism was growing, and the Kaiser was coming to believe that war with France was inevitable. "The whole of Germany is charged with electricity", Colonel House reported after a visit to Berlin in May, 1913, "Everybody's nerves are tense. It only requires a spark to set the whole thing off." In Paris the feeling was much the same, and a series of Franco-German incidents served to fan the flame of French chauvinism: the spirit of the spring of 1870 was in the air. From Vienna the French ambassador was reporting that "the feeling that the nations are moving towards a conflict, urged by an irresistible force, grows from day to day", while at the beginning of 1914 the Tsar said, "For Serbia we will do everything". No single statesman could, in these circumstances, prevent the breaking of the storm, but so long as the British and German governments refused to allow their hands to be forced there was a hope that war might be postponed. As late as June, 1914, an agreement was reached between London and Berlin regarding the vexed question of the Baghdad railway, by which Britain secured her position in the Persian Gulf while recognizing the whole of Mesopotamia north of Basra as within the German sphere of influence.

Whatever hopes there may have been of the preservation of peace were destroyed by the murder on June 28th, 1914, at Serajevo by Austrian Serbs of the Archduke Francis Ferdinand, the heir to the Habsburg throne; this set in motion the events which culminated five weeks later in one of the greatest catastrophes civilization has ever known. To what extent this crime was directly inspired by Belgrade is, perhaps, a moot point, but its immediate effect was to convince even the most moderate in Vienna that it was essential to administer a sharp lesson to Serbia. The attitude of Francis Joseph, who had more than once in the past restrained his wild men, is well brought out in a letter he sent to the Kaiser a day or two after the murder:

The crime against my nephew is the direct consequence of the agitation carried on by Russian and Serbian Pan-Slavists, whose sole aim is to weaken the Triple Alliance and shatter my Empire. Though it may be impossible to prove the complicity of the Serbian government, there can be no doubt that its policy, intent on uniting all Jugoslavs under the Serbian flag, must encourage such crimes and endanger my house and countries if it is not stopped. My efforts must be directed to isolating Serbia and reducing her size. After the recent terrible event I am certain that you also are convinced that agreement between Serbia and us is out of the question, and that the peace policy of all European monarchs is threatened so long as this centre of criminal agitation remains unpunished in Belgrade.

What had, in effect, happened was that the old strife between Teuton and Slav had broken out in a new form. If the Dual Monarchy became Triune, then in due course the Jugoslavs would look to Vienna rather than to Belgrade and St. Petersburg; therefore Francis Ferdinand was murdered. On the other hand, as the German White Book put it, "If the Serbs continued, with the aid of Russia and France, to menace the existence of Austria, her gradual collapse and the subjection of all the Slavs under the Russian sceptre would result, thus rendering untenable the position of the Teutonic race in central Europe. A morally weakened Austria under the pressure of Russian Pan-Slavism would be no longer an ally on whom we could count in view of the ever more menacing attitude of our eastern and western neighbours." Therefore Germany had to stand by her ally.

So far the situation was very much what it had been in 1908; Germany was ready to support Austria-Hungary, and Great Britain had certainly no intention of going to war for the sake of Serbia. On the other hand the forces making for peace were everywhere weaker, especially in Vienna, than six years before, and Berchtold, who had succeeded Aehrenthal as Austro-Hungarian Foreign Minister in 1912, was far from possessing the diplomatic skill of his predecessor. Aehrenthal had refrained from putting any real pressure on Belgrade until he knew that Russia would interfere, while Berchtold presented an ultimatum to Serbia in such circumstances that Russia was left no alternative save to support her Serbian client. Instead, therefore, of following the precedent of 1908 Berchtold preferred that of 1859, and thus made his country appear in the wrong, when, in fact, it had a very good case. In consequence, and as a result of conflicting counsels in Berlin, what Bismarck would never have allowed then took place, namely the Austrian horse bolted with the German waggon, and the Reich was forced into war with Russia.

On July 23rd, 1914, the ultimatum was presented at Belgrade with a time limit of forty-eight hours. The demands of Austria-Hungary, set out in ten articles, included not only the suppression of Pan-Serb societies and propaganda, but the co-operation of the officials of the Dual Monarchy in the measures required for that purpose. From the beginning it was clear that everything turned on the attitude of Russia, and Grey told the Austro-Hungarian ambassador that if the ultimatum did not lead to trouble with that Power he had no concern with it, and he went so far as to urge Serbia to promise the fullest satisfaction if any of her officials should prove to have been accomplices in the Serajevo murder. The views of the Russian government were not long in doubt, and Sazonoff, the Foreign Minister, described the ultimatum as provocative and immoral, while the military party at St. Petersburg were by no means averse from a conflict of which Constantinople might be the prize. With the clouds thus rapidly gathering, Grey suggested the cessation of all military operations pending a conference, and the Serbian acceptance of the ultimatum, save in the matter of the co-operation of foreign officials, afforded some slight hope that his efforts at mediation might be successful. Even at this late hour peace might have been preserved had Great Britain and Germany worked together as during the Balkan crisis.

There was, however, no controlling hand in Berlin as was shown at the Crown Council held on July 29th. The Chancellor was himself strongly in favour of peace, but he had lost all control of the situation, and the Kaiser was vacillating; on the other hand were those who said that a more favourable moment for war would never come, with Britain divided on the Irish Question and the Russian army in the throes of reorganization. Such being the case it is not surprising that the worst was made of both worlds. An attempt was made to buy British neutrality on impossible terms, while Vienna was warned not to precipitate matters. Berchtold and his colleagues, with the full support of their fellow-countrymen it may be added, however, took the line that operations against Serbia, which had already begun, must continue, that the British suggestion could not be adopted until the Russian mobilization had ceased, and that the ultimatum must be accepted as a whole.

Hostilities were now inevitable, though, as Mr. Lloyd George was later to write, "no one at the head of affairs quite meant war at that stage. It was something into which they glided, or rather staggered and stumbled, perhaps through folly". Certainly there was much indecision, and not a little treachery in high places; for example, when the Tsar ordered mobilization against Austria-Hungary alone in the hope of limiting the scope of the conflict the War Minister continued with a general mobilization, while concealing the fact from his master and denying it to the German military attaché. On July 31st an ultimatum was sent from Berlin to St. Petersburg demanding the cessation of mobilization within twelve hours, and on the following day Germany and Russia were at war. On the 3rd Germany declared war on France, and her troops crossed the Belgian frontier: this news put an end to the doubts and hesitations which had divided British opinion, and midnight of August 4th–5th marked the participation of Great Britain in the conflict. What future generations, as has been suggested above, may deem the Peloponnesian War of Europe had begun.

CHAPTER XXVII

THE FOUR YEARS' WAR, 1914–1918

IN time of war the objects of diplomacy are two: it has on the one hand to aid the armed forces by securing the adhesion of allies and by the prevention of any accession of strength to the enemy such as would result from the adherence to his cause of those who have hitherto remained neutral; on the other hand it must never forget that the object of war is peace, and such a peace as shall be in the best interests of those for whom it is working; for this reason it will often have to oppose the conclusion of agreements, or the raising of hopes, which may be justified on the ground of temporary military expediency, but which in the end are likely to create embarrassing complications. The Four Years' War, like that of the Spanish Succession and the Revolutionary and Napoleonic Wars, threw much light on these considerations.

The conflict began with Great Britain, France, Russia, Belgium, Serbia, and Montenegro on the one side, and Germany and Austria-Hungary on the other, for, as was expected, Italy and Roumania had proclaimed their neutrality. The war had not, however, been long in existence before the full benefits of the Anglo-Japanese Agreement were felt, for on August 15th Japan demanded the withdrawal of all German warships from the Far East, and the surrender of Tsingtau in a week. As no reply was received to this ultimatum she proceeded, with the assistance of a small British detachment, to capture the fortress: for the rest of the war she kept the Pacific clear of German ships, did valuable convoy work, and supplied Russia with munitions, but at no time did she throw, or was asked to throw, her whole weight into the struggle. Meanwhile, on September 5th, France, Great Britain, and Russia agreed not to make a separate peace, and in November of the following year Italy associated herself with this declaration.

All this was preliminary skirmishing, but the first resounding diplomatic success went to the Central Powers when, at the end of October, 1914, they were joined by Turkey. Years of patient work by Germany at Constantinople had brought their reward, and the results of this were far-reaching. The scope of the struggle was immensely enlarged, and both the prizes and the dangers were increased. Great Britain, in particular, was compelled to consider the effect upon the Indian Moslems, and she was heavily committed to defend her interests in the Near East. Her immediate reply was to annex Cyprus, to proclaim a Protectorate over Egypt, to depose the Khedive, to select a son of Ismail as Sultan of Egypt, and to invade Mesopotamia.

If the action of Turkey raised some difficult problems for such Powers as Great Britain and France, which had millions of Moslem subjects, it was hailed with delight in Russia, where its possibilities were at once realized. In the middle of November, 1914, the British government informed Sazonoff that it would raise no objection to the incorporation of Constantinople and the Straits in the Russian Empire. Throughout the winter of 1914-1915 nego-tiations continued between London, Paris, and St. Petersburg as to the disposal of the Sultan's dominions, and in March, 1915, agreement was reached. The main provisions were that the Cali-phate was to be separated from the Ottoman dynasty; the Sacred Places were to be put under an independent Moslem ruler; and the neutral zone in Persia was to be included in the British sphere; while British and French rights in Asiatic Turkey, to be defined later, were to be recognized. The wheel had, indeed, come full circle when the old antagonists of the Crimean War were united to drive the Turk out of Europe.

While the finishing touches were being put to these negotia-tions Italy came into the market. "What is needed", declared her Prime Minister, "is a freedom from all preconceptions and pre-judices, from every sentiment except that of sacred egoism", and in this spirit she put herself up for sale. Germany was quite willing to bid, but she could only do so at the expense of Austro-Hungarian provinces, with which Vienna was unwilling to part. At one time the Allies might have been able to buy Italian support fairly cheaply, but in the spring of 1915 they suffered a series of reverses in the field, and when they bought it was at the top of the market. The transaction was completed on April 26th, 1915, by the Treaty of London.

This agreement was between Italy on the one hand, and Great Britain, France, and Russia on the other. It was decided that Italy should at the end of the war receive Trentino, Alto Adige, Trieste, Istria, Gorizia-Gradisca, the islands of Cherso and Lussin, and Dalmatia to Cape Plonka. She was to hold in full sovereignty Valona, the island of Saseno, and a territory sufficiently extensive to secure the defence of these points, while in like manner she was to receive the Dodecanese. Outside Europe she was to be given territory in Asia Minor, in the province of Adalia, in the event of a partition of Turkey between the Powers, and if Great Britain and France augmented their African possessions at the expense of Germany then Italy was to have compensation. Never in all its long history of bargaining had the House of Savoy sold itself to such advantage : as Asquith was later to declare, "The French and ourselves were fighting for our lives on the Western Front, and the Treaty represented the terms on which Italy was prepared to join forces". If the terms were high, it must be remembered that Italian neutrality saved France in 1914, and that Italy did not throw in her lot with Germany was originally due to the skilful diplomacy of Grey at the time of the seizure of Tripoli. Italy declared war against Austria-Hungary in May, 1915, but not against Germany until more than twelve months later.

The Serbs soon found out what had been settled, and they were by no means pleased at the fate of Jugoslav territories being settled behind their backs. Later, President Wilson refused to recognize the Treaty of London because he had no knowledge of it. Actually, there was no reason why it should have been communicated to him, for the United States was neutral in 1915, and we have Balfour's authority for the statement that he was informed when his country entered the war.

In April, 1917, there was a further agreement, this time between Great Britain, France, and Italy, called the Pact of St. Jean de Maurienne. Its object was to clear up any uncertainty about the future of Asia Minor, and it stipulated that Italy was to have the Smyrna area as well as Adalia.

Some of this is to anticipate, for the spring and summer of 1915 had been marked on both sides by a further search for allies, and Greece, Bulgaria, and Roumania had all been plied with exhortations, promises, and threats. In the main the Central Powers were the more successful. King Constantine was too dubious of the ability of the Entente to implement its pledges to come to its aid when most necessary, and Bulgaria was in the pocket of Berlin and Vienna almost from the start. Austria-Hungary had been cultivating Ferdinand ever since the Balkan Wars, for Serbia was the common enemy, and Russia was her patron. The Entente put pressure upon its Serbian ally and on neutral Greece to satisfy Bulgarian ambitions, but the only effect was to exacerbate opinion in Belgrade and Athens, nor were the Serbs in any way

appeased by the British refusal to allow them to anticipate the
Bulgarian attack. In October, 1915, Bulgaria entered the war on
the side of the Central Powers, and the offer by the British government of Cyprus to Greece remained without effect. The general
war situation was unfavourable to the Entente, and alike in London, Paris, and St. Petersburg sight had been lost of the close
connection between diplomacy and force.

The complications which resulted from the agreements between
the Entente, to which reference will in future be made as the
Allies, and Italy were as nothing to those which made their appearance in connection with the proposed partition of the Ottoman
Empire. In the autumn of 1915 the British government had
agreed to recognize the independence of the Arabs within certain
territorial limits, which meant not the coast but the interior, and
in the following year there was an agreement between Great
Britain, France, and Russia to clear up the points which had
been left undecided in the settlement of March, 1915. To Russia
were to go the provinces of Erzerum, Trebizond, Van, Bitlis, and
Southern Kurdistan; France was to have the coastal strip of Syria,
the vilayet of Adana, and south-east Asia Minor; and Great
Britain was to receive South Mesopotamia, Baghdad, and the ports
of Haifa and Acre. The zone between the French and British
territories was to form an Arab state, but Alexandretta was to be
a free port, and Palestine was to have a regime to be determined
by the three Powers. As between Great Britain and France these
decisions were implemented by the so-called Sykes–Picot Agreement in May, 1916, which gave France virtually a free hand on
the Syrian coast with a veiled protectorate over the interior.
Finally, in November, 1917, Balfour, then Foreign Secretary, sent
a letter to Lord Rothschild informing him of the intention of the
British government to establish in Palestine a national home for
the Jews.

These various promises had the unfortunate result of encouraging Arab aspirations which it finally proved impossible to satisfy,
and many years were to elapse before a settlement was reached
between the claims of the Arabs and those of France. Indeed, it
is difficult to withstand the conclusion that in the Near East the
Allies were too inclined to sacrifice the future for the present.

At this point it is not without importance to discover what
efforts were made to put an end to the war while it was still in
progress, for these throw considerable light upon the attitude of

the Allies before they had won their victory. There is no proof of any concrete proposals for peace prior to November, 1916, but during the last weeks of that year suggestions for a termination of hostilities were made in several quarters. The reason for this is not far to seek. For the first time since the war began the prospect of a stalemate had become obvious to the most convinced chauvinist on either side. In the west the Germans had failed to overcome the French defence at Verdun, while the ground which had been gained by the British had only been won at tremendous cost. In the east the situation was more favourable to the Central Powers, but even there it was obviously idle to expect an early decision. Roumania, who had at last taken the field on the Allied side, was at her last gasp, though Bucharest did not fall until the beginning of December; General Townshend had surrendered at Kut in May; the Allied Forces at Salonika were clearly unable to take the offensive; and the Italians had made no real progress along the road to Trieste.

On the other hand, none of these successes was likely to bring the Allies to their knees, for in no case were the Central Powers in a position to push their advantages home, while there appeared a distinct possibility of a Russian revival in the near future. At sea, Jutland had been fought, and although both sides claimed the victory, the fact remained that the British blockade of the German coast continued without interruption. In effect, at the end of 1916 neither set of combatants appeared to have any real hope of forcing a decision in the field, and, such being the case, it is in no way surprising that in London, as well as in Berlin and Vienna, the possibility of securing peace by negotiation should have begun to be envisaged.

On November 14th, 1916, Lansdowne, then Minister without Portfolio in the Asquith Coalition government, laid a memorandum before the Cabinet in which he suggested that the time had come to examine the possible bases of peace, and to make it plain that the Allies did not aim at the total destruction of Germany. This seems to have been the first definite step which any responsible statesman in any belligerent country had taken in the direction of a cessation of hostilities since the war began over two years before: there had been repeated declarations that the sword would not be sheathed until this or that had been done, but the actual war aims of the antagonists were largely a matter of conjecture. Of course the Lansdowne proposal was unknown to the general public at the time, and it is impossible to estimate what effect it might have had, for the Asquith administration was already tottering to its fall, and within a month it had ceased to exist. It was replaced by the government of Mr. Lloyd George, which was pledged to a more vigorous prosecution of the war.

A week after Lansdowne had put his views before his colleagues Francis Joseph died. Whether the old monarch would have made an effort, had he lived a little longer, to bring the war to an end it is difficult to say, though evidence has been adduced which seems to show that he would have pursued such a policy. However this may be, there can be no question of the pacific sentiments of his successor, Charles. In a proclamation on his accession to the throne the new Emperor used the significant phrase, "I desire to do all in my power to end, as soon as may be, the horrors and sacrifices of the war". There can be but little doubt that this disposition on the part of their ally was extremely distasteful to the German government, and it was almost certainly responsible for the German offer to treat which was made on December 12th.

The Central Powers presented four identical notes in which they stated that they were willing to bring forward definite proposals, but they also announced their intention of fighting to a finish if these were rejected. Whatever chance of success this step might have had in other circumstances, an extravagant speech by the Imperial Chancellor in which he threw all the blame for the outbreak of war upon the Allies, completely ruined. Such being the case, one may perhaps be pardoned for questioning the sincerity of the whole negotiation so far as Germany was concerned, for she may well have had no other object in view than to forestall a move on the part of Austria-Hungary, and to place upon the Allies the onus of refusal to discuss terms of peace. This, at any rate, was the interpretation put upon her action by those to whom the offer was addressed, and the impossibility of negotiating upon such a basis was demonstrated in speeches by the leading Allied statesmen. The suspicions of the Allied Powers were also voiced in their official reply on January 29th, 1917, when they declared, in addition, that there could be no peace without restoration and reparation.

A week after the Central Powers announced their willingness to enter into negotiations, the President of the United States, who was still a neutral, addressed a note to all the belligerents asking for a statement of their war aims as an essential preliminary to any approach to peace. It is clear that Wilson had decided to take this step before he was acquainted with the intentions of the Central Powers, and the State Department was at considerable pains to show that the two proposals were entirely unconnected. This fact was certainly appreciated by the governments concerned, though the general public in the Allied countries, which had no great love at that time for the President of the United States, showed a decided disposition to confuse the two events, and in private, if not in public, Wilson's note was widely denounced as a deliberate attempt to second the efforts of the Central Powers. The only reply which this appeal elicited from the Allies was a paraphrase of that which was shortly afterwards sent to their opponents, and in it they declared that "their objects in the war will not be made known in detail with all the equitable compensations and indemnities for damages suffered until the hour of negotiations". It was, however, stipulated that the Turk should be expelled from Europe, but no mention was made of the retrocession of Alsace-Lorraine to France.

This interchange of notes, though it led to no definite result, cleared the air to some extent. It showed that Germany was not ready to treat upon any basis to which her enemies would agree, and that the Allies were not prepared to accept the mediation of a neutral, for although Wilson had not actually offered his services in that capacity, it was obvious that they were available if desired. On the other hand, the reticence of the Allies suggested either that they were not in complete agreement with regard to their aims, or that the latter were subject to negotiation. The new Austrian Emperor felt that in either case there might be a chance for him to secure a settlement, and so, in the early days of February, 1917, he got into communication with his brother-in-law, Prince Sixte of Bourbon-Parma, with this end in view. Thus originated the most determined of the attempts to bring the Four Years' War to an end by negotiation.

Sixte was at that time serving with the Belgian Army because no Bourbon was allowed with the French forces, and he readily obtained the permission of King Albert to co-operate with Charles. He was then informed of the terms upon which his brother-in-law considered peace to be possible. These were: firstly, the conclusion of a secret armistice between Austria-Hungary and Russia in which the question of Constantinople was not to be made an issue; secondly, the restoration of Belgium and of Alsace-Lorraine—the latter, incidentally, a concession which, as has been shown, had not yet been demanded by the Allies themselves; and thirdly, the formation of a Southern Slav monarchy which should include not only Serbia, Montenegro, and Albania, but Bosnia and Herzegovina as well. It should be noted in connection with these suggestions that there was at that time no idea in the mind of the Austrian Emperor of concluding a separate peace; all that he intended to do was to explore the ground and when he had arrived at a general understanding with the Allies, he proposed to place before Germany, Bulgaria, and Turkey certain definite recommendations based upon it.

As a French subject, Sixte naturally laid his brother-in-law's proposals before the President, Poincaré, in the first place, and he, in his turn, communicated them to Briand, who was then Premier and Minister for Foreign Affairs. Both French statesmen agreed that they might well form a basis for negotiations, but they warned Sixte that Italy would be the chief obstacle to any understanding. As a result of two interviews with Poincaré the Prince went to Vienna, where he saw the Emperor in the latter part of March, 1917. Unfortunately in the interval two events took place which were destined to bring about the failure of the negotiations, namely the outbreak of the Russian Revolution and the fall of the Briand administration. The first of these soon weakened Russia to such an extent that the more chauvinistic elements in Berlin and Vienna once more became convinced, with considerable justification it must be admitted, that the victory in the field which had seemed beyond their capacity to achieve at the end of 1916 was again within their grasp, while the second resulted in the installation as Premier and Minister for Foreign Affairs of Alexandre Ribot, a man whose capacity did not rise above mediocrity. In spite, however, of these drawbacks, Sixte continued his mission, and he was assisted by the fact that as the spring of 1917 was exceptionally late, and the Germans executed a retirement in the west, there was a comparative lull in the fighting.

On the return of Sixte from Vienna, where he informed Charles of the attitude of France, it was decided to acquaint the British government with what was afoot. Accordingly, Ribot told Mr. Lloyd George of the Austrian proposals, and the British statesman promised complete secrecy. As evidence of the relations existing between Vienna and Berlin it is to be noted that Sixte's chief reason for insisting upon such complete secrecy was the fear that if news of the proposals reached Germany the Austrian Emperor would be murdered at official German instigation within a week. On April 18th, Sixte had an interview with Mr. Lloyd George, in which the British Prime Minister showed himself extremely sympathetic, but, like Poincaré, he feared that Italian ambitions would prove an insurmountable obstacle, for Italy was supposed to be still demanding all that had been promised to her by the Treaty of London. At this point, however, it was discovered that the Italian government, unknown to its allies, was already engaged in a separate negotiation with Vienna on the basis of the cession of the Trentino alone, and in these circumstances there seemed to be no special reason why London and Paris should be unduly careful of Italian susceptibilities.

Sixte, therefore, came to England in May, and remained there until the first week in June, during which time he saw King George V and had several conversations with the Prime Minister. The position then was that both the Austrian Emperor and Mr. Lloyd George were extremely anxious to come to terms, and Charles had become so thoroughly convinced of the impossibility of inducing his German ally to listen to any proposals for bringing the war to an end that he was now prepared to negotiate a separate peace for his own dominions. On the other hand, Ribot was at least lukewarm, though whether it was his head or his heart that was at fault is a problem which is unlikely now to be solved. Count Czernin, the Austro-Hungarian Foreign Minister, also blew hot and cold, and Sixte found him to be an influence upon which no reliance could be placed. Lastly, the King of Italy refused to pay a visit to the Western Front, where it had been hoped to have arranged a meeting with the King of England and the French President at which the three rulers could have exchanged views on the Austrian proposals.

On the Allied side the protagonist of peace was Mr. Lloyd George. He at once suggested that he and Ribot should have a meeting with Czernin, and only the Frenchman's invincible obstinacy prevented the taking of a step that might well have shortened the war by some eighteen months. But when Mr. Lloyd George made up his mind something had to be done, as even Ribot soon recognized, and after a good deal of discussion Great Britain and France proposed certain terms to Austria at the beginning of August. These comprised the cession of the Trentino to Italy, and the establishment of Trieste as a Free Port, while in exchange

Austria-Hungary was to receive Silesia, Bavaria, and Poland, the last-named within the frontiers of 1772. In short, the Allies recognized that if the menace of Prussianism was really to be removed from Europe it was not only the verdict of 1870, but that of 1866, which had to be reversed: accordingly they proposed that the Habsburgs should once again exercise the predominant power in Germany. It is not a little significant that this offer was made within a few days of the Pope's attempt to bring about peace by negotiation, and there can be no doubt that the action of the Vatican was not unexpected in Vienna.

Unfortunately this step was taken too late, and the course of the actual fighting was such as to render the very continuance of negotiations impossible. A British offensive had been launched on the Western Front at the beginning of July, while the delivery of the Allied note coincided with an Italian attack that came within an ace of breaking through the Austrian resistance. This last thrust thoroughly frightened Czernin, and he succeeded in communicating his fears to his master, to whom he maintained that only the help of Germany could prevent the Austrian armies from being overthrown. In October, 1917, the Austrian counter-attack resulted in the Italian defeat at Caporetto, and British and French troops were hurried to the Piave, where, for the first time, they came into contact with the armies of Austria-Hungary. The vicious circle was complete, and Ribot took occasion to close the door upon any further negotiations in a speech of quite exceptional bitterness.

The responsibility of Ribot was very heavy indeed, and only two explanations of his conduct would appear to be possible. One is that he did not possess sufficient intelligence to realize that the Austrian proposal was entirely separate from the German, and so regarded the negotiations in which Sixte played so prominent a part as a trap set in Berlin and baited in Vienna. The other is that he was so fanatical a republican that he preferred the continuance of the war to the success of a negotiation for which a Bourbon prince would receive the credit. The truth probably lies between these two explanations. In any event defeatism was very prevalent in France at the time, and to a man of mediocre intelligence any resolute action probably appeared to be fraught with danger. It is deeply to be regretted that Briand did not remain at the Quai d'Orsay throughout 1917. Far more guilty was Czernin, for he knew his country's need of peace, and yet when the oppor-

Y

tunity arrived of concluding it upon the most advantageous terms, his fear of Germany got the better of him. In fine, it is difficult to resist the conclusion that by their cowardice and incompetence he and Ribot prolonged the Four Years' War by another eighteen months.

Up to this date no serious suggestion had been put forward by the Allies for any general disintegration of the Central Powers: the offer to Austria-Hungary represented the first suggestion that with regard to Germany anything more was envisaged than a paring of her claws; any spoils were to come from the dissolution of the Ottoman Empire. During the winter of 1917–1918, however, there was a hardening of opinion in the Allied countries, notably in Great Britain, and evidence of this is to be found in the hostile reception generally accorded to Lansdowne's famous letter in the *Daily Telegraph* on November 29th, 1917. This letter was almost identical with the memorandum which its author had laid before the Cabinet twelve months earlier, and in connection with it Lord Esher said he was "sure we could have detached Austria, had we had the skill to make her definite peace offers six months ago". In this he was, in ignorance of what had actually taken place, unfair to Lloyd George, but his opinion is further evidence of the fact that the summer of 1917 was a very critical period, and Lord Newton, Lansdowne's biographer, admits that the appeal was issued at the wrong moment. Had it appeared in the spring the result of so respected a statesman's intervention would probably have been very different, and it is doubtful whether the polemics of the Press would then have been able to prevail against him.

The Times had in the first instance rejected the letter on the ground that it did not reflect any "responsible phase of British opinion", and the Northcliffe Press as a whole was openly hostile. The *Morning Post* spoke of it as "a stab in the back", and Lansdowne was accused of uniting various people "who are working for Germany in one clamorous cry". Most significant of all, Bonar Law referred to the letter as a national calamity, and threatened a General Election if it evoked any support.

The early days of 1918 were marked by a speech by the British Prime Minister which showed that the government was not uninfluenced by the growing strength of opinion in favour of a fight to a finish. He put forward three main conditions of peace, namely, the re-establishment of the sanctity of treaties, a territorial settlement based on self-determination, and a territorial organization to limit the burden of armaments. He naturally demanded "the complete restoration of Belgium, Serbia, Montenegro, Roumania, and of occupied French and Italian territory". The return of Alsace-Lorraine to France was now required, and Lloyd George stated his belief that "an independent Poland, comprising all those genuinely Polish elements who desire to form part of it, is an urgent necessity for the stability of Western Europe". This, also, was a new departure, for only six months before Poland had been offered to Austria-Hungary. On the other hand he disclaimed any desire to destroy Germany or to alter her constitution. Lloyd George went on to declare that "the break-up of Austria-Hungary is no part of our war aims", but he proceeded to qualify this with a demand for "genuine self-government" for her nationalities, and added two very vague phrases about "the legitimate claims of the Italians" and justice for "men of Roumanian blood and speech". With regard to the German colonies, he repeated earlier declarations to the effect that "they are held at the disposal of a conference whose decisions must have primary regard to the wishes of the native inhabitants". With Russia in the throes of revolution a more generous policy towards Turkey became possible. "We are not fighting to deprive Turkey of its capital, or of the rich and renowned lands in Asia Minor or Thrace, which are predominantly Turkish in race." The Straits, however, were to be internationalized and neutralized, while Arabia, Armenia, Mesopotamia, Palestine, and Syria were entitled to a recognition of their separate national conditions.

Three days after the British Prime Minister had delivered this speech the American President outlined a peace settlement in Fourteen Points (*vide* Appendix II), and his subsequent insistence upon a change of regime in Germany, as well as the *de facto* recognition of the Czech government, was in flagrant contradiction of Lloyd George's pledge. Great Britain and France had not been consulted before this programme was issued, and they by no means agreed with all of it. At the same time the United States was an Associated, not an Allied, Power, and so had a certain liberty of action in these matters: whether this was misused is another matter.

The advocates of compromise received a further set-back in March, when the extent of the German appetite was made manifest in the terms imposed upon Russia at Brest-Litovsk. By this treaty Russia lost a territory nearly as large as Austria-Hungary and Turkey combined; 56 million inhabitants, or 32 per cent of the whole population of the country; a third of her railway mileages; 73 per cent of her total iron, and 89 per cent of her total coal production; and over 5,000 factories, mills, distilleries, and refineries; by a supplementary agreement she paid to Germany an indemnity of 6,000 million marks. The terms of the Treaty of Bucharest, imposed upon defeated Roumania, were certainly not less rigorous. The vanquished state was deprived of the whole of the Dobrudja; she had to cede certain frontier districts to Hungary, and to give that country control of the mountain passes: she was compelled to surrender her oil-fields and forests to the Central Powers, and to give them the right of pre-emption of all raw material and foodstuffs; while there was to be a German army of occupation of 90,000 men, paid for by Roumania, who was herself only permitted an exiguous allowance of arms and munitions for her own use. The mind of the rulers of Germany was too clearly revealed by these treaties to permit of any illusions.

Nevertheless, it was only very gradually that the Allied statesmen came to the conclusion that there must be a drastic revision of the *status quo ante bellum* in Central Europe, and as late as May, 1918, General Smuts said, "When we talk of victory we do not mean marching to the Rhine or Berlin, and we do not mean going on till we have smashed Germany and the German Empire, and are able to dictate peace to the enemy in his capital. . . . I do not think that an out-and-out victory is possible any more for any group of nations in this war." Meanwhile, in the spring and early summer the Central Powers had come very close to that complete victory of which General Smuts was so sceptical, and the Allies could not afford to neglect any weapon for their defence. Accordingly, there was created a department of propaganda under the direction of Northcliffe, and this devoted special attention to fostering discontent among the Slavs in Austria-Hungary, though it was not so successful in reconciling their ambitions with those of Italy. The result was that by August, 1918, the attitude of Great Britain and France was very different from what it had been when they made their offer to the Austro-Hungarian government twelve months before.

Then came the unexpected collapse of the Central Powers. On August 13th Ludendorff told the Kaiser that the war could not be won; on September 8th the German Army leaders informed the Imperial Chancellor that they desired peace as soon as possible; by September 15th Bulgaria had asked for an armistice, and Ferdinand had abdicated; and on October 5th the German government requested Wilson to undertake the restoration of peace on the basis of the Fourteen Points. For a rapid succession of epoch-making events the autumn of 1918 is only comparable with the spring of 1814.

Throughout the month of October there was an interchange of messages between Washington and Berlin, while Turkey was passing out of the war, and the Habsburg dominions were disintegrating. Realizing the weakness of the enemy Wilson insisted on the establishment of what he considered to be a democratic regime in Germany before he could advise London and Paris to draft conditions of an armistice. When he was satisfied on this point he passed on the correspondence to Great Britain and France, and on November 8th the armistice terms were communicated to Germany. They included evacuation of all conquered territories; withdrawal beyond the Rhine; the establishment of a neutral zone on the right bank of that river; the cancellation of the Treaties of Brest-Litovsk and Bucharest; the surrender of guns, aeroplanes, and rolling-stock; and the transfer of the fleet. The terms were accepted, and at 11.0 A.M. on November 11th, 1918, the Four Years' War came to an end.

CHAPTER XXVIII

THE DISINTEGRATION OF PEACE, 1918–1923

ON the morrow of the defeat of their enemies the Allied and Associated Powers had two courses open to them. They could follow the precedent of 1814, and come to terms with the beaten foe before embarking on a general settlement; or they could postpone the settlement with Germany and her late allies until the peace conference assembled. If the first of these alternatives had been adopted the blockade could have been raised, prisoners repatriated, and the wheels of industry restarted at a relatively early date. Nor should this policy have been difficult of accomplishment, for the Allies had granted the German request for peace on the basis of the Fourteen Points save for reservations in respect of nos. 2 and 11, while once the settlement with Germany had taken place there could have been, as in 1814, an interval before the meeting of the peace conference during which there would have been time for tempers to cool and for accurate information to be collected concerning the problems in dispute. This course, however, did not recommend itself to the victors, who preferred to leave all questions to be settled at a peace conference in Paris. In the circumstances it may well be that this choice was inevitable, for no Treaty of Chaumont bound together the Allied and Associated Powers, whose peace aims were neither clearly defined nor mutually compatible.

This is not, however, to say that the various nations came to Paris with a free hand, for such was certainly not the case, and in several instances the freedom of their representatives was extremely restricted.

Hardly had Germany been defeated than Mr. Lloyd George determined to hold a General Election. He based the necessity of this appeal to the country upon the fact that it was essential for him, when he went to Paris, to be sure that he had the electorate behind him, though his opponents were not slow to allege that he was chiefly actuated by a desire to turn the victory to personal and party account. However this may be, as the election campaign progressed the British government became pledged to proposals of an extreme and impracticable nature. The administration began with a manifesto to the effect that "our first task must be to

conclude a just and lasting peace, and so to establish the foundations of a new Europe that occasion for further wars may be for
ever averted": by polling-day it was promising, *inter alia*, to try
the Kaiser and to make Germany pay for the war. As Lord
Keynes has not inappropriately remarked, "To this concoction of
greed and sentiment, prejudice and deception, three weeks of the
platform had reduced the powerful governors of England, who
but a little while before had spoken not ignobly of Disarmament
and a League of Nations, and of a just and lasting peace which
should establish the foundations of a new Europe". This appeal
swept the constituencies, and the new Parliament was filled with
unknown men determined to hold Mr. Lloyd George to his
pledges.

The result of this election was unfortunate in more ways than
one, for before long the people both of Great Britain and Germany felt that they had been deceived: the British because the
pledges given so glibly on the platform proved impossible to
redeem, and the Germans because they considered that they had
surrendered on terms which were repudiated as soon as they had
laid down their arms. There was some justification for both
points of view. The British Prime Minister did not himself say
that Germany would be made to defray the cost of the war, but
that was the impression given by many of his supporters: when,
therefore, in due course the Budgets of 1919 and 1920 disclosed
huge deficits which necessitated a great increase in taxation, the
disillusionment was complete. As for the Germans, they bitterly
resented the fact that their fate should be made the sport of a
British General Election, and they declared that the conditions
upon which they had given up the struggle bore no resemblance
to those which they were subsequently compelled to accept. The
British electorate displayed its resentment at the deception which
it considered had been practised upon it by promises that could
not be fulfilled by getting rid of Mr. Lloyd George upon the first
opportunity, but in the German mind the bitterness continued to
rankle, and was not the least of the many causes which were one
day to carry the Nazis into power.

Then again there were, as at Utrecht and Vienna, the commitments, some of them contradictory, which had been entered into
while the struggle was still in progress. In the present instance the
embarrassment was the greater because Wilson refused to be
bound by these promises, and the position of those whose hands

were tied by them, in particular Mr. Lloyd George, whose government did not want to offend Washington, was rendered more than usually delicate. Indeed, it is no exaggeration to say that the Allied and Associated Powers were not ready for peace when it came, and were not agreed upon the principle by which it should be inspired: so far as Great Britain herself was concerned, she was as unprepared for the termination of the Four Years' War as she had been for its commencement. All this was soon reflected in the deliberations of the peace conference.

This met in the middle of January, 1919, and it was from the beginning dominated by the personalities of the British and French Prime Ministers and the American President. Of these Mr. Lloyd George had a slender equipment of detailed knowledge concerning the problems which had to be settled, but he possessed a very quick brain, and he had at his disposal excellent advice which he was not too proud to take. Clemenceau derived much of his strength from the singleness of his aim: he was not at the conference to create a better world, but to bring security once more to France by undoing the work of the Treaty of Frankfurt. Lastly, there was Wilson, whose knowledge of books was great, and of men small: academic in his outlook, yet at that moment hailed by half Europe as a new Messiah; the representative of the newest and one of the greatest World Powers, yet hampered in his actions by the constitution of his own country. The leading delegates in Paris had thus decidedly less in common than their predecessors at Utrecht and Vienna.

In contrast with previous conferences of a similar nature the representatives of the beaten foe were not allowed to take part in the discussions, though these were sufficiently acrimonious without them. The frontiers of France, the coalfields of the Saar, the trial of the Kaiser, Reparations, the relations of Italy and Jugoslavia, and the demands of Poland all gave rise to the most bitter controversy before the conditions of peace were handed to the German delegates on May 7th. In retrospect, it would appear to have been a mistake to exclude them in the first instance, for they came on behalf of a regime which had been set up largely to please the victors: unfortunately it was not to be the last occasion on which British and French statesmen failed to realize that if they would do nothing to satisfy moderate opinion in Germany they would sooner or later throw that country into the arms of the extremists.

On June 28th, 1919, the Treaty was signed by all the Allies, except China, and by Germany in the Galerie des Glaces at Versailles, where the German Empire had been proclaimed nearly fifty years before. Its terms may be briefly summarized. On the west Germany ceded Alsace-Lorraine to France, and Prussian Moresnet, Eupen, and Malmédy to Belgium, though in this latter instance a plebiscite was to be held after the transfer. The Saar valley was surrendered for fifteen years, Luxembourg withdrew from the Zollverein, and the left bank of the Rhine was to be demilitarized. On the Danish frontier north and central Schleswig were to determine their allegiance by a plebiscite. In the east the territorial sacrifices were on a considerably larger scale, for the larger part of the provinces of Posen and West Prussia was ceded to the reconstituted state of Poland. Another plebiscite was to be held in Upper Silesia. Danzig was to become a free city under the League of Nations, within the Polish Customs Union, while East Prussia was separated from the rest of the Reich, and more plebiscites were to be held in the south and east of the province.

Outside Europe the entire German colonial empire was surrendered, and was divided among the victors as mandatories. South-West Africa became part of the Union of South Africa, while East Africa went to Great Britain, who presented a small portion of it to Belgium. France secured almost the whole of the Cameroons and Togoland. The Pacific possessions of Germany were divided between the British Empire and Japan, the former taking those to the south of the equator, and the latter those to the north. These British acquisitions were assigned to Australia, except for Samoa which went to New Zealand, and the island of Nauru, which Great Britain retained herself.

Furthermore, the German Army was to be reduced to 100,000 men enlisted for twelve years, the General Staff was to be abolished, and large guns were forbidden. Only a small navy, without submarines, was permitted, and no air force was allowed. The total sum for reparation was to be fixed by an Inter-Allied Commission. Germany was to surrender all her merchantmen over 1600 tons, half those between 1600 and 800 tons, and a quarter of her fishing vessels. Large quantities of coal were to be delivered to France for ten years. Germany was to bear the cost of the armies of occupation, to make no tariff discrimination against Allied trade for five years, and to consent to the sale of all German property in the

Allied countries. The Kiel Canal was to be open on equal terms to warships and merchantmen of all nations, and German rivers were to be internationalized. The Kaiser was to be tried by judges of the five Great Powers, and the "war criminals" were to be brought before special military tribunals. Finally, the sanction for the treaty lay in the occupation of the left bank and bridgeheads of the Rhine for fifteen years, evacuation to be by stages as the indemnity was gradually paid off; if, however, there was any failure to pay indemnity or reparations, either during or after the fifteen years, the area might be re-occupied.

Few international settlements have been so productive of controversy as the Treaty of Versailles, but now that nearly three decades have elapsed since it was concluded it is possible to take a more objective view than that of the generation which made it. More than one subsequent difficulty was due to the course adopted by the Allies at the time of the Armistice. It is a well-established legal maxim that justice must not only be done but that it must also appear to be done, and had the Allies applied this dictum to their victory in 1918 many of their later embarrassments would have been avoided. They had won the war in the field, but no real effort was ever made to bring this fact home to the German people, and so the way was left open for the propagation of the Nazi myth that the overthrow of Germany was due to the collapse of the home front. There were victory marches in London and Paris, but it surely would have been much better had there been a victory march in Berlin. That was the policy of the Allies after the defeat of Napoleon, and of the Germans themselves in 1871 : there was probably no necessity for an occupation of the enemy capital, which would have been undesirable from several points of view, but a march through it by the victors would have created an impression which no amount of Hitlerian propaganda would have been able to efface.

As for the Treaty of Versailles itself, one of its greatest weaknesses was that the Allies, in opposition to their own interests, carried the work of Bismarck to its logical conclusion and completed the unification of Germany. The strongest centrifugal force lay in the dynasties which ruled the various kingdoms and duchies, and which were always restive under the tutelage of Berlin; yet the German people were deliberately encouraged to overthrow their ruling houses, to many of which they were deeply attached, as the price of peace, and so the last obstacle to a unified

Reich was removed by those most concerned in its retention. This was to follow the precedent of Napoleon I rather than that of Louis XIV. Once the dynasties had gone there was no reason for the continued existence of their former dominions as separate units, and so the way was cleared for that complete Prussianization of Germany which was to be the outstanding accomplishment of the Nazi regime. Few voices, it is true, were raised at the time against this mistaken policy, though Jacques Bainville crystallized the situation when he said that the war was lost in the first clause of the Peace Treaty, in that the settlement should not have been made with Germany as a whole, but rather that there should have been separate treaties, with Prussia, Bavaria, Saxony, and the other states which had composed the Hohenzollern Empire.

Another serious mistake was to associate the League of Nations with the peace settlement. The former claimed to be based on the principles of abstract justice, while the latter rested on the armed forces of the Allies; it was clear that the vanquished were unlikely to regard the peace settlement with any marked favour, and to connect the League with it was to attach to Geneva the odium which already pertained to Versailles. Moreover, under cover of the League some very doubtful transactions took place. The decision in respect of the Polish plebiscite, for example (*vide* Appendix III), was hardly calculated to render Germany enthusiastic about the League; nor was there any reason why that body should have continued to be tied to the Peace Treaties, for all difficulties concerning them could have been settled between the signatories direct, and disputes referred to the Permanent Court of International Justice at The Hague.

Lastly, in marked contrast to the treatment accorded to France at Utrecht and Vienna, at the conclusion of the Four Years' War no insult was spared to defeated Germany, while not only was she given every assistance to complete her unification, but she was left on her frontiers with weak states which could not be expected to offer any effective opposition to her ambitions once her inevitable revival began.

On the other hand, there is little substance in the complaint that the Treaty of Versailles was an "imposed peace", for it was neither more nor less imposed than most treaties which had terminated a war fought to a finish. In this respect, it bears a marked resemblance to the Treaty of Prague which terminated the Seven Weeks' War in 1866, and to that of Frankfurt five years later: in both cases Bismarck had made up his mind in advance as to the terms he meant to exact, and he took full advantage of the military position of his country to secure what he wanted. Even more recently Germany had imposed the Treaties of Brest-Litovsk and Bucharest in exactly the same way, and, as we have seen, the terms of those settlements were considerably more severe than the provisions of the Treaty of Versailles.

The later months of 1919 were marked by the settlements with Germany's allies, all of whom had surrendered unconditionally. In spite of a desperate attempt by Charles to reorganize his dominions on a federal basis the Dual Monarchy had fallen to pieces, and in September, 1919, the Peace of St. Germain was concluded between the Allies and the new Austrian republic. By this time Vienna not only recognized the independence of Czecho-Slovakia, Jugoslavia, Poland, and Hungary, but also ceded Eastern Galicia to the Allies as well as the Trentino, South Tyrol (or Alto Adige), Trieste, and Istria to Italy. At the end of November it was the turn of Bulgaria, and by the Treaty of Neuilly that country was compelled to surrender Strumnitza to Jugoslavia, was once more cut off from the Aegean, had her army limited to 20,000, and was burdened with an indemnity of ninety millions. Hungary was by the Treaty of the Trianon in June, 1920, treated even more severely, for she was reduced to little more than a third of her former territory and population. The liquidation of the Ottoman Empire was postponed until it was known whether the United States would accept the mandate for Armenia, and the Treaty of Sèvres, signed in August, 1920, was destined to remain unratified.

The ink was hardly dry upon these various settlements than there arose a fresh set of problems which were destined to trouble the world's statesmen for several years to come. They were primarily concerned with the policy of France, Germany, and the United States respectively.

France had originally demanded the annexation of the Saar and the separation of the Rhineland from the Reich, and she only abandoned this claim in return for a definite promise by Great Britain and the United States of military support in the event of renewed aggression by Germany, and a Treaty of Triple Guarantee to this effect was signed on the same day as the Treaty of Versailles. When, however, the American Senate repudiated

Wilson, the British government took the line that, as the guarantee was not individual but collective, it was no longer binding on Great Britain. From this decision many consequences flowed. France became alarmed for her security, and sought to ensure it by reverting to her ancient system of Eastern alliances as well as by the adoption of an intransigent attitude towards Germany; this policy in its turn alienated British public opinion, while the repudiation of the Treaty of Triple Guarantee by Great Britain deprived her of much of her influence in Paris. Nor were the French by any means always farsighted in the attitude they adopted. They did all they could to foster separatist feelings in the Rhineland, but often by methods only too well calculated to defeat their purpose, while they sternly discouraged all attempts to restore the Bavarian monarchy on the ground that this would be merely the prelude to the return of the old order throughout the Reich, whereas in all probability it would have been the first step in the disintegration of Germany. This search for security on the part of France was one of the chief features of European politics until the conclusion of the Locarno Pact.

Second only to this problem was that caused by the ineptitude or dishonesty of the various governments which came into power in Germany. The German is not, contrary to the general belief, naturally efficient in political matters, and he only becomes competent when driven; for some years after the Armistice those who had done the driving in the past, and were to do it again in the future, were in eclipse, and the result was that the various commissions of control set up by the Peace Treaty found it very difficult to do their work, or to decide to what extent the obstacles in their path were due to incompetence and to what to deliberate obstruction. All this bred suspicion not only between victors and vanquished, but between the Allies themselves, and still further poisoned the international atmosphere. The French, for example, were inclined to lay the blame for German obstinacy on British leniency, to which it was replied that a more conciliatory attitude on the part of Paris would go a long way towards making the Germans more reasonable.

Thirdly, the Peace Treaties had been signed and the League of Nations established on the assumption that the United States would continue to interest itself in European affairs, and when this proved not to be the case a fresh series of complications ensued. In the absence of Germany, Russia, and the United States the League of Nations was little more than an organization of the victorious European Powers; yet it was worked as if it was all-embracing, and this led to blunders which in the end were to prove its undoing.

Although the world's statesmen had not followed the precedents of 1814 in the conclusion of peace they did for a time adopt the procedure of their predecessors by holding a series of conferences between the interested parties. The first of these was held at San Remo in April, 1920, and it met in exceptionally difficult circumstances. As a result of the violation of the demilitarized zone by Germany, in the course of operations against the Communists in the Ruhr, the French had occupied Frankfurt and four other German towns, much against the advice of the British government, which had, however, then been forced most reluctantly to give its consent to the occupation of three more towns, this time at the entrance to the Ruhr valley. There was soon proved to be a fundamental cleavage between the views of Paris and London. The French refused to consider the idea of German participation, while the British and Italians opposed the French argument that one ally might act independently against Germany to enforce the Treaty of Versailles. The upshot was that a sharp Note was sent to Berlin demanding fulfilment of the disarmament clauses of the Treaty of Versailles, and refusing a German request for an increase in the standing army of 100,000 men fixed at the Peace.

To San Remo in April, 1920, succeeded Spa in July. This conference differed from its predecessors in that the representatives of Germany were admitted for the first time, chiefly owing to the insistence of Mr. Lloyd George. The atmosphere was not exactly cordial. There was much wrangling over coal, over reparations, over disarmament, and over war criminals. Finally, the Allied demands in respect of disarmament were conceded, and there was an agreement about coal. The much more difficult problem of reparations was left over to another conference, this time in London, early in the following year, which not only proved abortive, but resulted in an Allied ultimatum to Germany; this in its turn led to the fall of one German government, and the rise of another which duly gave way to the Allies. In the meantime there had been a triangular duel between Great Britain, France, and Germany over events in Silesia, and British troops had been sent there to restore order in the conflict between German and Polish bands.

In January, 1922, there was a conference at Cannes, which was held for the purpose of framing resolutions for another one at Genoa in two months' time, but it is chiefly remembered for having precipitated the fall of Briand. By this time Mr. Lloyd George had become anathema to the greater part of the French people, who considered him the personification of the Gallophobe and pro-German section of British opinion. Accordingly, there was considerable opposition in Paris to the idea of Briand going to Cannes at all. When, therefore, photographs appeared in the Press of the French Prime Minister apparently accepting with due humility instruction from Mr. Lloyd George in the art of swinging a golf club, this was taken as evidence that he was the Welshman's pupil in more important matters, and in consequence he was compelled to resign.

The relations between Great Britain and France, upon the co-operation of which two Powers the Peace settlement depended, had been steadily deteriorating, and they now reached deadlock. Briand was succeeded by Poincaré, who was not only a very difficult man with whom to deal, but who was also on the worst possible terms with the British Foreign Secretary, Lord Curzon. On one occasion Poincaré shrieked and roared at Curzon, raging up and down the room the while, until the Englishman could stand it no longer, and walked out. In these circumstances it is hardly surprising that Franco-British differences became enhanced, and the two nations drifted apart in a manner that boded extremely ill to the peace of Europe.

Mr. Lloyd George realized that an effort must be made to secure that general settlement which it was hoped had been reached three years before, and it was in this spirit that he went in May, 1922, to the conference at Genoa to which had been invited the representatives of all nations. It was doomed from the start, for Poincaré not only declined to attend himself, but insisted on a rigid restriction of the scope of the conference and the exclusion from its agenda of reparations or any other matter arising out of the Peace Treaties. Then the United States refused to be represented, and this deprived the gathering of much of its importance. Above all, when the stage was finally set it was suddenly announced that Germany and Russia had made an alliance, known as the Treaty of Rapallo, and as friendship and co-operation between the nations was supposed to be the object of the conference the other Powers could not but give their blessing, though this agreement was not in the least what most of them desired. The French said that the alliance was the natural result of weakness on the part of the Western Powers, to which it was replied in London that the harsh policy of France had thrown Moscow and Berlin into one another's arms. The conference of Genoa failed, and its failure was decisive; for although there were to be more conferences, the attempted reorganization of Europe by this means was henceforth abandoned as a definite policy.

Meanwhile, the Near East was in ferment, and Great Britain and France had no common policy there. The Treaty of Sèvres had been signed in August, 1920, and by it the Turks retained Constantinople and a small strip of territory in its immediate neighbourhood, but the Straits, henceforth open to all, were placed under an International Commission, while Smyrna (promised to Italy by the Pact of St. Jean de Maurienne) and a considerable *hinterland* were handed over to Greece. Unhappily the settlement was made with a Turkey which no longer existed save in name, for Mohammed VI at Constantinople under the guns of the British fleet represented nobody except himself, and all real power was in the hands of Mustapha Kemal Pasha, later to be known as Kemal Ataturk, away in the heart of Anatolia. The Greeks proved unable to hold the territory that had been assigned to them, and by September, 1922, the Turks had driven them back to the coast. France and Italy hastened to make friends with the Nationalist leader, and Poincaré, in particular, was by no means sorry to give Mr. Lloyd George his tit for tat for the British failure to implement the Treaty of Triple Guarantee.

Accordingly, when the Greek armies broke, and the victorious Turks were at the gates of Constantinople, the French troops were ordered not to co-operate with the British. For a brief space it looked as if there might be war between Great Britain and Turkey, and an open breach between London and Paris. These were, however, averted by the tact of the general on the spot, Sir Charles Harrington, but the crisis brought about the fall of Mr. Lloyd George's administration. The general settlement of the Near East proved no easy matter, and, with one break, the representatives of eight states discussed the problem at Lausanne from November, 1922, to July, 1923. In the end the Turks secured practically all they wanted, as well as the repudiation of the Treaty of Sèvres. The Arab provinces of the old Ottoman Empire were, it is true, not restored, but otherwise Turkey recovered everything which she had possessed before the Four Years' War. Moreover, unlike Germany and the other Central Powers, Turkey was not compelled to submit to any restrictions on her armed forces or to foreign control over her finances. Her success in this respect was in no small measure due to the violent disagreement between Great Britain and France, of which the conference at Lausanne afforded fresh evidence.

The year 1923 witnessed, indeed, a further deterioration in the general situation, and throughout the twelve months Great Britain and France were held apart by what the wits termed a *rupture cordiale*. The final breach came over reparations. These had been scaled down at Cannes, and for six months after that Germany met her revised obligations, but in July, 1922, she announced that she could do so no longer. The reasons put forward were her economic difficulties, the financial chaos, and the collapse of her currency. To this the French replied that Germany had made no serious attempt to put her house in order since the Armistice, and that successive administrations had been guilty of the most reckless extravagance. By the Treaty of Versailles provision was made for this contingency, for the Allies were empowered to take any action deemed necessary against Germany without that country being entitled to regard this as an act of war. Poincaré was determined to avail himself of this right, and nothing that the new British Prime Minister, Bonar Law, said could divert him from his purpose.

In very difficult circumstances the British government did everything in its power to bridge the gulf between London and Paris. Bonar Law proposed that the reparation debt should be reduced to £2,500,000,000; that bonds of that amount should be issued immediately, and that, subject to the establishment in Berlin of a foreign Financial Council to supervise the reorganization of German finance, a four-year moratorium should be granted. The British Prime Minister accompanied this proposal with an offer, in the event of his suggestions being accepted, to cancel the French and Italian war debt to Great Britain, less certain sums representing gold deposits already in British hands and various minor financial adjustments; and he added that should Germany fail to satisfy the Council that she was making adequate efforts to attain financial stability, Great Britain would be prepared to join in the forcible seizure of German revenues and assets, as well as in an extended occupation of territory. These proposals had much to recommend them, but they were made too

z

late, and the situation had got out of hand. There was nothing for it but for the Allies to agree to differ, and on January 11th, 1923, the French marched into the Ruhr.

This act had the most unexpected and far-reaching consequences. In the recklessness of her despair Germany deliberately debased her currency until it became worthless. The result of this was that by one stroke she got rid of her internal debt, but at the cost of ruining the middle-class which had been her backbone for so many years: the younger members of this class were thus denied the advantages which their fathers had enjoyed, and so it came about that the very section of the community which in normal circumstances is the bulwark of stability was ripe for revolution. Furthermore, the suffering caused by the occupation of the Ruhr did much to discredit the regime under which it had taken place, and this, too, helped to pave the way for a dictatorship. Whether or not France was the gainer in terms of cash by what she did is a subject upon which it is not easy to express an opinion, but she outraged public sentiment throughout the world by her use of coloured troops, and left memories in Germany which were not soon to be effaced. The British government made no secret of its disapproval of the Ruhr adventure, but it could not wholly divest itself of responsibility, for the invasion was in no small degree an expression of that desire for security which France had hoped to obtain by the Treaty of Triple Guarantee.

CHAPTER XXIX

THE SEARCH FOR SECURITY, 1923–1933

WHEN the French troops marched into the Ruhr in the opening days of 1923 relations between London and Paris were worse than at any time since the conclusion of the Entente nearly twenty years before, and yet the Versailles settlement depended upon the co-operation of Great Britain and France, the only two stable Powers in Europe. After the conclusion of wars in the past there had always been a number of strong states interested in the maintenance of the existing order, but the Four Years' War had wrought havoc in this respect. Austria-Hungary was only a memory, Russia was the champion of world revolution, Italy was in the throes of exchanging Liberalism for Fascism, Spain was no longer a Great Power, the United States had washed its hands of the Old World, and Germany, beaten and resentful, was already beginning to think of revenge. Everything thus turned upon Great Britain and France; they alone stood between Europe and chaos, and they were on the worst possible terms with one another.

Such was the state of Anglo-French relations when Ramsay MacDonald became Prime Minister of Great Britain in January, 1924. He fully realized that an improvement in the situation was an essential preliminary to any amelioration of the international position as a whole, and also that this was bound up with the question of French security. Fortune undoubtedly favoured him, for soon after he took office there was a General Election in France, and Poincaré was replaced by Herriot as Prime Minister. The Scot and the Frenchman had much in common both in tastes and outlook, and they worked hard through the summer of 1924 to bring their respective peoples together again. The method favoured at first was a Treaty of Mutual Assistance. At the Third Assembly of the League two years before resolutions had been adopted laying down the principle that disarmament and guarantees for security must go together. In 1923 the Temporary Mixed Commission prepared a draft treaty, known as the Draft Treaty of Mutual Assistance, for the purpose of giving practical effect to this principle. However, during the course of the following year the British government came to the conclusion that this arrangement was not acceptable, chiefly owing to the peculiar position of the

British Empire, for, as one authority put it, "the apportionment of liability on Continental lines cut fatally across the structure of the British Commonwealth with its world-wide responsibilities". In its place was evolved the Geneva Protocol.

This document proclaimed "the solidarity of the members of the international community", and referred to a war of aggression as "a violation of this solidarity and an international crime": it went on to propose the amendment of the Covenant of the League with a view to rendering more effective Article VIII, which prescribes "the reduction of national armaments to the lowest point consistent with national safety and the enforcement by common action of international obligations". The means by which this aim was to be attained may be summarized as follows:

1. Not to resort to war against other nations observing the Protocol, whether members of the League or not.

2. To recognize as compulsory the jurisdiction of the Court of International Justice in certain specified matters.

3. To refer political quarrels to the League or to arbitral bodies.

4. Not to mobilize armed forces during the course of arbitration of a dispute.

5. To consider as an aggressor any Power resorting to war in defiance of the agreement.

6. To consent that aggressor states should pay the costs of war to the limit of their ability, but that war indemnities should not include cessions of territory.

7. To take part in an international conference on the reduction of armaments as a preliminary to rendering the Protocol operative.

Finally, it was agreed that a state engaging in hostilities should be presumed to be an aggressor unless a unanimous decision of the League Council should declare otherwise. On October 2nd, 1924, without a dissentient vote the Protocol was recommended by the Assembly of the League to the various governments, while far away in a Bavarian prison Adolf Hitler was putting the finishing touches to *Mein Kampf*.

From the beginning the Protocol was more popular in Continental than in British circles. MacDonald defended it on the ground that it confirmed and restated, rather than extended, the national commitments under the Covenant of the League, but his argument carried little conviction outside the ranks of his own party. The ordinary Englishman was inclined to criticize the Protocol as an instrument to place the British Navy under the control of Geneva. Dominion opinion was especially critical, and it was only pressure from Downing Street that prevented the Dominion representatives from voting against it. In November, 1924, Mac-Donald's government, in which he was Foreign Secretary as well as Prime Minister, was defeated at the polls, and in the new administration Austen Chamberlain was at the Foreign Office. He enjoyed there a very free hand, for Baldwin interfered extremely little with his ministers' running of their departments. On the other hand he was subject to two handicaps which his predecessors before the Four Years' War had never known, namely the unreasoning optimism of the large majority of his fellow-countrymen and the one-sided disarmament of Great Britain which had been its result.

When Chamberlain arrived at the Foreign Office he was at once confronted with a difficulty. The result of the General Election had proved that the majority of the British electorate disliked the Protocol, and therefore one of the first tasks of the new government must be to reject it, but it was not going to be easy to do this without throwing Europe back into chaos, and dealing a severe blow to the new-found friendship between Great Britain and France. It had also now become clear that the French would not be satisfied with the Protocol alone; and that even if the British Government accepted this without amendment it would be at once confronted on the part of France and Belgium by a demand to supplement it with a tripartite treaty.

In these circumstances, after Chamberlain had ascertained the views of Herriot and Mussolini, the British government decided to discard the Protocol, but they were fully aware that they must put something in its place, and the only substitute of which they could think was a defensive alliance of the type which had been envisaged six years before. Service opinion was still in favour of such a policy, but much water had flowed under the bridge since the Armistice, and it was doubtful how far the ordinary citizen would approve. The invasion of the Ruhr had made France extremely unpopular, quite apart from the traditional and often illogical British sympathy for the under-dog, but all the same there seemed no other course. London's dilemma did not long remain a secret, and when the news of its proposed solution reached Berlin there was consternation. A bilateral Anglo-French alliance would be a re-affirmation of the Treaty of Versailles, and would perpetuate the division of the European Powers into victors and vanquished. This panic induced the German Foreign Minister, Stresemann, to make an offer which revolutionized the whole situation.

Towards the end of January, 1925, therefore, the German government intimated that it was willing to enter into an agreement guaranteeing the existing frontiers in Western Europe, but in doing so it committed one of those blunders which have so often marked German diplomacy since the fall of Bismarck by asking Chamberlain to say nothing of the offer to the French. Not unnaturally, he saw in the approach only a clumsy attempt to drive in a wedge between Great Britain and France, and he considered that "these overtures were premature, and that the moment was not opportune for their successful prosecution". Nevertheless, Stresemann persisted, and he put forward more detailed proposals, this time to the French, whom he endeavoured—unsuccessfully—to pledge not to divulge them to the British government. Germany was ready to join in a pact between the Powers interested in the situation on the Rhine, especially France, Great Britain, Italy, and herself, with a solemn undertaking over a long period not to go to war with one another. The German government further considered that a pact between the states interested in the Rhine might include a formal guarantee, both individual and collective, of the existing territorial position, and that the signatory Powers might further guarantee the fulfilment of the obligation in regard to the demilitarization of the Rhineland; this pact would be completed by a treaty of arbitration to be concluded by Germany with France and the other Powers. So far as her eastern frontiers were concerned, Germany was not prepared to guarantee them in the same way as those in the west, but she was willing to conclude a treaty of arbitration with Poland and Czecho-Slovakia. Finally, the German government considered that the pact of security could be formulated in such a way as to prepare for the conclusion of a world convention, to include all nations, on the model of the Protocol.

Such was the inception of the Pact of Locarno, but there was much to be done before it assumed its final form. In the first place, it was by no means certain whether the French would consider that the new proposals went far enough, or whether they would require some further guarantee. Then there were the eastern frontiers to be taken into account, for the German scheme might well result in a state of affairs in which Germany would be within her rights in crushing Poland while France was unable to come to her ally's assistance. Lastly, there was the attitude of the British electorate to be considered. The Liberal and Labour Parties were still wedded to the Protocol, and would oppose anything in the nature of a regional pact, while the Conservatives were all for a curtailment, rather than for an extension, of the national commitments. If Chamberlain had to walk warily, Herriot and Stresemann were in the same predicament. The French public was not yet in favour of any pact with Germany, in view of her failure to comply with the disarmament conditions of the Treaty of Versailles, while German opinion was highly suspicious.

From this moment the lead in the negotiations was taken by Chamberlain, who had to exert pressure both upon Paris and Berlin to produce the desired result. In the case of the former the situation was rendered easier by the substitution of Briand for Herriot. Not that the latter was more intransigent than his successor, but rather that, being heavily committed to the Protocol, it was not easy for him to work whole-heartedly for the pact which was to take its place. Chamberlain and Briand, who had not previously been well acquainted, speedily became personal friends, and such being the case the negotiations between Great Britain and France proceeded smoothly: thanks to the insistence of the Foreign Office the towns of Dusseldorf, Duisburg, and Ruhrort were evacuated at the same time as the Ruhr, and this reassured German opinion as to the intentions of France.

For the difficulties mostly came from the German side although the proposal itself had originated in Berlin. At one moment Germany pleaded her defenceless condition as a reason why she should be given special treatment, when she became a member of the League, in respect of Article 16 of the Covenant, though what lay at the back of this was fear of losing the Russian support which had been so valuable. On another occasion the German government began to quibble about joining the League at all, and had to be told quite firmly that this was a *sine qua non* of any pact: then the Germans tried to introduce some stipulations in connection with the occupied territory. Beaten on these points, Berlin declared that the question of war guilt must first of all be settled, and this procedure caused Chamberlain to write that "the

German government, like a nagging woman, must have the last word".

As if this was not enough, the German President died, and the ensuing election resulted in the victory of Hindenburg. One of the "war criminals" and an avowed supporter of the Kaiser, his triumph was regarded as the first step in the return of the old order in Germany, and in Paris and Brussels the alarmed crowds already seemed to hear the tramp of marching feet borne down the east winds of late spring. Gradually, however, these fears were set at rest, for the felon blow which the old soldier was to inflict upon his own country and the world was not to be struck for another eight years.

By summer France and Great Britain had come to an agreement, and it only remained to bring the negotiations to a conclusion in such a way as to avoid offending German susceptibilities. Accordingly Berlin was invited to send a legal expert to London to go over the draft, which he was to take away with him after having asked any questions he might think fit. This representative duly came to London, made some suggestions, obtained all the information he wanted, and ascertained the real intentions of Chamberlain and Briand without being asked to commit himself to anything. In this way were avoided the misunderstandings which otherwise might so easily have arisen from the presentation of a text between principals without any previous opportunity for exposition or explanation. The ground was thus thoroughly prepared when the statesmen of the Powers concerned met for their final discussions at Locarno in October, 1925.

The Pact, which was signed in London in December, consisted of eight treaties, of which that which concerned western Europe was a treaty of mutual guarantee between Germany, Belgium, France, Great Britain, and Italy. By it the first three Powers promised never to go to war against one another, and to settle all disputes between themselves by peaceful means. The five signatories, collectively and severally, guaranteed the maintenance of the territorial *status quo* in the west as fixed at Versailles, and the observance of the conditions laid down for the demilitarized zone. In all cases save one the decision whether a *casus fœderis* had arisen was left to the Council of the League. The exception was in the event of actual invasion or of a flagrant violation of the stipulations regarding the demilitarized zone, if the guaranteeing Power was satisfied that "the violation is an act of unprovoked aggression, and that by reason either of the crossing of the frontier or of the outbreak of hostilities, or of the assembly of armed forces in the zone, immediate action is necessary". In this case each party was to come to the aid of the victim. This was the only one of the Locarno treaties, it is to be noted, in which Great Britain was immediately concerned.

It will be remembered that Germany's most considerable losses at the Treaty of Versailles had been in the east, and it proved impossible to obtain her guarantee of the *status quo* there in the same way as in western Europe. On the other hand she was willing to enter into arbitration treaties with her eastern neighbours, though without in the last resort renouncing a subsequent revision of the territorial arrangements, and these were incorporated in the general settlement. French engagements with Poland and Czecho-Slovakia were also included. They provided that in the event of either of these states or of France suffering from a failure to observe the undertaking between them and Germany with a view to the maintenance of general peace these Powers undertook to lend each other immediately aid and assistance if such a failure be accompanied by an unprovoked recourse to arms. In this connection, and in view of what lay ahead, the statement of Dr. Benes to the Permanent Commission of the Czecho-Slovak Parliament is not without significance, "We must emphasize that the assistance in question would take effect automatically. This means that the contracting states have the full and only right to judge themselves whether they are confronted with a *casus fœderis* and that they are not pledged to wait for the result of any negotiations. Our former treaty with France thus acquires an entirely new character without losing anything of its effectiveness." It is also worthy of note that the Locarno Treaties were not subscribed to by the British Dominions.

Two main criticisms have been made of these agreements—that they were inconclusive so far as eastern Europe was concerned, and that some, at any rate, of the signatories did not possess sufficient armaments to implement their undertakings. That there was a good deal in the first of these observations subsequent events were to prove, but it must be remembered that France had special obligations towards Poland and Czecho-Slovakia. So far as Great Britain was concerned her Locarno engagement represented the absolute maximum that either Parliament or the country at that moment would concede. It may not have been far enough, but it was further than would have been tolerated a few years earlier: it may have been unfortunate, yet it is none the less true, that public opinion was not ready for the guarantees which Chamberlain's own brother gave in 1939, and had such a policy been attempted the government would have been defeated in the House of Commons. Moreover, so long as the demilitarized zone provided an open door into western Germany it was in the highest degree unlikely that Berlin would embark upon any adventure in eastern Europe. To maintain that the Locarno Treaties did not go far enough is to view the Europe of 1925 in the light of that of fourteen years later.

In the second contention there is more substance. In an earlier day statesmen were careful to stipulate the amount of armed force required to carry out an obligation, and it is not easy to understand why the Baldwin administration did not ask Parliament for such armaments as their Service advisers presumably told them were necessary if they were to implement their promises. This was not done, and the consequences were to prove extremely serious.

The Locarno Pact was meant to be not only an end but also a beginning. The first step was to elect Germany to a permanent seat on the Council of the League, and this was to have been done in March, 1926, but unexpected difficulties arose. Hitherto it had been only the Great Powers—that is to say, Great Britain, France, Italy, and Japan—which had enjoyed permanent seats on the Council, and the intention was that Germany should join this select company. However, the fact that an alteration was to be made raised the hopes of other aspirants to permanent seats, and Poland, Brazil, and Spain each put in a claim, while more or less openly threatening to veto the election of Germany, and then resign themselves, if they did not receive satisfaction. This was sufficiently embarrassing, but what was worse was that the Great Powers had their own favourites among these candidates. Brazil, it is true, had no supporters, but the Polish claim was favoured by France and also by Mussolini, who at that time took no particular interest in Spain. On the other hand, Great Britain favoured the Spanish candidature in principle, but was not actually committed to press it on this particular occasion.

The Germans claimed, with a considerable show of reason, that they had been promised election to the Council as constituted, and that if it were enlarged the value of membership would be proportionately diminished. To complicate matters still further some of the smaller Powers, notably Sweden, began to fish in the troubled waters in the hope of thereby increasing their own importance. To what extent Stockholm received direct encouragement from Berlin it is impossible to say, but the Swedes set to work to form a pro-German *bloc* at Geneva consisting of themselves, the Danes, and the Dutch: the most pressing requests were made to Spain to join this combination, and when she refused, Sweden and her associates announced that they would oppose the creation of any new permanent seat save for Germany. In these circumstances the task of Great Britain was far from easy, but the government was determined to honour its obligations to Berlin, and Chamberlain went to Geneva with instructions not to admit any change in the Council "which would have the effect of preventing or delaying the entry of Germany": Baldwin and his colleagues considered "it would be best that Germany should, as a member of the Council, have full responsibility for any further change in the Council beyond her own admission".

The upshot was that the election of Germany had to be postponed until the following September. In the last resort Spain and Poland had proved reasonable, but Brazil had shown herself impervious to argument, and a unanimous vote was essential. It may be added that the fact that this compromise was reached, and that there had not been a conflict between the signatories of the Locarno Pact, was almost wholly due to the efforts of British diplomacy.

That same autumn witnessed a meeting between Briand and Stresemann at Thoiry, and for a brief moment it looked as if there might at last be an end to those differences which had kept Paris and Berlin apart ever since Bismarck's accession to power. It was not to be, for both men were carried away by their surroundings, and when they returned to their respective capitals difficulties presented themselves which had seemed of small importance by the waters of a Swiss lake. Nevertheless, it is worthy of note that the number of Nazi deputies in the Reichstag dropped from 32 to 14 at a General Election.

Throughout 1927 the pacific influences of the Locarno Pact were felt throughout Europe, and save in the Far East there was a general relaxation in the international tension. Such being the case it is hardly surprising that the next year should have been marked by an attempt to do away with war altogether. The idea of outlawing war appears to have originated with a Chicago lawyer called Levinson, and in the spring of 1927 it reached Briand through another American, Shotwell. Whether or not the French statesman grasped all the implications of such a proposal it is impossible to say, and at first he probably regarded it merely as a welcome means to improve French relations with the United States, for these were at the time somewhat strained by the recent refusal of France to participate in a new naval conference; in any event he took it up as a Franco-American, not as a universal, policy. Accordingly, in June, 1927, a French scheme, with elaborate conditions for a pact, was sent to Washington, but several months elapsed before a reply was received from the State Department; when it did come the original French proposal was found to have been changed out of all recognition. Briand had thought that outlawry would in practice mean nothing more than the neutrality of France and the United States in one another's quarrels. Kellogg, Coolidge's Secretary of State, went far beyond this, and was determined to abolish war altogether as an instrument of policy; furthermore, he expressed a desire to have such an agreement signed by every nation in the world. There was a Presidential election due in a few months' time.

This scheme bid fair to wreck both the League Covenant and the Locarno Pact, and the British government was determined to save them. The line, therefore, that Chamberlain took was to adopt the idea of a multilateral treaty, but to persuade Kellogg so to word this that Great Britain and France could sign without abrogation of their previous engagements. Accordingly, he informed Washington that it was of the utmost importance to the British government "that the principle should be recognized that if one of the parties to this proposed treaty resorted to war in violation of its terms, the other parties should be released automatically from their obligations towards that party under the treaty". Chamberlain also made it plain that respect for the obligations arising out of the Covenant of the League of Nations and of the Locarno Treaties was the foundation of British policy, and that the government could not agree to any new treaty which would weaken those engagements. These points were duly met, and at the beginning of July, 1928, the British Foreign Secretary was able to notify the American *chargé d'affaires* that his government was ready to sign the pact, but in doing so he called attention to a speech by Kellogg declaring that the proposed treaty did not restrict or impair in any way the right of self-defence, and in this connection he stressed the importance of "certain regions with regard to whose welfare and integrity His Majesty's Government have special responsibilities"; he added that "interference with these regions or with the discharge of these responsibilities cannot be allowed. Their protection from attack is for the British Empire a measure of self-defence." The Kellogg Pact was finally signed on August 27th, 1928, in Paris.

Unfortunately the result was not to outlaw war, but to cause a formal declaration of war to fall into disuse, with the most disastrous effects upon the whole system of international law which had over a long period of years been so carefully built up to safeguard the rights of belligerents and neutrals. At once mankind went back to the practice of the sixteenth century, when Elizabeth and Philip II brought to a fine art the waging of war against one another without any formal rupture of relations, and in consequence it became almost impossible to say what was and what was not justifiable when hostilities were in progress.

The years 1925-1928 represented the highwater-mark of peace. The economic blizzard soon began to blow across the world, and in the distress which it caused old suspicions and enmities were revived and new ones were created. The situation was further embittered by a deterioration of Anglo-French relations after Chamberlain had left the Foreign Office in 1929 in consequence of the defeat of the Baldwin administration at the polls. Much criticism was levelled at Chamberlain on the score of his alleged excessive partiality to France, and his successor, Arthur Henderson, had hardly taken office before he announced that he was not going to play second fiddle to Paris. The summer witnessed a somewhat heated exchange of uncomplimentary epithets between Snowden, the new Chancellor of the Exchequer, and the French statesmen at a conference at The Hague on the subject of reparations, when Snowden publicly declared the figures of the Finance Minister of France to be "grotesque and ridiculous". The British public, which had been taught to believe in Chamberlain's subservience to France, heartily welcomed what it considered to be a reaffirmation of British independence, but the only result was to place a strain upon Anglo-French relations at a time when this was more than usually undesirable.

Nevertheless the real disintegrating force among the nations was the question of disarmament, and it was largely as a result of their failure to agree in this matter that Hitler came into power and a fresh era began in the history of the world.

So long ago as the Peace Conference it had been felt that the armaments' race which had preceded the Four Years' War had not a little to do with the outbreak of that conflict, and it was felt that steps should be taken to prevent the repetition of so unfortunate a sequence of events. In 1921 there was a naval conference at Washington when Great Britain, the United States, and Japan agreed—most unwillingly on the part of the last-named—to limit their navies on a 5–5–3 ratio, and in the same year Great Britain decided not to renew the Anglo-Japanese Agreement. After the signature of the Locarno Pact a Preparatory Commission was set up to prepare the way for a Disarmament Conference, but it made little progress because while some of its members did not know what they wanted, others too obviously did, and it was to deprive potential enemies of offensive armaments while retaining their own. The work of this body was not rendered any easier by the failure, owing to lack of adequate preparation, of a Three Power Naval Conference at Geneva in June, 1927. A year later Chamberlain announced in the House of Commons that Great Britain and France had arrived at a compromise on naval disarmament and trained reserves, and that this was based on a scheme prepared by Paul Boncour at a meeting of the Preparatory Commission.

This announcement was badly received, for the proposal upon which the agreement was founded had already been rejected by the United States and Italy, and neither Power was any too pleased that it should have reappeared in the form of a bilateral treaty between Great Britain and France. Then occurred one of those "leakages" in Paris for which it is not always easy to account. An "important French official" gave an interview to an English journalist in which he declared the agreement to be the most outstanding diplomatic event since the Armistice. He said that while it appeared to be merely a technical agreement, it was in fact of the first diplomatic importance, being nothing less than a return to the relations which had existed between Great Britain and France before 1914. He even declared that the agreement could "be considered as a sort of unified command of the naval and military forces of the two countries". Such an interpretation at once gave rise to the rumour that there were secret clauses by which the Mediterranean was to be divided into British and French spheres of influence, and this roused in the mind of Mussolini suspicions which it had for years been the object of British diplomacy to lull to rest. It is true that the storm died away almost as suddenly as it had arisen, but some damage was nevertheless done.

A Naval Conference was held in London at the beginning of 1930 at which the representatives of Great Britain, France, Italy, Japan, and the United States were present. Its object was disarmament, but from the beginning it was clear that the main issue would be the Italian claim to parity with France. There was more than one lively passage of arms between Tardieu and Grandi, the French and Italian delegates respectively. In such an atmosphere it was idle to expect the conference to result in a general agreement, and although a naval treaty was signed by Great Britain, Japan, and the United States, it was found impossible to bring France and Italy within its scope.

By this time the whole international situation was deteriorating rapidly, for like some fell disease the slump was sweeping across the world. It had begun on the New York Stock Exchange towards the end of October, 1929, and ere long banks were closing by the hundred, while the number of unemployed was in the neighbourhood of eight millions. The next two years witnessed everywhere a crash almost without precedent, and by the end of that period the finances of central Europe were once more in chaos, while Great Britain was off the Gold Standard.

The repercussions of these events in the field of politics were serious, for the catastrophe came at a more than usually unfortunate moment. The men who had given Europe what it was hoped would prove to be new life, which now turned out to be a breathing-space, were no longer there to ride the storm. Stresemann was dead, Briand was dying, and Chamberlain was out of office. A reaction set in against everything for which they stood, and while Baldwin's followers were seeking a promise from their leader that in any future Conservative administration Chamberlain should not be Foreign Secretary, elsewhere Parliamentary Government itself was beginning to rock on its foundations. This was notably the case in Germany, where the new Reichstag elected in September, 1930, was found to contain 107 Nazis and 77 Communists. Three months earlier the last Allied soldiers had been withdrawn from the Reich, that is to say four and a half years earlier than was stipulated in the Treaty of Versailles, so this Nazi success was an interesting commentary upon the state of German public opinion.

In a desperate effort to recapture its waning popularity the

German government in March, 1931, concluded a customs union with Austria, but handled the negotiations in so maladroit a manner as to defeat its own purpose. The rest of Europe was suddenly confronted with the *fait accompli*, and those who might have given their blessing had they been consulted in advance were forced into opposition. French opinion in particular was definitely hostile, and saw in the agreement the dreaded *anschluss*, which was a violation of the Treaty of Versailles. The German government was forced to refer the arrangement to the Permanent Court of International Justice at The Hague, which declared it inadmissible. The bungling procedure adopted thus had the effect of further weakening the German government's prestige, and so played straight into the hands of the Nazis, who declared that their country was still clearly under foreign tutelage.

On February 2nd, 1932, the Disarmament Conference opened at Geneva. All the nations of the world were represented with the exception of Ecuador, Nicaragua, Paraguay, and El Salvador, so that the subsequent failure could not be attributed to the abstentions, and the president was Arthur Henderson, in his private capacity. From the first the omens were unpropitious, for on the very day the conference met the Japanese guns were firing on Shanghai, and the delegates had to adjourn for an hour while the Council of the League discussed the matter. There was certainly no dearth of suggestions for disarmament, for each of the Great Powers came forward with its own scheme, though none of these met with general assent.

It soon became obvious that, so far as Germany was concerned, time was a very important factor, for in April the Nazis made extremely substantial gains in the state elections, and the Imperial Chancellor, Brüning, was under no illusions but that his last chance of preventing the advent of the Third Reich lay in securing some settlement at Geneva which would remove the stigma of inferiority in the matter of armaments. Accordingly, on April 26th, 1932, conversations began between the British, American, and German statesmen. France was not, of course, excluded, but she was in the throes of a General Election, and so the Prime Minister, Tardieu, was absent from Geneva, but it was decided that if the basis of an agreement came in sight he should be recalled.

Brüning then proposed that, in return for an undertaking given by Germany not to increase her armaments for five years, or until a second Disarmament Conference, she should be permitted to reduce the twelve-year period of service in the Reichswehr, laid down at Versailles, to five years; to organize a militia which should not exceed the number of 100,000 men allowed for the Reichswehr; and to purchase the war material hitherto forbidden. He also asked that the prohibition of the possession by the Reich of weapons of offence, such as aeroplanes and tanks, should be abrogated, but he declared that Germany was prepared to renounce these on the condition that all the other Powers did the same; if neither of these suggestions met with approval, his country would be satisfied with "samples" of the weapons in question. The British and American representatives, MacDonald and Stimson, agreed that the German argument was both justified and reasonable, and Grandi took the same view when Brüning's scheme was communicated to him.

Such being the case, it is not too much to say that an agreement appeared to be in sight when a turn in the German political situation brought the scheme to nought. A few weeks before there had been a Presidential Election in Germany, and almost entirely owing to the efforts of Brüning the aged Hindenburg had been returned for a second term by a majority of nearly six million votes over Hitler. Gratitude and loyalty, however, were never among the most prominent characteristics of Hindenburg, and in spite of what he owed to Brüning he allowed himself to come increasingly under the influence of the *camarilla* of his son Oscar, Dr. Meissner, and General von Schleicher, who were working for the overthrow of the Chancellor. When Brüning put forward his disarmament proposals this little group determined to frustrate him. Von Schleicher met the French ambassador in Berlin at an evening party in a private house, and advised him not to negotiate with Brüning, on the ground that his fall was already virtually accomplished and that his successor, who was named, would be found more amenable. Tardieu accepted this advice, and he refused, on the score of an attack of laryngitis, the pressing request of his colleagues to return to Geneva to consider the German scheme.

It is a moot point whether a different attitude on the part of the British government would have brought France into line, or, again, whether acceptance of the German proposal would have prevented the accession of the Nazis to power. What happened was that no action was taken, and matters were allowed to drift,

A A

with the most disastrous consequences both for the future of the conference and for the peace of Europe. In Germany the results were soon to be seen. The President replaced Brüning by von Papen, and a General Election in July gave the Nazis 230 seats in the Reichstag. Thereafter events moved to their allotted end, and on January 30th, 1933, Hitler became Chancellor. A new epoch in international relations had begun.

THE MONROE DOCTRINE

PRESIDENT MONROE's message to Congress was delivered on December 3rd, 1823; the main contents were as follows:

The occasion has been judged proper for asserting, as a principle in which the rights and the interests of the United States are involved, that the American continents, by the free and independent condition which they have assumed and maintain, are henceforth not to be considered as subjects for future colonization by any European Powers. . . .

It was stated at the commencement of the last session that a great effort was then being made in Spain and Portugal to improve the condition of the people of those countries, and that it appeared to be conducted with extraordinary moderation. It need scarcely be remarked that the result has been, so far, very different from what we then anticipated. Of events in that quarter of the globe, with which we have so much intercourse, and from which we derive our origin, we have always been anxious and interested spectators. The citizens of the United States cherish sentiments the most friendly in favour of the liberty and happiness of their fellow men on that side of the Atlantic.

In the wars of the European Powers in matters relating to themselves we have never taken any part, nor does it comport with our policy to do so. It is only when our rights are invaded or seriously menaced that we resent injuries or make preparation for our defence. With the movements in this hemisphere we are of necessity more immediately connected, and by causes which must be obvious to all enlightened and impartial observers. The political system of the Allied Powers is essentially different in this respect from that of America. This difference proceeds from that which exists in their respective governments, and to the defence of our own, which has been achieved by the loss of so much blood and treasure, and matured by the wisdom of their most enlightened citizens, and under which we have enjoyed unexampled felicity, this whole nation is devoted.

We owe it, therefore, to candour and to the amicable relations existing between the United States and those Powers, to declare that we should consider any attempt on their part to extend their system to any portion of this hemisphere as dangerous to our peace and safety. With the existing colonies or dependencies of any European Power we have not interfered and shall not interfere. But with the governments who have declared their independence and maintained it, and whose independence we have on great consideration and on just principles acknowledged, we could not view any interposition for the purpose of oppressing them, or controlling in any other manner their destiny, by any European Power in any other light than as the manifestation of an unfriendly disposition towards the United States. In the war between those new governments and Spain, we declared our neutrality at the time of their recognition, and to this we have adhered, and shall continue to adhere, provided no change shall occur which, in the judgment of the competent authorities of this government, shall make a corresponding change on the part of the United States indispensable to their security.

Our policy in regard to Europe, which was adopted at an early stage of the wars which have so long agitated that quarter of the globe, nevertheless remains the same, which is, not to interfere with the internal concerns of any of its Powers; to consider the government *de facto* as the legitimate government for us; to cultivate friendly relations with it, and to preserve these relations by a frank, firm, and manly policy, meeting, in all instances, the just claims of every Power, submitting to injuries from none. But in regard to these continents circumstances are eminently and conspicuously different. It is impossible that the Allied Powers should extend their political system to any portion of either continent without endangering our peace and happiness; nor can anyone believe that our Southern brethren, if left to themselves, would adopt it of their own accord. It is equally impossible, therefore, that we should behold any interposition in any form with indifference. If we look to the comparative strength and resources of Spain and those new governments, and their distance from each other, it must be obvious that she can never subdue them. It is still the true policy of the United States to leave the parties to themselves, in the hope that other Powers will pursue the same course.

PRESIDENT WILSON'S FOURTEEN POINTS

1. Open covenants of peace openly arrived at.

2. Absolute freedom of navigation upon the seas alike in peace and war, except as they may be closed by international action for the enforcement of international covenants.

3. The removal, so far as possible, of all economic barriers.

4. Adequate guarantees that armaments will be reduced to the lowest point consistent with domestic safety.

5. An impartial adjustment of all colonial claims on the principle that the interests of the population must have equal weight with the equitable claims of the Government whose title is to be determined.

6. The evacuation of all Russian territory and the independent determination of her own political development and national policy.

7. Belgium must be evacuated and restored, without any attempt to limit her sovereignty.

8. All French territory should be freed, and the invaded portions restored, and the wrong done in 1871 in the matter of Alsace-Lorraine should be righted.

9. A readjustment of the frontiers of Italy should be effected along clearly recognizable lines of nationality.

10. The peoples of Austria-Hungary, whose place among the nations we wish to see safeguarded and assured, should be accorded the first opportunity of autonomous development.

11. Roumania, Serbia, and Montenegro should be evacuated, occupied territories restored, Serbia accorded free access to the sea, and the relations of the Balkan States determined along historically established lines of allegiance and nationality.

12. The Turkish frontiers of the Ottoman Empire should be assured a secure sovereignty; but the other nationalities under Turkish rule should be assured an undoubted security of life and an absolutely unmolested opportunity of autonomous development, and the Dardanelles should be permanently opened as a free passage to the ships and commerce of all nations under international guarantees.

13. An independent Polish State should be erected which

should include the territories inhabited by indisputably Polish populations, which should be assured a free and secure access to the sea, and whose political and economic independence and territorial integrity should be guaranteed by international covenant.

14. A general association of nations must be formed for affording mutual guarantees of political independence and territorial integrity to great and small states alike.

THE PLEBISCITE

THE word itself has a respectable ancestry. The Roman *plebiscitum* was a law enacted by the plebs in the *concilium plebis tributum* on the rogation of a tribune: originally these resolutions needed confirmation by the Senate, but after the constitutional struggle which succeeded the long Semnite Wars the *Lex Hortensia* was passed in 286 B.C., and they became binding upon all citizens without reference to any other body. The terminology of the Roman Republic appealed to those who governed France at the close of the eighteenth century, so the plebiscite was, along with consuls and eagles, rescued from oblivion and launched upon a career of which the end is certainly not yet.

There are, however, certain differences between the plebiscite of antiquity and that of more recent times. To the Roman a plebiscite meant one thing and one thing only, but since the revival of the institution it has been employed in two different ways: that is to say, as a verdict on a particular regime, or as an expression of choice by people in a specified area with regard to the state to which they wish to belong. Sometimes the two have been confused, as in the case of the Italian plebiscite in the days of unification, when the voters were in fact called upon to condemn both the form of government and the state which they had previously known. In the twentieth century there is also a marked difference, though this is not always appreciated as it should be, between the referendum and the plebiscite, which are often regarded as two words for the same thing. Actually, there is a sharp distinction between them: the referendum is a normal method of voting in use in a number of countries, applied on a general system to certain classes of legislation, whereas a plebiscite decides a specific question *ad hoc* and *pro hac vice*. Nor is this all, for a referendum is usually held on some step about to be taken, whereas a plebiscite is generally to ratify a *fait accompli*. It may, perhaps, also be observed that the referendum is essentially democratic in its nature, while the plebiscite has often been employed for anti-democratic purposes.

Indeed, the plebiscite commenced its career in eighteenth-century France as a protest against Parliamentarianism, and it was a useful instrument in the hands of those who were responsible for that return to authoritarianism which marked the policy of the Directory and the Consulate. Guido de Ruggiero, in his *History of European Liberalism*, says of plebiscites that they are "in fact nothing but a reminiscence of the old social contract converted into a national contract". For this reason they made a strong appeal to those who were attempting to put some water into the heady wine of Rousseau's doctrine. The plebiscite possessed the double advantage of upholding the theory of the social contract and of weakening the Parliamentarians, for on no democratic ground had they any right to criticise a regime which had received a direct mandate from the people. In all ages dictatorship has owed much of its success to the skill with which it has turned the weapons of democracy against the latter, and as a method of rendering universal suffrage not only innocuous but positively helpful the plebiscite has been found extremely useful by successive dictators.

No one who has had any practical experience of elections will deny that, more often than not, their result depends not so much on the issue on which they are fought as on the way in which that issue is put. The late Earl Balfour, for example, always held that he had been improperly kept out of office in the autumn of 1910, and that if there had been a Conservative government he could have won the second General Election of that year by stressing the fact that any diminution of the powers of the House of Lords would merely pave the way for Home Rule, for which there was no mandate. The election, it is true, was fought on the question of the Upper House, but this was posed in a different way, and the emphasis was placed on the alleged hostility of the Peers to all progressive legislation. The government of the day enjoys a great advantage in being able to decide both the time and the issue for a General Election. In the case of a plebiscite those who are responsible for its conduct enjoy an even greater advantage, for their opponents must answer with a direct negative (often to a question of the have-you-left-off-beating-your-wife type) since any attempt to side-track the issue is impossible.

The French plebiscites were marked by many features which have remained unaltered. The voter was always confronted with the fact that there was no practical alternative to the regime which he was asked to support: the choice lay between the existing order and chaos. He was not given the opportunity, for example, of saying whether he preferred the Bourbons or the Republic, and the results showed the success of this manoeuvre. In the Year VIII the plebiscite on the Consular Constitution, in which the voting was open, gave 3,011,007 for and 1526 against; in the Year X there was another plebiscite on the proposal to make Bonaparte First Consul for life, and this showed 3,568,885 for and 8374 against; and in November, 1804, there was yet a third on the establishment of the Empire, when there were 3,572,329 votes for and 2569 against. On the third occasion it is to be noted that Napoleon showed himself no mean exponent of the art of propaganda by holding the plebiscite immediately after the discovery of the plot of Pichegru and Cadoudal against his life: "We hoped to give France a King," observed the Chouan leader in prison, "but we have given her an Emperor instead". In all three instances the only possible answer was a definite affirmative or negative.

It was not, however, only in France itself that plebiscites took place in these years. Napoleon held one in Holland in 1801 on the constitution with which he had endowed that country, and there was another in Switzerland. Unfortunately the Swiss refused to provide a majority for the proposals which had been put before them, but faced with this difficulty, which might well have daunted a lesser man, Napoleon merely announced that those who abstained were to be considered as having voted in the affirmative, and so what he recommended had in reality been approved by the Swiss people.

With the fall of the First Empire the plebiscite went out of fashion. It was a contradiction of that conception of legitimate monarchy upon which the settlement of Europe at Vienna was based, and it recalled the two things which the high priests of the new order were, not without reason, most desirous of consigning to oblivion, namely the social contract and Napoleon. The lapse of a generation, however, brought its revenge, and as the Second French Republic began to yield to the Caesarism of Louis Napoleon, the plebiscite once more came into its own. There was the same reaction against Parliamentarianism that there had been fifty years before, and the nephew, like the uncle, proved an adept at turning the chosen weapon of democracy, universal suffrage, against itself. He was also well aware that the way the question was put was everything, and that the voter must be confronted with no choice but to vote either for the existing order or for chaos. Accordingly the *coup d'état* of December 2nd, 1851, was followed by a plebiscite on the 20th of the same month when the French electorate was called upon to accept or reject the following proposition—"The people wishes to maintain the authority of Louis Napoleon Bonaparte, and delegates to him the powers necessary to frame a Constitution on the bases proclaimed in his proclamation of December 2nd". The votes were 7,439,216 for and 640,737 against. In view of the precautions taken to ensure the desired verdict, it is difficult not to share the astonishment of the great historian of the Second Empire, Pierre de la Gorce, at the number of negative votes. Since the Republican leaders were for the most part either in prison or in exile, these votes must be taken as an indication of the strength of the Legitimist and Orleanist opposition.

The procedure of more than one subsequent dictator was anticipated by the Prince-President in consequence of the plebiscite: for a short space it rained decrees, and the administration of the country was remodelled in accordance with the views of its ruler. When the legislature met, it found itself not only with little to do, but also in a definitely subordinate position to Louis Napoleon, who had himself received so marked a vote of confidence direct from the people. Such being the case, the reestablishment of the Empire was a mere question of time, and, following a resolution of the Senate, a plebiscite was held on this subject in November, 1852. Little opportunity was given to the opposition to make its voice heard, though it is to be noted that the *Moniteur* published the proclamations of the Comte de Chambord, and the Republican leaders. The government, it was soon proved, could well afford to be generous in this way, since the voting showed 7,824,189 for and 253,145 against. It was a more notable triumph than that of the previous year, though there were 2,062,798 abstentions, chiefly in the districts of La Vendée, Maine-et-Loire, and Morbihan, which were Royalist, and of Bouches-du-Rhône, Rhône, and Gironde, where there were many Republicans. Once again, in May, 1870, Napoleon III held a plebiscite, when he asked for his subjects' approval of the Liberal Empire. On this occasion there voted 7,358,786 for, 1,571,939 against, while there were 1,894,681 abstentions and 113,978 spoilt papers. Even Gambetta, the inveterate foe of Napoleon, believed that the Empire was stronger than ever, yet in four months it was a thing of the past, and some valuable evidence had been provided as to the exact value of a plebiscite.

The influence and example of Napoleon III gave the plebiscite a wide popularity in the sixties of last century in the countries that were dependent upon France, notably in Italy. The Emperor remained wedded to the plebiscitary principle, and when Nice and Savoy were ceded to him as compensation for Victor Emmanuel's annexation of Lombardy and the Central Italian Duchies, he insisted that this cession should be ratified by the people concerned. The result had been carefully prepared, and the votes for France were in Nice 25,000 to 160 and in Savoy 130,000 to 235. As in the French plebiscites, the issue had in fact been decided before the vote was taken, and the participants had actually no alternative save to ratify a *fait accompli*. The real decision had been taken elsewhere.

The House of Savoy had little cause to complain of plebiscites, even if they lost their ancient home by one, for the plebiscite proved an extremely useful method of compelling Napoleon III to acquiesce in the unification of Italy, which had been carried a great deal further than he intended when he commenced his campaign in Lombardy. The Italian plebiscites conformed closely to the French model in that they were so contrived as effectually to prevent the opposition from expressing an opinion. In the Two Sicilies, for example, the electorate had to vote in the affirmative or negative on this proposition: "The people wishes for Italy one and indivisible with Victor Emmanuel as Constitutional King, and his legitimate descendants after him". The voting on the Neapolitan mainland was 1,302,064 for and 10,312 against; in Sicily it was 432,053 for and 667 against. In the Papal dominions the vote was in the Marches 133,072 for and 1212 against; in Umbria, 99,628 for and 380 against. Perhaps the most apposite comment is that of Professor Trevelyan in *Garibaldi and the Making of Italy*: "The voting was open, and every one who voted 'no' did so in the face of a disapproving world. No doubt, therefore, the real minority was a very much larger proportion of the citizens. But if the plebiscite exaggerated it did not belie the opinion of the people."

In Tuscany there was hardly even the pretence of impartiality, and Ricasoli literally marched the people to vote:

The bailiffs at the head of their own administrations, the most influential peasant proprietor at the head of the men of his parish, the most authoritative citizen at the head of the inhabitants of one street, one quarter, etc. . . . will order and lead his voters in a troop, in a file more or less numerous, but always disciplined and marching in good order, to the urns of the Nation. The Italian flag will be at the head. Each one will lay in the urn his paper, and then retire, and at a fixed point the troop will be dissolved with that quiet and dignity which comes from the consciousness of having performed a high duty.

All this has a curiously modern ring, and so has the announcement that the polling-booths were beflagged, while municipal officers were present to watch, "helped by good patriots". Supporters of the old dynasty could only abstain, as the voting formula gave them no opportunity of stating their will, and those who tried to distribute a manifesto of the Grand Duke Leopold II were severely handled by the police. The result of these precautions was seen when there voted 386,445 for union with Italy and 14,925 for a separate kingdom; there were, however, no less than 127,630 abstentions. In the Central Italian Duchies it was the same.

As after the fall of the First Empire, so after that of the Second the plebiscite in its Napoleonic form was frowned upon for a time. It was the age of democracy and of Parliamentarianism, and the statesmen of Europe had seen enough of the uses to which a plebiscite was put by the two Napoleons to have recourse to it themselves. There was, indeed, one in Norway, after the separation of that country from Sweden, but that was taken not upon the question of a republic but upon the acceptance of Prince Charles of Denmark as King. Once again there was no real choice, but in this case there can be no question but that the voting was perfectly free.

The close of the Four Years' War witnessed a revival of the plebiscite as it had been applied in the case of Nice and Savoy. The Allied and Associated Powers had, at any rate in the later stages of the conflict, laid great stress upon the principle of self-determination, that is to say the right of races to say to which particular state they wished to belong, and the plebiscite was a convenient method of putting this into effect. It soon appeared, however, that plebiscites of this type were at least as doubtful a means of ascertaining public opinion as those by which the two

Napoleons consolidated their position or Italy was unified: in the one instance the secret of success lay in the way the question was put, and in the other in the extent of the area in which the voting was held. To take an example from the British Isles, if a plebiscite was held in the whole of Ireland on the question of unification there would be an overwhelming majority for it; if it were held in Northern Ireland alone there would be an appreciable majority against, and if it were held in Northern Ireland, less the counties of Fermanagh and Tyrone, there would be a very large majority indeed against. The technique of selecting just the area to give the verdict required was soon appreciated, and it has now become highly developed.

In consequence of the provisions of the Treaty of Versailles several plebiscites were held during the years 1920 and 1921. The northern part of Schleswig opted for Denmark, and the southern part for Germany. This plebiscite was, it may be noted in passing, admirably conducted, and the Danish government showed commendable restraint at a moment when a different attitude might well have resulted in a considerable accession of territory, though probably at the cost of serious complications in the future. No such encomium can be passed on the Silesian plebiscite. The poll there resulted in 62·3 per cent of the votes going to Germany and 37·7 going to Poland, but all the same Poland was awarded fifty out of the sixty collieries, and 400,000 out of 570,000 tons of iron ore. It was travesties of justice such as this that were responsible for so many subsequent difficulties.

One of the most interesting plebiscites of all time was that in the Saar, which was most elaborately conducted. By Article 4 of the Treaty of Versailles the French obtained for fifteen years the exclusive right to exploit the coal mines in the Saar Basin as compensation for the German destruction of the mines in the North of France during the war; at the end of that time the inhabitants were to vote whether they wished to be united to Germany, to join France, or to retain the existing order. When the date approached on which the vote had to be taken a Plebiscite Commission was established consisting of the representatives of the smaller Powers not immediately affected, and this body drew up regulations for the compilation of voting lists; for examining the claims of those to be inscribed or the objections to the names already there; for fixing the polling districts; and, finally, for setting up tribunals to inflict punishment upon those who offended against the regulations. To maintain order an international force was drafted into the area, and it consisted of 1500 British, 1300 Italians, 250 Dutch, and 250 Swedes. In actual fact these troops were under British command, and the headquarters staff was entirely British, except for liaison officers attached from the other contingents.

Never was there a fairer plebiscite, and there have been very few that were so fair. The voting took place in a manner reminiscent of a British election, the "tellers" being all German-speaking neutrals. At the close of the poll the boxes were placed in charge of soldiers of the international force, and then, accompanied by neutral tellers and witnesses, were sent by lorry or train to Saarbruck, where they were counted by the tellers under the supervision of the Plebiscite Commission. The ballot boxes were subsequently sent to Geneva, where the papers were taken out of them and destroyed. It was all very different from the methods of Ricasoli, and the crushing majority for union with the Reich certainly did not exaggerate the feelings of the voters. The Saar plebiscite was the exception that proves the rule. It had been provided for fifteen years in advance, the voters had three different solutions between which to choose, and it was organized by those who had no interest whatever in the result. In other words, it was unique. No plebiscite before or since has been held in similar circumstances, and no arguments can, therefore, be based on it.

In view of the rising tide of anti-Parliamentarianism which set in during the twenties and thirties of the present century, it is in no way surprising that there should have been a recurrence to the plebiscite on the part of the dictators. Primo de Rivera held a plebiscite, arranged in the traditional manner so that all his opponents could do was to abstain, but it must be admitted that he obtained an impressive number of affirmative votes which testified to his undoubted popularity with the mass of the people. General Elections in Italy during the latter years of the Fascist regime partook of the nature of plebiscites, but they can hardly be classified as such, partly because they were a normal part of the constitution and partly because there was an alternative should the official list of candidates fail to secure a majority. Hitler, too, was not slow to grasp the uses of the plebiscite: he soon assimilated the lesson of Napoleon I and his nephew, and showed remarkable skill in turning the weapon of universal suffrage against the champions of democracy.

Hitler's use of the plebiscite was, in fact, so adroit that his skill would often appear to have escaped the notice of his critics. After the annexation of Austria in 1938 there was a plebiscite of the whole Reich, including the newly incorporated territory, to approve of what had been done, but when it was proposed to apply the principle to the Sudeten German area no one suggested that the whole of Czecho-Slovakia should vote. The Führer was, too, very wise from his own point of view not to give Schuschnigg time to hold a plebiscite; he knew too much about both plebiscites and Austrians. The story goes that in some remote village in the Tyrol a heavy fall of snow cut the inhabitants off from contact with the outside world for a few days, and the Schuschnigg plebiscite was held; it gave a hundred-per-cent. majority for the Austrian Chancellor; then the snows melted, the news of what had happened reached the village, and in due course the Hitler plebiscite took place: it gave a hundred-per-cent. majority for the Führer.

In one country, Greece, the plebiscite has been more or less regularly employed when a change was in question. When, in the sixties, King Otto was forced from his throne by the so-called Protecting Powers there was a plebiscite to choose his successor, and in 1920 King Constantine refused to return to Athens until another had been held. Four years later the establishment of the Republic was confirmed in the same way, though in spite of every sort of official pressure no less than 325,322 votes were cast for the monarchy, as against 758,742 for the new order. In November, 1935, there was a plebiscite on the Restoration, when no less than 97 per cent of the voters declared in its favour. King George II and his immediate advisers, it may be added, were not enamoured of the idea of a plebiscite, and they were criticized in some Royalist circles for insisting upon one being held. Such criticism was in reality beside the point, for, in different circumstances from those prevailing in October, the King had, earlier in the year, given his consent to a plebiscite, and it was felt both in Greece and abroad the worst possible impression would be created if it appeared that he had gone back on his word.

Moreover, it was essential that he should not owe his return to military support, as would have been the case had he returned to Athens on the invitation of General Condylis. King Alfonso XII was unhappily restored by the *pronunciamento* of General Martinez Campos rather than by the civilian Cánovas, and the effects of this were felt in Spain throughout the whole of his reign and that of his son; the army was continually interfering in politics, with results that in the end proved disastrous for the monarchy. Above everything else, King George was determined to reign as King of all the Hellenes, and a plebiscite seemed a good method of calling attention to this resolution.

This policy was certainly justified by results. Conscious of the fact that he had behind him a majority to which no politician could aspire, the King was able to take a firm line with General Condylis over the question of the amnesty, and it strengthened his hand in many ways. The Greek plebiscite of 1935, therefore, can be classed among the few against which no objection can be raised. No other monarchy has been restored by this method, which in normal circumstances is open to a good deal of criticism. Nevertheless, it might have been an asset to the Archduke Otto in the struggle with Hitler for Austria had he at least professed willingness to put his claim to a plebiscite; he was, however, advised against it, for better or for worse, by his principal supporters in Vienna.

This brief survey of the history of the plebiscite, incomplete as it necessarily is, would appear to lead to certain conclusions. The first is that although in theory the plebiscite is essentially democratic, yet in practice the reverse has proved to be the case. If this was so in the days of the two Napoleons, when the art of propaganda was still in its infancy, it is far more true at the present time, when the exploitation of mass psychology has been developed almost to perfection. To group a large number of people in one electoral unit, and then to subject them to an intensive propaganda from the platform, over the wireless, and in the columns of the Press until on the appointed day they are stampeded into voting as they had been told, may be good politics, but it is certainly not democracy; yet that is what happens in a plebiscite under modern conditions. No opportunity is given for reflection, and if the other side of the question is put at all it is in such a way as to appear unacceptable. In electing a representative to a legislative body the citizen does not abandon his right to reverse the decision, for if that representative proves unsatisfactory he can be removed in a few years' time; in a plebiscite a blank cheque is given to a man or a group of men, and there is no opportunity of going back on the verdict. In effect, it is generally little more than a sop to Cerberus on the part of those who hold democracy in the greatest contempt.

This is probably the reason why the plebiscite has always appealed to the dictator: it gives the people the illusion of power, while the reality is carefully withheld from them. It is, indeed, an interesting commentary upon human nature that those who most loudly proclaim their contempt for democracy are never so happy as when they have a cheering mob at their heels. Their methods of diplomacy, too, are those of the market-place, and are calculated with at least one eye on the gallery. Such being the case it is hardly surprising that by dictatorship, which is only democracy standing on its head, the plebiscite should always have been so greatly favoured.

Another consideration which arises from a study of the past is that even if the principle of a plebiscite be admitted as an equitable means of ascertaining public opinion upon a specific issue, the plebiscite itself is open to every kind of manipulation: so much depends upon the way the question is put or the area in which the voting is held that it is putting humanity to too hard a test not to expect advantage to be taken of these opportunities. Nor is this all, for the circumstances of a plebiscite are usually such that the fiercest passions are unloosed and the prestige of powerful individuals and nations are at stake. The plebiscite in the Saar, as has been shown, was an exception in that it had been envisaged years in advance; it was held in relative calm; and there was an international force standing by to keep order. In normal circumstances, as in Italy at the time of unification and in Central Europe immediately after the Four Years' War, a plebiscite is held in a hurry, and at a moment when passions are inflamed. Furthermore, the result has generally been allowed for in advance and the interested parties leave no stone unturned to ensure that the outcome shall be in accordance with their calculations.

What, then, is the lesson to be drawn from the history of the plebiscite? Where the area is compact and the issue one of local interest only, it is an admirable method of gauging public opinion. In England it is widely used to decide such questions as whether cinemas should be open on Sundays, and to solve problems of this sort it serves an extremely useful purpose. The problem to be solved is one that is easily understood, it is possible only to have one of two opinions, and if there are a large number of abstentions it shows, what is extremely valuable, that the district as a whole is indifferent. On the other hand, it would be absurd to elect even a rural district councillor upon so narrow an issue. He might

B B

hold the views upon the Sunday opening of cinemas which his constituents shared to the full, but on housing and a water supply he might differ from them fundamentally. Such being the case, a plebiscite would serve a very useful purpose.

It is when one comes to the more important questions and the wider areas that the difficulties occur. It is of no interest either to the Government or to the Opposition at Westminster whether or not the one cinema at Little Puddlescombe is open on Sunday; it does not concern them greatly if the whole county of Blankshire votes for Sunday closing, though one could imagine so firm a stand for Sabbatarianism intriguing the various party organizers; but if one of the provinces of Ruritania, especially if it be rich in minerals or oils, suddenly demands a plebiscite owing to its refusal any longer to be governed from Streslau, then the chancelleries of Europe will at once be agog. Neighbouring Powers, if they have not actually instigated this agitation, at once begin to fish in the troubled waters, while there is sure to be a very vocal minority which has no desire to shake off allegiance to Streslau and which also has powerful friends beyond the borders of Ruritania. Especially is this likely to be the case in these days of conflicting ideologies, when in so many countries men regard foreigners of their own way of thinking as closer to them than fellow-countrymen with whom they are not in agreement. If, after repeated disturbances, a plebiscite is eventually held, it will only be as the last resort of embarrassed diplomacy: the voters will make their choice after being worked up to a delirium of excitement, and the result will be one that could as easily and far more satisfactorily have been reached by a few statesmen sitting in privacy round a table several months earlier.

In fine, if the League of Nations had ever come to attain that power not only over the bodies but also over the consciences of mankind which was the intention of its founders, and if Article 19 of the Covenant had been applied in the spirit in which it was framed, then the plebiscite might have become an extremely useful instrument of impartial international justice. As it is, it is likely to remain, what it has generally been, namely a pseudo-democratic mask for aggressive and often undemocratic purposes.

SELECT BIBLIOGRAPHY

Chapter I

Churchill, W. S.: *Marlborough: His Life and Times.* London. 1933–1938.
Coxe, W.: *History of the House of Austria.* London. 1807.
Petrie, Sir Charles: *Bolingbroke.* London. 1937.
——: *Louis XIV.* London. 1938.
Trevelyan, G. M.: *England under Queen Anne.* London. 1930–1934.

Chapter II

Armstrong, E.: *Elisabeth Farnese.* London. 1892.
Atkinson, C. T.: *History of Germany, 1715–1815.* London. 1908.
Chance, J. F.: *George I and the Northern War.* London. 1909.
Gaxotte P.: *Le Siècle de Louis XV.* Paris. 1933.

Chapter III

Carlyle, T.: *History of Frederick the Great.* London. 1858–1865.
Gaxotte, P.: *Frédéric II.* Paris. 1938.
Lodge, Sir Richard: *Great Britain and Prussia in the Eighteenth Century.* Oxford. 1923.
——: *Studies in Eighteenth Century Diplomacy, 1740–1748.* London. 1930.

Chapter IV

Bain, R. N.: *Peter III, Emperor of Russia.* London. 1902.
Rousseau, F.: *Règne de Charles III d'Espagne.* Paris. 1907.
Soltau, R. H.: *The Duke de Choiseul.* Oxford. 1909.
Williams, B.: *The Life of William Pitt, Earl of Chatham.* London. 1913.

Chapter V

Broglie, Duc de: *Le Secret du roi.* Paris. 1878.
Kaus, G.: *Catherine the Great.* London. 1935.
Smitt, F. de: *Frédéric II, Catherine, et le partage de Pologne.* Paris. 1861.
Temperley, H. W. V.: *Frederick the Great and Kaiser Joseph.* London. 1915.

Chapter VI

Namier, L. B.: *The Structure of Politics at the Accession of George III.* London. 1929.
Petrie, Sir Charles: *The Jacobite Movement.* London. 1932.
Rose, J. H.: *Life of William Pitt.* London. 1923.
Williams, B.: *Carteret and Newcastle.* Cambridge. 1943.

Chapter VII

Gaxotte, P.: *La Révolution Française.* Paris. 1929.
Hobhouse, C.: *Fox.* London. 1948.
Rose, J. H.: *The Life of Napoleon I.* London. 1934.
Sorel, A.: *L'Europe et la Révolution Française.* Paris. 1908–1911.

371

CHAPTER VIII

Cecil, A.: *Metternich*. London. 1943.
Cooper, A. Duff: *Talleyrand*. London. 1932.
Mahan, A. T.: *Influence of Sea-Power on the French Revolution and Empire*. London. 1892.
Petrie, Sir Charles: *George Canning*. London. 1946.

CHAPTER IX

Coulaincourt, A. A. L.: *Mémoires*. Paris. 1933.
Webster, C. K.: *The Foreign Policy of Castlereagh, 1812–1815*. London. 1931.

CHAPTER X

La Gorce, P. de: *La Restauration*. Paris. 1926–1928.
Lockhart, J. G.: *The Peacemakers, 1814–1815*. London. 1932.
Phillips, W. A.: *The Confederation of Europe*. London. 1920.
Webster, C. K.: *The Congress of Vienna*. London. 1934.

CHAPTER XI

Temperley, H. W. V.: *The Foreign Policy of Canning, 1822–1827*. London. 1925.
Webster, C. K.: *The Foreign Policy of Castlereagh, 1815–1822*. London. 1925.

CHAPTER XII

Petre, F. L.: *Simon Bolivar*. London. 1910.
Rippy, J. F.: *Rivalry of the United States and Great Britain over Latin America, 1808–1830*. London. 1929.
Robertson, W. S.: *The Life of Miranda*. University of North Carolina Press. 1929.

CHAPTER XIII

Crawley, C. W.: *The Question of Greek Independence*. Cambridge. 1930.
Isambert, G.: *L'Independance Grecque et l'Europe*. Paris. 1900.
Marriott, Sir J. A. R.: *The Eastern Question*. Oxford. 1940.
Phillips, W. A.: *The War of Greek Independence*. London. 1897.

CHAPTER XIV

La Gorce, P. de: *Napoleon III et sa politique*. Paris. 1933.
Marriott, Sir J. A. R.: *Makers of Modern Italy*. Oxford. 1937.
Paleologue, G. M.: *Cavour*. London. 1927.
Urban, M. B.: *British Opinion and Policy on the Unification of Italy, 1856–1861*. Scottdale. 1938.

CHAPTER XV

Bulwer, Lord: *The Life of H. J. Temple, Viscount Palmerston*. London. 1871–1874.
Dodwell, H. H.: *The Founder of Modern Egypt: A Study of Muhammad 'Ali*. Cambridge. 1931.
La Gorce, P. de: *Louis-Philippe*. Paris. 1931.
Roux, Marquis de: *La Restauration*. Paris. 1931.

CHAPTER XVI

La Gorce, P. de: *Histoire de la seconde république française*. Paris. 1925.
——: *Histoire du second empire*. Paris. 1894–1905.
Parry, E. J.: *The Spanish Marriages, 1841–1846*. London. 1936.
Walpole, Sir Spencer: *Life of Lord John Russell*. London. 1889.

CHAPTER XVII

Holland, Sir T. E.: *Treaty Relations of Russia and Turkey, 1774–1853*. Oxford. 1877.
Kinglake, A. W.: *The Invasion of the Crimea*. Edinburgh. 1863–1887.
Lane-Poole, S.: *The Life of the Rt. Hon. Stratford Canning, Viscount Stratford de Redcliffe*. London. 1888.
Stanmore, Lord: *The Earl of Aberdeen*. London. 1893.

CHAPTER XVIII

Henderson, W. O.: *The Zollverein*. Cambridge. 1939.
Ludwig, E.: *Bismarck*. London. 1927.
Robertson, Sir C. Grant: *Bismarck*. London. 1918.

CHAPTER XIX

Cecil, Lady G.: *Life of Robert, Marquis of Salisbury*. London. 1921–1932.
Monypenny, W. F. and Buckle, G. E.: *The Life of Benjamin Disraeli*. London. 1910–1920.
Morley, Viscount: *The Life of William Ewart Gladstone*. London. 1903.
Sumner, B. H.: *Russia and the Balkans, 1870–1880*. Oxford. 1937.

CHAPTER XX

Andrassy, Count J.: *Bismarck, Andrassy, and Their Successors*. London. 1927.
Bainville, J.: *La Troisième République, 1870–1935*. Paris. 1935.

CHAPTER XXI

Bülow, Prince von: *Memoirs*. London. 1931.
Crewe, Marquess of: *Lord Rosebery*. London. 1931.
Garvin, J. L.: *The Life of Joseph Chamberlain*. London. 1932–
Lee, Sir Sidney: *King Edward VII*. London. 1925–1927.

CHAPTER XXII

Amery, L. S.: *The Times History of the War in South Africa*. London. 1900–1909.
Cromer, Earl of: *Modern Egypt*. London. 1911.
Milner, Viscount: *England in Egypt*. London. 1904.
Temperley, H. W. V. and Penson, L. M.: *Foundations of British Foreign Policy*. Cambridge. 1938.

CHAPTER XXIII

Bland, J. O. P.: *Li Hung-Chang*. London. 1917.
Joseph, P.: *Foreign Diplomacy in China, 1894–1900*. London. 1928.
Newton, Lord: *Lord Lansdowne*. London. 1929.
Renouvin, P.: *La Question d'Extrême-Orient, 1840–1940*. Paris. 1947.

CHAPTER XXIV

Adams, R. G.: *A History of the Foreign Policy of the United States*. New York. 1924.
Fish, C. R.: *American Diplomacy*. New York. 1919.
Mowat, R. B.: *The Life of Lord Pauncefote*. London. 1929.
Randell, J. G.: *Lincoln the President*. London. 1947.

Chapter XXV

Miller, W.: *The Ottoman Empire and Its Successors*. Cambridge. 1936.
Pears, Sir Edwin: *Life of Abdul Hamid*. London. 1915.

Chapter XXVI

British Documents on the Origins of the War, 1898–1914. London. 1926–
Grey, Viscount: *Twenty-Five Years*. London. 1925.
Jerrold, D.: *Britain and Europe, 1900–1940*. London. 1941.
Poincaré, R.: *Au service de la France*. Paris. 1926.

Chapter XXVII

Baker, R. S.: *Woodrow Wilson: Life and Letters*. New York. 1927–1939.
Churchill, W. S.: *The World Crisis*. London. 1923–1931.
Dugdale, B. E. C.: *Arthur James Balfour*. London. 1936.
Lloyd George, D.: *War Memoirs*. London. 1933–1936.

Chapter XXVIII

Clemenceau, G.: *Grandeurs et misères d'une victoire*. Paris. 1930.
Temperley, H. W. V.: *History of the Peace Conference of Paris*. London. 1920–1924.
Zetland, Marquess of: *The Life of Lord Curzon*. London. 1928.
Woodward, E. L., and Butler, R.: *Documents on British Foreign Policy, 1919–1939*.
    London. 1947.

Chapter XXIX

Petrie, Sir Charles: *Life and Letters of the Right Hon. Sir Austen Chamberlain*.
    London. 1939–1940.
Vallentin, A.: *Stresemann*. London. 1931–
Wheeler-Bennett, J. W.: *The Disarmament Deadlock*. London. 1934.
——: *Hindenburg, The Wooden Titan*. London. 1936.

INDEX